C000178253
KICK-OFF 3.00 p.m.
STOCKPORT
COUNTY
OFFICIAL PROGRAMME 1/-

JOHNNY HAYNES

THE MAESTRO

JOHNNY HAYNES

THE MAESTRO

A celebration of the career of Fulham Football Club's greatest player

MARTIN PLUMB
and
KEN COTON

First published in March 2008

Designed and published by
Ashwater Press
68 Tranmere Road, Whitton, Twickenham, Middlesex, TW2 7JB

www.ashwaterpress.co.uk.

Printed by Ian Allan Printing, Hersham, Surrey

ISBN 978-0-9548938-7-3

JOHNNY HAYNES

1934–2005

Johnny Haynes

The Maestro

During his career Johnny Haynes was known as The Maestro.

It's a name forever associated with him.

MAESTRO

A term of address from the original Latin 'magister' meaning master,
then from 18th-century Italian 'maestro'.

A master in any art
A person whose creative work shows sensitivities and imagination
An artiste of consummate skill
An eminent teacher
A distinguished figure in any sphere
A great performer

Virtuoso
Conductor
Expert
Genius
Captain
Director

Said about Haynes:

In jest

"A perfectionist is someone who takes great pains, and gives them to everyone else..."

In seriousness

"He had the unmistakable gifts of genius, and genius is always hard to understand and hard to love."

Said by Haynes:

"Footballers are entertainers, and the public wants to see goals and sparkling movements. That is what the game was designed for."

Foreword

by Jimmy Hill OBE

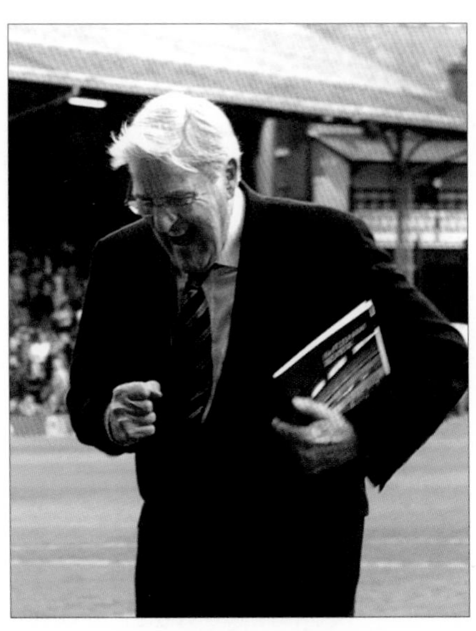

JOHNNY HAYNES WAS a natural sportsman and could probably have been a professional at whatever sport he tried, be it with a golf club, tennis or badminton racquet or a cricket ball. He had this marvellous and completely natural ability.

In the event it was with a football that he chose to demonstrate his amazing prowess. He just loved playing the game and being for twenty years such a talented part of Fulham Football Club. John was a very intelligent boy and studied all the aspects of association football meticulously, and became a football academic. He mastered virtually every area of the soccer arts, and this magic enabled him to dictate the shape of matches for years.

Although he was dubbed a perfectionist, really it was his great love of the game alongside his tigerish and perpetual competitive spirit that sometimes provoked words and gestures of frustration—unfortunately other mortals couldn't be supermen all the time. However, all of that was quickly forgotten once the final whistle blew!

His skill and his absolute dedication to training and fitness were an example to any aspiring professional footballer. He worked so very hard at his game that it was no surprise at all that he became a legend in his own lifetime.

When the maximum wage was abolished, Johnny Haynes was the first player to be paid £100 per week—and deservedly so. A gifted craftsman, the first real superstar, he was admired by all. It came as no surprise that with such skill he captained his country with distinction and won over half a century of England caps.

But it will not be just on the football field where John will be remembered. What makes a true star is their all-round persona. Despite his astounding abilities, he always remained a lovely person, a man who showed great humility, courtesy, wit and charm and one who bestowed gifts on friends. Johnny was a man of the people, he adored his fans and was always available for supporters and charitable events.

He was called 'The Maestro' by Fulham fans, an accolade generally to be used with caution but in this instance, wholly appropriate. The world of football will be fortunate to see the like of him again.

I am delighted to provide the introduction to this tribute book to Johnny Haynes, and I can do no better in closing than to repeat the words I wrote and delivered at his memorial service:

One wonders how John became so skilled,
Professionally always to be top billed,
He appeared to have eyes in the back of his head,
To avoid interception, leaving defenders for dead.
But in order to inflict such match-winning pain,
He delivered each pass in destructive vein.

Memories of his special talent will live for years to come,
To pass the ball through a needle's eye was ecstasy for some.
But apart from being a football genius,
So many adored him as a much-loved friend of us.
His other talents, his charm, his sense of fun,
Meant no-one could forget the game's fantastic son.

There's no doubt now that he's in Heaven,
Having earned his place in God's eleven.

Jimmy Hill.

About this book

WHENEVER IN LATER life Johnny Haynes was asked whether he would like a book written about him he usually respectfully declined. This was for two main reasons. Firstly, he was a private man, and he didn't want the details and minutiae of his private life documented. Secondly he was also a very modest man and truly considered that, almost fifty years on no-one would remember him or be much interested in his career. However, the fact remains that at Fulham and elsewhere in the country he is still talked of as much today as the current team turning out at Craven Cottage.

Almost two generations have now grown up since England put nine goals past Scotland at Wembley to win the British Championship and Johnny Haynes received the trophy from the Queen and was carried shoulder-high by his colleagues off the pitch. Some fortunate Fulham supporters witnessed his entire playing career, some saw part of it. Those who saw him all have everlasting memories of his play. But what about the younger generation of supporters who did not have such an opportunity?

The author's son-in-law, born almost ten years after Johnny Haynes last kicked a ball professionally in South Africa, asked: "What was he like, what made him such a special player? Why was he sometimes controversial, how did he dominate games?" To where could he be directed to find answers to these questions?

Many people have assumed, wrongly, that Johnny Haynes' playing career is fully and completely documented. If it is, then the author has never found it. If you possessed twenty complete years of Fulham programmes and waded through the entire five hundred of them, you may get a flavour of his greatness. The internet will probably provide you with a few snippets—generally information of the 9–3 win over the Scots and the fact that he was the first £100 per week footballer, but not much else. There was a great deal more to Johnny Haynes than that. This book draws together many fragmented sources from far and wide and consolidates them all together.

This book already stretches to a considerable number of pages. Even at this size it provides just a thumbnail sketch. The book documents many of his outstanding games, the goals he scored and perhaps more importantly the goals he created and crafted for his colleagues. If it were to record every time he hit the bar or post, had stupendous shots clawed away at the last by despairing goalkeepers, had efforts kicked off the line or efforts a fraction wide of goal—well, it would be a thousand pages long!

The book covers competitive matches played for Fulham, England and various clubs in South Africa. In this context 'competitive' covers the principal league and cup games, but it doesn't include the many friendlies, testimonials or charity matches for which he frequently turned out.

The book documents how the Fulham club, the local press, the national press and his colleagues saw it all. There are only so many superlatives that can be used. There are only a limited number of ways of describing great moves and goals, so a number of complimentary adverbs and adjectives are necessarily repeated! Which is why the author has sometimes borrowed phrases and descriptions from journalists more eloquent than himself; it is hoped that they will be understanding and forgiving.

The help of a number of former players is gratefully acknowledged. They have given willingly of their time to provide reminiscences and anecdotes, and quotes from them are used throughout the book.

This is a story of a schoolboy footballing prodigy who could have joined any football club that he wanted but chose little Fulham simply because one of his schoolboy chums had joined them. He joined a First Division club, but by the time he made his debut at eighteen they were, once again, a Second Division team.

He was pretty much an overnight sensation, soon demonstrating all the skills and crafts that would become the hallmark of his career. He made his England debut before he was twenty as a Second Division footballer. He joined, played with and was comfortable among some of the greatest English players ever: Stanley Matthews, Nat Lofthouse and Tom Finney. He won a significant number of England caps as a Second Division player.

He became Fulham's captain at the age of twenty-one. He improved Fulham's scoring rate in the Fifties to the point where they scored almost a hundred or more goals each season, though unfortunately they also conceded that many as well, so initial progress was slow. However, with the gradual arrival of a number of classy players over the years from inside and outside the club, Haynes captained Fulham back to the First Division in 1959.

From this point Johnny Haynes almost single-handedly kept Fulham in the top flight for almost a decade, fighting and beating off relegation season after season. Under his captaincy, Fulham twice reached the semi-finals of the FA Cup, both times unluckily beaten in a replay. He was made England captain in 1960 at the age of twenty-five. He played in two World Cups, captaining England in Chile in 1962.

At the height of his career in 1962, he was badly hurt in a car accident and lost virtually an entire season. Many predicted he would never play again, but he recovered to play another seven seasons for Fulham, but never again for England; he had won fifty-six caps in total. As Haynes' mercurial powers inevitably waned, Fulham dropped out of the First and the Second Division. Johnny Haynes played the last of his eighteen seasons as a first-team player in the Third Division. He was that rare breed of footballer, the 'one club man', staying with his beloved

Fulham through fluctuating fortunes for twenty years. During all his time with Fulham he won no domestic honour.

When the inevitable time came to move on, Johnny Haynes extended his career in South Africa for over five years, winning two championships and three other cup trophies with Durban City. He finally retired with Maritzburg at the age of forty-one.

Johnny Haynes was a pivotal figure in British football, one of the first to have an agent. In the years between 1958 and 1962, he was one of the most important figures in sport, and one of the most talked about men in the whole country. He was as important then as was David Beckham at the height of his fame.

The story of Johnny Haynes is invariably inextricably linked with the fortunes of Fulham Football Club, so this book in some ways is also about what Ken Coton called 'the golden years' of the popular west London club by the Thames, from Stevens–Jezzard–Mitten in the Fifties to Conway–Earle–Barrett in the Seventies.

Johnny Haynes never lost his love of the club, whether he was in South Africa or Edinburgh (his home in later life). It was the first result he looked for. He was actively involved in saving the club through its darkest hours in the early Nineties and also lent support to keeping Fulham at Craven Cottage when a move was mooted. Nobody was more delighted than Johnny Haynes when Fulham finally returned to the highest level of English football after an absence of thirty-three years. Happily Johnny returned to the Cottage as a guest on occasions to see his team once again play and win in the top flight.

Throughout Johnny Haynes' career the badge of Fulham Football Club was closely based on this crest of the former Borough of Fulham. The shield incorporates a representation of the River Thames; it is beside this river that the club's Craven Cottage ground has stood for over a hundred years.

THE PRODUCTION AND PRINTING *of this book has been underwritten by Robert Fennell and Graham McDermott, two life-long Fulham fans. Without their help and encouragement, which is gratefully acknowledged, this book would not have been possible.*

PICTURE CREDITS

Thanks are due to the following for reproduction of copyright photographs and illustrations: Ken Coton, Solo Syndication, PA Photos, Popperfoto, Getty Images, Robert Fennell, Alan Williams, Avril Haynes, David Roodyn, Ed Holford, Melvin Tenner, Ken Simpson, Peter Raath, Roger Slater, Morris Smith, David Newman, Winchmore Hill Cricket Club, England Schoolboys FA, Marjorie Haynes, Sheila Seymour and the author's private collection. In spite of best efforts, it has not been possible to trace the owners of a small number of photographs used in this book; any such owners are requested to contact the publishers.

BIBLIOGRAPHY

Football Today – Johnny Haynes (1961); It's All in the Game – Johnny Haynes (1962); An Autobiography – George Cohen (2003); Tales from the Riverbank Part 1 – Martin Plumb (2005); Tales from the Riverbank Part 2 – Martin Plumb (2006).

Contents

Contents

A note from Ken Coton

I WAS LUCKY enough to see nearly all of Johnny Haynes' Fulham career—and thrilled to be able to photograph some of it. I still remember his Boxing Day debut against Southampton, and from then on he provided us all with countless displays of sublime football, unsurpassed even today. He remains Fulham's greatest player.

I am proud to be part of this tribute book to my footballing hero. I have spent many long, but satisfying hours putting this book together, incorporating Martin Plumb's superb research and writing, and I am delighted to be able to display many of my Johnny Haynes photographs within. It is a privilege to be associated with this book, which I hope goes some way towards being a fitting tribute.

Acknowledgements

MANY PEOPLE HAVE been kind enough to help with research, photographs, anecdotes, interviews, advice and encouragement in connection with this book, as have many libraries, newspapers and other institutions. ***Grateful thanks are extended to them all.*** *Among them are the following:*

Former Fulham players who provided so much time, insight, fun and recall of former times: Sir Bobby Robson CBE and his very helpful personal assistant Judith Horey, George Cohen MBE, Jimmy Hill OBE, Alan Mullery MBE, Roy Bentley, Tom Wilson, Fred Callaghan, Steve Earle and Stan Brown.

Libby Haynes Marx and Marge Haynes for conversations and memories beamed across the world.

Avril Haynes for her wishes of good luck with the book.

Winchmore Hill Cricket Club for their hospitality and excellent recall of events; club secretary Chris Langford and members Denis Metson, John Tait and Martin Pryke in particular for their time.

Roger Slater, club secretary at Wealdstone FC, for his research and information.

All those kind people who responded to the request for information on the maestro's South African times: Peter Raath for his diligent research and words and for assisting in sourcing pictures, the editor of the Durban Mercury, Durban library staff, the librarian for the South Africa High Commission, London, Harry Weir, Morris Smith, Judy Thesen, Jay Nanthnall, Peta B'Alac, Fred Forge, Ron Roe and Jack Young.

Journalists David Instone and Rob Hughes; James Lawton for permission to use George Cohen's autobiographical material.

Sarah Harvey at the Hornsey Journal; Graham Dalling at the local history unit, Enfield council; Alan Power, the Bucks County Council librarian.

The staff at the British Newspaper Library at Colindale, particularly Vic and Stewart Gillies; staff at the British Library, Wetherby; Anne and the helpful staff at the Hammersmith and Fulham archives; Martin Hilditch, formerly of the Fulham Chronicle; research staff at several libraries including Burnley, Blackpool and Newcastle and the National Football Museum staff at Preston.

Alan Swain; the school secretary, Houndsfield Primary School, Enfield; and from Latymer School, Andrew Granath, Doreen Buckland and Dame Eileen Atkins. David Newman for the information on Edmonton Boys.

David Barber, historian at the Football Association for his support and quick, accurate and positive help with statistical information and for permission to reproduce those statistics; Patricia Brown at the Football League; John Read, chief executive, and Sue Gifford at the English Schools Football Association.

Steve Torrington for helping to connect us with pictures.

Alan Pinnock of Associated Newspapers' archives and Danny Howell of Solo Syndication, for their tremendous help and assistance with images and letting me have the time of my life in their library! This book has been significantly enhanced by their personal help and their professional football knowledge.

Crispin Thomas of The Football Poets, for the reproduction of his poem.

The long list of long-term Fulham supporters eager to support and make a contribution includes: David Roodyn, Melvin Tenner, Peter Hammond, Ed Holford, Kevin Shea, Dave Wilson and David Lloyd.

Debbie Silver, former head of retail at Fulham Football Club for promoting the idea and for giving the green light to start the project.

Dorothy Ravenswood for her scholarly proof-reading and marking of the text, and letting me off with just a few canings; also to my daughter Jessica Hutson for religiously going through every line of the book despite other pressures.

My daughter Joanna Plumb for long hours on the Mac and assistance with improving the images; the rest of the Plumb family for their patience whilst I locked myself away to put down the words.

Alan Williams for his contacts and advice.

Ken Coton—"without whom…"

Last, but certainly not least, a great big thank you to Sheila Seymour, a long-term friend and devoted fan of the great man. Sheila has been in on the project from day one. To call her a foot-soldier, researcher or assistant would be wholly inadequate, and throughout the last, very busy, year she has taken on a great deal of the administration, and assisted me in every way with the leg work; I owe her a great deal and this book would not have been produced if it hadn't been for her. I hope the final result has been just as satisfying for her—and sorry to husband John for all the phone calls!

Martin Plumb

Notes to the text

England:

During some of Haynes' career:

* England had a 'B' team.
* World Cup qualifying matches were called World Cup preliminaries.
* Qualification for the World Cup usually consisted of just four games, due to the smaller number of nations taking part.
* England often played league sides like Chelsea or Liverpool in 'behind closed doors' training matches, as part of their get-togethers.
* During the Fifties and early Sixties, England would often complete a 'summer tour' of friendlies as well as World Cup qualification matches.
* There was no European Championship in between World Cups until 1960, and then England didn't take part in the inaugural competition, competing initially in 1964.
* There was a British Championship (England, Scotland, Wales and Northern Ireland). This was spread out across the season. Two games were played in October and November (Wales and Northern Ireland) and the competition was completed *before* the end of the season against Scotland in April whilst teams were still battling it out for promotion or against relegation.
* The British Championship games were later re-named the Home Internationals, and the three matches were all played in May following the end of the domestic season. They were withdrawn completely from the domestic calendar in 1984.
* The Football League played representative matches (a kind of probables v possibles). To all intents and purposes they were experimental England sides. Games were played against other Football League teams, like Scotland and Ireland, and occasionally against foreign opposition.
* Like cricket, the England team had a team manager and nine other 'selectors' right throughout the reign of Walter Winterbottom and Haynes' England career. Team selection was not down to one man.

Fulham:

* Up to season 1961–62 the Fulham programme delighted in stating that the club played in black knickers. After that knickers became shorts. Stockings had been dropped many seasons previously.
* In the early seasons covered by this book, players often lost two years of their career to a stint in the forces performing National Service.
* Teams were awarded only two points for a win, not three points as today.
* Players in each team were numbered from 1 to 11 in every match, and did not have squad numbers.
* There was no League Cup (now Carling Cup) competition until 1960.
* Up until 1961, there was a maximum wage of £20 per week during the season, and £17 in the summer. This basic wage had gone up from £15 per week in the Fifties.
* Up until 1965, substitutes were not allowed on the field for even injuries let alone tactical reasons. Even then only one substitute was allowed.
* It was also an era where control on tackling was fairly lax and very often teams played with only ten men on the field, sometimes for a considerable part of the match.
* Fairly often teams were left after ninety minutes with only eight or nine fit players on the field. It was quite common for an injured goalkeeper to end up playing on the wing during a game with an outfield player deputising in goal.
* First Division games were very rarely postponed just because players from either side were 'away' on international duty.
* Games in the Fifties were played on frozen surfaces, muddy and boggy pitches and virtually waterlogged grounds. Unless there were several inches of snow on the ground, games were rarely postponed.
* For three quarters of Haynes' career, 'systems', apart from the renowned 2-3-5 and the W-M formations, didn't exist.
* Football was pure entertainment in the Fifties and the game was very attack-minded; high scores were common. Fulham's squad, like most others, would normally have more forwards than goalkeepers, full backs and half backs put together!

South Africa:

* South African football seasons do not cross year boundaries (such as 1969-70) and are therefore given in single years (e.g. 1972).

General:

* Haynes' side's score (Fulham, England or South African sides) is given first.
* Unlike Chelsea, Arsenal and Tottenham, Fulham were a Second Division side for most of the Fifties. Whilst cameramen would be seen at First Division matches in abundance, far fewer would be seen at a Second Division match. As a consequence of this, action shots of Johnny Haynes playing for Fulham during this period are few and far between.

Introduction

I FIRST SAW Johnny Haynes during the 1963–64 season. My initial reaction as a twelve-year-old was—if he is this good now what must he have been like before his car accident? He always looked the captain, perfectly turned out, pristine white shirt, with brilliantined hair reflecting off the sun.

The centre circle and an imaginary square box surrounding it was Haynes' domain. Always alert, invariably calling for the ball, palms outstretched, pleading for a pass in order to weave his magic. Then, upon receipt of the ball, it would be a minimum of movement, a quick swivel, or a turn on a sixpence, head down, never looking at the man.

What followed were passes flying out to either wing, inside, outside or over the defenders, or through the centre of the defence. Slide-rule passes, lobbed passes, curling passes, all seemingly perfectly timed, straight to the feet or head of a colleague, like an express train linking with a slower branch line train at a junction station. Short ten-yard passes, and passes half the length of the pitch!

You almost felt that every time Johnny Haynes received the ball, something was going to happen; a frisson of excitement rippled through the crowd, another attack would be set up, and another chance would be created for the Fulham team. Not many would argue that for many seasons Johnny Haynes was Fulham Football Club and that almost single-handedly he carried Fulham FC along and kept them in the First Division spotlight.

It is clear that Johnny Haynes was an intelligent, colourful, highly complex and in some ways controversial character both on and off the field. Haynes was a visionary who saw that the game of football was one to be studied and mastered. He wanted to throw off the mantle of muddy pitches and working class, male dominated Saturday afternoons during a dull, grey February. He understood business and wanted football to be a colourful spectacle to be enjoyed. He could see the future of television and the involvement of local industry and sponsorship.

He wanted better facilities and first class pitches if you wanted to see proper, calculated football. Having said that, he once said that English footballers were underpaid and that if you wished them to perform like artists, then they should be paid as such. He boldly predicted that if British players were paid the correct wages, and given the correct incentives and facilities, it would enable them to beat any club or international side in the world. Perhaps we're still waiting for that particular vision to be fulfilled!

This book has tried not to beatify Haynes, but to show the different moods, temperaments and mannerisms that so many great players have. It is meant to magnify and glorify a wonderful career.

Johnny Haynes was playing at a time when football was really fun and a pure entertainment; a time that produced a welter of real characters of which Fulham had more than their fair share. Already we have lost Bobby Keetch, Johnny Byrne and more recently Bedford Jezzard, Maurice Cook, Arthur Stevens and Jimmy Langley; what stories would there have been from them! It's very sadly too late to talk to them, but hopefully, amongst those remaining, we can capture more than just a flavour of those times gone by.

Martin Plumb – Ascot, 2008

Author Martin Plumb was born in Hammersmith and has been a regular at Craven Cottage since 1963. He was trained in accountancy, but has subsequently spent thirty-five years in I.T. consultancy, working with many leading software houses. He is a teacher of mathematics and a professional guitarist and keyboards player with a long career in music. He is a respected author, a school governor and a devotee of heritage railways. He has been with his partner Jean for 40 years, has three daughters, and lives in Ascot in Berkshire. He is author of the acclaimed 'Tales From The Riverbank' books about Fulham's history.

1: The pass master

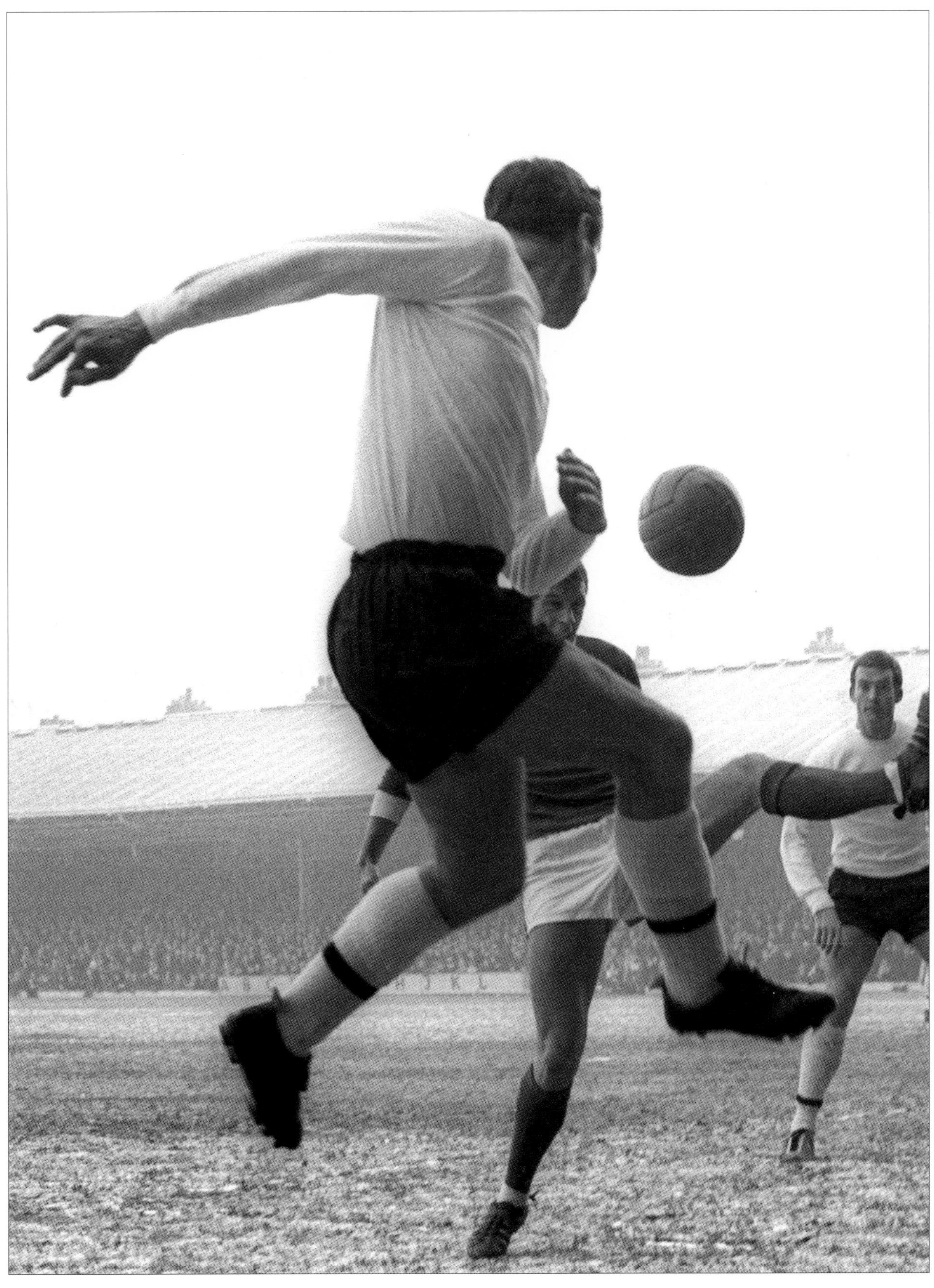

1: The pass master

Whatever controversial circumstances followed Johnny Haynes around during his career, in one area there are no arguments. He was the outstanding inside forward of post-war English football. During his entire career in England, he was a 'one-club man' sitting alongside some of the greatest single-club stalwarts that the game has produced: Billy Wright at Wolves, Bobby Charlton at Manchester United, Nat Lofthouse at Bolton Wanderers and Tom Finney at Preston North End.

In his book *Striking for Soccer* in 1961, Fulham colleague Jimmy Hill described the best player in the country thus: "It is necessary to consider what makes a great player. He must, of course, have superb control. When he decides to pass the ball, his kicking ability must be such that he makes the minimum number of mistakes over any distance. He must have an accurate and powerful shot; he must be very agile, strong in the tackle, and able to get through a tremendous amount of work.

"He must know how to manoeuvre out of tight situations with other players, and be able to dribble and hold the ball against fierce-tackling defenders. He must also have great courage and great speed. In any of these skills except possibly the last, I would put Johnny on a par with, or ahead of, any other player in the country."

Michael Parkinson described Haynes as the most complete footballer in the land in the Fifties and Sixties. He stated: "Any suggestion that he lives anywhere other than the Pantheon is an insult to anyone who saw him play. If you compile a list of English players of equal calibre, only Bobby Charlton, Bobby Moore, Tom Finney and Stanley Matthews come to mind. Together they comprise the crown jewels of English football."

Truly great sportsmen like Haynes, Matthews and Finney are like colours in the spectrum. If you tried to imagine a new one, it would be impossible to do so. It has to be said that modern sports media appear to be happier to opt for shallow celebrity in lieu of the genuine talent and the life force of the great performer.

Johnny Haynes played in an era when crowds would flock to see individual players as much as a team, and not necessarily one of their own team either. Opposition post-war supporters of the time would readily admit that Haynes was the finest player they had ever seen.

He was a supreme artist in a doomed breed, the midfield genius, those all-seeing footballers who would later disappear from the beautiful game by a combination of close marking and suffocating tactical formations. The centre circle was his personal stage. Players such as Johnny Haynes stamped their authority on matches. Tom Wilson, a playing colleague from 1950 to 1956, said of him: "On the field, whenever your side got possession of the ball he wanted it, didn't matter who had it, where you were on the field, even if you had to get it through the eye of a needle to get it to him—he wanted it!"

Alan Mullery confirms this absolutely: "One of the first things he said to me when I got in the team was, 'No matter what position I'm in, when I ask for the ball—give it to me.' But there would be times where he would have three men immediately surrounding him, but if you didn't pass him the ball, he'd give you one hell of a bollocking. However, it didn't matter what the score was, you'd never see him hide in a game—he always wanted the ball."

One eminent writer described such midfield geniuses thus: "They were as smooth and invidious as panthers, shrewd and devastating in midfield as they seamlessly linked defence to attack, often conducting play as if the other side didn't exist." Haynes' style of play was to pave the way for the midfield playmakers of today.

Opponents as well as spectators marvelled at Haynes' control, privileged to watch a schemer who seemed to be able to play without the bother of having to look at the ball. He and his kind illuminated the humdrum lives of millions. For years, the names of Haynes and Fulham were synonymous. He scored almost 160 Fulham goals himself, but how many did he craft, scheme or create for his colleagues? Who can guess, probably a figure around 600 to 800.

He had natural ability as George Cohen confirms: "We had one spotlight on the Cottage and we used to run around in the dark almost. In those days we didn't have track suits or jumpers, there just wasn't anything around, we couldn't afford it, you had to have the determination in those days to get on and do things or you'd just...go under.

"This is what a great player like Haynes didn't ever have to worry about with his unbelievable natural ability, skill, vision and flair, whereas people like myself had to make themselves a player. Whilst I had the strength, power and the speed, there was no real substitute for skill—which Haynes had!"

Build

Johnny Haynes wasn't tall, between five feet nine and five feet ten. He was full in the thighs, stocky in the legs and very hard to shake off the ball. He was an extremely strong player too, exceptionally good at screening and protecting possession. He had the innate ability to shield the ball, and then change direction in a completely unpredictable way, often throwing an entire defence off balance. He used his posterior to great effect!

Jimmy Hill elaborated: "It never surprises me that the most enthusiastic tributes to him come from those who had tried to mark him out of a game. This was almost impossible to accomplish because John had the capacity to screen a ball, using his more than amply-muscled backside to emphatic effect against even the strongest tacklers."

When Haynes was asked in retirement what he missed most about the game, he replied: "The training." One of the first pictures taken of the young Haynes soon after he arrived at Craven Cottage was the one above of him training with other newcomers Archie Macaulay, Reg Lowe and Eddie Lowe. The picture at right, taken a few years later, shows Haynes leading the training with, from left, Jim Langley, Tony Macedo, Jimmy Hill and Trevor Chamberlain.

Training and fitness

Of all the qualities Johnny Haynes brought to the beautiful game the chief ones were style and skill—and of course work rate. No-one worked harder in training than he did. He was superbly fit. As captain of Fulham and England he consistently preached the following advice, especially to young players: "Over and above everything else, there is a need to keep yourself thoroughly fit, I cannot stress this too much. Don't be taken in by the blasé attitude towards training which you might see in others. No player gets to the top without being wound up for his job. There is always that moment of truth, when training sins of omission will find you out.

"It may be a pitch inches deep in mud, when the don't-care types have their tongues hanging out long before the end. Or it could be a run of several matches in a short spell, as happens near the end of the season, maybe in extra time in cup competitions. All the skill in the world is useless when limbs and wind won't answer the call. Keep fit, take pride in your physical condition—it will pay you in the long run."

Even when he was England's captain, he was incredibly dedicated; he would be the first to arrive at training and the last to leave. Sir Bobby Robson said of him: "He was a great trainer, *loved* training, he never missed training and he was very fit." Tom Wilson confirmed: "He wasn't a slacker—ever!" Johnny

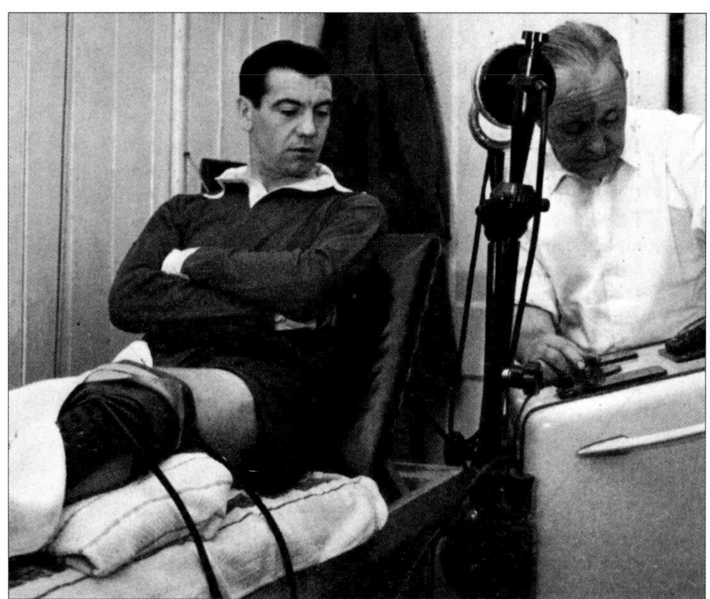

A rare sight, indeed—Haynes on the treatment table. Despite treatment, he was almost always ready for the next game.

Haynes was a normal guy, he liked a drink, he was a great socialiser and was certainly no 'early bird', but he never abused his body; he was the supreme trainer. Whatever he had done the night before, he would always be raring to go next day.

Often the senior players would be allowed days off, but as Fred Callaghan recalls: "Johnny would always turn up and we would have to get out a load of gear for him. He may have been out the night before, but he would still go out there and do endless laps of the field. By the time he had finished, and I'd picked his kit up, you could have wrung his shirt out in a bucket."

The view is echoed by George Cohen: "After John went out for a drink or for a late night for whatever reason it may be, he would be out there lapping, getting 'a good sweat on' for training; he never neglected his training, Johnny. The other thing is although he may have got in late, he always got seven hours sleep. For whatever you do in this game, you can't afford to lose your sleep!"

The club's general manager, Frank Osborne, once said of him: "Johnny Haynes is the grandest fellow I've ever met in football. Although he is one of the biggest stars we've ever had, he is entirely unspoilt and trains harder than anyone on our books."

Haynes worked just as hard in training and in training matches as he did in the real thing. When asked by Archie McPherson just a few years before his death in Scotland what he missed most about the football world, he replied honestly, "The training." Not many of today's current crop of internationals would say that.

The fitness and strength of Johnny Haynes is well and truly brought home when you look at just how many games he played. If you remove the season of his car crash, the times he was on duty for England and the times he was rested from the team (by Bobby Robson during season 67–68 and by Bill Dodgin during 69–70), then Johnny Haynes appeared in *over 90% of all Fulham matches* played over a period of eighteen seasons—a marvellous achievement.

George Cohen pointed out: "He played in well over six hundred games in an outstanding career. It was a huge, huge effort quite frankly. In those days I played regularly between thirty-nine and forty-two league matches a season, and that was a hell of a good going. I was injured when I was twenty-eight, and I wouldn't have kept going past thirty-two unless I was absolutely really enjoying it, as I thought there were other things to life besides football, but John kept going. The fact is he was a tremendous competitor, even when he was slowing down a bit, the speed as far as Johnny Haynes was concerned was all in the brain."

To the current Premiership players who struggle to play thirty games a season, it should be pointed out that in his heyday Haynes regularly played sixty highly competitive matches a season, and the number of times during a season where Haynes had no midweek fixture of some kind to fulfil was small indeed. The final word to Johnny: "I loved every minute of it, I even loved training. I enjoyed myself at the weekends after the game, but during the week it was business."

Intelligence and vision

Haynes talked about how he thought about the game as a boy: "If you use your brains from the start, you will develop into an intelligent footballer, and whilst you need to have ability, it will be largely the thought you have given to the game in your tender years that will decide whether or not you become a successful tactician."

He was a player who seemed to possess an uncanny sixth sense on the football field, a brilliant ball player whose sheer coolness in tight situations often completely bamboozled opposing players. He was constantly on the go, consistently finding space, always asking for the ball and moving smoothly into position. He was also extremely quick over five yards. One scribe said, "There was liquid, subtle movement—so very mobile."

He knew exactly what he was going to do with the ball a second before it actually arrived, as if he could sense an opening without actually having to see it. Senior players would often swear that he literally had eyes in the back of his head, he seemed to have a 360 degree panoramic view of the game and knew what was happening all over the field.

Bobby Robson confirms that, saying, "He would be facing his own goalkeeper and receive the ball, and he literally knew where the five opposing defenders were. He would turn and hit the diagonal pass, the pass up to the centre forward, the through ball or lob—just marvellous."

Jimmy Hill agreed: "It was accurate to say he had eyes in the back of his head, he was an exceptional talent. He had that bit of magic, a very bright boy, who

The pass master of swerve.

used his head and his feet. He had such confidence, he knew without looking down what his feet were doing and where the ball was, so he could look up. It was a result of both experience and talent."

It was all like an elaborate chess game to Haynes, and he loved to scheme and outwit and be three moves ahead of the play. His delight was to create goals. Sometimes berated because of his own few goals in a season, he would smile and say, "I am a maker of goals." He was ahead of his time inasmuch as he did not concentrate on passing to feet, he concentrated more on passing into space, and allowing the colleague to anticipate the pass and move into the space.

After his playing career was over, Haynes said: "Looking back I think I always had peripheral vision. It was a very important part of my game. I knew where everybody was on the field. It was instinct; that's the way I played."

Control and touch

It wasn't all about passing. He also had superb close control and could worm his way through a defence on his own if there was no player available for the pass. One description was that he had an eel-like quality in his forward play that would allow him to wriggle free and slip away from the tightest of defences.

Roy Bentley confirms: "He had a superb first touch, it was very rare that his first touch was no good; he could control the ball coming at him from all angles, chest, thigh or foot it made no difference. His major asset was that if the pass was received at the right pace and the target was there, if he could, he would play the ball first time."

George Cohen had this to say: "He had an unbelievably good first touch which would allow his body position on the ball to be such that he could play it anywhere he wanted to, and he was always able to know where he was going to play the ball anyway, so his first touch was quite incredible even if he wanted to do it on a half turn. He was a master of any situation, Johnny Haynes; I wished I'd had half of his skill in that direction; mind you, he did say he wished he'd had half my speed!"

Passing the football

The great master Pelé once remarked, "He's the best passer of the ball I've ever seen! It was as if he possessed his own internal guided missile system." Others frequently said about his passes that the length couldn't be more accurate if they were produced by a slide rule. He did not very often bother to beat his man; he let the ball do that.

Johnny Haynes was a technician of unrivalled finesse, and an elegant right-footed inside forward of rare vision. It is strange to consider that for the vast majority of his career he wore the inside left (number 10) shirt, but was predominantly right-footed. Alan Mullery however says, "The shirt number didn't mean a great deal in those days. Most good footballers were two-footed, and he could hit a ball with his left foot equally as well."

Many consider that comparisons with David Beckham are rendered redundant when Haynes' total two-footed dexterity is taken into account. Jimmy Hill said: "His control of the ball was immaculate, and he was a completely two-footed player. He could drop a forty-five-yard pass from the old inside left position equally well with his left or his right foot."

Tom Wilson agreed: "His forte was these defence-splitting passes; I mean, they marvel at Beckham sometimes when he knocks the ball from somewhere approaching out on the right touchline to somebody standing wide on the left of the field; well, Haynesey was doing that every week fifty years ago."

He was the best passer bar none in the English game in the second half of the twentieth century, equalled perhaps only by the great Raich Carter of Sunderland, who, like Haynes, was an inside forward and cricketer of considerable skill, with Derbyshire and Durham. Carter was considered the finest inside forward of all time, but said of Haynes when at the age of just twenty-one, "He's the best prospect I've watched."

Johnny Haynes had great positional sense, and an eye for an opening. He realised that there was space to be exploited by a man who could make accurate long diagonal through passes. It is difficult to convey to a younger generation just how glittering a talent he was. He could strike a fifty-yard pass on to the toecaps of a fleeting winger with inhuman accuracy.

His main skill was the long accurate through ball inside the full back to the winger, but his signature was also the diagonal through ball played behind the centre half, often delivered on the turn.

He was not limited to these of course; there was also the cross-field pass and the reverse pass. He could chip it, drive it, bend it, whatever the situation demanded. Johnny Haynes made passes of five yards or forty-five yards.

One writer summed it up perfectly: "Haynes would calm the ball, caress it, then half-turn, or feint, to allow an extra moment's work-space and a split-second upsum of possibilities—then the right-footed inside left would draw his bow and let go a pass of twenty, thirty, often forty yards into the very stride of a confrère.

"No British footballer this century has hit cleaner, longer, more breathtakingly imaginative passes than Haynes—not Alex James, nor Jim Baxter, not Bobby Moore, nor Glenn Hoddle, nor the young Paul Gascoigne."

He was always the fulcrum of the attack.

When new defensive strategies tightened things up at the back, Haynes was happy to adapt to this. A player who could regularly find his man with passes of forty yards and more became lethal when the

The pass master at practice.

requirement was only for ten. Though, as Haynes once admitted of the new, shorter-range game: "I used to get bored and frustrated and wanted to try something more ambitious."

Tom Wilson said this of Haynes' play: "The only comment I would make about his style of play would be that safety wasn't in John's make-up, certainly in the early days. He could be a bit ambitious when trying to put people through other teams' defences. He would demand it and then what would emerge from that would either be a chance on goal or he'd give the ball to the other side. The goalkeeper or defender would pick it up and we'd have to start from scratch—cover your man, get it off them, give it to him and go through the whole thing again! That's an over simplification of course!

"I think in his later years he developed a 'bread and butter' ball because he had to. In the later years [Sixties] due to defences and his slightly declining reflexes and speed of turning, etc, he had to perhaps play the ball back to give himself a chance to manoeuvre himself into position."

Johnny in later years still showed the same timing and leverage that enabled him to execute the long pass.

George Cohen added glowingly: "The old Webber-T ball was a bitch of a ball and it picked up water irrespective of how much dubbin or Vaseline you put on it and it picked up a lot of weight. But he, with his timing and leverage, could actually still kick a moving ball from one side of the pitch to the other on the run. He had tremendous hips and was able to hit such passes. I bet you any money you like that players today given the same ball in such conditions wouldn't get anywhere near it."

Haynes' dedication to practising was renowned. Alan Mullery recalls: "When I was a kid on the groundstaff at Craven Cottage sweeping the terraces, I'd watch the team train on the pitch—there was no separate training ground at the time. The team would run around the track for half an hour, do their training then go. After everyone had left the pitch, Haynes would come back out with a bath towel, lay it down by the entrance to the Cottage just by the corner flag and take a bag of footballs over to the half-way line on the far side. He would start hitting cross-field balls over to the towel and by the time he'd finished, he was getting ten out of twelve on target. The accuracy was absolutely amazing. I would just stand there on the terraces thinking, 'I'm watching the England captain practising his passing.'"

Man marking

It was an era of unsubtle opponents more than eager to decommission any parts of those artistic legs they could get near enough to kick. Haynes took terrible punishment week in and week out with little protection from referees, frequently falling victim to the tackle from behind. He only really retaliated once, as this book will tell.

Even so, hardly any player really got the better of Johnny Haynes in his prime. Even in the early days with the freedom to tackle from behind, opportunities to get a tackle in on him were rare. The only professionals who did a fairly good job stopping him on occasions were his England team-mate and former England captain Ronnie Clayton of Blackburn and maybe Everton's Jimmy Gabriel.

Haynes' only real nemesis was a journeyman professional, Andy Malcolm of West Ham; they engaged in several skirmishes during some bitter London derbies. Malcolm was about the same age as Haynes and would have studied the maestro's skills and technique whilst in the England schoolboy and England youth fold. Malcolm learned to put what he had observed to good effect, and it was said that "Malcolm played in between Haynes' shoulder-blades, virtually inside his shirt."

Shooting

Johnny Haynes also had a real eye for goal. He had, when he chose to use it, a fierce shot with either foot. He could hit goals from near-impossible angles from thirty yards. He specialised in the long-range rocket from outside the penalty area. He was sometimes criticised that he didn't use this particular weapon often enough. Being such a perfectionist he didn't like missing the target. Roy Bentley agreed, saying: "He had two very good feet; he really ought to have scored more goals."

Strength and stamina

What was most remarkable was that he displayed all his superhuman skills on a weekly basis on quagmire pitches that were often more mud than grass, sometimes

Heading was not Haynes' favourite football skill!

inches deep in places in the goalmouth or down the centre of the field, using a wet, laced leather football that weighed as much as a dense neutron star.

The loyal Haynes knew that Fulham didn't have the money for star names, and he was once quoted as saying, in the nicest way possible, that Fulham had probably only fifteen players of league quality, not just First Division, the rest of the squad probably being just about good enough for the Southern League. For a man of his talents supplementing these shortcomings must have been excruciatingly difficult at times. Such was his strength and stamina that he was often reported as doing the work of two or even three players on a Saturday afternoon.

Weaknesses

Incredibly he had a couple. Johnny Haynes wasn't the greatest header of a football, something he freely admitted and often joked about. However, people often pointed out that the late, great Alex James of Arsenal rarely, if ever, headed the ball. In more recent times the same was said of Bobby Moore. This didn't stop Haynes spending hours trying to improve that skill.

Like all great players, he was quick off the mark and very sharp over five to ten yards. He wasn't the fastest over a longer distance, but then he often didn't need to be.

I'll leave it to the others

It almost seemed as if Haynes instinctively knew when he had to turn on his special brand of soccer. When Fulham scored sixes, sevens, eight or even ten, you would expect Johnny to be amongst the feeding frenzy, but the match reports say otherwise. He rarely scored in these matches nor appeared to create that many either. It was almost as if he knew that the 'mere mortals' in the team were capable of winning this kind of match on their own without his hard input. It was when the going was tough, which it was frequently, that Johnny Haynes came into his own.

2: *The all-round sportsman*

2: The all-round sportsman

The cricketer

Johnny Haynes was introduced to Winchmore Hill Cricket Club by a master at Latymer School, Jack Hurst. His parents also actively encouraged him to play the game. He was also a member of the Winchmore Hill tennis club, and initially he wasn't sure whether he was a tennis player who had been converted to cricket or vice versa.

Between the years of 1952 and 1955, and with the blessing of Fulham Football Club, Haynes played regularly for Winchmore Hill every Saturday and Sunday during Fulham's close season. He was thrilled to be part of a "great bunch of guys". He remembered the great times he used to have practising his reflexes and catching using the slip cradle.

Haynes joined as a colt, but progressed very quickly under his coach, Norman Long. In 1952, not yet in the cricket first team, Haynes topped the batting averages with 42 and once took five wickets in an innings. Winchmore Hill had a significant number of cricket elevens at the time, often putting out in excess of ten sides. At that time the first eleven were looking for a wicket-keeper; John was presented with the chance to play, impressed and stayed in.

He was a very good wicket-keeper; he was also a more than able batsman, but never bowled for the first team. He batted down the order at number seven, the usual slot for a wicket-keeper; in one league game against Chingford he demonstrated his proficiency with the bat by scoring a century.

He was joined at Winchmore Hill by the then Arsenal centre forward Cliff Holton, and he enjoyed the cricket so much that he joined the club on a tour of the south coast. One match at Westcliff due to start in the morning was delayed because of rain, so the Winchmore Hill team played an impromptu football match instead against the local side on an adjoining pitch. It must have been incredible for the local lads to be facing the Arsenal spearhead and the England inside forward, but it was all played in a great spirit. On occasions, once the cricket matches had been played, a game of football took place afterwards.

Although he cut down on the cricket to give his troubled ankle a rest in 1956, he returned to play matches again in 1957. The fact that he was Fulham's captain and England's inside forward at the time was rarely mentioned, and Johnny was content to be anonymous, just one of the team. He never asked for any preferential treatment and was never given any.

He would often return to the club socially, and would also play sporadically in benefit matches. In

Wicket-keeper/batsman Johnny Haynes (right) takes to the field for his club, Winchmore Hill, during the Fifties. Below: a relaxed Johnny Haynes (seated third from right) pictured with his cricket club colleagues. On the right of the back row is fellow footballer Cliff Holton of Arsenal.

SCORE CARD PRICE 6d.

WINCHMORE HILL CRICKET CLUB
v
THE PROFESSIONAL FOOTBALLERS XI

at the Paulin Ground, Ford's Grove, Winchmore Hill, N.21.
Sunday August 2nd 1959. Hours of play—2 to 7 p.m.

The PROFESSIONAL FOOTBALLERS XI.

‡ 1. E. Baily
2. R. Tindall
3. A. Biggs
4. D. Bennett
5. J. N. Haynes
6. J. Chisholm
7. J. Standen
8. M. Charles
9. P. Baker
10. B. Jezzard
*11. E. Ditchburn

Extras

Extras B. L.B. W. N.B.

Fall of Wickets— **Total**
1. 2. 3. 4. 5. 6. 7. 8. 9. 10.

Bowlers 1 2 3 Bowlers 4 5 6

WINCHMORE HILL C. C.

1. H. J. Felton
2. B. J. Felton
3. D. A. Metson
‡ 4. M. N. G. Pryke
5. J. C. Tait
6. C. C. Holton
7. P. N. Pizey
* 8. L. A. Lambert
9. J. Taylor
10. B. Avent
11. J. N. Marshall

Extras

Extras B. L.B. W. N.B.

Fall of Wickets— **Total**
1. 2. 3. 4. 5. 6. 7. 8. 9. 10.

Bowlers 1 2 3 Bowlers 4

‡ Captain

WINCHMORE HILL C.C. SCORECARD PRICE 1s.

JACK ROBERTSON BENEFIT MATCH

WINCHMORE HILL C.C.
v.
MIDDLESEX C.C.C. XI

PAULIN GROUND, FORD'S GROVE, SUNDAY, AUG. 16 - 2 p.m.

MIDDLESEX C.C.C. XI from

J. J. Warr
J. D. Robertson
D.C.S. Compton
F. S. Trueman
A. E. Moss
F. J. Titmus
R. A. Gale
W. E. Russell
J. T. Murray
R. W. Hooker
P. H. Parfitt
E. Clark

Extras
Total

WINCHMORE HILL C.C.

H. J. Felton
B. J. Felton
D. A. Metson
M. W. G. Pryke
J. C. Tait
C. C. Holton
P. W. Pizey
J. N. Haynes
R. W. Morgan
B. H. Avent
J. Marshall

Extras
Total

TEA AND REFRESHMENTS ARE AVAILABLE ON THE GROUND
Your free lucky scorecard number for an autographed bat is on the otherside of this card. The draw for which will take place at close of play

Top: Haynes turns out with Beddy Jezzard for the footballers against his Winchmore Hill colleagues. Bottom: Haynes plays for Winchmore Hill against a Middlesex team including his hero DCS (Denis) Compton and Fred Trueman.

Haynes holds four catches

Winchmore Hill, set to score only 58 runs to beat Alexandra Park, at the Pauline Ground, lost a wicket with only three runs scored.

Earlier, the Park collapse began in the second over of their innings when Johnny Haynes, England and Fulham footballer, took a great catch at finger-tip stretch far to his right to dismiss Munro.

This was the first of four grand catches taken behind the stumps by Haynes.

Davies sound

Only Con Davies, a sound 21.

games where Winchmore Hill played the Professional Footballers XI, Haynes sometimes played for Winchmore Hill, and sometimes for the footballers. In these matches he was often joined by Fulham stars Beddy Jezzard and Jimmy Hill.

He maintained his interest in cricket throughout his life. One of his biggest thrills later in life in Scotland was to be put on the same dinner table as the West Indian legend Sir Garfield Sobers. Sobers was his hero, and he couldn't wait to get back home and tell everyone about his experience!

The golfer

Johnny Haynes could also have been a top golfer. With Jimmy Hill, he won the amateur foursome golf prize at Guildford in 1961. Fulham included a golf day as part of the training regime at the time. Haynes said: "It's healthy, there's plenty of fresh air and walking to keep you fit. Then you get the 'bug' and want to start playing every spare second—like I did."

Haynes normally played on Sunday afternoons and Mondays, either at the RAC course, situated just a stone's throw from his Epsom home, or with other players at Wimbledon Park. At that time he had a twelve handicap. Jimmy Hill said: "Johnny has got the same talent for golf that he has for football, despite his atrocious grip! Only a natural games player could get anything like a game from that grip."

After retiring from football, Haynes played a great deal more golf, and in the end reduced his handicap to a single figure.

The tennis player

Haynes joined Winchmore Hill Lawn Tennis Club and promptly won the junior singles lawn tennis title in 1952. He played consistently during his lifetime, and was also skilled at most racquet sports including badminton and squash.

The snooker player

After training, was there a better place to be than upstairs in the Cottage on the snooker table? Frank

Golf remained a favourite relaxation of Johnny Haynes throughout his lifetime. Here he watches Bobby Robson tee off alongside colleagues Tony Macedo and John Ryan. Note that the ever-fit Haynes is carrying his clubs whilst lesser mortals have resorted to golf trolleys!

Style, grace and stamina on the tennis court.

Osborne, Jimmy Hill, Beddy Jezzard, Charlie Mitten, Arthur Stevens were all excellent players; the younger players coming in could rarely get on the table. Robin Lawler was the artiste, the potter capable of generating some serious breaks. Bobby Robson spent more time watching. Needless to say, Johnny Haynes was also a good snooker player.

The swimmer

Swimming was another sport where the young Londoner shone, but he had to take this strenuous sport easy because of ear trouble.

The folklore

There is a persistent rumour that Haynes once played in a representative football game for Fulham in the morning scoring a hat trick in the game, played a cricket game for a Winchmore Hill XI in the afternoon scoring a century, and rounded things off by winning a major tennis tournament either in the evening of that day, or early the following day! You wouldn't have bet against it.

3: A Jekyll and Hyde character?

3: A Jekyll and Hyde character?

Johnny Haynes was often termed a complicated man, and a man of many faces. Some consider that very few people got truly close to him. By his own admission he was a perfectionist in all walks of life, and he expected the same standards from everyone else. Like all exceptional talents his greatness came as part of a complete package alongside his faults and frailties.

Dr Jekyll

The superstar

It is considered by many that Johnny Haynes was the first genuine football superstar in England. He was the David Beckham of his day, immaculate in character and appearance, always smart and very nicely dressed. Even late on in his career in South Africa, he was entirely amiable, always available for interviews, always turning up five minutes early and always smartly attired. He had an air like Bobby Moore, a natural charisma; when he walked into a room people took notice. He was, in his prime, a very handsome man, having inherited his ebony dark hair from his mother Rose and his sapphire-blue eyes from his father Eddie.

From owning sports cars to dating TV stars, Haynes displayed all the trappings of the celebrity lifestyle, with none of the arrogance and petulance of many of today's leading lights. He never wanted to be splashed across the papers outside of the football arena and was a private man. He never flaunted his relationship with show business personalities.

Johnny Haynes was somewhat of an enigma and was often seen out on the town with cricketers and boxers, and he seemingly took television appearances coolly in his stride. On the other side, there was the 'boy' who lived at home with his parents, refused to go out with the footballers on a Wednesday evening as he had promised to take his Mum to the cinema instead, and the studious man who would spend hours writing encouraging letters to youthful fans who considered him a friend.

He always had time after the game to emerge from the players' door, sign autographs and chat to fans for half an hour. He was even a perfectionist with autograph hunters; he often made the boys stand in line, and he would then count them. To ensure every boy received one and just one signature, any latecomers would

Tidiness counts. Haynes is as neat off the field as he is on it.

Below, a star relaxes . . . with gramophone records and an appreciative budgerigar.

On the doorstep of Fulham's homely stadium.

Always immaculately smart and very presentable. Left: a young Haynes featured in a Fifties football magazine; right: in 1963, visiting a hospital for treatment and continuing to attract admiring glances.

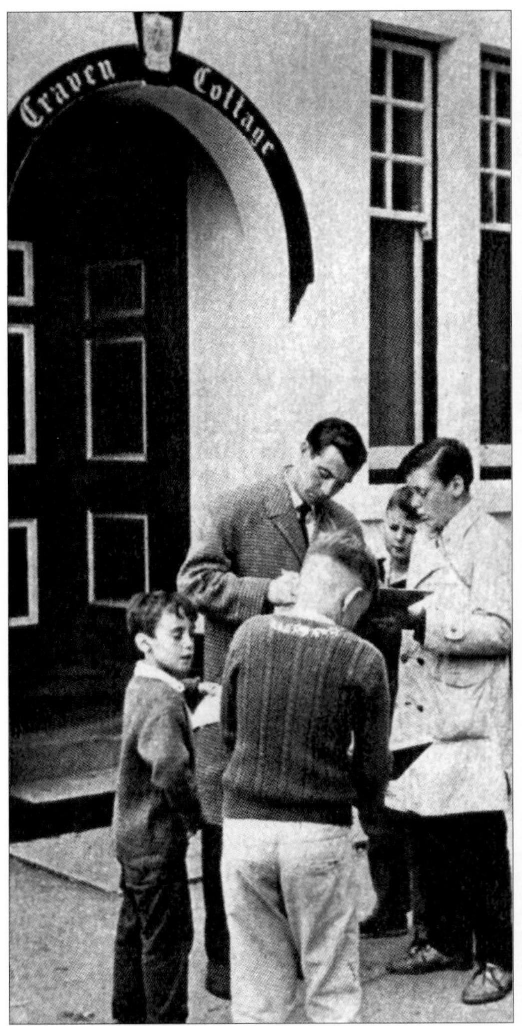

Always ready, willing and able—Johnny pictured at various stages of his career signing for his young fans.

apparently have to argue their case with the England captain. Those observing these rituals maintain that he was never unreasonable, always fair, but sometimes difficult to warm to.

Socially

The press, who never really got to know him, attempted to paint a picture of the off-the-field Johnny Haynes that was similar to the footballer on it, but nothing could have been further from the mark.

Roy Bentley commented: "It was scandalous what the papers were allowed to print about John's temperament, calling him this and that—it was all just a load of old rubbish. Selfish, big-headed and conceited? Just rubbish. He was quite the opposite; you couldn't have met a more polite or helpful bloke, which you would have found out for yourself if you'd met him a few times. He certainly wasn't the man the papers made him out to be."

Without any doubt at all, Johnny Haynes was a nice human being. He could be quite shy and reserved and was not a natural conversationalist, some saying he could be "spare with words". However, he also had a ready dry wit and strong sense of humour when the need arose. Several sources come up with the same descriptions of Haynes' persona: polite, courteous and modest, with an utter lack of vanity that was endearingly engaging.

He was a real gentleman with grace and charm. Off the field of play he was described as the mildest of men, friendly and wholly likeable. Fulham legend Fred Callaghan concurs: "Within the club, he commanded and could have demanded the greatest of respect, but he never did, and he was the politest man you could meet."

Despite his charisma and star status, he was rarely at the forefront socially; once he had made his 'entrance', he was content to blend into the background. George Cohen summed it up succinctly: "Off the field you wouldn't know he was in the same room." In a group he was the retiring sort, and the last person one would notice; he preferred to be an onlooker rather than an active performer, which was in stark contrast to his behaviour on the football field.

Johnny Haynes was a thoughtful individual and could be quite a serious man, though Fulham's chirpy, extrovert and funny squad brought Haynes out of his shell. Haynes would often wish that he had the panache of Bobby Keetch and his 'front' when wooing the ladies, or that he could emulate the carefree, clowning of Rodney Marsh or maybe just be Tosh, but he was content to be amongst these personalities, drinking in the atmosphere that they generated.

Sir Bobby Robson recalls: "He was very well mannered, courteous and polite, but he was good company, very good company. He would always be the first to the bar, and would always order the first round of drinks. He liked a joke and he liked a laugh—you would never be bored with Johnny Haynes."

His former cricket colleagues remember him fondly as just a regular guy who liked to socialise. He was good fun in the bar afterwards. He liked a drink in moderation, and mixed freely with the lady tennis players. It was a place where he could escape the stresses and rigours of high-level football. He was a happy guy who was seemingly always singing, and, as his cricketer colleagues recalled: "Who could forget his rendition of 'April Showers'?"

Therefore to imply that Johnny Haynes was in some ways an introvert would be quite wrong. He had a very good singing voice, and in the right company he would be asked to sing. Johnny would frequently take the microphone and give excellent renditions of, amongst other songs, 'The Shadow of your Smile' or 'The Nearness of You'. Such was his talent that it was suggested seriously that Haynes make a few recordings when he finished playing; however there is no indication that he actually took up the challenge.

He also loved dancing and, predictably as a master of balance on the field, his steps were just as fleeting on the dance floor. His first wife Libby likened him to Nureyev as he was so graceful and well co-ordinated.

The hardest thing Haynes found about being captain of England was having to deliver the after-dinner speeches at the banquets, and it took him time to grow into this role. However, he admitted that he had long got over that initial stage fright. He said in 1962: "I haven't had to make anywhere near as many speeches as Billy Wright, but I have now climbed to my feet often enough to feel more able to tackle this social part of my job."

Journalists

Renowned journalists like John Arlott found a courteous Haynes. In 1956 Arlott said: "Haynes is a young man whom any father would be proud to own as a son. He knows where he is going; he has no need to bluster about it, and his conversation is neither boastful nor mock modest but straightforwardly intelligent. Above all he has natural good manners and, with them, a love and respect for the game of football."

However, at the height of his fame Johnny Haynes tolerated the press rather than embraced them. Discussions about matches were kept succinct and to the point, and his responses could be laconic. Often journalists found the situation difficult when confronted with an intelligent footballer, capable of writing books and penning a column for a newspaper. One called his interviews with him "a polite joust".

Another journalist said of his guarded stance: "You weren't sure whether to shake his hand or try to goad him in an attempt to improve matters. It was as difficult to get under his skin as it was to draw confidences out of him through false adulation." Haynes would spar with journalists, and always appeared to be asking the questions rather than answering them.

He would answer questions after considered thought and would always be on the boundaries of politeness; however, the shutters would come down very quickly whenever he was asked about his private life. Off the field he was a private man, and wanted at all times to protect his parents and acquaintances, both male and female, from any unnecessary intrusion.

Johnny was always available and happy to attend supporters' club functions.

A happy Haynes with lifetime supporters and close friends, Reg and Nell Weller. When Johnny had just two of his England caps left, he presented one of them to Reg.

He also retained a very honourable stance in public with journalists, and would never dream of openly criticising his less illustrious Fulham team-mates. In fact many will agree that they never heard Johnny Haynes say a bad word about anyone. Being loyal to his team-mates was important to Haynes; if a team-mate had a stinker of a match, he would say that "the ball wasn't running too kindly for him today," or that "he had a lot of bad luck."

Charity

Sid Huggett, chairman of the supporters' club at the time of Haynes' testimonial, said: "We never needed to ask Johnny twice to attend one of our functions. He was always willing to captain the darts team or help pick the beauty queen or sign autographs. I can remember many great nights at our headquarters where he would lead us all in a sing-song. Then there were the discussions where Johnny would constantly surprise us with his memories of famous comedians as well as football subjects. We value him highly and also greatly appreciate the long support of his mother and father."

Journalist Ray Hepburn recalls times in Edinburgh: "I will remember forever his generosity to dozens of charities up here, after he moved from South Africa to live with Avril, which left him with just one memento from his career.

"Almost all the shirts and caps from his fifty-six games for England, twenty-two of them as captain, were given away at charity dinners, along with many other treasured items of memorabilia.

"All that he retained was his first cap for his country, against Northern Ireland at Windsor Park, Belfast in 1954, his only tangible link with a glittering career.

"I recall berating him for giving away a Pelé No 10 Brazil shirt from the 1958 World Cup finals in Sweden but he just shrugged and replied: 'It was for the kids.'"

Mr Hyde

Johnny Haynes was a perfectionist in an imperfect football world. In his own book *Football Today*, published at the height of his career, he admitted: "Team-mates say I can be moody—it's true. I can be bad-tempered and over-demonstrative on the field—I won't deny it. I can get so worked up about this fabulous game that I hardly know myself."

Showing probably his most paradoxical face, Johnny Haynes said of his gestures and withering looks to team-mates: "No, it wasn't like that at all. It was *myself* I was getting the hump with for not getting the pass quite right. I was a bit of a perfectionist; it was me cursing myself rather than a mate."

He also said: "It was directed more at my own incompetence, rather than the faults of others." However, later in life he once said about his reactions: "I accept that I gave this image of myself as a footballer, and even if I didn't express myself in quite the same way later in life, my reaction was always the same." He summed up: "Maybe others are better actors, and have learned to disguise their emotions better than I do."

The quest for perfection

Johnny Haynes' personality appeared formed and hewn even before he set foot inside Craven Cottage. Many footballers who had known him from his earliest days right up to the end of his playing career have said that he had been basically the same person since he entered into, let alone emerged from, his teens. His later gestures and looks were caused more by his quest for perfection than any arrogance on his part. Haynes never demanded from a team-mate any effort he wasn't prepared to put in himself. He had a relentless need to deliver the best he had.

Haynes sometimes felt he was responsible for taking on the mantle of all ten outfield players. He wanted to start the move, provide a winger with a through pass, get the cross in and then be on the end of it. Haynes was a player who wanted to be in the thick of the action from first whistle to last—a player who would fight everyone's battles.

He would sometimes berate himself for not being on the end of a cross, when he had initiated a move five passes and twenty seconds earlier: "I should have been up there," or "I should have seen it coming." Colleagues would say that it wasn't a bit of good trying to console him—it was best to let him get on with it. One player said, "It would take just seconds for Haynes to be plunged into despair, but a few seconds after that his recovery would be complete!" His fellow professionals sometimes called this his 'carrying on'.

In the early stages of his career, he liked to be told about his mistakes and eagerly sought advice from almost everyone. In one unimportant midweek reserve match Haynes missed a penalty. He was inconsolable; missing a penalty was an unpardonable crime to him. He was in tears in the dressing room, asking other professionals how on earth he could have missed it. The next day he asked for several volunteers so he could spend extra hours just taking penalties.

In truth, Johnny Haynes was no different, therefore, to a number of perfectionist performers or divas (men may also exhibit 'diva-like' behaviour...) at the top of their profession and at the height of their professional fame. Be they opera singer, model, pop star, actor or footballer, there are those who want it just right.

It was all about standards

Johnny Haynes wasn't a good loser on the field of play; every defeat was like a slap in the face to him. He had a short fuse when players slipped below standards. George Cohen recalls in his autobiography: "He expected the same total application from others, as well as the best of their ability."

He had worked so hard at his own game, he expected the same dedication from others; he had little time for the hangers-on and wasters inside football. Haynes always said, "You can't afford to make an error especially in the 'danger areas' on the pitch, you've always got much more of a chance if you do things the simple way."

Roy Bentley recalls: "He would get frustrated with players who he thought hadn't mastered the basics. Being professionals he thought it was the first thing they should have done, learn how to pass properly with the inside of the foot or the instep for longer passes. He wondered why fellows kept flicking the ball or back-heeling it. He thought why be fancy; the ball could go anywhere, you risk losing it, why not just turn and pass it? Of course he was right.

"His distribution of the ball was so good that he expected everyone to be the same. He felt that all those lads coming up through the ranks should be able to do what he could do at fourteen. He couldn't accept less. I had to say, they're not all you, John; you have to allow some margin of error!"

Tom Wilson spoke similarly: "I saw him remonstrate many times. He got angry because he didn't sympathise with mistakes which in his book were blatantly 'unforced'. If you made a 'cods' of it, then he was unforgiving. It was in his nature to be that way. By unforgiving I don't mean that he was malicious or that he'd hold it against you, he'd note it and maybe talk about it after the game.

"Not too many had the courage to give it back to him, but some of us did from time to time—he didn't like it of course! I think because he was so good, people tended to given him a little bit of licence."

George Cohen varied this slightly when he said: "I don't think he always expected players to be as good as him, but his view was, 'You're in the first team, I expect a first-team performance.' You had to be sensible about it; you were going to have to be grown up when you were in that team. You couldn't expect as a young player to come into a team and not be told something!

"Although players like Jimmy Hill, Tom Wilson, and Roy Bentley would give you the coaching, John would come up and say, 'Do this or do that' with just the odd nudge or a wink, and that made a great deal of difference. I think the people here at Fulham understood the presence that he had here over many years—that you were playing with a true master."

Stan Brown added: "I think he got frustrated when people couldn't get the ball back to him. In those days centre forwards were big, clumsy players and they often fumbled around with it, the ball got caught up between their feet and they couldn't return it. I had fairly good control and could play the ball back. He always encouraged me and I didn't get too many rockets."

When he was made Fulham captain, he felt it was his duty to provide leadership in *all* areas. Maybe his only flaw was *how* this leadership sometimes manifested itself on the field of play. These reactions were described beautifully by a journalist as "head-hanging shrugs of despair, and the fairly obvious imprecations flung at colleagues or himself and the heaven-invoking look where you could almost feel the intensity with which he pleaded for more patience with lesser mortals." They became an inveterate part of his nature.

Johnny Haynes admitted to this, saying: "It manifested itself very early in my career and although I mellowed in later years, I always set my standards very high. It was natural that having become captain of Fulham at twenty-one, I was always exhorting my players to greater efforts. Mistakes annoyed me because I was a perfectionist and demanded a competent display from everyone, including myself."

"Much hands on hipping"

The phrase "much hands on hipping from Haynes" was used by renowned journalist Bob Ferrier. Gestures and words flowed from Haynes in an almost Tourette's-like fashion: head-flinging, foot-stamping, shoulder-shrugging, pitch-kicking—and of course the famous 'hands on hips' gesture. When 'the verbals' erupted, expletives were sometimes spat out momentarily at the height of his frustration. His depressed looks sometimes made you think that if he could have hanged himself there and then, he probably would have done! One former player said, "He would rip people to shreds. Of course, he made mistakes too, but not too many people had a pop at him."

The little nark

Haynes was the big fish in a small pond and controlled things on the pitch, and whilst others ran and puffed, he would often stand still, shrug, moan and become visibly fed up when things didn't go his way. He was affectionately known as 'Narky' and he was *always* moaning. Some would comment that at certain stages of his career, the gestures were talked about almost as much as his play.

Sir Bobby Robson smiled when he recalled: "He liked it right, he was a perfectionist and outstanding. He wanted people to play to his standards and ability all the time—which was impossible, because he was way above most people anyway and was a master craftsman. He sometimes got irritated with people who were not as good as he was. We called him the little nark because he was always moaning; the pass wasn't good enough, you've lost the ball, first touch wasn't good enough! He had high standards and expected high standards from everybody else."

Tom Wilson added: "Everything he played at, whether it was darts or billiards, he had to win, and if anything went wrong when he was playing, he *always* complained!"

The captain's role

At the height of his fame there were rumours that he was too tough with his criticism and that his relentless search for perfection had promoted dressing-room rows at Fulham, and this had even led to disillusioned young players hoping to follow in his footsteps having to leave the club. This charge was always vehemently dismissed by Fulham officials who countered by saying that demands for trials at Fulham shot up considerably as Haynes came to prominence.

However, despite Fulham's smokescreen the charge laid at Haynes' door was sometimes accurate. Alan Mullery recalls: "Unfortunately I saw him ruin quite a few kids. Allan Jones used to be a centre forward here, but Haynes ripped him to shreds, and Jonesy was as honest as the day was long. It affected him, but it didn't affect me or George [Cohen]; we had similar attitudes to the way we played the game."

Despite these imperfections, and constantly 'shouting the odds', he was a good captain, and he knew which players would respond to rollickings and which ones wouldn't. He never belittled or patronised his suffering team-mates. Johnny recognised that they were adults with families.

Of the earlier days of his captaincy Roy Bentley recalls: "He didn't F and blind at his team-mates, I never heard him do that. He certainly would have a go, but it was on a level of 'You should have been a lot tighter' or 'You allowed him to get away'. He would dictate to top internationals, he expected them to know what their job was. He was nearly always right."

Bobby Robson recalls that senior players accepted his criticisms without comment. He explained: "They knew he was a better player. He would speak his mind at half-time, and say a few words if it wasn't right. He was made captain at a very young age, and saw it as part of his responsibility, and he wasn't afraid to put up and say something. But he knew the game so well, and was a great analyser of the situation, so what he said always rang true."

Veteran Charlie Mitten spoke of Haynes as follows: "He was a perfectionist and was inclined to give the impression he was big-headed. Onlookers would walk away thinking that Haynes was a 'naughty boy', and it was true that he was rather outspoken in the dressing room. But if there was any criticism at all, it wouldn't be from me.... But Johnny like many youngsters before him learned his lesson in time and he turned out to be a very successful England player.... He sometimes found it difficult to conceal his exasperation for the shortcomings of lesser mortals. It earned him a reputation of being arrogant which was unfortunate and certainly not warranted."

Alan Mullery says of Haynes at his peak: "Sometimes the language that came out of his mouth was... I mean, he was a real gentleman off the pitch, but on it—oh dear! Every word you could possibly think of as a swear word—and after knowing him for all that period of time I think I heard every one! But he was a lovely man."

Around 1959, Haynes said this about the Fulham captaincy: "I know I do a lot of shouting during the game, I always have done; and when things are not going as they should then somebody *has* to shout—as captain it is my job. In any case, nobody has ever seen a match without a lot of noise. To most players shouting is instinctive. I make as much noise, often far more, as the rest. But there it is; I can't see myself changing now."

As skipper of England in 1962, Haynes added: "I am a demanding skipper. I ask a lot from players at country and at club level. But I make no apologies for this, because I demand a lot from myself and however I am judged in my role as captain and player I would not wish that judgment to be by anything but the highest measure. So, if I find my team-mates failing in that respect then it is up to me to try and set it right. That

Trevor Chamberlain and Johnny Haynes. One writer affectionately referred to Chamberlain as being the stone to Johnny Haynes' flint.

is the yardstick of my own performances when they don't come up to scratch."

At the end of the day

However, Johnny Haynes did not let football overwhelm his life. George Cohen says, "After handing out almighty rollickings to a team-mate, when the final whistle blew they would still go off for a drink together after the game. Off the field, he quickly regained his perspective that unfortunately not all were superhuman."

George also added: "That was Haynes' style; he cared passionately about football, but when it was over, he wasn't going to let it dominate his life, and that, when I think about it, may have been the reason he settled so happily for life at Craven Cottage."

Elaborating on this, George said: "He would have a go and could curse and F and blind at team-mates in moments of exasperation. He and I had stand-up rows about various things, but we ended up having a drink in Sean Tracey's pub (The Queen's Elm) and it was not even mentioned. There was never ever *any* malice about Johnny Haynes. He just wanted Fulham to win and Fulham to do well."

Haynes and Trevor Chamberlain

Of all the players who were the victims of Haynes' ire, no-one received more flak than Trevor Chamberlain. This book will later document the way Johnny and Trevor became lifelong friends through football. When an attempt is made to document all the on-field events between the two, they will fill a book on their own.

Haynes and Chamberlain formed one of soccer's great double acts: Chamberlain's Falstaff to Haynes' Henry V; Haynes a single-minded, meticulously prepared perfectionist, Chamberlain whimsical, a creature of tides and moon. Their on-field rows were spectacular. They were also described as chalk and cheese, night and day, and the strangest of left-wing partnerships.

Johnny Haynes admired his mate Tosh, but often they would be on different wavelengths. Stand-up rows on the pitch were common, at least one per match; they were however always quickly patched up. Tosh would always defend his mate with a typical quirkish quote: "Anyone tells you Johnny Haynes is a big 'ead, needs a new hat, I'll tell you!"

Like the alleged incident when Maurice Cook demanded parity with Haynes' pay during the summer because Haynes wasn't a better player than him during the close season, there are many versions of the Haynes/Chamberlain incident where a referee tried to book Haynes or Chamberlain or both because of words exchanged between the pair on the pitch. Stories like these are apocryphal, but still serve to embellish Haynes' character—and will no doubt forever be recycled!

4: The early years

4: The early years

John Norman Haynes, the son of a shoetree manufacturer who later became a GPO (Post Office) engineer, was born at Kentish Town, north London, on 17th October 1934. He was born in the year Stanley Matthews made his international debut. His father Edward, a quiet man, was from Walworth and his mother Rose (born Newton), lively and gregarious, came from St John's Wood; that Haynes, an only child, was a dyed-in-the-wool Londoner was entirely predictable. Rose and Eddie were married in April 1934 and John was born just days after Rose's eighteenth birthday.

The family lived in a maisonette in Tramway Avenue off the North Circular Road near Jubilee Park. The young Haynes attended the local primary school in Houndsfield Road, situated just a goal kick away from the family home.

How every boy starts

His early youth, like that of most others, was spent kicking a ball round the streets of Kentish Town.

These are Haynes' recollections of this time: "Even in my earliest days, I managed to fit in about three hours a day kicking and heading a ball; again luck was on my side. We lived next door to Jubilee Park, Edmonton, and there were always young fellows who were as keen and ambitious to kick and head a ball as myself. However, you don't have to live next door to a park. Ball control can be learned equally well in the back-yard provided the pupil is sufficiently dogged not to tire of his lessons, and needless to say, doesn't break too many windows!"

Early school

His school never showed much of an interest in rugby, so it was soccer all the way. It was the first sport the young Haynes tried, and he was good at it—so much so that, because of the number of wartime evacuations, he made the school team, Houndsfield Road's under-eleven side, at the age of just seven. A local greengrocer offered Johnny an orange for every three goals he scored. He remembers, "I settled down at Houndsfield Road to earn oranges as fast as I could."

Even at a tender age Haynes was concentrating on his eventual game. At his peak he recalled: "I always gave much thought to how a ball should be passed, even when I was around seven, and the art of accurate passing had come to me by the time I was playing inside left at the Houndsfield Road School at Edmonton when I was eleven. I am not suggesting that I had mastered the art at that age because I am still learning, and hope to go on learning for many years to come, but I had acquired quite a bit of ball control, and only because of the thought and the hours of practice I had given to it."

His first memories were of something that interrupted his soccer progress—war. And John's first recollections, like those of many other children of his age, revolved around air raids and frightening nights spent in the shelters. His mother Rose worked in the factories during the war, whilst Eddie served in the Ordnance Corps and saw service in Burma during 1943–45, leaving Haynes without a father figure for two years.

As well as playing school football with older children, Haynes extended his adventures to park football. He was indeed a 'midget' at this time, and as he was always playing with kids who were three or four years older, he was always the smallest player on the pitch, and was often roughed up by the older children. But it was all part of his football education, and he more than matched his elders with ability on the field.

To further test his skills, the young Haynes was given a bicycle and embarked on a paper round. The bicycle allowed him to venture further afield and find new playing colleagues. The new pitches were the crucibles that would enable him to find his true métier.

Haynes evacuated

Haynes had originally been evacuated with his mother in 1940. They had taken a train to a small village near Braintree, Essex, but were away for just four days, and returned hitching a lift back to Enfield on a fruit and vegetable lorry. Then in October 1942 his parents decided to evacuate him once again. He remembers: "I was one small boy put on one large train, and in my heart there was a void as big as Wembley Stadium." To Haynes the industrial north was like travelling to a foreign country.

Haynes later went to live with a family in Droylsden, Manchester; the family were friends of Haynes' parents. The couple had a boy of Johnny's age and the two shared a bedroom. The family were very kind to him, and were devout Catholics. This meant a great deal of religion and very little football. Johnny didn't fancy the northern cinder pitches anyway. He was shipped to a convent school for four months, where he had to attend mass every day and fulfil the duties of altar boy. He had few fond memories of his time there.

It was rumoured that after those four months, the Houndsfield Primary campaigned vigorously to have him returned, as the school's football results had deteriorated dramatically! Despite the dangers of living in London at the time, Johnny didn't need to be asked twice about returning.

He was very glad to be home and was immediately put back in the Houndsfield Road team. In his first

Previous page: A young Johnny Haynes, fifth from the left in the front row, is pictured aged seven at Houndsfield Road Primary School in Edmonton. The broken windows are a grim reminder of the prevailing World War conditions.

match, he scored eight goals, and described it as "one of the happiest days of my life." Johnny's sponsoring greengrocer in his exultation happily presented him with three congratulatory oranges.

Off to Latymer

Academically, John was a bright lad and won a scholarship at ten to attend a good school, the Latymer School in Edmonton, starting in September 1945. According to the official canon, the school's aims were to provide "a first class, liberal education where pupils achieve their full potential and show consideration for others." The school already had a 300-year-old history, and had as its motto *Qui patitur vincit*, 'Who endures wins'. Haynes would learn a great deal about endurance during his years at Craven Cottage.

Latymer was, and still is, exceptionally strong academically. Haynes' school reports would confirm that he was "quite an intelligent boy", but this was coupled with the usual "doesn't concentrate enough, mind on other things." A former school colleague recalls a Haynes who was often in trouble for not doing his maths homework, waylaid by yet another soccer match; his female maths teacher would often berate a young Johnny saying, "Football will get you nowhere, Haynes." Strangely, mathematics was Johnny's favourite school subject.

But there really was only one other thing on his mind, a career as a professional footballer. As Saturday approached, John freely admitted that his mind incessantly wandered from his scholastic tasks towards those beckoning on the pitch the following day.

Haynes did occasionally take his mind off football, as witnessed by an incident recalled by the marvellous actress Dame Eileen Atkins, the co-creator of *Upstairs, Downstairs* and *The House of Eliott.* Dame Eileen was a contemporary of John at Latymer, and once at Christmas—she thinks they were about fourteen—John asked her to the school party, but she turned him down as he was so much smaller than her!

Learning from his heroes

By birth and upbringing Johnny Haynes should not have been a Fulham player at all. Born and raised in Edmonton, north London, he should logically have joined nearby Tottenham Hotspur. With his father and Uncle Jack (Eddie's brother, also named John Norman Haynes), the young Haynes was regularly taken to both Highbury and White Hart Lane during and after the war.

His father had also been a keen and very able footballer himself in his day, playing at inside or outside left for local sides. The young Haynes was also a very keen cricketer, and his father and uncle regularly took him to Lords to see his hero, Denis Compton.

He was well loved by his parents; by his own admission he had a very happy early life, and even during a time of rationing and turmoil he never wanted for food or clothes. After seeing his natural ability, John's

Playing with sixth-formers and schoolmasters, the diminutive Haynes has already made the Latymer cricket team.

parents never discouraged their son from attempting to become a professional footballer and always ensured that there were new boots or a new football as birthday or Christmas presents. Even at this young age Johnny recognised the efforts and the sacrifices that were being made on his behalf, and would never forget the part his parents played in his future success.

He was actually an Arsenal fan, and pictures of the Highbury stars of the day festooned the walls of his Edmonton home. His very early inspiration was watching Denis Compton play First Division football for Arsenal and cricket for Middlesex and England from 1946 to 1949, and very early on he decided that if he could, he would like to emulate him.

Originally Haynes wanted to join Arsenal, a crack team, and he thought he might have a decent chance of advancement there. His original Highbury inspiration was the diminutive Scotsman Jimmy Logie, similar in stature to himself but a great dribbler.

He recalls: "I was not in favour of young boys playing and never watching; you can learn so much from watching footballers who are better than yourself. When I was a boy at Edmonton I never missed watching Arsenal or Tottenham. I played my own football on Saturday morning before dashing over to either Highbury or White Hart Lane to see a top-class game.

"Jimmy Logie of Arsenal and Eddie Baily then with Spurs were truly great inspirations to me and I confess that I picked up plenty from them whilst standing on the terraces. Baily particularly inspired me soon after the war years when Spurs had such a splendid team, and Eddie made up a dangerous left-wing partnership with Leslie Medley, who is now in Canada."

Haynes was also a great fan of the legendary Wilf Mannion of Middlesbrough, and he recalls: "Living in Kentish Town I knew I had to take every opportunity I had to watch Wilf Mannion whenever his team, Middlesbrough, visited the capital. He really was something else, his balance, his work rate and the inch perfect passes made a huge impression on me. I recall in later years after becoming a regular member of the Fulham side, I hit a long crossfield pass for our winger

The Edmonton District team of 1948. The proud captain is in the middle of the front row—and he's got the ball, of course.

He was in the junior Edmonton team that won the Sun Shield in 1947, and then played three full seasons with the senior side from 1947 to 1950. In that side, he won the Corinthian Shield in 1947–48 and in 1949–50. The reward for young Haynes and his victorious colleagues for winning the Sun Shield was a meal out and a trip to the Windmill Theatre!

As he improved he was, in his own words in 1952, "lucky enough to have been selected for London boys in both 1949 and 1950, Middlesex boys in 1950, junior schoolboys international against Eire and reserve for the senior schoolboys international against Wales in 1949."

In the London boys' side, Haynes played in matches against Birmingham and the Midland Counties Federation. He was then chosen for the London team which departed from Victoria Station and toured West Germany for ten days in April 1950, competing against boys' teams from Cologne, Frankfurt, Mainz and Nierstein.

Tosh Chamberlain to chase. As the ball ran out of play for a throw-in he yelled at me across the pitch in disdain, 'Who do you think you are, Haynes—bloody Wilf Mannion!'"

The school versus district dilemma

School football at Latymer was a hit-and-miss affair for Haynes, although he practised as most kids did then, with a tennis ball in the school quadrangle. He played only in a series of form or house teams that competed against one another during the week. He was placed in Keats House. Many people who played against him in school during the Forties still have nightmares; a 15–0 defeat was a letting off.

He was more interested in the formalised district team that played regularly in fierce local competitions. The district team was picked from a plethora of local schools and from hundreds of kids, but it soon became abundantly clear that he would command a regular place there.

This led to him facing up to the first football 'crisis' of his life, when the head teacher at Latymer, Mr Victor Davies, gave him, and others at Latymer, an ultimatum: they could play for the school year side on a Saturday or for the district—but not both. After deliberating with his parents, he chose the district side.

Success with Edmonton and elsewhere

So he began with the Edmonton district side, of which he was, inevitably, captain. There were in fact two Edmonton district sides—junior and senior—and Johnny often played in both; and when playing with the seniors, he was again frequently competing against players who were two years older than he was. Former team-mates recall a player who was already streets ahead of anything else on the pitch.

Originally Johnny was a one-man show; his entire game was based on dribbling with the ball and solo work. Although he excelled in this dimension of the game, he was somewhat isolated as a team player. His mentor at the district, a Mr Sanders, took John aside and showed him how "the ball can travel faster than the man," and gave him the first clues on how to "send it rather than take it." It was the first real coaching John had received and it opened his eyes to aspects of integration and team play.

It was at this tender age of twelve that John fully realised that passing the ball accurately and at the right pace was the key to winning games, a lesson he never forgot: "As I climbed the higher grade school football, I began to realise that an inside forward can be more helpful to the rest of the team if he cuts out the tendency to hang on to the ball for too long. Quick and accurate passes to colleagues often bring better reward to the team. My change in policy [from dribbling] helped me and my school team considerably. We won more matches, and as I graduated into the England Schools team I realised that the quick pass paid off best of all."

In those days, the football activities were intense, and Haynes was coached twice a week. The district boys all travelled to White Hart Lane, and although they were not allowed to utilise the pitch facilities, they would train on the cinder track and use the club's gymnasium and associated facilities beneath the stand. The coaching was actually carried out by the Tottenham Hotspur stars of the day, inside forward Eddie Baily and goalkeeper Ted Ditchburn.

Haynes was also a member of the Boys' Brigade. The brigade also trained twice a week, and so at least four out of five weekday evenings were already used

The Edmonton District team at Norwich, winning away from home to reach the semi-final of the English Schools' Shield. Haynes (front row, second from right) looks younger than all the rest!

up. The brigade also played on a Saturday afternoon. So it was not unusual for Haynes to play twice on a Saturday, once for the district and once for the Boys' Brigade, with a clean football shirt and shorts for each game, but in the afternoon game often playing in the same wet and muddy socks and boots he had worn in the morning.

Such was the intensity of this training and playing regime that his time was totally occupied with organised football, and he freely admitted that he never had to dribble a tennis ball all the way to school and back each day. On the rare occasions when he was not involved in any kind of match, his father would accompany him to Jubilee Park in Edmonton and help him with his dribbling, passing and shooting skills.

The district team's regimen was a veritable smorgasbord of cups and competitions, and to complete a full season's worth of fixtures, a team merely had to keep winning and progressing to further rounds of each competition. However, there was one competition that stood out above all the others—the English Shield.

First successes and first disappointment

Haynes was already being recognised, both in the local press and nationally. The young lad used to follow their words slavishly. In one season, the Edmonton team did phenomenally well. After seeing off the likes of Acton, Heston and Islington in the divisional aspects of the English Shield, the Edmonton team made it into the 'proper' rounds.

He was a prodigy even at this very young age, and that was extremely rare in the world of football at the time. His later chum Trevor Chamberlain played for the nearby Islington district and often played against Haynes when he turned out for the Edmonton equivalent. Chamberlain refers to him affectionately as: "A little snide, he was only four feet eleven which made him an elusive little sod. He was one of those players you felt like you wanted to kick, because he was driving you crazy, but you couldn't get near him to kick him. He was an amazing talent even as a schoolboy."

In the fifth round Edmonton played Walsall at White Hart Lane in front of 10,000 soprano schoolboys. A draw at home was followed by a 2–0 win at Walsall's Fellows Park ground. In the sixth round it became better still, with the London team winning 2–1 at Northampton, in front of the Mayor and Mayoress of Edmonton. The quarter-final produced another draw at White Hart Lane, before Norwich were overcome on their own ground. Haynes' first opportunity for

The young Haynes always loved playing cribbage with his father Eddie. Pictured here in his teens, it looks as though he's about to win another game with Dad. Winning was something Haynes always wanted to do.

glory was scuppered at the semi-final stage when they were beaten 0–3 by Leicester. It was the first sporting disaster he had been forced to suffer, and he recalled "there were a few secret tears."

Football was so organised in those days that there were networks of hundreds of ordinary people working behind the scenes building a tree structure to enable the youngsters to find a platform on which to demonstrate their skills. Even at schools level, the young Haynes had experienced the atmosphere of playing on Football League grounds in front of pretty large crowds, as well as the training, the tactics, the travel and even the publicity.

He had shot to prominence, with the national press reporting that he was a quick, alert type of player and that his ball control was delightful. One report pointed out that Haynes formed an effective link with the defence. There was more to come.

5: England Schoolboys

5: England Schoolboys

His footballing displays and the accompanying publicity had put the young Haynes in line to receive schoolboy honours, and after playing in a number of trials he was selected to play for England Schoolboys.

The first honours

He always admitted that selection had been a priority: "The opportunity of playing in schoolboy internationals was a great incentive." At the age of fourteen, this was an enormous step up and he recognised its seriousness. His first England Schoolboys match brought with it his first international trip to Belfast, which required a long train ride, a trip on a big ship and staying in a decent hotel. Although the lightweight Haynes (still under seven stone) struggled on a bog of a pitch against Northern Ireland, the game overall was excellent, and his joy was complete when England rammed home two late goals to come away victorious 4–3.

After his fifteenth birthday, he played again for England Schoolboys against Wales in front of a stunning crowd of over 40,000 at Hillsborough. He scored in the midweek match, as did Cliff Jones for Wales, who would join him at Fulham late in his career. Early in the game the score stood at one-all, but England then produced what was described as a copybook exhibition to demolish the Welsh 6–1. This put Haynes in line for the 'big one' the following week—Scotland.

Previous page: Johnny Haynes in action on the famous green turf at Wembley during the slaughter of the Scottish Schoolboys; and a starring role on the cover of a famous boys' magazine of the day.

A star is born

He was still trying to give as much time as possible to his academic studies, and was working hard revising for his School Certificate at Latymer when he was told that he would play against Scotland—at Wembley! He recalled: "What a thrill it was to get the opportunity whilst still at school to play on the famous green turf upon which so many cup finals and internationals had been played!"

So on 15th April 1950 a tiny fifteen-year-old played for England Schoolboys against Scotland at Wembley—and he simply turned the opposition inside out. A huge crowd of between 50,000 and 60,000 watched the game at the Empire Stadium. It was also shown live on television. This was a rare event, as permission for the transmission of live matches of any description was seldom granted at the time. So little Haynes became, at fifteen, a national figure, and here were the very early signs that he would be a famous player.

England beat Scotland by a huge 8–2 scoreline, and Haynes scored twice. Reports also say that he made most of the other six goals. One of his goals was a cheeky 'one step and shoot' penalty, but the other, the third England goal, was described by the young Haynes himself as a "picture goal". Collectively the England team had played exceptionally well, but the supremely competent and confident Haynes was far and away the most impressive player on the field.

In the *Boy's Own Paper* of September 1950, the great inside forward Alex James said: "His brain

Johnny Haynes (second player from left in the front row) lines up with the other English Schoolboys that put Scotland to the sword in April 1950.

Haynes slots home England's third goal in the schoolboys' 8–2 rout of Scotland at Wembley, April 1950.

worked as fast as his twinkling feet, and that's saying something."

He had a marvellous match, and everything went right for him: the dribbles, the passes and the shots. He felt that, once on the pitch, he could do no wrong. He had stolen the show against Scotland, and become a *wunderkind*, famous thanks to television and his own precocious talent. It was a display that had the critics raving, and he became a household name overnight.

Trevor Chamberlain recalls: "It wasn't until England Schoolboys demolished Scotland Schoolboys and he starred, that people sat up and took notice, and he quickly became the talk of the town."

He actually appeared on television as a fifteen-year-old soon afterwards and gave a talk to youngsters on football tactics and demonstrated a few moves before the cameras.

He said in 1960 about that eventful match day: "How grateful I was that I had devoted so many hours to putting the ball into the open space and perfecting the long through ball. Because of my youth, I suppose, I made the headlines in the national press after that match and football writers seem surprised at my knowledge of the game…all due I repeat to the study I had given to the game soon after I had raised myself from the kindergarten."

He was instantly famous, and after the Scotland match a reporter barged into the dressing room, accosted a startled Haynes and demanded an interview, asking him which were the professional clubs that were clamouring for his signature. The interloper was quickly ushered out of the door.

The local Edmonton and District Schools' Association Jubilee Handbook (1902–1952) said of him: "Aged fifteen, height five foot and seven stone five pounds he was the smallest player on view. His uncannily directed passes constantly split the Scottish defence wide open. As the match was also televised, he had the distinction of being the first schoolboy to score a penalty seen by televiewers."

Although he could have done without the pressure, he had to resign himself to the fact that he was a schoolboy prodigy, and was going to be coveted by all the major clubs following these displays during the schoolboy international matches. He knew that he would have to work hard on his physical development in terms of both height and weight, but if he could master this, then he felt that nothing else could stop him. Yet even at this early stage, some of the 'wise men of soccer', whilst acknowledging his considerable skills, considered that young John would never make the grade in top-class football—too short and too frail.

He played in two more internationals for England Schoolboys in 1950: a 3–1 win over Scotland at Ibrox and a 3–2 win over Eire at Dalymount Park in Dublin. England Schoolboys won all the five matches involving Haynes, notching up twenty-four goals in the process. In the squad of sparkling players that demolished Scotland at Wembley, a number of others also went on to become seasoned professional footballers, notably Ron Cope with Manchester United, Eddie Clamp with Wolves, Ray Parry with Bolton, Colin Booth with numerous clubs and Frank Blunstone with Chelsea.

Haynes became an instant celebrity after his Wembley display against Scotland's schoolboys. He immediately found himself the object of press attention, and here he shows the television cameras and his fellow schoolboys how he controlled the ball during the Wembley victory.

Five days after the Scotland game, Haynes joined his London schoolboy colleagues for a ten-day tour of Germany where they played against school teams in Cologne, Frankfurt, Mainz and Dusseldorf. Pictured here in the window of their train at Victoria Station are, top, Bryan Twaites and Philip Norman, and below them Fred Cooper and young Johnny sporting a smart new raincoat. Cooper played a few games for West Ham, but the other two failed to make the grade in league football.

6: Arsenal or Tottenham? No, it's Fulham!

6: Arsenal or Tottenham? No, it's Fulham!

People have wondered whether it was because of Haynes' initially short and light stature that bigger clubs than Fulham—a club much loved but never very successful—did not seem to want to acquire and secure his services. He was, after all, born and brought up virtually on the doorstep of the Tottenham ground in north-east London, while it was known that he was also a great fan of some of the Arsenal players, at the other great north London club.

Other famous clubs at the time, especially Portsmouth and Wolverhampton Wanderers, were also very keen to get Haynes under their wing. It seemed, however, that he just had to join Arsenal; he dreamed of the day that he could wear the red and white. During the late Forties and early Fifties, Arsenal had enjoyed success in both the League Championship and the FA Cup.

He looked carefully at both London clubs. It was illegal for clubs to make an official approach to a schoolboy player, so Haynes' father took the young starlet to meet the Arsenal manager Tom Whittaker. Although it is not known exactly what transpired, it seems certain that the young Haynes felt overwhelmed at Highbury. The marble halls, the dressing rooms and the offices were all superb. He felt that "it was more like the stock exchange." This was football on a grand scale, and Arsenal were a successful club with a succession of household names in their ranks. He just couldn't see himself breaking through there.

Later the Spurs manager, Arthur Rowe, visited Haynes' home on a Sunday afternoon, presumably at his father's request, and outlined his plans for the boy. He was kind and straightforward, but Spurs, too, were an excellent side at the time, with a number of top stars in their squad, and Haynes again considered that he probably had little chance to make an early impression. He had seen a number of young local players signed up by Spurs who had subsequently disappeared into the ether after progressing no further than the youth team.

Even at his young age, he had his head firmly screwed on, and didn't want to commit to anything without viewing all the options. This is thankfully where fate took a hand. His final decision was partly sentimental, but also partly based on common sense.

Previous page: The young Haynes, with his first medal, flanked by fellow Edmonton colleagues, about to ponder his future. Spurs and Arsenal were interested in him, but he finally plumped for homely Fulham, where he began working in the office, being instructed in the secretarial side by Charles Reed, Fulham's assistant secretary.

Trevor Chamberlain was slightly older than Haynes. He had been born in Edmonton as well, but played for Islington schools. Haynes and Chamberlain always seemed to be in opposition to each other in the various cups and shields played out at district level, and they were also colleagues at England youth and England schoolboy international level. So they got to see a great deal of each other and became very firm friends.

Fancy a look at Fulham?

Chamberlain, who admitted that he had not been as clever a student as Haynes, had joined the ground staff at Fulham Football Club a year before. Haynes had only ever seen Fulham play once before, at Highbury, and had described them as "one of the roughest, toughest mobs I had ever seen"!

Trevor knew that the two north London giants were chasing John, and said to him in hope rather than expectation: "Why don't you come along to Fulham with me?" Fancying that he couldn't tempt him and expecting a firm "No," Chamberlain was delighted when his pal said, "Fine, I'd love to." Haynes valued the opinion of his friend, and Trevor had continually extolled the virtues of Fulham FC. Therefore Haynes accompanied Trevor and another schoolboy friend, Luigi Carretta, to Fulham for some kickabouts and ad-hoc training—and soon fell in love with the place.

First impressions

He initially visited Craven Cottage at perhaps the worst time, the close season. The place was deserted, save for a few workmen. It seemed a little shambolic to him, but there was just something about the little place: the river running alongside the ground, the long, low, wooden stand, its odd little 'Cottage' at the corner, and most of all, its tradition of an excellent playing surface. The people at the Cottage all seemed very friendly too. Most of all, his friend Trevor was very happy there. It reminded him of a 'real' football club.

Later general manager Frank Osborne confirmed that story: "I shall always remember that day, the Cottage and the ground have not looked in a more depressing state. We had decorators all over the place, the pitch was partly dug up prior to re-turfing—even the tide was out! I had a talk with the lad and offered him a job working in the office. He said little and when we went outside to have a look around I thought the depressing vista would kill any hopes of signing him. You can imagine my surprise and delight when he came back and said 'Yes.'"

Haynes could see straight away that this was a family club, full of colour and character. There was Tommy Trinder, one of the directors, at the height of his showbiz fame, as well as the genial pipe-smoking Frank Osborne, another father figure. The club had also retained links with previous Fulham teams, with coaches and trainers around like Frank Penn and Johnny Price. These were complemented with mature and helpful senior professionals like Joe Bacuzzi and Arthur Stevens. Roy Bentley says: "John also liked the experience that was at the Cottage, international players like Bacuzzi, Taylor, Campbell and Brennan, very experienced players that would help him improve his game."

The playing surface swung it in Fulham's favour. Haynes was looking for a pitch that would suit and promote his passing skills, and he had just found it. There was an additional incentive in that Fulham were also in the top division at the time, having been promoted in 1949. The promotion had seen the club fork out almost £100,000—an astounding amount of money at the time—on half a dozen players who would help cement their foothold in the First Division. Although Fulham had a number of quality players, it was a club without giants and stars, and Haynes saw the opportunity of an early chance of a first-team place.

Fulham were the club for him, and so he turned down overtures from the more glamorous clubs to join the friendly, homely and somewhat lowly Cottagers. Surprisingly, Fulham put no pressure on him to join them, content for the youngster to make his own mind up, based on what he had seen and experienced down by the river. As in his later life, the characters, manners and personalities that surrounded his 'football mania' were also very important to him. He liked the honesty of the club, and he was utterly sure that he would be welcomed.

Even at this early stage, some questioned his judgement, and suggested that perhaps this decision was a sign of a slight insecurity and that maybe he didn't consider himself good enough then for the 'big time'. In truth it was a shrewd move to get himself into the first team and the spotlight at the earliest possible moment. Haynes' other eventual long-term pal, Bobby Robson, also signed for Fulham around this time, after coming down from the north-east.

Although he had studied the game intensely, he hadn't neglected his school work. He was academically bright, and could, if he wished, have gone further and continued with his education, as he had successfully matriculated. As George Cohen commented: "He had plenty of brains." However, in July 1950, three months before his sixteenth birthday, he left Latymer and joined Fulham Football Club.

Haynes' parents took to Trevor and he became part of the family, perhaps as the brother that John never had. The fact that he was a surrogate brother, and a fairly decent footballer as well, possibly cemented his place in John's parents' affections. Equally, Trevor's parents regarded Johnny Haynes as part of their family. Many, indeed, thought that the two were brothers.

The office boy

By employing Haynes, Fulham shrewdly kept him away from the clutches of other clubs. At first, he was literally the office boy. He did all the basic tasks: licking stamps, brewing tea for the staff, polishing

Bright-eyed and ready for action, Haynes pictured shortly after arriving at Craven Cottage in the summer of 1950.

the boardroom table and running errands, mainly for Tommy Trinder's cigarettes. He was later 'promoted' as a ground staff boy, which allowed him to clean boots. So dedicated and keen was he that Trinder later remarked: "We used to have to kick him out so we could lock up for the night."

It is unlikely that he spent much time sweeping the terraces or clearing up under the stands. Tom Wilson pointed out: "The football and the training would have come first, then he would have probably done a little office work, and then probably upstairs to play snooker."

Sir Bobby Robson joined the club around the same time, and recalls: "I was seventeen, a year older than Johnny, and I came straight into the club as a pro. When I arrived Johnny was in the office, being a year younger than I was, but he couldn't sign professional forms. The trick was to employ him as an office boy, but he trained every day like I did."

Haynes was very slightly built in those days, and only five feet tall; even he described himself at that time as 'frail'. The club used to measure him rather anxiously every week against the office door, the safe or the walls of the secretary's office. The right food and continuous exercise would eventually see him rise to five foot ten inches and a weight of twelve stone.

Sir Bobby Robson continued his reminiscence of that time: "Being from Langley Park I hadn't come across John, but on joining the club I was aware of his reputation. He had played for England Schoolboys and I hadn't! He was a titch, absolutely tiny, but I knew that he had had this memorable game against Scotland. Bill Dodgin (senior) said that he was very proud that he had persuaded John and me to sign. He said that Fulham had signed probably the two best young inside forwards in the country; not Manchester United or Tottenham—but Fulham!"

The first trophy

The first mention of Haynes in the Fulham programme came in December 1950, when he and Trevor Chamberlain were amongst six Fulham players selected to play for Middlesex in the FA County Youth Trophy. Haynes qualified for the Middlesex team rather than the London side because he was turning out for Feltham regularly as a Fulham junior.

The excellent Middlesex team lifted the trophy. After a bye in the first round, they won 5–0 in Sussex, Haynes responding to his "smashing win and coach ride into the country" with two goals. The following rounds saw a 2–0 victory over London and, following a long trip to St Austell, a 5–1 win over Cornwall. In the semi-final, the team, on top form, demolished Essex 6–0.

The final was a two-legged affair; again Middlesex were at their best to win 2–1 at Leicester in the first leg and then held out doggedly to force a draw at Wealdstone in the second leg to lift the trophy. It was Haynes' first success, and the victory over Leicester was particularly sweet, as it levelled out the semi-final district defeat as a schoolboy playing for Edmonton in the English Shield. The win and higher profile could have done his chances of an England youth cap no harm at all; this was what he was setting his sights on.

Feltham, Wimbledon, Woodford Town

Amazing as it may seem today, at the time Fulham, like most other clubs, had no football academy and possessed no junior, under-17 or under-18 sides at all. Instead, clubs had arrangements with local amateur or semi-professional sides. Fulham helped with equipment and the local teams helped blood the Fulham stars of the future.

Haynes would train with the Fulham players and be photographed as part of the first team squad, but never played competitive games with them. Although he said he played "some games for Fulham" in the midweek league, the young star would be shepherded away elsewhere. Tom Wilson elaborated: "The midweek league would have been physically a lot harder for him at that stage of his career as this league was a mixture of first team and reserve team players, but *all* were full-time professionals. It would have been easier for him in these other leagues." The journey out to Feltham (United), on the border between Middlesex and west London, was an exhausting one for the young Haynes, all the way from north London down to Waterloo followed by a Southern Railway expedition to the little hamlet sandwiched between Richmond and Staines.

The matches in the Middlesex League were initially hard work, and a hungry and exhausted Haynes would trudge off to a local café to polish off bacon and chips. He would also carefully carry an egg with him to the ground alongside his kit. Eggs were still rationed in 1950, so players, well off enough, provided their own, and the café owner would cook them. Haynes admitted he was often so hungry he "could have eaten boot leather."

Eventually he became frustrated at being sent to an outpost like Feltham; the standard of football was not particularly good, and the team usually overwhelmed their opponents, often winning by ten or more goals. Unfortunately, there is little recorded information relating to Haynes' time there. He felt that it was contributing little towards his career; even so, he lasted a full season (1950–51) with Feltham. During the close season, with the first-team squad in America, he returned to his 'office job' and during that time he confided in club secretary Charlie Reed that he felt he wasn't getting anywhere.

Reed had connections with the Wimbledon Football Club and managed to get Haynes in there. At least it was nearer to home. John started with a couple of games for Wimbledon reserves in August 1951, before forcing his way into the first team, where he stayed for six months.

Little is known of his time there, except that he found Isthmian League football very hard. He was often playing against grown men much larger than himself. In his own words he was "knocked about a bit," but he had no doubt that this type of play hardened him up in readiness for the physical challenges ahead. From there he was back on his journeys again, moving into the wilds of Essex to play for a short period for Woodford Town in the newly formed Delphian League.

Have I made the right decision?

In some ways it was probably beneficial that Haynes wasn't around the Cottage much during those two years. The atmosphere had been fairly poor during the 1950–51 season. Manager Bill Dodgin had a large squad, but there were a number of ageing players.

There had been a great deal of chopping and changing, and many players were frustrated that they weren't getting a decent run in the side. There were also seemingly no young reserve players coming through. Results deteriorated further, and by the time Haynes returned to base camp following his two-year flirtation with amateur football, Fulham FC were, once again, a Second Division side, the disastrous 1951–52 season

Haynes signed professional forms with Fulham in 1952. Here he poses with defender Jim Taylor at the start of a career that would reverberate throughout the world.

seeing them finish bottom of the pile with just eight league wins all season, two of these being the final two matches.

Although Haynes had no quarrel with Fulham, he was feeling slightly black about his future, and he was, at seventeen, impatient to get on. During this period in the doldrums, he made an impetuous mistake that haunted him for the next decade. Patience is not a quality of the young, and he decided to pay another visit to Arsenal manager Tom Whittaker and ask to be taken in there. He was still an amateur player, not bound by contract. He really only needed to give the Fulham club a modicum of notice and he would be free. He was now old enough to sign forms.

Whittaker listened intently and he knew he would love to have Haynes under his wing, but although it sounds almost impossible today, it was a question of ethics. Whittaker, although sympathetic, thought that this was not something that either he or Haynes should enter into, and advised him to go back to Fulham, be patient and wait for his inevitable opportunity.

Selected for England Youth

The gloom of Fulham's relegation scarcely affected Haynes, who was more focussed on winning an England Youth Cap for himself. After playing in a grandiose-sounding game for a Youth Representative Games FA XI against Public Schools, the opportunity duly arrived when he was selected to play for England Youth in the fifth FIFA under-18 tournament in Barcelona during Easter 1952. If you exclude Ireland, it was his first-ever trip abroad, his first time in an aircraft and the first time he had experienced the sights and sounds of a Latin city.

He had picked up an ankle injury playing for Woodford, and almost didn't make the trip at all. In the first match, he collected his first cap as England beat Switzerland 4–0. This, however, was followed two days later by a 1–4 defeat by the hosts, Spain. Technically Spain were superb and all over the England side. England's tour was completed two days after that with a remarkable 5–5 draw with Austria, although Haynes was dropped from the England side that day.

His ankle had troubled him during the Spain match, and he admitted frankly, "I had played so badly." He won his third and final youth cap in another international at the end of the week when the England team were beaten 0–2 by Northern Ireland in Belfast. He didn't find the net at all as an England youth player.

I'll sign professional forms

He had been eligible to sign professional forms with Fulham during the previous six months, but had delayed during his 'uncertain' period. Fulham were sweating more than a little at this point as they felt sure that Haynes, still an amateur and not under contract, would be poached by a top club and coerced away from the Cottage.

This time the club did apply some very gentle pressure on him to sort out his future. Then one day, after winning England Youth honours, he just walked into the club office, quietly announced that he was ready to sign, and did so straight away. He was paid sixteen pounds a week when he joined Fulham. It was now up to him to force his way into the first team.

Here fate took another turn. Now a professional, Haynes was placed under the aegis of Eugene 'Taffy' O'Callaghan, who had joined Fulham in the autumn of 1937 and had remained there until the outbreak of the Second World War. His total league record read 125 goals in 375 appearances (a 1 to 3 ratio). After the war he became the coach to the younger Fulham players and ultimately the reserve side.

Taffy was a great influence on the young Haynes, and this is where the maestro received his first real professional tuition. It was sheer happenstance, but here was someone whom Haynes respected and from whom he could learn. O'Callaghan was a former Welsh international inside forward whose game and playing style were very similar to John's. O'Callaghan would often give the fledgling Haynes one-to-one coaching on the Cottage pitch with a ball, repeatedly going over a few points and making helpful suggestions.

At the same time, Haynes was also studying the play of talkative Fulham first-teamer Jimmy Bowie. Although he was now concentrating more on his passing game, he marvelled at the ball control and weaving ability of the little inside forward. Another skill that Bowie had which was to be added to his armoury was the ability to be off the mark very quickly.

He was amazed how quick Bowie was over five to ten yards, and saw the advantages of such an asset on the field of play. He would make sure that he built this particular art into his repertoire as well.

By the time Haynes was England captain almost a decade later, Frank Osborne was candid enough to admit: "We couldn't teach Johnny anything really, he had it all from the start; in fact the most brilliant game I ever saw him play was for England Boys at Wembley, before we even thought he would join us."

7: The first season 1952–53

7: The first season 1952-53

Johnny Haynes signed professional forms in May 1952, seven months after his seventeenth birthday. During the two years he had been at the Cottage he had shot up several inches to five feet eight and put on a considerable amount of weight. With advice from the club doctor and under his Mum's careful eye, the milk, steak, rice pudding and fruit diet was doing the trick. Haynes considered that he could now compete physically in the real world of league football.

Now it was just about pace. He recalled at the peak of his game: "I think the pace of professional football was one of the greatest lessons and tests I had to overcome. It is one of the big stepping-stones in the game."

National Service—no thanks!

Both Haynes and Bobby Robson somehow contrived to fail their medical examination for National Service, compulsory at the time for young men at the age of eighteen, and so were able to avoid 'serving the nation'. A number of other Fulham players passed, however, and were forced to see out the two years. Certainly eyebrows were raised as to how two such superbly fit young professional sportsmen could be so unfit for conscription.

Haynes' reason was that he had, earlier in his life, suffered perforated eardrums. It appears that this was one of the 'good' ways of getting round being drafted. The Army were very nervous about having people suffering this condition around guns, which could have repercussions for the Army or the sufferer. Once the necessary doctor's certificate had been prepared, Haynes was clear.

Robson had a similar ear condition—mastoids—which precluded him from being conscripted, and he was mocked with the nickname 'cloth-ears' for several months afterwards. Trevor Chamberlain jokingly reckoned that Haynes wheedled his way out of National Service only by feigning this kind of deafness, as he suspected that John could hear a five-pound note dropping on the ground behind him from ten yards.

In August 1952, Haynes played his first game for Fulham reserves in an away fixture at Southampton. Following this, he took part in his first home game for the reserves, against Chelsea. In a strong team performance, both Chamberlain and Haynes found the net in a 7–0 victory. It was Haynes' first goal in the name of Fulham, rather than Feltham or Wimbledon.

Under the experienced eyes of hard-man Archie Macaulay, who was more or less coaching the reserves from his right half position, Haynes' game improved. This gradual process wasn't going to be all plain sailing, however, as the Fulham first team hit its usual injury crisis, forcing many of the reserves to be unexpectedly drafted into the first team.

So bereft were the reserves of quality players that in one reserve game Fulham, with Haynes in the side, lost 1–9 at White Hart Lane to a Spurs reserve side galvanised by Tommy Harmer. However, they say it's an ill wind, and one of those Fulham first-team players struck down by injury was inside forward Bobby Brennan.

Fulham debut

Johnny Haynes came into a team that had been relegated the previous season, one that had finished rock bottom, something that he would eventually get used to. Bill Dodgin (senior) was desperately trying to return Fulham to the top flight at the first attempt, and he turned to Haynes and gave him his opportunity.

This was the era of the five-man front line, an age which was somewhat reckless of defensive skills. Protection for the goalkeeper was afforded by a centre half and two full backs who regarded it as their task to mark wingers out near the touchlines.

You're playing!

December

Johnny Haynes made his debut for the first team against Southampton on Boxing Day 1952, due to the significant injury list. It was just two months after his eighteenth birthday. Although his name had been pencilled in alongside others, it wasn't until thirty minutes before the start of the match that he knew he would be playing. He had a sixth sense that he might be chosen, and hadn't slept well the night before.

While the rest of the team were getting stripped, young Johnny was sitting on the dressing room table looking hopefully at everyone who came into the room for the tip to get ready. When the news finally came, he jumped to it with alacrity. His debut in the league side was something he had been waiting months for. He couldn't have asked for a finer Christmas present. This was what his mother and father had sacrificed so much for—it was his big day.

He was very nervous and felt sick as he ran out on to the field, but soon "got into it." He later said, "I felt so sick, it was all I could do not to turn around and scuttle back to the dressing room."

The pitch was heavy and overpowering, and for a lightweight player it was difficult going, but he survived. It wasn't long before young John in his first game was drawing applause for his skill both in working the ball through the mud, and in putting well-placed passes either down the middle or out to Charlie Mitten on the wing.

It might have been a winning debut as well, but Fulham had a goal unluckily disallowed and Charlie Mitten blasted a last-minute penalty straight at the

Previous page: The programme for Haynes' debut match, Boxing Day, 1952, the best Christmas present he could have wished for!

Bill Dodgin, senior, was the Fulham manager who gave Haynes his first taste of league football. Exactly what's going on between the two of them in this training photograph is hard to surmise, but the picture provides a nostalgic look at the Bishop's Park corner of the Craven Cottage ground.

Southampton goalkeeper, and the match was drawn 1–1. The press said: "He did well in his first game for Fulham."

After his debut, Haynes said: "I was very nervous, more than I have ever been before or since. The ground was terribly heavy, but Fulham continued to play very well and outclass Southampton, but failed miserably to score."

Haynes was left out for the return match the following day because of his age and the heaviness of the pitch, but he returned the following week for the game against Birmingham City, which Fulham won 3–1. He held down his place for the remainder of the season, and became the bedrock on which Fulham teams were founded for the best part of the next two decades.

Haynes creates his first goal

Against Birmingham, he almost had his first goal but slipped in the mud. Then, a minute before the interval, came the first Fulham goal that he created. Showing fine understanding with Bedford Jezzard, he placed a judicious pass goalwards for the centre forward to run on to and score with a powerful shot. The local press said of the Birmingham game, "Haynes stakes his claim." This was the start of the Robson–Jezzard–Haynes partnership—and his first Fulham win.

The club programme was quick to praise his contribution against Birmingham, saying: "Our judgement on Haynes on this performance is that a stranger on the ground would have almost certainly thought that the lad had been playing first-class football for years and if the same person had been told he was wrong, he'd have thought his leg was being pulled!"

Bobby Robson, then in his third playing season, said of Haynes' incipient skills: "When I played alongside him, he was only eighteen, but even then he stood head and shoulders over everyone else, mainly for his maturity; that was truly remarkable. That is something you are born with. Johnny wasn't the complete player then, but he was very good indeed.

"You could see from those early days that he was absolute class. Johnny had such great control; he could turn on a sixpence with the ball at his feet, one touch movement, great vision, the complete package really. He also had a great footballing brain, and this amazing defence-splitting pass ability."

The first FA Cup tie

Haynes had the opportunity to play for the first time against higher league opposition when he was in the Fulham side that played away against Bolton Wanderers—Nat Lofthouse et al—in the third round of the FA Cup. It was just his third game. Fulham eventually went down 1–3, the third clinching goal not arriving until the last couple of minutes. In truth, the pitch was again much too heavy for the young Haynes and in the end he moved out to the drier right wing position, swapping places with Bobby Brennan.

He acquitted himself well in the game, however, and felt reasonably confident, only three weeks after his league debut, that he could hold his own in the top sphere. The First Division Bolton team must nevertheless have been fairly useful as they went all the way to Wembley, dramatically losing out at the last, 3–4 in the famous 'Matthews final'.

Haynes would experience league defeat in a Fulham shirt for the first time in just his fifth league match, when Fulham lost to Plymouth Argyle in Devon by 1–3.

Although he hadn't yet grabbed the headlines in his first few games, there were glimpses of what was to come.

The first headline

January

Less than a month after his debut, he made his first press headline—"Haynes inspires Fulham"—in the 2–1 win over John Charles' Leeds United. The report said: "Young Johnny Haynes, the schoolboy wonder of four years ago, was, however, the real brains of Fulham's attack. There was studied thought in everything he attempted and his distribution of the ball was unsurpassed by any other player."

February

In the 2–2 draw at Lincoln in February came his first recorded effort at goal, a match where Stevens and Jezzard all had good shots saved. The following week against Hull, the press were already talking about the 'snappy' forward line of Robson, Jezzard and Haynes.

March

At Blackburn, it was reported that alongside Stevens and Brennan, Haynes was an "outstanding attacker." He gave his best performance to date, robbing a full back and supplying winger Stevens with a perfectly weighted pass described by manager Dodgin as "one of the finest passes I have ever seen." Stevens' shot was parried but Mitten made no mistake with the rebound.

At Everton in a 3–3 draw, the passing movement was replicated and Haynes made the first goal for Jezzard and Fulham's second. The youngster began to get more confident and in a 5–0 thrashing of Brentford, he was unlucky with several shots—just wide, blocked, into the side netting, with one hitting the outside of the post.

Even though it was early days, the 'Haynes frown' was mentioned in the programme, as he brooded on why his first Fulham goal was still eluding him. The local paper, the *Fulham Chronicle*, said: "Fulham have seldom played better, partly due to Jezzard and the two exciting inside men Bobby Robson (twenty) and Johnny Haynes (eighteen)."

Robson, Jezzard and Haynes—how much?

Haynes remembers: "We were scoring a lot of goals using the 'double centre forward plan'. When we started this move, it involved the inside right Bobby Robson sharing the role with Bedford Jezzard. My part was to lie deep and play the through ball. It is then up to the centre forward to draw away the centre half and for the inside right to run through the middle with the space clear.

"We didn't overdo the through ball, but the main aim was to have the centre half in two minds all the time, so that he was never sure whether to move away or stay put and mark only the centre forward. This alone made the plan worthwhile."

So impressive were the golden inside forward trio of Robson, Jezzard and Haynes that after witnessing another particularly impressive performance at the beginning of the month, the directors of Newcastle United, watching from the stands, enquired what was the asking price—for all three. Whether the sum of £60,000 was ever formally offered by Newcastle, or whether the Fulham management had just clutched the figure out of the air by saying: "Gentlemen, even if you offered us £60,000…" was never fully resolved.

The British record transfer at the time lay at just £34,000 and even that was considered inflated and rather obscene in austere post-war Britain, but this was something entirely different; this was a figure that almost doubled the transfer record—coupled with the fact that the three were playing in the Second Division.

Haynes was the new kid on the block, but the stylish Robson and the goal-machine Jezzard had already been transfer targets for other clubs. The golden trio immediately became the subject of media frenzy. Their lives were analysed and all sides of their private life became matters of public scrutiny; they became public property. It was the first time as an adult that Haynes had been put under the spotlight.

The Fulham board immediately poured cold water on the deal, emphasising through the club programme that they were trying to build a team not sell one. It

Early league action from the young Haynes, in the 2–1 victory over Hull City at the end of February.

was unlikely that either Jezzard or Haynes would have moved anyway, as both had strong family roots in London; Jezzard's family ran a public house. It may have been very tempting, however, for Robson, who was from Newcastle. In the end, the proposed record-breaking transfer did not take place, and slowly things returned to normal.

During that period, Haynes rather enjoyed the early publicity and coped well with the press intrusion for an eighteen-year-old. From a personal point of view, he was staggered at the power of the press, the figures being bandied about, and the amount of column inches in the newspapers given over to the three players.

He was unnerved by the fact that the other eight members of the Fulham team were dismissed and hardly given a mention. He was also amazed that Fulham were wealthy or self-financed enough to decline such sums. However, in the event of a Haynes move, all the young lad would have been entitled to was a £10 signing-on fee. How times have changed!

Later he reminisced: "We were all pretty young at the time, Beddy was maybe three or four years older, and Bob and I were almost the same age. But we were highly thought of as Newcastle tried to buy all three of us. But we were just mates enjoying our football. I've known Bobby all my life—we're old mates."

The first goal

April

Haynes had to wait over three months for his first goal in the Fulham first team, which finally arrived in a disappointing 2–3 home defeat against West Ham on Easter Monday. Both Jezzard and Mitten sustained

HIS FIRST GOAL

Johnny Haynes who was not too successful in the mud redeemed himself with a great goal from the edge of the penalty area, eight minutes from time. A corner from Mitten was partially cleared, and Haynes hit a screamer from the edge of the penalty area. It was his first league goal.

As the local press saw it.

early injuries in the match and were only half effective. Haynes' goal came eight minutes from time. From Mitten's corner and following a mêlée, the ball came to him on the edge of the area. He volleyed it straight back and although the experienced Gregory in the West Ham goal got his fingers to it, he couldn't keep it out.

The star begins to shine

The game where his first real impact was made came against Swansea Town at Craven Cottage when Fulham won 3–1. The match had no significance in terms of promotion or relegation, but both teams played as if the championship itself were at stake.

Under another headline of "Haynes is great", after he'd been involved in all three goals, it was reported: "Fulham took the lead in the twelfth minute with a picture goal, a great Haynes-Mitten movement being rounded off by Robson. Haynes looked as if he might shoot, but cleverly played the ball back to Robson who was better placed.…Three minutes later in an identical move, Haynes split the defence again with an accurate centre and Groves in the Swansea goal blundered to give Robson a second goal."

After half-time, the report continued: "Haynes with the help of Stevens drew Charles out of the middle and laid on the goal scored by Jezzard with a sliding

Great to be in the league side! Even with a supposedly dodgy leg...

pass.... Haynes is a great young player in the making, but one could wish that he had more confidence in his own goal-scoring abilities."

Near the end of the season, he was described as "brilliant in his approach work" following a 2–4 defeat against Huddersfield Town at Leeds Road. Since his arrival at Christmas, the Fulham team had scored thirty-nine league goals, and had failed to find the net only twice in matches in which he took part, and the golden trio had amassed twenty-eight of that total (over 70%). The Fulham side had hovered around mid-table all season, finishing a respectable eighth.

Summary

By the time eighteen-year-old Johnny Haynes had reached the end of his first season as a professional he had broken into the first team, scored his first league goal, and experienced playing in front of large crowds. He had played a number of games in front of 25,000 or more and had also shared the pitch with a number of his boyhood heroes, including Tommy Lawton (Brentford), Nat Lofthouse (Bolton) and John Charles (Leeds).

He was also learning how to pace himself and how to conserve energy for the last vital twenty minutes, during which so many matches were critically won and lost. He was also being educated in integration and team play at the highest level: how to get a return pass, how and when to track back, how to be on the move at all times, and—certainly for the first time in his life—the defensive side of his game.

Folklore from 1953

When Haynes first established himself in the Fulham first team as a teenager, the Fulham director, Tommy Trinder, was still at the height of his showbiz career as a comedian, actor and presenter on what was then fledgling television.

Tommy was appearing in a show in Southsea when he received an invitation from the president of Portsmouth Football Club, Field Marshal the Viscount Montgomery of Alamein, to a Saturday match at Fratton Park. After the game Tommy was in the boardroom listening to the results on the radio. Finally, the presenter announced that Fulham had won 2–0 and that one or both goals had been scored by Johnny Haynes.

"That Haynes boy, he's going to be a great player," said Tommy, glowing with pride and satisfaction. "He has a great football brain and is an excellent passer of the ball. Mark my words, sir, Johnny Haynes will captain England one day. He's a brilliant player and only eighteen years of age."

"Eighteen years old?" said Viscount Montgomery sternly, immediately quelling Tommy's joy and delight. "What about his National Service?"

"Well, that's the only sad thing about him," said Tommy, thinking on his feet. "He's got a dodgy leg!"

8: The first full season 1953–54

8: The first full season 1953–54

Haynes was desperate to build on the excellent start he had made to his Fulham career during the previous season, but he saw that, as football was a team game, he couldn't do it all himself.

August

He found the net on the opening day of the season, a Thursday, being part of the team that drew 4–4 in a highly entertaining encounter at Eastville against Bristol Rovers. It was a game of fluctuating fortunes, with both sides having the lead at one stage. Haynes had already seen a thirty-five-yard shot brilliantly saved and it was he who scored the seventh goal with a powerful strike to give Fulham the lead for the first time. However, newly-promoted Rovers stormed back to take a fortunate point.

Fulham lost their next match just two days later at the Cottage to newly-relegated Stoke 0–1. The away goalkeeper made brilliant saves from Haynes, Jezzard and Robson. The press said: "Fulham should have made better use of Haynes whose superb ball control stamps him as a grand schemer." It was admitted that Haynes at this stage of his development found the going much tougher against the former First Division club.

First away goal—and first blunder

John scored his first away goal in a Fulham shirt in a 2–2 draw at Leicester City in a midweek game, following a slick four-man passing movement which ended with him shooting home. It was also a match that saw his first major mistake, when a poor crossfield pass was intercepted by a Leicester forward who passed for a colleague to equalise. The young Haynes was aghast and in tears, and it took many team members on the pitch to console him. After the match he was said to be forlorn and contrite.

September

Fulham also drew their midweek return match, 1–1, against Leicester at the Cottage. Haynes was unlucky with a volley on the drop that was somehow turned away by the visiting keeper, but he ended the match unconscious having tried to prevent Leicester's injury-time equaliser after Charlie Mitten had put Fulham ahead with a penalty minutes earlier. Half an hour after the game, he was still glassy-eyed and his neck was so stiff that he could hardly raise his head.

Previous page: The Fulham first team squad for the 1953–54 season. Back row: Gordon Brice, John Chenhall, Eddie Lowe, Ian Black, Jimmy Hill, Reg Lowe, Joe Bacuzzi, Robin Lawler, Norman Smith; front row: Arthur Stevens, Bobby Robson, Jeff Taylor, Bedford Jezzard, Johnny Haynes, Charlie Mitten, Bernard Newcombe.

Fulham's form was poor defensively and little was seen of Haynes in the next three games; Fulham lost them all, conceding nine goals in the process. In one of those games at Rotherham, Haynes was unlucky. He hit the post with one shot, scrambled a goal late on from close in and was then unfortunate with another close shot near to time. He picked up an injury in the match which caused him to miss the subsequent 2–4 Rotherham home defeat.

It was the only match he would miss that season, and it corresponded with Fulham's worst performance, although a severe eye injury to Eddie Lowe early in the game caused the whole side to be reshuffled.

In the 2–2 draw at Birmingham, Haynes was involved in the four-man move that created the opening goal for Jezzard after just fourteen seconds. Against Forest the following week, Fulham finally pulled off a 3–1 victory. Haynes helped with the final goal: "Jezzard ran on to one of Haynes' specials, took a neat touch, and then crashed it into the back of the net to put the result beyond doubt."

Although Haynes picked up three goals in the first seven games, the team failed to record a single victory in August and up to the final days in September. Fulham were the only team in the entire league without a win at this stage of the season, ending the month just outside the relegation slots of the Second Division, having drawn just four other games.

October

Haynes was not unduly worried about his own game, but was concerned about his prospects of playing at a higher level, if he and the team were permanently outside the spotlight and struggling in the Second Division. Thankfully, after the end of September the results did begin to improve, and the team began to move, albeit slowly, towards the top half of the table.

They won the first game of the month at Luton Town, where Haynes pushed the ball forward to Bedford Jezzard who looked well offside, but had been played on by a Luton player. It was a lucky break, but it turned out to be the winner in a 2–1 victory.

The next game was a pivotal 5–2 defeat of Derby County, when Beddy Jezzard netted four goals, and the crowd were treated to a series of delightful moves from Bobby Robson and Johnny Haynes. Arthur Stevens created the first three goals and Haynes masterminded the last two. One was a perfect centre for Jezzard's head, and the other a typical through pass from the halfway line. Derby had pulled the score back to 3–2, so Haynes' contribution settled the match. The press commented: "Johnny Haynes was the architect of Fulham's success. He really knows how to split a defence."

He tried to follow this performance up the following Saturday on his nineteenth birthday, but Fulham were dumped 1–5 at Blackburn Rovers due to poor teamwork and defensive mistakes. It was noted, however, that he was the best forward on view, though inclined to overdo the fancy stuff.

Manager Bill Dodgin (senior) departs

Bill Dodgin, having failed in his quest to return Fulham to the First Division, was relieved of his duties three months into the season. He left after the club's directors had politely asked for his resignation. Fulham decided not to replace the team manager immediately, and the general manager, Frank Osborne, took on the jobs of both administration and team selection. He was a great admirer of the young boy from Edmonton and persisted with his selection.

Osborne was a pre-war international player and, like Haynes, an inside forward, and he knew a good footballer when he saw one. He said in 1953, "This boy is a natural and is bound to play for England. There are things in Johnny's play I have not seen in any other player in twenty years."

Against Doncaster the following week at the Cottage it was reported that Haynes toiled hard to create opportunities, but Fulham lost by the odd goal. Against Bury in the final match of the month at Gigg Lane, Fulham were emphatic winners 3–1 and all through the game Jezzard and Haynes brought danger to the Bury defence.

Haynes made the second goal for Jezzard and the third for Robson with a superb pass. Soon afterwards he worked an opening for himself. He waltzed through the Bury defence, but placed his shot straight at the keeper. It was a pity, as the Fulham programme noted: "It would have rounded off appropriately one of the finest displays he has ever given. The manner in which he used the ball and opened out the game was in the highest tradition."

November

The true scope of his talent was now beginning to emerge, and in a 3–1 win over Oldham his astute pass put Charlie Mitten away on the left and his hard centre flew straight into goal. The second goal was again a peach, with an intricate four-man move ending with Bedford Jezzard firing home Haynes' final pass. It was reported thus: "Haynes played a brilliant game strategically. Mitten put Haynes through and the inside forward laid it on a plate for Jezzard." Haynes then went through to hit the side netting. For the third goal, he was involved again and Jezzard headed in from Arthur Stevens' final cross.

The first brace of his career

Haynes' goals had temporarily stopped flowing, and in fact he hadn't netted for ten games. But all that changed when he scored the first brace of his career in a 5–1 thrashing of Hull City at the Cottage. This was a tremendous match for the young lad. At 1–1, he let fly a 'stinger' that the Hull goalkeeper couldn't hold, and Bobby Robson followed up to score.

He effectively put the seal on the game midway through the second half when he converted Jezzard's cross with a flick of the head. Five minutes from time he scored another; Hull keeper Bly parried his first shot, but he rammed in the rebound. Finally, a very shrewd pass from Haynes presented Jezzard with the fifth. A great day all round—scored two and made two of the other three.

Fulham drew a blank at Notts County the following Saturday, but right at the end, following a short pass from Stevens, Haynes belted the ball towards the far corner of the goal; it rebounded off the chest of the home goalkeeper, who knew little about it. It was the first time that the Fulham rearguard had managed to keep a clean sheet in twenty matches.

Educated by the Hungarians

Later that month, Haynes also had the opportunity to witness football played at a vastly higher level than he had experienced previously. The Hungarian international side, the Olympic champions, visited England in November 1953. Prior to their international game at Wembley they used the Craven Cottage pitch for pre-match preparation. Haynes was astounded at what he saw as a spectator sitting in the stands. Their training methods and training games were light-years ahead of what he was doing.

There was hardly any physical side to their preparations at all; it was nearly all ball work. No running or lapping; instead, practice matches, ball control, specific exercises and set plays for each area of the team, with emphasis on passing and shooting, from all distances and all angles.

He was also amazed at the amount of short passing, five to ten yards, instead of his own raking twenty or thirty-yarders. He vowed that he would spread the word and incorporate this short passing into his game as well. He marvelled at what he had witnessed and felt angry that such innovative techniques were being ignored by our own FA, and in fact by Fulham.

As the weather worsened, he saw further evidence of the prehistoric English set-up. Fulham had no training ground—not even a second pitch. The club didn't want the pristine Cottage pitch ruined by practice matches. There was a perfect pitch right next to the ground in Bishop's Park, but strict covenants prevented Fulham playing on it. Without a pitch, team play and practice matches were impossible and the intelligent young Haynes experienced his first real frustrations with the domestic professional game.

He witnessed the Magnificent Magyars destroy England's unbeaten record at Wembley a few days later. England lost a first-minute goal, and were at one stage 1–4 down, then 2–6 down, before a late penalty by Alf Ramsey brought some scant respectability to the final 3–6 score. It was, though, a footballing education, and Puskas' goal would remain firmly in Haynes' mind.

December

The month started well with a 4–1 victory over Lincoln City at Craven Cottage. Again it was a typical canny through pass from Haynes that gave Bedford Jezzard Fulham's second goal, and Haynes put the seal on a

Haynes leaps forward to head home Stevens' centre, the second goal in a 3–1 FA Cup replay victory at home to Grimsby Town. This was the young Haynes' first-ever FA Cup goal. He also scored Fulham's third goal that afternoon.

fine team performance with the fourth Fulham goal seven minutes from the end, when, following a quick move, the ball was slipped into the net before the Lincoln defence were alive to the situation.

He liked to practise his shooting, especially the long-range stuff, and the hard work started to bear fruit again at Bristol Rovers. Although Fulham went down 1–2 to a last-minute goal, it was reported that Stevens' goal arrived after a twenty-five-yard piledriver from Haynes had been pushed out.

The following Saturday, in a solid 3–1 win over Stoke City at the Victoria Ground, Haynes' flashing header from Charlie Mitten's centre six minutes from time put Fulham ahead (2–1), and his pass inside the full back enabled Bobby Robson to settle the match with a third goal just a minute later.

Although Haynes only hit the post and had two twenty-five-yard shots turned over in the Christmas Day match at home to Plymouth Argyle, the following day was better. Exactly a year after his debut, Plymouth took the lead inside thirty seconds in the return match at Home Park, but fifteen minutes from the end, Haynes' sublime pass created the important equalising goal for Jezzard in a 2–2 draw. Haynes also had a powerful header pushed away by the goalkeeper. At the end of the year, Fulham were lying ninth, having lost only three of their last fifteen league games, and won nine.

January

At the start of the New Year, Johnny Haynes was bang on form against Brentford in a misty match at the Cottage, setting up the first goal with a beautiful through ball to Bobby Robson. He then hit the angle of post and bar with a thirty-five-yard shot, finally sealing the win with an astute free kick right at the very end of the match that enabled Bedford Jezzard to claim a headed fourth in an emphatic 4–1 victory.

Haynes and Fulham then took part in an amazing 5–5 draw with Grimsby Town from the Third Division (North) at Blundell Park in the third round of the FA Cup. The midweek replay was abandoned at half-time when torrential rain turned the pitch into a lake.

An international reserve

Haynes' performances in the Second Division during the previous three months had influenced those watching, and the nineteen-year-old was selected as a reserve for the first-ever England Under-23 international match against Italy in Bologna. It was his first adult international honour, and he had been a league player for little more than a year.

The Under-23 team had been the brainchild of national manager Walter Winterbottom. Realising that throwing youngsters into a full international game without any relevant experience often produced disappointing performances, the England manager set up a nursery team in which the country's bright young talent could develop, before parading its skills on the world stage.

By instituting an Under-23 level he had created a sense of continuity within the broad England set-up, and a team spirit between the youngsters and senior players. The team was a success from the start. Haynes didn't actually get on the pitch for that first match, but was a spectator who witnessed England lose 0–3 to the Italians in the snow.

Just before the second attempt at a Grimsby replay, the enigmatic Fulham side were at their worst. Against West Ham at Craven Cottage they notched a three-goal lead on thirty minutes. Jezzard received Haynes' through pass for the second and rounded several defenders before scoring, and then Haynes took the third himself, pouncing on a misjudged defensive clearance by Hammers defender Malcolm Allison.

The visitors hit back to a one-goal deficit before the interval, and much to Haynes' despair, more poor defending saw the Irons escape with a 3–4 victory, scoring four times in just eighteen minutes. Haynes hit the post with a rasping drive late in the game, but Fulham couldn't get the ball in the net again.

First FA Cup goals

Haynes polished off the Humberside team in the replay 3–1 on the following Monday afternoon. He played well, being described as the man of the match, and he contributed the two goals that turned the tie. The goals were his first ever in the competition. He scored goals two and three, his first being described by the club programme as "as grand a goal as we've seen at the Cottage for many a day." A marvellous move involving five players ended when Haynes leapt and headed into the net from ten yards from Arthur Stevens' centre.

The third was scored just four minutes after the interval; again it came from a Stevens centre, with Haynes killing the ball and hitting it into the net in one movement. Grimsby's goal was merely a late consolation. Fulham were then shocked to go out of the FA Cup to lower league opposition in Leyton Orient in the following round.

February

Haynes was beginning to be taken pretty seriously now by opponents, but they couldn't stop him playing a major part in Fulham's 5–2 victory over Birmingham on a bitingly cold afternoon. The press said: "The man chiefly responsible for Fulham's great win was Johnny Haynes, the lad with magic in his boots. Whenever he had the ball, he had the Birmingham defence foxed, and his through passes were a model of accuracy."

If it hadn't been for famous Birmingham goalkeeper Gil Merrick, it would have been ten. Bedford Jezzard scored in two minutes, then Robson scored the goal of the game: Haynes, from fifty yards, dropped a long ball into the goalmouth, where Bobby Robson, just on-side, scored acrobatically from ten yards with a magnificent header. Haynes' sublime pass crafted the third as well. His pass to Jezzard was met with a full-blooded shot. Merrick could not hold on and Robson was again on hand to pick up the pieces.

Haynes also netted Fulham's fourth following a great run from Charlie Mitten on the wing, driving low past the stranded keeper. Amazingly, Haynes was also part of a four-man move that finished with Arthur Stevens putting away Fulham's fifth. The Midlanders put away a late consolation goal.

First hat trick in senior football

Fulham's results continued to improve and they were now eighth, the position in which they would ultimately finish. They were scoring goals aplenty, and Haynes was both making and taking them. The highlight of this improvement in form was a 5–1 home victory over Luton Town, where Haynes scored his first-ever league hat trick. The headline read "Fulham smash dainty Luton."

Again the press were very impressed. "The star and man of the match was undoubtedly Johnny Haynes, who scored three and played soccer right out of the top drawer. He and Mitten form one of best left-wing partnerships in the country."

What a match it was, a fluent Fulham overwhelming the Hatters! Jezzard opened the scoring after ten minutes, Haynes laying on the perfect pass. Before half-time, he scored two "grand" goals himself. The first came in the thirty-sixth minute, when Stevens' low square pass was met in his stride by Haynes, who slammed the ball into the net. Only four minutes later, a through pass from full back Lawler was driven powerfully into goal by Haynes from a tight angle.

Four minutes after the interval Haynes put Jeff Taylor through for the fourth, and then completed his hat trick two minutes from the end, when Jimmy Hill's energetic run and pass set up the chance for the youngster to easily ram home goal three. The direct Fulham attack had looked full of goals.

Haynes always enjoyed playing with Charlie Mitten and was learning a lot from the senior professional. He said later: "As a thirteen-year-old I had seen Charlie in the 1948 [Cup] final against Blackpool, and there I was four years later playing with him on the left wing—I couldn't believe it. He was my first left-wing partner in the Fulham first team, and I've got fond memories of him. He was an electrifying player with a great left foot."

Charlie Mitten held Haynes in similarly high regard: "I played alongside Johnny Haynes for three years and it was obvious he was going to be a fine player; it was just a question of time as he developed. It was true that he was a bit of a hothead in his early days, but that was because he had an intense love of the game."

To complete the month, Fulham came from behind three times to get a 3–3 draw against Derby County away from home. It was an excellent result, considering that Mitten played in goal for most of the second half and didn't concede any goals! As in the previous week, Haynes made the second for Taylor with a replica of the fourth against Luton, and was then involved in the four-man move that gave Jezzard the final equaliser. It was only a superb save from Derby goalkeeper Middleton late on that prevented Haynes from notching a winning goal.

His first 'B' international cap

March

So well was he playing that Haynes was selected for the next rung of the international ladder—the 'B' international. The local press wished him well, saying "It will be a big test for the Fulham boy who is not yet nineteen. Provided Johnny is not overawed by the occasion, I think he might stake a claim for a full cap." The only major surprise was that Bedford Jezzard had not been selected as well.

Haynes won his first cap for the England 'B' side against Scotland at Roker Park, Sunderland, in front of 21,000. The game was played in appalling conditions of ice and snow and freezing temperatures. The teams battled out a 1–1 draw, West Ham's Harry Hooper scoring for England. Haynes, showing changes of pace, received a good press, some declaring that he was the best player on the field—mobile, full of ideas, a player who opened up the game. One headline read: "At eighteen Haynes is star of England 'B' draw". In his mind, though, he considered that in those conditions "I was probably the one who made least mistakes!"

Fulham then lost disappointingly at home to Blackburn Rovers despite Haynes' best efforts. He seemed to be on a telepathic wavelength with Jeff Taylor as well as Jezzard, and made both goals for Taylor in a 2–3 defeat. Then, in a 2–2 draw at Doncaster Rovers, Mitten scored a brilliant goal from an astute pass from Haynes who was described as "a grand schemer".

The following Saturday Fulham demolished Bury 3–0, and the papers said: "Haynes was his usual brilliant self, always keeping the Bury defence on tenterhooks with sweeping passes." The forwards had just too many tricks for Bury. Charlie Mitten and Haynes combined in the twelfth minute and Haynes' beautiful centre was converted by Taylor. The second-half goal was described as a gem. Newcombe and Haynes took part in a spot of jugglery before Haynes served up the ball to Jezzard who scored easily. It was the first time Fulham had kept a clean sheet at home that season—and it was almost April.

Charlie Mitten, Haynes' first left-wing partner.

Three weeks after the award of the first, came his second England 'B' cap when England played in the Glueckauf Stadion in Gelsenkirchen in front of a huge 42,000 crowd against Germany 'B'. The match was the first between the two countries since the end of the Second World War, and there were many British troops in the crowd. England demolished the home side 4–0, with Haynes' team-mate Bedford Jezzard scoring three, and Les Shannon, who would later to return to the Cottage as manager of Bury in 1969, taking the other following a peach of a through pass from Haynes. A few of Haynes' through passes went astray, but this was mainly down to the uneven surface. In the programme, the club expressed its delight that "Johnny gave the kind of dazzling display that our supporters know he can produce."

There was a slight blip in a 1–2 defeat at Hull City, played in a nasty atmosphere, but the game was lit up by a magnificent goal from Haynes in the closing minutes. Jezzard and Haynes had played all the football at Boothferry Park with accurate long and short passes, but once again the defence had not been so clever. The report read: "Haynes' goal came three minutes from time and beat Forgan all the way from over twenty yards. The keeper could only stand and watch the ball go in." A heavy tackle on Haynes gave rise to a scare that he was badly injured at the end of the game; fortunately, it was just a severe shaking.

April

Following the 4–3 home victory against Notts County, the press talked of the indomitable spirit of Mitten, Jezzard and Haynes; the youngster had again provided a last-minute winner for Jezzard. Although the defence conceded goals, the livewire attack could seemingly score at will. Fulham had been 1–3 down at half-time, and won with two goals in the final four minutes.

Three more goals arrived against doomed Oldham Athletic, and once again the superlatives rang out. "The brilliance of the Fulham attack was just too much for Oldham, fine goals by Haynes (two) and Robson paving the way for this win. The trio of Robson, Jezzard and Haynes seemed to be able to cut through the Oldham defence at will."

Bobby Robson scored the first in the thirteenth minute, cutting between the full backs to curl a shot in following a Haynes pass. Five minutes later, Haynes added the second with a well-placed shot following a pass from Bedford Jezzard. After Oldham had reduced the arrears with a penalty, Haynes spotted a gap and immediately went to the other end to hammer into the net a bouncing ball that the Oldham defenders were too slow in clearing. Fulham were 3–1 up inside half an hour, and then relaxed.

The month was concluded perfectly by a 4–3 victory over Swansea Town at the Cottage on Easter Monday. Haynes' slick brain was complimented once more. He made the two Jezzard goals, and had a brilliant first half. For Jezzard's first, Haynes lobbed the ball down the middle, perfectly beating Swansea's offside trap. The second was a repeat, his through pass catching the Swansea defence off guard.

Haynes closed the season as he had opened it, with a goal; at Lincoln City he put Fulham into the lead after only fifteen minutes. It didn't last, however, and the suspect defence conceded four to eventually lose the match 2–4.

Representing the Football League for the first time

Just days after the end of the season came the next honour for Johnny when he was selected to play for the Football League against the Scottish League at Stamford Bridge in front of a crowd of almost 50,000. On a bone-hard pitch, England won comprehensively 4–0. Graham Leggat played for the Scottish League, and amongst England's scorers were Jezzard, again claiming two, with one provided by Haynes, and Johnny Haynes himself with his first international goal. It was the final England goal of the match and came seven minutes from the end, Portsmouth winger Harris unselfishly setting up Haynes to score with a neat finish.

Summary

Fulham finished the 1953–54 season in eighth place, occupying the same position with exactly the same number of points as the previous year, but with some amazing statistics. In this, his first full season, Haynes had missed only one league game, and in all competitions had scored an impressive eighteen times.

Fulham had scored at will under his direction and amassed an amazing 107 goals in forty-five games, 65 of these at the Cottage. Jezzard profited most, with a truly spectacular haul of 38 goals in forty-two league games. Fulham failed to score in just four of the forty-five matches played. They scored more goals than any other Second Division side; in fact they were the leading scorers in the entire Football League! The press described Haynes and Mitten as having an almost perfect understanding.

A welcome break from training. The golden trio of Robson, Jezzard and Haynes take time to relax on the Putney End terracing.

Even though the outlaw and 'Bogota bandit' Charlie Mitten was being overlooked by England, many considered that the three Fulham players—Mitten, accompanied by Haynes and bolstered by defender Eddie Lowe at left half—would form the finest left-side triumvirate in the England team of all the players in the country.

However, life on the other side of the club's balance sheet was not so rosy. In the liabilities column were ninety-three goals, which was why Fulham had never been seriously in contention for promotion.

Forty-five league and cup matches had produced exactly 200 goals for and against. Haynes would later rue that, pointing out: "As fast as we were scoring 'em, we were giving 'em away again at the back!" Although the remark was made with a smile and it had all been very enjoyable initially, Haynes was not a defender and was beginning to become upset at some of the basic errors in defending that had contributed to that large total.

Fulham didn't keep a clean sheet until the end of November, and kept out the opposition only five times in the forty-five games. They conceded two fives, five fours and seven threes; fifty-one goals in these fourteen games. In fact they conceded more goals than any team in the division, except the hapless Oldham Athletic, who had duly finished bottom and been relegated.

First international tour

May

Johnny Haynes, however, had done enough to justify his position internationally, and won a place on the summer tour with the FA squad and the England 'B' team in the Balkans. In Ljubjana, Zagreb, in front of 30,000, England lost 1–2 to Yugoslavia with Bedford Jezzard scoring again to give England the lead initially. Haynes in his third game played well. Here he experienced real gamesmanship for the first time, with tripping and elbowing accompanying basic blocking and blatant obstruction techniques.

The England squad arrive back home looking dazed and sheepish, after the 1–7 drubbing they received in Hungary. Haynes, who was 'reserve' for the match, is third from right in front. At far right is one of his great heroes, Tom Finney. Beddy Jezzard had the misfortune to play in the match—not the best occasion to win your first cap!

In the English game, such tactics didn't occur, and the games provided a real eye-opener for the nineteen-year-old Haynes. He played well enough to be promoted to the 'A' group (seniors), and neither he nor Jezzard played in the next 'B' match against Switzerland in Basle. Many speculated that Haynes was poised to make his full debut against Hungary in Budapest on that tour, but in the end it didn't happen. Perhaps for him it was good that it didn't.

Embarrassed by the Hungarians again

Instead, Haynes accompanied his team-mate Jezzard, who, being older, was selected for the first time for the full England team. Haynes travelled as a full England 'reserve/observer' and witnessed, from the touchline, the 'disaster on the Danube' when England were again comprehensively outplayed by the rampant Hungarians, who recorded their second massive win against England in just six months. This time the score was 1–7, but the home side were so much in control that England could have easily conceded double figures. When the seventh Hungarian goal went in there were still twenty minutes to play.

The result left the whole of English football totally dazed. Haynes would often admit: "They were the best team that I ever saw." Their game was based on skill, passing and control, rather than raw power and physical excesses. He had witnessed domestic league games played with the ball being booted into orbit, the result hinging on uncontrolled skirmishes. This team were able to extemporise, do the unexpected and change the game and its direction in an instant.

Even at a tender age, the watching Haynes bristled with indignation and felt humiliated at what he saw. He recognised that British football was no longer the best available and that the dinosaur FA needed to see the facts that were right in front of their eyes.

The intelligent Haynes, thinking ahead, was going to model his game on what he had seen at Wembley and in Budapest from the 'Magnificent Magyars'—accurate passing, close control and quick thinking. At nineteen he was already plotting England's future.

Reserve for the 1954 World Cup squad

Such was his progress that Haynes was selected for the original squad of forty for the World Cup of 1954 as a reserve. The party was then trimmed to twenty-two and England eventually took just eighteen. Jezzard and Haynes both missed out, England favouring the 'golden boy' of the moment, Sheffield Wednesday's Albert Quixall, later to command the British transfer record, over the young Haynes.

Haynes was able to rest and enjoy another close season of high-level cricket matches with Winchmore Hill. He watched the World Cup on television, and saw England beat Switzerland 2–0, before drawing 4–4 with Belgium and losing 2–4 to Uruguay. The defeat was enough to see England eliminated from the competition at an early stage.

9: First international honours 1954–55

9: First international honours — 1954–55

In their pre-season warm-ups, Fulham usually played the club's reserves in a 'public trial' match. This season was no exception. Haynes played for the first team and contributed to a 7–1 demolition of the second-string team. Bobby Robson scored four goals that day, three of them supplied from passes by Haynes. The *Fulham Chronicle* said: "Haynes was showing all the arts and crafts that made him the talking point of soccer last season. He will surely be knocking on the door of the England selectors this season."

Four goals in the first four games

Johnny Haynes started the 1954–55 season as if he meant business. He found the net in the opening four games of the season, registering five goals in all, as Fulham took thirteen points out of a possible fourteen, and found themselves riding high and sitting at the top of the table jointly with Stoke City.

August

In the opening game of the season, Fulham outclassed and crushed Blackburn Rovers 5–1 at Craven Cottage. The press described the match as some of the best football and crisp passing seen for almost ten years. Haynes was the inspiration for Fulham's dazzling first-half display. From his feet came a constant stream of passes down the middle and out to the wings, most passes being superb one-touch efforts.

Fulham scored four times in the opening nineteen minutes of the season, and missed three other chances. Haynes' sweeping pass had made the first for Arthur Stevens, and then a four-man move involving Haynes, who supplied a beautiful, traditional defence-splitter, gave Bedford Jezzard his first of the season. Haynes later hit the post with the keeper beaten, and for the final goal, he ran on to a Charlie Mitten pass and slammed the ball past Blackburn keeper Elvy. Bobby Robson was the only forward not to find the net.

The midweek game away against Derby County was equally dramatic and exciting. Jezzard scored from a cleverly presented opening by Haynes after only nine minutes. Three minutes later Derby were level, but Haynes immediately took matters into his own hands. Defenders laid off him, expecting a pass, but he advanced and belted a left-footed thirty-yard drive which was a goal all the way. After Fulham had gone 2–3 behind to an own goal and a penalty, he netted the equaliser for his second goal. Stevens' flying header rebounded from a post and he made no mistake. Following a Derby mis-kick in defence, Robson scored a late winner.

At Bury the following Saturday, Fulham won yet again. The scheming and industry of Robson and Haynes worried Bury, and Haynes combined with

CHIX No. 2 SERIES
Numbers 1 to 48

FAMOUS
FOOTBALLERS
No. 14

Johnny Haynes
(Fulham and England)

There is no need to despair for the future of English soccer with young men like Johnny Haynes playing. Johnny, appointed captain of Fulham this season, has made the England inside-right position deservedly his own and is worthy to carry on in the Carter-Mannion mould.

The Best Chix Bubble Gum

CHIX CONFECTIONERY Co. Ltd.
SLOUGH, ENGLAND

Stevens to allow him to score at the second attempt with twenty minutes to go.

He secured the victory with the third goal just two minutes from time in a 3–1 win. Mitten and Haynes criss-crossed their way down the wing, and Haynes took the ball inside and shot; the effort was blocked by a defender, but he made no mistake with his second attempt.

September

Bedford Jezzard repaid Haynes in midweek during a 2–0 win over Derby County, when he made a brilliant twenty-five-yard run. He then squared the ball to Haynes who, with perfect timing, finished with aplomb. His shot was described as unstoppable, flying in just under the bar.

Fulham had been struggling up to that point, but then the perfectly rolled passes from Haynes began to flow. Such was his performance that the reporter covering the game said: "The former schoolboy international had more ways of beating defenders than I have seen an inside forward show for many a day." Haynes' rallying capability had brought a steadying influence and order to Fulham's approach work. He was described as "the nineteen-year-old with the twinkling feet and quick brain." Haynes was now the club's leading scorer, and it was refreshing to see the defence keep a clean sheet so early in the season.

In the 2–2 draw at Swansea Town, Arthur Stevens and Haynes fashioned the opening score, scheming a headed goal for Robson, and then Haynes combined with Charlie Mitten in a beautiful movement that got the Swansea defence into a real tangle and created a goal for Jezzard to put Fulham ahead.

And so it continued when Fulham thrashed Doncaster Rovers 5–2 at the Cottage after the visitors had taken an early lead. Although Haynes didn't score, his masterly control and the flow of openings he created made the first goal for Robson with a perfect cross, the second goal for Jezzard with a clever twist and screwed

The Chix card (opposite page) used the photograph that is featured on the opening page of this chapter. The card was issued in 1956, and added painted-on colour (and a pitch line). The magazine illustration, above, went one better and added a crowd.

pass that enabled the centre forward to finish with a cannonball shot and then the fourth goal for the same player. The headline left no-one in doubt, "Haynes puts it right for Fulham."

England selectors come to watch

The quality of Haynes' play was sending shockwaves through the Second Division. It wasn't long before those reverberations reached the ears of the Football Association. England manager Walter Winterbottom and FA selectors turned up in force to watch Fulham's 3–1 victory over Notts County in the middle of the month. It turned out to be a groundbreaking match, with Haynes in great form.

For the first Fulham goal, he put Jezzard through to create a goal for Mitten after his shot had been hacked off the line by a defender. He scored the second himself on the half-hour with a brilliant shot from thirty yards which left the crowd gasping. In one movement he controlled the ball and shot; the keeper appeared to have the shot covered but its pace and power meant that he got nowhere near it.

The press said: "Instead of passing, he slipped past the full back, and his power drive had the goalkeeper groping the air." Jezzard scored the third, taking a pass from Stevens after Haynes' initial pass to Stevens had split the defence. Some described the game as "an England cap performance by Haynes". At this stage, Fulham had already banged in twenty-four goals!

Whether all the furore surrounding the prodigy Haynes affected his performances is not entirely certain, but Fulham took two canings in their next two away fixtures, losing 0–4 at Doncaster Rovers and then 1–4 at Liverpool. The Liverpool game undoubtedly flattered the home side. Liverpool icon Billy Liddell scored a hat trick, including a couple of dubious penalties. Haynes had another good game but the Fulham team felt that they had been harshly treated by the officials.

Haynes partners Tom Finney

On the 22nd of the month, Haynes was selected to play for the Football League for the second time, against the League of Ireland at Dalymount Park. It was another milestone, as he played for the first time with Preston's Tom Finney, an experience he thoroughly enjoyed. England, against vastly inferior opposition, cantered home 6–0, thanks to a hat trick from Don Revie and, of course, a goal from Haynes which came ten minutes from the end following a four-man move. Haynes, applauded for his magnificent passes, had set up Revie with a beautiful through pass as early as the second minute. The scoreline flattered England somewhat as four of their goals came in the last eight minutes against the fast-tiring Irish.

After this international experience, it was back to basics with a home fixture against Bristol Rovers. The dynamic duo were at it again; Jezzard crashed in a Haynes pass to put the home side ahead in the twentieth minute. Haynes was a real star in the second half, with lovely, accurate, defence-splitting passes in abundance, and in another raid Jezzard scored yet again from a Haynes assist. Unfortunately it was one of the defence's sleepy days and the home side literally threw it away 2–3, with gift goals arising from very poor marking.

England debut

October

The Football League performance, coupled with his exceptional league form, led to Johnny Haynes being awarded his first full England cap. He was picked to represent England against Northern Ireland. In doing so, he became the first footballer ever to have represented England at all five levels other than amateur—Schoolboy, Youth, Under-23, 'B' and the senior team. For the statisticians, Haynes was the 739th player to appear for England. He missed Fulham's match against Plymouth Argyle as a result.

He was still only nineteen, the match taking place just a fortnight before his twentieth birthday, and less than two years after he'd made his league debut in a Second Division team. He had reached the peak of his profession, and for him it was a deep and personal experience. An emotional Haynes knew that the first

This squad picture features a number of hopefuls who never made it through to the first team, but all those in the front row made the grade. They are, from left: Chenhall, Barton, Cronin, Robson, Hill, Haynes, Mitten and Dwight.

match was vital, and that he had to fully justify his selection.

He joined a demoralised English side and football-loving nation, lately exposed so brutally by the Hungarians, and a team that had performed pretty inconspicuously in the summer World Cup. The England selectors were chopping and changing the side around, and the team in which he played showed seven changes from the previous match, and included the future Leeds United manager Don Revie. Haynes would have to bed in quickly with experienced internationals like Billy Wright, Nat Lofthouse and Stanley Matthews.

The previous Saturday a reporter had phoned him at his home in Edmonton with news of the England call-up. But Johnny was staying with Jimmy Hill and his wife at the time, and he only found out the exciting news at almost midnight, too late to go out and celebrate.

He would be awarded an enormous £50 match fee for playing for England, but what would a nineteen-year-old lad do with so much money? For the young player this sum constituted almost a month's wages. Haynes was in no doubt what he would do, and it was typical of the man that he used his first England fee to fly his parents over to Belfast to watch his England debut and stay overnight in a good hotel—the first step towards saying thank you.

His first England goal

Haynes was the only southerner in the England team and he travelled to Manchester on his own to join up with Walter Winterbottom and his England colleagues. He admitted to being tense before his debut.

So it was that on 2nd October 1954 Haynes made his debut for the full senior side, scoring a goal in a 2–0 England victory over the Irish at Windsor Park, Belfast. His initial nerves quickly dissipated in a fine performance.

His goal was nicely taken, sidestepping a defender with a neat dribble before shooting low past keeper Uprichard fifteen minutes from the end. He also provided the excellent and beautifully judged pass inside a defender that laid on the second England goal for Don Revie just three minutes later.

Some of the press also thought he had managed pretty well, one remarking: "Haynes' precise distribution, allied to his astute reading of the play and

Crunch! Birmingham's centre half Newman slides in on Haynes, indicative of the sort of attention that the Fulham star would receive throughout his career. Haynes was hurt in the tackle, but managed to carry on playing. Fulham won 2–1.

incisive finishing, offered a glimmer of hope for the country's future at world level." Another added: "Here is a player of real class who showed maturity beyond his years. His superb passing and two-footed skills were the main feature of the match."

Haynes thoroughly enjoyed his debut and thought he'd done all right. Showing creditable business acumen, he realised that his England performances could boost his annual salary by between £200 and £400, almost doubling his annual Fulham pay. He became aware of his commercial potential, and that if he could remain an international, there could be articles, advertisements, endorsements and public appearances; there could be many advantages to being a public figure.

The debut match saw the future Haynes very much in evidence. Ray Barlow of West Bromwich Albion won his only England cap in that match, and Sir Bobby Robson recalls: "Back at the Hawthorns, Ray Barlow was talking to me about this little cockney twit, great little player, who had far too much to say at half-time, talking to Matthews and Wright of all people about how the match was going on!"

Despite his outwardly confident appearance, the chattering masked an inward inferiority complex which he was suffering as he lined up with all those great players.

The first major disappointment

In spite of the two-goal victory and initial reactions, it had been a poor England performance overall. Haynes received his first taste of press criticism when, later in the week, he was labelled as one of England's many flops. He was immediately dropped after the match and replaced in the next international against Wales by the experienced Len Shackleton. The balloon containing his immediate plans for stardom had been pricked right in front of him.

Haynes would miss the next eight England internationals, and his exile would last a full twelve months. His next opportunity would, ironically, also be against Northern Ireland.

He was angry about the dropping; it was the first real slap in the face for him. His pride was badly hurt, and he felt indignant that he hadn't been given more of an early run in the side to prove his capabilities; however, he could do little about it.

He thought that he'd made "a fair contribution" and was "not the worst player by far". His only consolation was that stars like Raich Carter and the great Stanley Matthews had also been dropped following their first England appearance.

In his memoirs, England captain Billy Wright recalls that it was very rare for the England selectors to put

A midweek England 'special training' session with manager Walter Winterbottom. It may not be exactly what the manager was talking about, but the picture clearly shows the heavy leather ball in use at the time. An attentive Haynes is the third player from the left.

their faith in youth: "I was impressed with the debut performance of Johnny Haynes. He was just nineteen, and already looked an assured and confident player who could hit accurate forty-yard passes with either foot; but the powers that be decided he was too young to trust with the role of midfield general and he was dropped along with Don Revie and six other players."

England continued to change the side around, and Haynes' frustration mounted as England started to perform well with Nat Lofthouse and Wolves' Dennis Wilshaw up front.

On that October day when he was absent playing for England, Fulham had no luck either. In the match at Plymouth, the Fulham goalkeeper tossed the ball into his own net when down injured, and a goal was awarded. Fulham played with Mitten in goal for most of the match. Fulham had been stuck on thirteen (unlucky for some) points for three games, and this 2–3 defeat made it four consecutive losses.

After recovering from the initial England snub and disappointment, Haynes came back stronger and redoubled his efforts. In the next home match, Fulham won 2–1 against Birmingham City, Haynes and Jezzard working together for the first goal for Stevens. Haynes had a pile-driver headed over the bar. He was then the victim of a hard tackle from Birmingham's Newman, but was able to carry on after attention. Finally he and Mitten linked up, enabling Jezzard to provide the knockdown for Robson to shoot the second.

The following week Fulham were again on top form, winning 4–2 at Ipswich. Haynes had to play slightly deeper due to an injury to Jimmy Hill. Despite being a goal down in the first five minutes, Haynes and Jezzard combined to give Stevens the equaliser just seconds later; and with Haynes moving the ball sweetly and dangerously into open spaces, it enabled Bobby Robson to rise twice to head Fulham two goals to the good by the interval.

Haynes was unlucky when a fabulous run and shot in the second half saw the schemer-in-chief shake the crossbar. The press heaped praise on the young man again, although he had failed to score: "Brilliant Haynes was the inspiration for three of the Fulham goals."

In the next home match Fulham were again victors, this time over fourth-placed Luton 3–1. Haynes received the ball from Norman Smith and parted with it immediately to Stevens, who scored. The press agreed: "The vital third was taken by Robson after fine work by Jezzard and Haynes."

This excellent form saw Haynes picked by the England selectors for special training with England Probables ahead of the international with Wales. Despite this promotion, and excellence in this special training, Haynes wasn't picked to play. England won 3–2, with Roy Bentley claiming a hat trick in eighteen minutes.

Confronted by Nottingham Forest's Bill Morley, Haynes shows delicate control in the 1–1 draw in December. The Stevenage Road stand, now named after our hero, is packed, and in addition there are extra fans sitting on benches in front of the railings.

A fourth league win in a row was secured the following Saturday, when Fulham staged a dramatic comeback after falling two goals behind by half-time at Millmoor. The midfield then put themselves to work, with Haynes and Robson baffling the Rotherham defence with their play and constant switching of position.

Robson on the hour took a magnificently placed ball from Johnny Haynes and scored with a powerful rising shot. Haynes and Stevens then engineered the equaliser for Jezzard. Jezzard's winner followed soon after that. The 3–2 match was observed by England selector Harold Shentall. By the end of the month Fulham were sitting comfortably in the second promotion spot.

Haynes is not himself

November

Things were looking extremely rosy for the young Haynes but, after helping to inspire the first goal at Ayresome Park, he received a nasty ankle injury in the 2–4 reverse against Middlesbrough, which caused him to miss Fulham's next two league games against Lincoln City and Hull City. He missed the winning debut of his friend Trevor Chamberlain in that Lincoln match and the goal he scored, which was a real beauty, a shot from thirty-five yards with his very first kick in league football.

Without Haynes against Hull City, Fulham failed to score for only the second time that season, but still secured a point. However, their form remained good, and the team were still firmly in the league's runners-up position at the end of the month.

December

Haynes returned to the fray but it appeared that he had been rushed back too soon. He played against struggling Nottingham Forest in a 1–1 draw, and started in international form, but an unpredictable ball and appallingly heavy conditions, coupled with strong, wild winds, ensured that he faded from the game pretty quickly.

At Elland Road Leeds, Haynes combined with Bobby Robson and Bedford Jezzard to allow Len Newcombe to score with a first-time shot that was deflected in, but little else was seen of him. Haynes, Jezzard and Charlie Mitten also all had worthy goalscoring shots miss the target by the narrowest of margins and Fulham eked out a point in a 1–1 draw.

After a barren patch, Haynes netted his first goal in thirteen games in the 1–3 defeat at Blackburn. "A dash through the defence by Mitten enabled him to cross

Action from the encounter with Italy at Stamford Bridge in January, the first-ever Under-23 match to be played in this country. England's Ron Flowers is pictured with the ball, and Haynes cuts inside to support the move. A superb Haynes performance contributed to a 5–1 victory.

a ball which Johnny Haynes headed beautifully into the net." It was the best goal of the game; but on a quagmire pitch, it had not been a day for ball-playing artists. This, however, was a very important loss, as Blackburn were right up at the top with Fulham, and it was certainly not the Haynes of two months before. The press said: "Haynes was in trouble with his fitness which was well below international standard, his lack of pace and speed of passing demonstrate that he has not fully recovered from the ankle injury."

Haynes celebrated his eighth goal of the season in a 3–1 win over lowly Port Vale on Christmas Day at the Cottage. He had already been unlucky with two magnificent shots, but the goal was a beauty: "In the twentieth minute, Jezzard nodded back a Mitten centre for the onrushing Haynes to fire an unstoppable shot from fifteen yards." The goalkeeper could only watch the power drive sail past him into the net.

In the last match of the year Fulham played on an appalling surface at Port Vale, where half the ball was not visible when it was on the ground. There was probably six inches of mud. Haynes considered that they were the worst conditions he had ever seen. For a football-playing side it was a day to forget. Vale were extremely fortunate that the referee allowed the match to be played. It was hardly surprising that Fulham lost 0–4, and by the New Year they had slipped to sixth.

January

The Fulham team were then turfed out of the FA Cup 2–3 by a Tom Finney-inspired First Division Preston North End in the third round at Craven Cottage. This was despite another goal from Johnny Haynes, who scored the first goal of the afternoon in the twenty-eighth minute from Charlie Mitten's pass when virtually unmarked. It was a fine goal and all five forwards contributed to the move. It was hard to believe, but it would prove to be his final goal of the season! Classy Preston replied with three goals, but a fighting Fulham almost forced a replay.

Severe winter weather set in not long after, and no match could be played for a month because of persistent snow and ice. The only game Fulham squeezed in took place three weeks later, a 2–1 friendly against First Division Cardiff City; Haynes scored the winner with a shot that gave the keeper no chance.

First caps for England Under-23s

On the 19th of the month, the fledgling England Under-23 side thrashed the experienced, settled and strongly fancied Italians 5–1 at Stamford Bridge. Peerless Haynes, on his Under-23 debut, was in devastating form, inspiring the team with his passes. The match, like the reciprocal encounter in Bologna the previous year, was played in snow, and the ground was frosty and unbearably hard and uneven. Haynes, however, skated over the surface like a gazelle, and won applause from all quarters. This experimental England side also contained the young Ron Flowers and Duncan Edwards.

Haynes had the ball in the net with a studied header from Flowers' free kick as early as the second minute, but with everyone celebrating, the French referee ruled out the goal because of an infringement only he could have seen. He kept probing until he found ever-widening gaps in the desperate Italian defence. Time and again he pivoted to send long through passes into the Italian defence.

With the score at 1–1, Haynes worked the ball along the goal-line, and Bristol City's John Atyeo fired a terrific header from his chipped pass to give England the lead. Minutes later, Haynes sent a perfect pass for Harry Hooper to run on to. Hooper crossed, and Frank Blunstone ran in to meet the ball and shoot to make the score 3–1. Still it wasn't over. Five minutes from time, Haynes received the ball and immediately sent a brilliant pass inside the back for Hooper to again run on to. Hooper beat the advancing goalkeeper and crashed the ball into an empty net. A rejuvenated Haynes, basking in the headline: "[wing] Halves and Haynes rout Italy," had done his international future a power of good.

February

Domestically the second half of the season saw a dramatic turnaround, as Fulham's form slumped alarmingly. As the snow began to recede, Fulham lost at home to Liverpool 1–2, but Haynes won his second England Under-23 cap in midweek when he was selected to play against Scotland in Glasgow.

This resulted in another resounding victory for England, by 6–0. Duncan Edwards, playing an emergency role at centre forward after Charlton's Ayre had dislocated his elbow in the first minute, scored a sensational hat trick in eighteen minutes and the final goal of the night was netted by Haynes. Haynes played superbly well again, providing a stream of deadly accurate passes that finally destroyed the Scottish defence who visibly shuddered every time he received the ball. His passes set up four of the England goals, two for Edwards, and one each for Blunstone and Atyeo.

His own goal came just three minutes from the end. Taking a pass from Blunstone, he hurdled Duff the luckless Scottish keeper to shoot in and round off a great night's work. This vibrant performance would ultimately catapult him back into the England 'B' side. The critics called it Haynes' match, and although it was an up and down season, he knew that his time "would come again."

When league matches fully resumed, the cold, boggy conditions didn't suit Haynes' game at all, although he was still competing well. In the snow at Eastville on another grassless mudheap, Fulham lost 1–4 to Bristol Rovers. Haynes and Charlie Mitten combined to make the goal for Bedford Jezzard and Fulham also saw two very disappointing decisions go against them with regard to goals that were clearly offside.

It's the ankle again

Against relegation-haunted Plymouth at Craven Cottage, where the home side lost again, 2–3, the playing conditions were again poor and this allowed defenders to go beyond the rules. Haynes was clattered early on, a tackle that required him to have prolonged treatment. He was described as being out of sorts, and there were no incisive passes inside the full back. The slippery conditions led to him turning the ankle again during the game, and he missed a further two league games. Fulham had now slipped right out of the promotion race down to mid-table.

March

Inclement weather forced the postponement of the next match against Birmingham City, which was fortunate for the young Haynes as he would not have played, as he was still struggling with the injury he had received against Argyle. The injury forced the club to withdraw him from the imminent Football League versus Scottish League match, saying that "the damage caused is slow in mending and requires careful nursing."

He missed the 4–1 victory over struggling Ipswich Town at home, and the disappointing but expected 0–3 defeat at promotion-challenging Luton. He returned gingerly for the home 1–1 draw with high-flying

Smiles were hard to come by during March, when Haynes' ankle injury forced him to miss matches, including a representative Football League fixture.

Rotherham United, but was reported as making no significant impression.

In midweek, he was selected for the friendly England 'B' international against Germany 'B' at Hillsborough, winning his fourth cap. Despite missing those two recent league Fulham matches, he played in this international, probably unwisely, as he wasn't fully fit. Some of his passes went astray, and the Germans who had watched Haynes dismantle the Italians earlier in the year were able, through tight marking and swift tackling, to cut off the supply to the dangerous Hooper. The match ended in a 1–1 draw in front of over 32,000, with Wolves' Roy Swinburne scoring the England goal from a long Haynes free kick.

Still struggling after his midweek exertions, Haynes made little impression in the 1–1 home draw with Stoke. In midweek for the rearranged match at St Andrews, however, he combined well with Tony Barton to give Roy Dwight a goal on his debut. Top-of-the-table Birmingham won with two goals in the last ten minutes, one being a very dubious penalty for hands against Robin Lawler. This 2–3 result made it a month to forget.

April

Against Middlesbrough, without the experienced Charlie Mitten, Arthur Stevens and Bedford Jezzard, all injured, Fulham played a forward line with an average age of twenty. This was handicapped even further when a crude and deliberate tackle took out Fulham's dangerous scorer Bobby Robson.

Johnny Haynes and Jimmy Hill combined for Johnny to push a great through pass down the middle for Dwight to convert, but the final outcome was yet another 1–2 home defeat. Haynes tried to set up late goals but shots were blocked or halted with fierce tackles.

Over Easter, Haynes skimmed the crossbar with one shot against West Ham, and Jezzard was just wide from a Haynes corner, but after the impetus of a third-minute goal from Jezzard returning from flu, Fulham went down 1–2 on Good Friday. At Lincoln the following day, Haynes failed to get a mention, and it was only due to a fine penalty save by Ian Black that Fulham clung on to a 2–2 draw. In the third game in four days, Haynes headed fractionally over the crossbar against promotion-chasing West Ham at Craven Cottage but it turned out to be the first goalless draw seen that season.

First medal as a Fulham player

Fulham took time out two days after the gruelling Easter programme to compete in and ultimately win the *Evening Standard* London Championship five-a-side trophy. The Fulham side was Ian Black (goal), Eddie Lowe and Jimmy Hill, Johnny Haynes and Bobby Robson. Although they were not real matches, it was an excellent night's entertainment, and the final match was televised.

The first match, against Arsenal, stood at 2–2 at full time, the scorers being Haynes and Hill. This necessitated extra time to get a result—one minute each way. During those remarkable two minutes, Haynes scored twice to secure a 4–2 win. Charlton Athletic were the next opposition and they were comfortably disposed of 5–1, with goals from Robson (3), Hill and Haynes.

The final proved to be an easy win. Playing against West Ham for the third time in six days, Fulham won 4–1 with Haynes rounding off the win with the last two goals. It meant five goals for Haynes on the night. Not only did Fulham receive the trophy, Haynes received his first medal as a Fulham player.

Any hope that winning the trophy might inspire the Cottagers failed miserably and Fulham lost 0–1 at home to lowly Hull City in the poorest home game of the season. Visiting keeper Bly saved a number of certainties, before Hull broke away to win the match with an offside goal twenty minutes from the end. One report said that Jimmy Hill was doing the work of two men; it probably meant his own work and that of Haynes. Fulham hadn't yet won at home all year, in a total of eight attempts.

Thankfully that was put right at the ninth attempt when Fulham pummelled mid-table Swansea Town 5–1. The game turned out to be Johnny's best for several

The victorious Fulham team after winning the Evening Standard five-a-side tournament: Bobby Robson, Jimmy Hill, Johnny Haynes, Ian Black and Eddie Lowe.

weeks and he was the architect of most of the goals. Haynes and Jezzard's passing movement created the first for Robson. Haynes' pass found Jezzard to score a solo second goal, and the move was repeated for the fourth, giving Jezzard a 'real' hat trick. Tony Barton rounded off a memorable day with the fifth.

Unfortunately the temporary upsurge in form didn't last. Fulham went back to over-playing and tip-tap football and were easily beaten in midweek 0–2 by a mediocre Nottingham Forest. The season petered out with one point gained at Notts County and a defeat at home to promotion hopefuls Leeds United. Haynes had been forced to play the last nine league games in the space of just twenty-nine days.

A disappointing season finishes

Although Haynes continued to craft and scheme as best he could, he didn't score a league goal after Christmas Day, and ended the season with a disappointing return of eight goals from thirty-seven starts. After the injury against Plymouth, he created only a few goals and chances, a country mile away from his pre-Christmas displays. Fulham's form had literally disintegrated when he was under par.

After Christmas Day, Fulham won just twice more in the league. Five extremely poor months had seen them drop out of a solid promotion slot to finish a very dispiriting fourteenth. The goals-for column again showed a healthy figure of two short of eighty, but the team had conceded eighty-two. So 160 goals for and against had gone in that season. Once again the team had managed to keep only five clean sheets, which hampered and neutralised Haynes' sterling inside forward work.

Bedford Jezzard had netted another amazing twenty-three goals, giving him a total of over sixty for the last two seasons; Bobby Robson had also netted twenty-three, giving him a two-year total of thirty-six. The 'golden trio' had amassed an incredible 125 goals between them in just two seasons—truly remarkable.

However, Haynes' confidence at some stages had seemed a little low, and he remained reluctant to have a shot, a point not lost on Robson, who commented: "Johnny was concentrating too much on his passing game, he could hit thirty-yard passes, but he could also hit thirty-yard pile-drivers too. He was so much of a perfectionist, he didn't like to miss or put the ball into the crowd." After he had burst on to the footballing scene so dramatically and been such an instant success, the second half of the season had proved to be a dreadful disappointment for young John.

He didn't travel with the England team during the close season for their matches in France, Spain and Portugal in the summer of 1955. Some Fulham players went off to the West Indies with the FA, including Bedford Jezzard, Bobby Robson and Jimmy Hill. Haynes was still definitely feeling the effects of the ankle injury, and wanted to give his leg some decent rest and rehabilitation.

The London XI and the first Inter-Cities Fairs Cup

In June, however, he did play in a competition, the first Inter-Cities Fairs Cup. The competition was created on 18th April 1955, and the first tournament took *three years* to complete. The entrants were the major football teams of all the cities which held trade fairs, hence the name of the competition.

Originally twelve clubs were split into four groups, but Vienna and Cologne withdrew before the competition started. This left just Barcelona and Copenhagen in group A, Birmingham, Milan and Zagreb in group B, just Lausanne Sports and Leipzig in group C, with London, Basle and Frankfurt in group D. Matches were played on a home and away basis.

Like many cities taking part, London had several strong teams; however, the rules stated that there could only be a single team from each city. It was therefore decided to create a team especially for the tournament, using players from several London-based clubs. Membership of the team varied considerably between matches. The London XI was managed by Chelsea chairman Joe Mears.

Haynes was part of a London team that travelled to Switzerland and won 5–0 against a Basle XI. The highlight of the game was a hat trick from his Winchmore Hill cricket colleague, Arsenal's Cliff Holton. Haynes played and although he didn't score, the match proved a good workout for the injured ankle.

Thinking about cricket

A somewhat downcast Haynes then stayed at home and played more club cricket with Winchmore Hill. Despite what he said publicly, he loved cricket and to him it was more than just a close season hobby. With his reactions, timing and hawk-eyed vision, he had become a first class batsman and wicket keeper. So good had he become that the Middlesex County Cricket Club offered him a professional contract to join the ground staff.

Haynes' boyhood idol had been Arsenal's Denis Compton, the original 'Brylcreem Boy'. Compton had managed to combine football for Arsenal and England with cricket for Middlesex and England. If he could juggle the two, why couldn't Haynes? His colleague, Cliff Holton, was a spin bowler and played higher level cricket, for the county Middlesex's second eleven.

Haynes said of Compton: "Denis Compton had it all; talent, charisma, determination, looks and a wonderful love for competition. He possessed modesty and charm and his sporting gifts were such that he played cricket and football for England. Throughout both careers he insisted that sport at the highest level should be enjoyed rather than taken too seriously.

The sight of those fearsome Australians Keith Miller and Ray Lindwall directing bouncers around his ears in the days long before protective helmets only seemed to make his smile grow broader. And he made a point of being sociable with his opponents once play was finished.

"We shared similar north London upbringings, him in Hendon and me in Kentish Town. He learnt his batting skills in the street, playing in front of a lamppost chalked with a wicket. Being a fan of cricket as well as football, the highlight of my summer holidays was being taken to Lord's by my uncle. I was twelve in 1947 when Compton had his finest year for Middlesex and England, scoring almost 4,000 runs, including eighteen centuries. He made 163 in the first Test at Trent Bridge against South Africa and I was there as he topped that with 208 in the second Test at Lord's. Still not satisfied, he hit another couple of centuries at Old Trafford and The Oval.

"Every schoolboy wanted to be Denis Compton and I was so inspired by him that I initially aimed to emulate him by playing football and cricket for my country. To begin with, I thought there was a chance when I was offered a contract by MCC after playing a reasonable standard of club cricket for Winchmore Hill. Cricket always took preference for Compton and I'm sure he was grateful that it got him out of pre-season training, but he still played fourteen wartime and Victory internationals on the left wing for England and collected league championship and FA Cup winners medals."

Initially Haynes gave the contract offer very serious thought indeed, and for a few days in his blackest moments even considered giving up football altogether to become a full-time cricketer, but this notion soon faded. He later said, "Life without football would hardly have been worth thinking about."

It was soon apparent that the year-round demands of modern football made mixing the two sports on a serious level manifestly unworkable. Football was more important to him, and in order to rest, he cut down on this close season's cricket and ultimately turned down the cricket county's offer.

As far as can be accurately ascertained, he never actually turned out for Middlesex in any professional capacity at this time. However, he didn't keep all his eggs in one basket, and decided he would see how he felt the following season. Publicly, he stated that he wouldn't rule out professional cricket if he was approached again the following year.

10: England, Newcastle and Brazil 1955–56

10: England, Newcastle and Brazil 1955–56

After a dismal and disheartening six months, Johnny Haynes returned refreshed and renewed, harbouring a burning desire to get Fulham's promotion push back on track and to force his way back into the England team and stay there. The club's board of directors had issued a positive statement, promising attacking football again and a commitment to retaining its nurtured talent, saying: "How would you, our supporters, have felt if we had parted with Bedford Jezzard, Johnny Haynes or Bobby Robson and a few more?" Fulham were proud that the ten principal forwards at the club had all been signed for just the £10 signing-on fee.

August

On the domestic front, Fulham went off like a train as they usually did, winning their first three league games. They were a joy to watch in their opening 5–1 victory over Bury away from home. It took Bedford Jezzard a mere three minutes to open his and Fulham's account. Then Haynes got into the match, pulling the ball back from the by-line for the second. The press commented: "Haynes' perfect cross from the left resulted in a diving header from Stevens for the second goal."

The fourth goal was a fine piece of anticipation from Haynes who positioned himself perfectly for a back pass, and when it came he hit the ball so hard that it entered the goal with the speed of a rocket. Haynes also hit the fifth. The paper's summary was: "Haynes scored the final two goals in the last fifteen minutes showing what a ball artiste he can be."

The midweek home game with Blackburn Rovers was just as good. Haynes and Jezzard, showing perfect understanding, made the second goal for the maestro, which he put away with an unstoppable shot. Haynes and Charlie Mitten then put together a wing movement for Jezzard to score another beautiful goal. It was a comprehensive 3–0 victory.

Against Barnsley at the Cottage in the twenty-seventh minute, Haynes spotted a gap and from his perfect pass, Jezzard scored the second goal. Haynes, Mitten and Arthur Stevens were all involved for the goals that gave Bedford Jezzard an individual four-goal tally. Fulham had won 5–1 again in front of England manager Walter Winterbottom, who was apparently observing Bobby Robson this time. After three games, Fulham had six points, Jezzard already had seven goals and Fulham had scored thirteen.

Previous page: A typical hand-coloured picture from the period, featuring Haynes, Jezzard and Mitten in the Fulham dressing room.

FOOTBALLERS
No. 42
JOHNNY HAYNES
(Fulham and England)
Haynes is the inspiration behind Fulham's rise to best form. He is also automatic choice for England at inside-right. Shrewd player and adept at long passes. Young and very talented.
A series of 50 issued with
CADET SWEETS
TRADING ESTATE, SLOUGH, BUCKINGHAMSHIRE

In Fulhamish style, the team managed just two draws from the next three games. They were unlucky to go down by a single goal in the return match at Blackburn Rovers, where a Haynes header cleared the bar by an inch.

September

In the 1–1 draw at Middlesbrough, Haynes made the opening for Charlie Mitten to score. Following a below par display and a 1–1 draw against Notts County in midweek, where Haynes banged a long ball down the middle for Stevens to score with a scrappy toe-poke and Mitten missed his first penalty of the season, Fulham and Johnny bounced back against second-placed Bristol City in a comprehensive 3–0 win.

Fortunately Bedford Jezzard was back after a two-match absence with an ankle injury. It was a rough-house atmosphere, in which Jezzard was booked. The deadlock was broken in the fifteenth minute when "Mitten swept a free kick over to Haynes who in one movement turned and sent a daisy cutter into the corner of the net. It was a perfect goal." Haynes then turned provider and Bristol's fate was sealed with two fine goals from Jezzard, both the result of defence-splitting passes from Haynes. The team had delivered a powerful performance, and it was noted that "no-one worked harder than Haynes whose pin-point passing had the Bristol defence baffled."

A hat trick away from home

The following Thursday afternoon, Fulham played just as well at Meadow Lane, a ground and a pitch where Haynes always did well, and he contributed a fine hat trick in a 4–3 win. The club programme admitted: "Johnny was outstandingly brilliant. Wiseacres of football said it was the greatest exhibition they had ever seen from one man."

It was an incredible game. Fulham had the lead three times but each time were pegged back, before finally squeezing out the winning goal. The fireworks began in the first thirty seconds. Fed by Jimmy Hill, Haynes raced to goal and his powerful shot never left the ground. After an equaliser, Mitten gave Fulham the lead for the second time with a penalty on the stroke of half-time, but again County pulled back.

Twenty minutes from the end Haynes scored one of the finest goals seen at Meadow Lane. As a cross came in, he had his back to goal, but he turned and met it on the volley, and the ball sped in like a rocket.

Time was beginning to run out after County's third equaliser, but Haynes had other ideas. With the referee looking at his linesman for a 'time's up' signal, the County defence retreated. Haynes was twenty-five yards out, but gave one last shot all he had and the ball flew along the wet turf, through tangled bodies and the goalkeeper's legs, for a memorable winner. The programme said: "His three goals were just reward, for not only was he the hardest worker on the field, but he was the mastermind, the tactician, the dictator!"

Two days later, a tired Fulham team lost 1–2 at Upton Park, where Haynes and winger Tony Barton combined to create a goal for Jezzard that gave Fulham an early lead. The game wasn't lost for the want of Haynes' endeavours. The papers said: "Fulham had their own youthful star scheming and fooling the opposition.

"He led a great side in the first half. He was the inspiration to older craftsmen. He showed sound judgement which sometimes defeated his own team-mates. It was their fault that all the good work done by this skilled young player failed to come to something." Fulham were eventually undone by two goals, both unfortunately deflected in off their own defenders.

They then had the shock of their season. After taking a second-half lead against Port Vale at the Cottage, when a four-man move including Haynes created the opening for Mitten, the away defence tightened up and Fulham were hit by a four-goal avalanche from the visitors in the last half hour, leaving the home side dazed with a 1–4 score.

Another sensational show for the England Under-23s

The two defeats were not the best preparation for an international match. However, Haynes was now firmly in the eyes of the selectors and he turned in three very good international performances during the next four weeks. These displays immediately put him back into contention for a restoration to the full England side.

In the first of these, Haynes was selected for the third time for the England Under-23 side to face Denmark Under-23 at Fratton Park, Portsmouth. The England side scored five, with Bobby Robson, just recovered from his ankle injury and making his international debut, scoring one goal, and Alf Stokes, later to join Fulham, scoring two. The other two goals fell inevitably to Haynes.

The match was televised, and gave Haynes the ideal platform on which to display his wares. He turned on a brilliant display in front of 25,000 spectators, especially in the second half when the entire team ran riot, and for the first time he took on the role of master tactician at international level. England romped to a 5–1 victory.

After the match, Haynes received an exceptional press, one headline reading: "Haynes is soccer's greatest on this form." One eminent sportswriter called his performance "the greatest one-man soccer show I have ever seen." Another remarked: "Master Haynes became Haynes the master." Haynes agreed that it had been a good night, saying: "Sometimes footballers feel good, sometimes they feel not so good. On the night, I just happened to feel good!"

The press made it very clear to the England selectors: "When the full England team fly tomorrow to play Denmark in Copenhagen on Sunday, the greatest inside forward in soccer will be missing from the party. He is Johnny Haynes who last night dominated this Under-23 international at Portsmouth." They concluded: "On the brilliant green of the Fratton Park pitch, the Danes chased a slim shadow in the white shirt numbered ten."

October

He followed up this display at the weekend with a 3–2 Fulham victory away at Rotherham United, and the press said, "The home side had no answers to the sparkling Fulham trio." How true that was, and it was Haynes' through passes that laid on all three goals! Bobby Robson and Bedford Jezzard took the first two, and after the away defence had allowed Rotherham back into the game with two casual goals, Jezzard nailed his second, the winner, from another slide-rule Haynes pass.

Surprisingly, it wasn't a performance that the club were happy about, naming in the programme the only four players they thought had played up to standard—and Haynes was one. Pointing a finger at senior and more experienced colleagues, the programme said:

"Let us say here and now that Johnny stood out head and shoulders not only as a pure footballer, but also as a tigerish, tireless worker. He proved that all the words of high praise written about him for his performance in the England Under-23 team against Denmark were true to the very last letter."

Jezzard was letting his boots and his head do the talking. In the next league match at the Cottage, he remarkably scored all five of Fulham's goals in a 5–0 victory over bottom-of-the-table Hull City, who had their goalkeeper injured. Haynes and Jezzard appeared on television after the match, and goalscorer Jezzard heaped glorious praise on his colleague for his significant contribution to the haul.

What made it all the more remarkable was that Haynes almost didn't play in the match. Due to traffic congestion, he had to take a taxi from King's Cross and arrived at Craven Cottage just ten minutes before the start.

It was, however, a hollow victory. Hull centre forward Patterson was taken ill before the match and

Haynes gets in a shot as Hull defender Berry closes in. Jezzard scored all the goals in the 5–0 victory.

didn't even start, so Hull began with ten men; after just ten minutes the Hull centre half Berry was hurt and had his thigh strapped. Finally the Hull goalkeeper was injured before half-time and also had to leave the field, so effectively Hull were down to just eight fit players.

Fulham should have scored a hatful, but played abysmally against the eight, the final two goals coming in the last three minutes. The club were not pleased by the performance and let the players know in no uncertain terms. Although Jezzard praised Haynes, the records show he was really only involved in one goal. It was probably one of those days when he could leave the engine idling, saving his energy for the forthcoming internationals.

Fulham lost the next game, at Nottingham Forest, by a single gift goal, and again the club criticised the attack and the team, though they omitted Haynes from their criticism. "Only Johnny Haynes produced the football we know they can all play. The others just couldn't get going at all."

Farewell to the England 'B' team

Haynes' performance for the England 'B' side at Maine Road in midweek was just as good as the one for the England Under-23 team the previous month. The match marked his fifth and final appearance for the 'B' team. Left back Jim Langley, then with Brighton and later to join Fulham, played in the game, alongside Fulham's Jezzard. Jezzard claimed two more England goals, both created of course by Haynes.

The first was a powerful strike following a precision pass, and the second a powerful header following a delicately chipped lob into the area. Blackpool winger Bill Perry also netted a brace, with Bristol City's John Atyeo scoring the fifth. Once again the gifted goal-maker provided a performance full of the shrewdest of passes. The match was a brilliant display of fast, attacking football, and 5–1 was an appropriate score.

Haynes then starred in Fulham's next home match, which ended in another victory, this time 3–2 over Leicester City. This was a much tighter match, where "Johnny Haynes made the winner for Robson just three minutes from the end." Haynes and Charlie Mitten had already crafted the second goal for Jezzard, after Robson's opener, but two goals from star striker and former Fulham favourite Arthur Rowley put Leicester back on level terms.

With time running out, Haynes won a tackle from deep, looked up and launched a forty-five-yard pass forward. Robson sprinted through in anticipation, neatly killed the ball and turned it in from twenty yards out; this was sheer delight for the Fulham faithful. The match saw Haynes become a man in more ways than one. He had just celebrated his twenty-first birthday and had already made well over 100 first team appearances. He received over 130 cards from well-wishers.

His third representative match in four weeks was against the Scottish League at Hillsborough. This third appearance for the Football League ended in a 4–2 victory and his long diagonal passes were a feature of the match. He made all four England goals, the first three inside the first sixteen torrid minutes, one for Turner of Luton and the other two for Nat Lofthouse. The plucky Scots pulled back to within one goal, but Haynes then laid on the clincher for Tom Finney.

Haynes was now reported as being an absolute must for re-selection for England, his passes being described as his "passport to Wembley". During the period of these three important representative matches, the full England side lost disappointingly 1–2 to Wales in the British Championship, and many pointed out that this was probably due to the absence of a player like Haynes.

The selection for the Football League caused Haynes to miss the second of the group Inter-Cities Fairs Cup matches for the London XI against a Frankfurt XI. Robson, Jezzard, Mitten and Roy Bentley (who would come to Fulham in the next season) all played. The match took place at Wembley Stadium. The London XI finally squeezed home 3–2 after being behind, and the goals were a family affair in the second half, with Jezzard scoring two and Robson scoring the other.

At the weekend, Haynes and Robson were again praised for their stylish footwork, but as usual a

England captain Billy Wright introduces Johnny Haynes to the Earl of Derby before the Home International Championship match against Northern Ireland at Wembley. On Haynes' right is Fulham colleague Bedford Jezzard. This match was the first occasion when Fulham had two representatives in the England team. England cruised to a 3–0 victory.

benevolent defence threw away any chance of victory, with Doncaster Rovers winning 2–4. Haynes poached a goal near the end, apparently the best goal of the afternoon, but it was scant consolation, as it had little effect on the final result. Perhaps he was preoccupied by his potential England recall. Despite this fifth defeat, Fulham were still handily placed just outside the top two at the end of the month.

Haynes the upstart?

A lazy press had attempted to stoke up a story that Haynes' omission from the senior squad was due to the fact that his style clashed with that of the mature greats like Nat Lofthouse and Stanley Matthews, and that the upstart Haynes had had the temerity to advise them how they should be playing. The mediocre performance of the England team that day in October 1954 had added fuel to the fire. So when the team against Northern Ireland in 1955 was discussed, with Haynes back in the frame coupled with the omission of the two legends, the story merely fanned the flames.

It was even mooted that the bad feeling extended beyond the field of play. It was all nonsense, of course, but at the tender age of just twenty-one, new-boy Haynes was being given his first real media mauling. He coped quite well, realising the only way to lay such ghosts was to perform well on the field of play in England colours, and let his boots do the talking.

The real reason for a delay in his reselection was down to the fact that to play him meant altering the entire team strategy. The England selectors were hesitant and wanted to be very sure before they committed themselves to 'the Haynes way'.

Before Haynes, roving wing halves like Bill McGarry and Jimmy Dickinson would support Don Revie in midfield. Now they could retreat further and merely chip the ball forward to Haynes, who became the central hub of England's midfield. He received this ringing endorsement from the great inside forward Raich Carter: "He is unquestionably the greatest inside forward in the game. He is so accurate, that once he distributes the pass, the player receiving has only to run on to the ball; there's no manoeuvring."

Haynes is recalled by England

November

In the end pressure told, and the headlines read: "At last, England build on Haynes." This return match against Northern Ireland was regarded by Haynes as "an easy win". For the first time ever, Fulham had two players in the England team. The Cottagers' Bedford Jezzard received his second cap and enhanced his growing reputation by almost scoring in the first minute following a perfect pass from his Fulham colleague. Working closely with Haynes' pin-point passes, Jezzard laid on two of the England goals scored by Wolves' Dennis Wilshaw, and the third from Finney, and from then on it was plain sailing. England cruised home to a 3–0 victory, and Haynes' probing passes had done most of the damage. The press lauded his performance saying, "Haynes the 'Governor-General' took charge straight from the kick-off and is obviously on the threshold of a very long international career."

Again captain Billy Wright was pleased: "I was delighted to see Johnny Haynes recalled. There was no question that he was the most accurate passer of the ball in the league. I almost used to purr when watching Johnny play his beautifully disguised reverse pass with either foot. He used to be able to land those crossfield passes on a handkerchief from distances up to fifty yards."

On return to league action, Haynes experienced another frustrating afternoon at the Cottage when Bristol Rovers, up in the table with Fulham, hit the Fulham defence for five. Fulham made a fight of it, coming from two down to be three-all at one stage. Haynes made the first goal for Jezzard with a long pass, and from a Haynes free kick and a clever movement with Jezzard, Arthur Stevens equalised. The two final Rovers goals in the 3–5 defeat came in the last five minutes. The press said that Haynes had a good game, but couldn't do it all on his own. The headlines made that clear: "Even Johnny Haynes can't save Fulham."

Just when everything seemed to be going right for him, Haynes was the victim of a severe ear infection that caused him to miss the 2–1 win at Stoke City. Jimmy Hill deputised well for him. Haynes travelled with the team but told Frank Osborne he didn't feel well enough to play. He was immediately sent back to the team hotel.

He travelled back on the train with the team, but was met at Euston station by the club doctor, who after an examination ordered him straight to St Stephen's Hospital. By now he was in a very distressed condition. He remained in hospital for five days, receiving treatment for an abscess, and then went to recuperate in Worthing, with his mother.

Haynes leaves St Stephen's Hospital in Fulham on November 17th, after having treatment for an ear abscess. The infection prevented him from joining the England team in special training at Birmingham.

At the weekend he surprisingly returned in the 2–1 home victory over relegation-threatened Plymouth Argyle, but didn't look well or fit, merely a pale shadow of his normal self. Yet even in this debilitated condition he made both goals, with two fine passes, one to Jezzard, a delicate long-range pass down the middle, and one to Charlie Mitten. Although he turned out for Fulham, he did not attend the 'special training' sessions with England in advance of the forthcoming international against Spain.

Certainly he was very far from his best when Fulham were demolished 0–7 at Anfield the following Saturday, in the final week of the month. The northern press crowed that Jezzard and Haynes were both in the side. Fulham were very poor, however, and Liverpool were excellent, having threatened a performance like this for several weeks.

Fulham were a goal down in thirty seconds and three adrift at the interval. They were not helped when goalkeeper Hewkins sustained a nasty facial injury that turned out to be a fractured jaw whilst trying to prevent the fourth goal. Every Liverpool forward scored and the result was the Merseysiders' biggest post-war win and Fulham's heaviest defeat for some years.

It was a testament to Haynes' resolve and character that he pushed himself to be fit for the next England game. Here he would receive his first test against real foreign opposition when Spain visited Wembley for the inauguration of the new floodlights. The match was billed as a potential brawl, following a hot-tempered match the previous summer that ended (without Haynes) as a 1–1 draw. The tough encounter never really materialised and England ran out 4–1 victors.

Haynes had a more than competent game, linking very well with Blackpool's skilful winger Bill Perry. It was Haynes' pass that put Perry through for England's second goal. The Haynes-Perry left-wing partnership worked well, Perry understanding the need to keep running to receive Haynes' passes in the spaces. This was in contrast to the previous match against Ireland, in which John had found it a little more difficult working with Tom Finney, who always seemed to want the square pass high up the pitch in front of the full back, so that he could do all the work himself.

December

Haynes returned home with a press report that he was suffering from concussion after the international match; it was totally unfounded and he was fine in a practice match the next morning. His head was probably dazed at the weekend, however, as Fulham slid frustratingly to yet another home defeat. In this match Haynes wore the unfamiliar number eight (inside right) shirt for the first time.

Fulham had the lead when a Bobby Robson corner found Haynes, and his brilliant pass across the penalty area found Jimmy Hill, who drove Fulham one up midway through the first half. However, two more defensive blunders and a missed penalty from Charlie Mitten donated fourth-placed Sheffield Wednesday a 1–2 win.

In midweek after this game, Haynes won his fourth cap for the Football League against the League of Ireland at Goodison Park. He didn't score, but impressed as England won 5–1. This appeared to be a common score when he played.

As Christmas was approaching, in the next game the Fulham defence decided to hand out early presents in the form of gift goals, and Lincoln won comprehensively 1–6 at Sincil Bank. Haynes looked completely demoralised and was marked out of the game. Most of the goals conceded were poor ones brought about either by poor marking or by defenders trying to play football in their own penalty area. To make matters worse, Mitten had yet another penalty saved.

Haynes turned matters around to a degree in a 3–1 success over the hapless Bury a week later, completing the double over the Lancashire side. Bury lost their keeper with a broken leg, and Fulham took second-half advantage despite going a goal behind initially. From Arthur Stevens' corner, Haynes presented Jezzard with an open goal, but the star marksman hit the stand-in keeper from just three yards; fortunately he netted the rebound. Haynes then ran to the by-line with the ball apparently tied to his foot, stopped dead and snapped the ball back for Jezzard to score.

The press were in raptures and said, "Haynes was at his best in the second half; racing through to meet a long throw-in by Robin Lawler, he provided a deft pass to Jezzard to score with a great drive." Ten minutes from time Haynes himself made the score three when he glided a hard, low centre from Trevor Chamberlain over the line to put the match beyond doubt.

The following Saturday, on Christmas Eve, he had a particularly quiet match at Barnsley, where the home side walked away with an easy 0–3 win after a freakish own goal from centre half Ron Greenwood, the former West Ham and England manager.

You're the new penalty taker

In their usual way Fulham then turned the form book around, smashing third-placed Swansea Town, a side containing Cliff Jones, Terry Medwin and Ivor Allchurch, 4–1 at the Cottage on Boxing Day. After a goalless first half, there were fireworks in the second.

After just six minutes, Norman Smith's shot was handled on the line, and Haynes, in his new role as penalty taker after Mitten's two misses, slid the ball in. This was followed by a stupendous goal from Chamberlain. Fed by friend Haynes, the winger embarked on a fifty-yard run before shooting in from eighteen yards.

Haynes grabbed the last goal himself in the final minute, firing in through a crowd of players, following yet another intricate four-man wing movement. Unfortunately, this form didn't carry itself through to the next day, when Fulham lost the return match 0–2 at the Vetch Field.

A happier Haynes, restored to the full England side.

Fulham's form was now very patchy, to say the least; the Cottagers had lost five out of the last seven matches, conceding a disastrous twenty-six goals in the process, almost four a game. They had also lost six of their last seven league games away from home. Unsurprisingly, they had slid right down the table to tenth.

On New Year's Eve, Fulham reclaimed some respect by putting the skids under Middlesbrough with a 4–1 victory at the Cottage. Jimmy Hill's goal after just two minutes was a picture; a dream pass from Haynes dropped right at his feet ten yards out, and the ball was in the net before the keeper could move. Then, in the twenty-fourth minute, Hill started a move which was followed by a defence-splitting pass from Haynes that gave Chamberlain a chance, and his fast, angled shot flashed into the far corner of the net. Haynes also had a hand in the fourth, allowing Chamberlain to cross for Robson to score.

January

Early in the month, Haynes returned to Meadow Lane, where he had registered a hat trick in September, to notch the winner against Notts County in the third round of the FA Cup. His goal in the twenty-ninth minute was the reward of opportunism, when he crashed the ball into the net from fifteen yards, after outside right Jimmy Hill had back-heeled the ball on to his colleague's right foot following Bobby Robson's assist.

It was a game of countless missed chances from both sides at the fog-shrouded stadium. The result was Fulham's first clean sheet for almost three months. It was also a win that pitched Haynes into a game against First Division cup holders Newcastle United. The Geordies were the current 'cup kings', having lifted the trophy three times in the past five years.

Fulham were still patchy in the league. They lost 1–2 at third-placed Bristol City and were two down before they finally went rampaging into the City goal area. Haynes scored after Bristol goalkeeper Anderson had stopped a terrific initial drive from the inside left, the ball being driven in from an impossible angle.

After disposing of West Ham 3–1 in a much improved performance, Fulham prepared for a mouth-watering cup tie at home to Newcastle.

That Newcastle FA Cup tie

The club were hoping to attract a record 50,000 spectators for the match, but in the event 'only' 40,000 turned up. In the first half-hour, Newcastle looked 'the team of the century', and Fulham were bewildered by their accurate, sweeping movements and deadly shooting.

Soon the visitors had amassed a seemingly unassailable three-goal lead, and it seemed as if Fulham would be routed. Newcastle's star-studded forward line looked world class and they put away their three goals in the space of eleven minutes through Jackie Milburn (seventeen), Bob Stokoe (nineteen) and Tom Casey (twenty-seven). However, Fulham fought back to prove without doubt that they had some forward line of their own.

Haynes' run and accurate low cross was powered in by local hero Trevor Chamberlain, playing in his first FA Cup game, to give Fulham a lifeline six minutes before half-time.

Soon after the interval came one of the turning-points of the match when Chamberlain had a goal very

Newcastle celebrate, whilst Fulham keeper Ian Black and the ball sit forlornly in the goal after being barged over the line for Newcastle's equalising goal at 4–4.

YES, FULHAM —THERE AIN'T NO JUSTICE!

By Maurice Smith

How the headline from The People saw the great match.

harshly ruled out by young linesman Jack Taylor (who would later referee the 1974 World Cup final). To those in the stand it was a perfectly good goal; Chamberlain had definitely been on-side when Jezzard crossed the ball, and had got ahead of the Newcastle defence due to sheer speed before slamming the ball in. It was described as the best 'goal' of the match.

From then on, a Haynes-inspired Fulham saw Chamberlain net two further goals to complete his hat trick, both from slide-rule Haynes passes, the third also involving Jezzard. Haynes and Chamberlain were now a devastating left-wing partnership, completely mesmerising the Newcastle defence.

The visitors began to lose their polish. Robson and Haynes came into their own, and sheer joy surged through Fulham's ranks when Jimmy Hill put them ahead for the first time in the match. Then came the second controversial incident, when Fulham goalkeeper Ian Black was charged into the net whilst airborne for Newcastle's equalising goal that made it 4–4.

Years later Black would recall: "It was one of the worst refereeing decisions I've ever come across. It was a tragedy. I'd jumped to collect a cross, and as I caught it, their centre forward Keeble came rushing in and whacked me into the back of the net. I was three feet up in the air at the time, and the referee was about three feet away watching it. Diabolical!"

Then Black, probably still shaken and hurt, missed a fairly routine cross which allowed Newcastle's Keeble to head home the winning goal with just nine minutes to go, and the First Division side sneaked away with a 4–5 win. The local reporter said: "In all my years of watching First and Second Division football, I have never seen a finer game; it was replete with all the soccer arts."

After the match, Haynes confessed: "We were out of the cup in a match we had lost, saved, won and lost again, but we went off the field arm-in-arm with Newcastle. Those of us who played and those of you that saw it will never forget it."

Much later, Haynes described this as probably the best game and atmosphere he had ever experienced in a match at Fulham. He recalled: "They were cup holders, we were in the Second Division. It was a great draw for us to get the cup holders. After twenty minutes we were 0–3 down, then five minutes after

New manager Dugald Livingstone (right) meets with a group of Fulham superstars: Trevor Chamberlain, Jimmy Hill, Tom Wilson and Johnny Haynes.

half-time we were 4–3 in front which would have been a tremendous result if it had stayed that way. Unfortunately Newcastle scored twice in the last few minutes and we ended up getting beaten 5–4, but it was a tremendous game of football."

February

In a league match that was a total anticlimax, and in appalling conditions of snow, ice and rain in the Potteries, a tired Fulham were beaten by Port Vale 1–2. After going two goals down, Fulham rallied and scored through Bobby Robson, who slapped the ball in from a Johnny Haynes cross after fifty-two minutes.

Captain of the England Under-23s

In midweek, Haynes travelled north and played for the England Under-23 side for the fourth time, cementing a fairly routine 3–1 win over Scotland Under-23 at Hillsborough. Awarded the captaincy of the team for the first time, he contributed two further goals to his growing repertoire, with Everton's Jimmy Harris scoring the other—from a Haynes pass, naturally.

Albert Quixall was unlucky with four of the maestro's passes, foiled by outstanding goalkeeping each time. The first Haynes goal came ten minutes before half-time in a move involving Pegg of Manchester United and Quixall. Pegg was also involved in his second which Haynes drove home with twenty minutes to go.

Haynes was applauded from the field by the crowd after as fine a show of inside forward play as Hillsborough can have seen for many a year. Scotsman Willie Walker, one of the all-time great inside forwards, said of Haynes after the match, "A wonderful player … one of the best I've seen … there's no-one like him in English football just now." One headline summed it up perfectly: "Haynes is scourge of young Scotland."

On his return in Arctic weather, and in terrible ground and goalmouth conditions, Haynes scored the goal in the 1–1 draw against lowly Rotherham United. He gave Fulham the lead after nineteen minutes, following a movement created by Jimmy Hill and Bedford Jezzard. He netted from four yards and would have been offside, but the ball came to him via a Rotherham deflection. All afternoon he created opening after opening, only to see them all frittered away. Inevitably the Millers escaped from the Cottage with a draw, due to an undeserved scrambled equaliser just two minutes from the end.

Livingstone is the new manager

Following this dismal performance, and after a two-and-a-half year hiatus, Fulham appointed Dugald Livingstone as manager. Livingstone had been in charge of the Newcastle United team that had just beaten Fulham. The new manager's first match in charge saw a goalless draw at relegation-threatened Plymouth Argyle, where "nobody had the answer to the wiles and scheming of Haynes' play" but the forwards' marksmanship was way off target.

March

A fortnight later at Leicester City, where the hosts were in a promotion place, Fulham's form in a 1–2 defeat had improved, but the results were not turning their way. It was a match described as having thrills galore. Haynes put in the best two shots of the match, but was thwarted on both occasions by the Leicester goalkeeper. For Fulham's goal, Jezzard's pass found Haynes who drew the defence before crossing accurately for Robson to tap in. It would be Bobby's last appearance in a Fulham shirt for six years.

Bobby Robson is transferred

Haynes' mood regarding Fulham's current form was not improved when the club sold star inside forward Bobby Robson to First Division West Bromwich Albion for £25,000. It was a very large fee, as the British record at the time was £34,500. Robson had scored in his last game, and had contributed ten further goals to his Fulham total that season.

The club directors said the money was necessary, commenting on the "serious financial position" that "impelled" them to make such a decision. A frustrated Haynes didn't really believe the story, but at twenty-one felt that he couldn't do much about it. So within three years of its formation, the first of the free-scoring Bobby-Beddy-Johnny trio had left the Cottage.

After the sale of Robson, other clubs were quickly in on the carcass and Fulham were inundated with offers for Haynes. They felt that as Fulham had started to break up the exciting golden trio, they would soon capitulate and agree to his transfer as well. Fulham still maintained that they were short of cash, but chairman Charles Dean stood firm. He said, "They can sack me, sell up and build flats over Craven Cottage if Johnny Haynes ever leaves Fulham."

Haynes misses his first penalty

Fulham improved and won against mid-table Lincoln City 3–0. The press agreed: "The supremacy of the Fulham attack was solely due to the brilliant passing of Johnny Haynes." In the thirty-second minute of this match, however, came another Haynes 'first'. Fulham were awarded a penalty, and he stepped up to take his second as penalty-taker. With the keeper diving the wrong way, he tried to glide the ball just inside the post, but succeeded only in pushing it a couple of inches outside. It was his first penalty miss for the first team. He said afterwards, "I changed my mind in my run up. It was a stupid thing to do."

He did atone for this rush of blood with the first goal four minutes from half-time, deflecting in Trevor Chamberlain's shot close to the line. Then in the fifty-seventh minute he made a glorious solo run, beating two defenders before giving the perfect pass for Bedford Jezzard, who scored the second goal from close range.

Next came Bristol Rovers, who were gunning for promotion, and an exciting match at Eastville ended 2–2. Fulham were two goals down on the hour when they were awarded a penalty. Haynes showed no signs of nerves after the previous week's miss and opted to take the kick. This time he was successful, side-footing the ball just inside a post.

Then Arthur Stevens drove home from a nice Haynes pass that made it possible for Fulham to secure the draw. In the closing minutes of the game Fulham should have sewn it up, but Trevor Chamberlain's shot, following a surging solo run, hit a post. The press said, "Haynes was again the saviour of the attack and he made many chances for the forwards most of which went begging. It wasn't a lucky point, Fulham were unlucky not to have won!"

Haynes hit the headlines the following week as well—"Haynes peps up Fulham." He was brilliant in the second half against Stoke City at the Cottage, and for the second clinching goal in a 2–0 victory he and Stevens combined to enable Chamberlain to score with a first-time rocket shot.

Fulham then suffered a deeply unimpressive Easter; they first lost at home to Leeds, 1–2, on Good Friday. Leeds, who were on a great run of form, paid Haynes the ultimate compliment of having two and often three men mark him. He worked like a demon to get the passes through and was unlucky with two shots, but it wasn't his day.

On Easter Saturday at virtually relegated Hull City, Fulham snatched a point in a 2–2 draw. A dull first half was lightened up only by a grand goal from Haynes that gave Fulham the lead. Stevens made a great cross, Haynes snapped up the pass, sized up the situation, went on a couple of paces and thrashed the ball into goal. After Hull had missed a penalty shortly after half-time, they levelled, but Haynes gave Fulham the lead again with a quarter of an hour to go, with a beautiful header following a long lob by Stevens. The goal was described as follows: "Haynes throwing himself through the air, connected accurately with his head, and steered the ball into the net." Hull came back yet again to scramble a draw. Another press report said that Haynes was the only forward to play up to standard.

April

On Easter Monday, Fulham looked a worn-out side at Elland Road and took a sound beating from in-form Leeds United 1–6; all the press could say was that the hard-working Johnny Haynes again scored Fulham's goal.

After some discussions concerning recent performances, Fulham pulled their socks up a little and racked up four straight wins to complete their league season. In the first of these, the manager included forward Roy Dwight for his first game of the season in place of the injured Bedford Jezzard, and was instantly rewarded. Dwight had been at Fulham since Johnny Haynes' arrival, but it had taken him almost six years to claim a regular first-team berth.

Fulham beat Liverpool at Craven Cottage 3–1, with Dwight claiming a fine hat trick, completely avenging the mauling Fulham had taken at Anfield in November and at the same time virtually killing off Liverpool's promotion hopes. A three-man move including Haynes fashioned the first goal midway through the first half. The second was similar, with Haynes and Chamberlain creating the opening. The third for Dwight's triple arrived in the same fashion fifteen minutes from time. Haynes had again assisted in all Fulham's goals.

The only thing missing in the game was a deserved goal for Haynes, but he was thwarted twice by brilliant saves from goalkeeper Dave Underwood, who would

A stern and focussed Johnny Haynes follows skipper Billy Wright on to the Hampden Park pitch. Haynes earned a below-par England a 1–1 draw with a goal in the last few seconds.

later join Fulham. Although Dwight claimed the headlines, the press reported that Liverpool's big headache was the elusive Johnny Haynes, who provided many of the chances for Dwight. Another report said, "The architect of this win was Johnny Haynes showing England form with some brilliant touches, particularly the back-heeled passes that opened up the Liverpool defence."

The performance was even better the following Saturday when Fulham visited Hillsborough to vie with Sheffield Wednesday, who were promotion favourites and had the champagne ready to be opened. Haynes was absent on England duty at Hampden, and Fulham were also without Jezzard, goalkeeper Ian Black and centre half Gordon Brice. Full back Tom Wilson was rendered a passenger on the wing after only ten minutes. Fulham naturally won 3–2, with Chamberlain netting the winner with only four minutes to go. It proved that when necessary, Fulham could score, play very well and win without 'JH' in the side.

Haynes saves England's bacon

Instead of being at Hillsborough, Haynes was playing in 'the big one' in the British Championship, the game against Scotland. A vast congregation of 134,000 packed into Glasgow's ancient coliseum. Winning his fourth cap, it was the first time Haynes had played there with the senior side. Just behind him was the priceless gem of a half back line, Dickinson–Wright–Edwards; the forwards, too, tripped off the tongue—Finney, Taylor, Lofthouse, Haynes, Perry.

Aberdeen winger Graham Leggat scored for Scotland on the hour. The England team in general were not playing at all well and Haynes was the only forward shining in a very mediocre display. He had already been unlucky with one shot that hit the post.

In the ninety-first minute, with the last few seconds allowed for injuries trickling away, a final long England cross from the wing was headed back across the box by Manchester United's Taylor. Haynes breasted the ball down and whipped home a superb low shot, picking his spot with careful deliberation. There was no panic at all; Haynes provided a really cool head at a time like that. The ensuing but optimistic Scottish protests of handball were quickly waved away.

Haynes recalled: "I was just a kid. It was an incredible experience, more daunting than I can possibly describe or you can imagine. We were getting well beat 1–0 and every single voice of that immense crowd was singing them home. With just ten seconds left on the clock, Tom Finney swung a last ball into their box, Nat [Lofthouse] got up and headed it back. I was about fifteen yards out. I chested it down and hit it, half-volley sweet as a nut, and it whistled into Tommy Younger's net. 1–1.

"Like I'd switched off a plug, there was dead silence, as if 134,000 had been turned to stone. For a few seconds I thought the ref had disallowed the goal. Then I realised they were all filing out, quiet as if they'd lost a war—which, in a way and even with a draw, they had."

Temporary captain for the first time

Towards the end of the season, Haynes received his next honour when he was given the Fulham captaincy for the first time in the match against Doncaster Rovers while Jimmy Hill was away in Trinidad at the start of a summer coaching tour. He was still only twenty-one.

Fulham thrashed Doncaster Rovers 4–0, with all four goals coming in the first half. Maybe because of the captaincy, Haynes was singled out for 'special treatment' by the Doncaster defence, and he limped to the dressing room at half-time with a badly swollen ankle after several illegal attempts to stop him. He had created the second goal for Chamberlain.

Fulham were also awarded another penalty in the match. Haynes was the usual taker and he placed the ball on the spot and walked back. Chamberlain, despite being on a hat trick, didn't appear keen to take it. Haynes, with his injured ankle, insisted that his mate took the kick. Chamberlain finally agreed and fired the ball into the net.

The Doncaster goalkeeper Harry Gregg, however, complained that he had been caught unawares as he thought Haynes was going to take it. The referee upheld his protest. So Chamberlain re-took it, scored again

Haynes adopts his trademark 'hands on hips' stance, but this time in amazement at the Brazilian team's antics at Wembley. The visitors walked off with the ball after what they considered to be a harsh penalty award. Despite missing two penalties, England won their first-ever encounter with the Brazilians 4–2.

with the second kick, and ambled past the prone keeper to retrieve the ball from the net. The press said: "Once more it was Johnny Haynes who inspired Fulham's first-half dominance. He baffled the Doncaster defence with his elusive turns and accurate passing."

A very busy Haynes had just about time to squeeze in another appearance for the Football League against the Irish League in Belfast in midweek. This time he was tired, for once having a quiet game, and he tasted defeat for the first time in this representative team, the Irish League winning easily 5–2.

He was flown back on a special plane after the match, as Fulham were playing the crack Russian side Spartak Moscow in a friendly the following day. During that game he dazzled the continentals with his wizardry, and his long, sweeping passes to the wings were in striking contrast to the close football of the visitors. Stevens, Haynes, with a lovely header from Stevens' centre, and Dwight provided the goals for Fulham in an entertaining 3–1 victory.

May

In the final game of the season and as temporary captain, Haynes guided Fulham to a 4–3 midweek victory over Nottingham Forest. As usual he laid on the chances, but failed to score. The press concluded that he had had a wonderful season.

Another mediocre season

Haynes may have had a marvellous season, but for the Fulham team it was another mediocre finish in the league. Haynes had inspired his team to a hatful of goals—just six short of another ton—but the Cottagers' continuing defensive frailties had seen them concede eighty-four, so that promotion was never a serious possibility after October.

In their ten worst defensive performances, Fulham had conceded forty-six goals. From a red-hot start and from a promotion position at the end of October, the Cottagers had once again slithered down the league to mid-table, before recovering to finish ninth.

Haynes' personal contribution was an excellent nineteen. Jezzard had had another remarkable season with twenty-seven goals; his three-season haul now stood at a stunning eighty-eight goals. The haul for the star trio of Robson, Jezzard and Haynes was now a massive 181—averaging a remarkable sixty a season! If the season of Haynes' debut was taken into account, the four-year total for the three players stood at 236, again around sixty per season. Bedford Jezzard's four-year goal total stood at a staggering 123. Jezzard had missed just seven league games in those four seasons.

Haynes was now exhausted, and didn't take part in the third group match of the Inter-Cities Fairs Cup, as it was just five days before England's game with Brazil. The London XI beat the Basle XI 1–0 at White Hart Lane, thanks to a goal from Tottenham's George Robb three minutes from time.

Haynes plays against Brazil for the first time

Haynes finished the season with a friendly against Brazil at Wembley, the first time the two great countries had ever played each other—the Old World versus the New World, as the game was described. England started brilliantly and were two goals up in four minutes.

Somehow, by way of two freakish goals in the space of two minutes after half-time, Brazil hauled themselves level, but five minutes later, England were donated a penalty kick in hilarious circumstances.

England were awarded a free kick; Haynes, thinking quickly, chipped it in at once, only for the Brazilian defence to be caught off guard, and the ball was instinctively caught by defender Nilton Santos in the penalty area, thinking that the referee had not given permission for the kick to be taken. The Brazilian Alvaro Valente then walked off with the ball, refusing to play on. Sanity was eventually restored after a lengthy hold-up of over three minutes and when the game resumed England, through John Atyeo, managed to fritter away the penalty, Atyeo's kick being saved

Johnny Haynes and Bedford Jezzard (second from left and far right) depart from England for the tour of South Africa. Travelling with them are Mansell (Portsmouth), Mullen (Coventry), King (Stoke) and Burgin (Sheffield United). The tour would end tragically for Jezzard.

by the goalkeeper. Fortunately England took the lead again a few minutes later, and could even afford the luxury of missing another penalty with Roger Byrne this time firing feebly at the goalkeeper.

All ended well, however, and a late goal gave rise to a 4–2 England victory. Johnny Haynes had asked Stanley Matthews for his autograph in the dressing room before the match. Johnny's hands were shaking so much that he could not hold the pen properly, and Matthews asked him to wait until after the game!

Johnny Haynes was surprisingly accused by Valente after the game of bad manners and poor sportsmanship with regard to the free kick, but he was not supported by his Brazilian management, who carpeted the defender for his comments.

On the strength of these performances, Haynes was a natural selection for England's forthcoming close season tour. It would be his first overseas tour with the senior England team. England travelled without either Matthews or Tom Finney. The tour was a successful one, and one that improved with each game.

England initially fought out a goalless draw with Sweden, lucky to escape with a draw in a match ruined by a near gale-force wind. Goalkeeper Reg Matthews made three stunning saves to stop the Swedes. Haynes worked like a galley-slave to get his forward line moving, and had a terrific right-foot shot brilliantly saved. He was one of only four England players given praise for his performance.

Four days later, England beat Finland 5–1, with a Haynes goal midway through the first half, smashed in from around the penalty spot, the second goal for England in the match. In the second half, Haynes was directly involved in three-man moves that led to goals three and four.

Haynes and England beat the world champions

The tour concluded six days later with a spirited and skilful display against World Cup holders Germany in front of almost 100,000 spectators. It was a new-look and new-style England, and Haynes was again the star. To the delight of the loud and boisterous soldiers stationed in Germany, England's display was rewarded with a 3–1 scoreline, Haynes again being one of the scorers.

The opening goal was scored by Manchester United's Duncan Edwards. Sheffield United's Colin Grainger, set up by Haynes, doubled the lead, and Haynes sealed the match himself with a third goal twenty minutes from time, gliding the ball in with the inside of his foot. The German goal in the last five minutes was a mere consolation.

The tour of South Africa

June

By now, Haynes was a much more satisfied man, having achieved a number of the goals he had mentally pencilled in for himself at the start of the season. He rewarded himself with a one-month holiday in South Africa without any close season cricket.

Bedford Jezzard had told Haynes what a nice place it was. Haynes quickly loved what he saw in South Africa, and it is no surprise that the country had a big influence on his life fifteen years later. He set sail on the 7th of the month and spent a happy few weeks in Cape Town as the guest of Barney Joel, a fervent London football supporter.

One of his reasons for going to South Africa was that his pals and Fulham colleagues Beddy Jezzard and

Bobby Robson were touring there on a three-month trip with an FA party. Following his England duties, Haynes went along to join them and support his friends. In today's climate, such a punishing schedule after a very long season would seem unthinkable. Sir Bobby Robson recalls: "It was a very hectic schedule. We played something like eighteen games in six weeks, all over the country. I think we played four international 'tests' against South Africa, and places like Bulawayo and Salisbury (Harare). I played in around fifteen of those matches!"

Bedford Jezzard is hurt

In one match against Southern Transvaal, the FA XI won 2–1, and Jezzard scored with a fine opportunist effort into the top corner of the net from the edge of the box. In the match against Southern Rhodesia which the FA XI won 3–1, Jezzard again scored twice, one a spectacular thirty-yard effort. The FA touring team then beat South Africa 4–2, but tragically Jezzard sustained a fracture to the left ankle in the second test.

Whilst travelling at full tilt, he was tackled very strongly by a full back. He fell and immediately realised that something was broken. Although all the games in South Africa had been won by the FA team, the over-tough tackling had been unwelcome and the English stars had received little protection from the domestic referees.

It was hoped that Jezzard would only miss six weeks of the season, but it looked like a bad injury, and was described as "fearsome"; he returned to England encased in plaster and on crutches. He had initially undergone surgery at a nursing home in South Africa to have the bones screwed together, and had spent eleven days in hospital. Following this recuperation, he undertook the long journey from Durban to Cape Town, where he was reunited with Haynes.

A saddened Haynes remained in Africa to support his colleague and close friend, and accompanied him on the long trip aboard the Winchester Castle back to England. The three-week voyage took them up the west coast of Africa before returning to Southampton.

Although they joined their fellow passengers for meals, Jezzard was in obvious discomfort, and he and a glum Johnny Haynes fraternised little during the journey; potentially Jezzard's career might have been over. In just three months, the golden trio of Robson–Jezzard–Haynes had been completely blown away, leaving Haynes as the sole survivor for the next season, having to pick up the goalscoring and goalmaking threads himself.

Haynes is off to Chelsea

Even being away on holiday, Haynes was not immune from the clutches and skulduggery of the press. On his way out to South Africa, he was asked whether he would like to join west London neighbours Chelsea by what he thought was a supporter.

He offered nothing but a noncommittal off-the-cuff remark, which was immediately blown up into a full sensation by the *Daily Sketch,* which categorically stated that Haynes was to join First Division Chelsea for £34,000 on his return from holiday, but that this would only be announced after the majority of the Fulham season tickets had been sold.

This story led to a furious row, with both clubs issuing firm denials. The furore only died down when the clubs threatened litigation and the 'scoop' was finally retracted with a grovelling apology. Haynes was unaware of the goings-on until he returned to the country. He knew he would need to watch his back even more closely and be more guarded with his remarks, even casual ones, to avoid being the victim of the press. He once said that he found it difficult to ignore press criticism and manipulation early in his career: "It took me the first four years of my professional career to do that."

King of the Cottage?

It was clear that Haynes' very early success, the award of the club captaincy, albeit temporarily, and his England status had got under some people's skin, particularly opposition supporters and sections of the media. There had been no proof whatsoever that as an only child, he was used to getting his own way or that he had been over-indulged by his parents, but he was regularly hearing shouts of "spoilt boy", "big head" and "King of the Cottage".

Some went further to suggest that he dictated all manner of affairs at the Cottage, including club policy and team selection. Again, there was not a shred of truth in the allegations.

He had not aided his cause by indulging, perhaps rather too frequently, in showing his disgust when things weren't going his way on the pitch. There were many different types of gestures. In the vast majority of these cases they were due to the fact that he had made an error, but sometimes they *were* directed at a Fulham colleague.

These gestures had been surfacing since the season after his debut. Colourful and flamboyant, they were earning him some ridicule, especially up in the north, but try as he might, it would be years before the antics were totally eradicated from his game. He declared five years later that he had exorcised the demons and 'cured' himself of his tantrums and arm-throwing. Although the physical aspects did probably wane, he would continue with the 'verbals' when required right up to the end of his career.

Even at this stage, although Haynes was an emerging star, he was happy at Second Division Fulham. He didn't feel constrained there, and because of the club's league status, there was not too much intrusion or pressure on him. He didn't ask for any star treatment, and wasn't given any. He thought of Fulham as a very civilised club, which didn't set down too many house rules, a club that allowed players to be responsible for their own conduct. He felt very settled and ready for next season's challenge.

11: The new Fulham captain 1956–57

11: The new Fulham captain — 1956–57

FOOTBALLERS

(A Series of 25)

No. 19

Johnny Haynes

Fulham & England
(Col.: White)

Down Fulham way they are convinced they have the finest inside forward today in Johnny Haynes their new captain, a youngster who seems destined to be the regular schemer for England for many years.

MITCHAM FOODS
LIMITED
MITCHAM IN SURREY, ENGLAND

The start of the new season saw highs and lows for Johnny Haynes. The happy personal news was that Fulham Football Club announced that he, just twenty-one years old and the youngest player in the team, would skipper the side for the coming season. The new team manager, Dugald Livingstone, was highly experienced and had quickly identified his team-leading potential.

Even this incident didn't pass without commentary in the press, a press that Haynes described as starved of any real footballing stories. One national paper reported that the Football Association had pressurised Fulham into making Haynes captain so that he could ultimately succeed Billy Wright in the England team. Frank Osborne was quick to dispel that myth: "The FA had nothing to do with it—we have asked Johnny to be captain and that's all there is to it." Johnny's only comment was, "I feel honoured and very proud. I only hope I give satisfaction."

This joy was tempered by the passing, during the summer, of his only real professional mentor, Taffy O'Callaghan, at the age of just forty-nine. The former Welsh international had guided Haynes through his early years on the ground staff and during his time as an apprentice. His influence on the young skipper would be greatly missed.

Joe Bacuzzi, who had been at the club as a player for almost twenty-two years, replaced him. Also, the depressing news came through that Bedford Jezzard's injury was indeed serious. He had a broken bone, another bone dislocated and torn ligaments. When he could resume training was anybody's guess.

This left Fulham with a much depleted squad for the season's start. Because he had accompanied the stricken Jezzard back to England, Haynes returned late for pre-season training, so had to put in even more effort than usual.

Outside the football playing area, Johnny Haynes was shrewd enough to know the value of self-publicity and self-promotion. Being a fairly good looking chap, he decided on his promotion to team captain to cash in on his assets and he employed an agent, Bagenal Harvey, to be his promoter. Together they began to seek out ways to bring the Johnny Haynes 'brand' even more into the public eye.

Crocked on the first day

August

Things didn't go to plan, of course, as so often happens at Fulham. In his first game as club captain, the team were firmly trounced 1–4 by West Ham United in a fairly bitter match at the Cottage. Haynes ran himself into the ground, but couldn't weld the attack into a strike force.

He was as usual closely marked by his nemesis Andy Malcolm, and managed to pick up an ankle injury which would plague him on and off for the remainder of the season. He was carried off, and was absent from the field of play for a number of minutes.

He resumed, but limped throughout the rest of the game. Fulham were ahead at half-time through a Roy Dwight goal, but West Ham snapped in three quick goals after the interval and it was game over. Haynes' injury forced him to miss the next two league games. Just when he had firmly re-established himself in the England team, he was out injured again.

A poor start

In his absence, Fulham made an unfamiliarly feeble start to the campaign, losing their opening four fixtures in the month, with Sheffield United, the league leaders, completing an early season double. Fulham were riddled with injuries, and apart from Bedford Jezzard they were also without Jimmy Hill. The four games saw Fulham concede fourteen goals and slump to the bottom of the table. The only consolation was that Jezzard's replacement, Roy Dwight, had scored in each match.

September

In this month, matters thankfully began to improve, and Fulham started by beating Huddersfield 1–0 at home. Due to injuries, the match saw the debut of young John Doherty, straight out of National Service. Haynes was marked tightly in an impressive display by former Fulham favourite Len Quested, but escaped just once to carve out the opportunity for Roy Dwight to score after fourteen minutes.

Dwight had a point-blank shot stopped on the line, and when the ball came back to Haynes he feigned that

Previous page: A wistful Haynes contemplates a new season.

Haynes' injured ankle needed lots of rest—and plenty of good home cooking from his Mum.

he was going to shoot, but instead lobbed it back with amazing accuracy for Dwight to nod in. Dwight later had the ball in the net again from another sublime Haynes pass, but was fractionally offside.

Fulham then had a 3–0 midweek win at Ashton Gate against Bristol City, the first time they had ever played under floodlights. They led from the sixth minute, when Eddie Lowe, Jimmy Hill and finally Haynes all combined to give Trevor Chamberlain an early goal. Fulham were three goals to the good by half-time, and when Roy Dwight scored the third, he had scored in six matches in a row, the only player in the entire Football League that season to accomplish the feat. City were demoralised enough to even miss a second-half penalty.

Sneaky defenders, knowing that Haynes was not at full fitness, targeted his suspect ankle once again, and Fulham supporters had their hearts in their mouths near the end when he went down heavily and had to be carried from the field. Fortunately he returned a few minutes later.

Fulham next took on Swansea Town, and were 0–2 down before Stevens coolly netted, thanks to a brilliant pass by Haynes. Fulham then went goal crazy, coming from 2–3 behind to demolish Swansea 7–3. In a crazy match, both sides scored an own goal and each scored a penalty.

Haynes did not score or take Fulham's penalty and was clearly still struggling with the ankle injury, coasting through the last twenty minutes out on the wing. Scoring a hat trick made Roy Dwight's record an amazing fourteen goals in his last eleven games. Even in his subdued state, Haynes again outshone Ivor Allchurch in midfield.

He recovered to play during the following midweek, and took part in a 2–1 win at the Cottage against now struggling Bristol City, his accurate pass setting Chamberlain free on the halfway line to run through and score from a narrow angle. Fulham had completed the double. Having lost the first four league matches, Fulham had promptly won the next four.

Out for a month

The impetuosity of youth had made Haynes try to return too early from the ankle injury, which led to it being aggravated. The ankle was black and blue and badly swollen again, and meant he was back on the sidelines for the next four league games, his longest spell out of the first team since his arrival. The possible ligament injury caused him to miss a number of representative and international matches—the Football League versus the Irish League, and the England Under-23 games against Denmark in Copenhagen and against France in Bristol. He also missed the full England international match in the British Championship against Northern Ireland in Belfast, which was drawn 1–1.

He was diplomatic about the opening day incident that put him out: "This is the first time I have ever been hurt during a match, and it may keep me out of football for weeks. It was a complete accident; as I ran in fast to shoot, Brown the West Ham centre half put his foot behind the ball, and it was just as if I had kicked a brick wall. I felt something go, but we won't know what until the swelling has gone down, and an x-ray can be taken."

Roy Bentley arrives

During Haynes' enforced absence, and to patch up an attack now devoid of Robson and Jezzard, Fulham signed the veteran international forward Roy

Roy Bentley makes his Fulham debut in the 3–1 home win against Rotherham. The experienced Bentley's arrival from Chelsea significantly strengthened the Fulham side; Haynes often called Bentley Fulham's best buy, and relied on him during his first season as captain.

Bentley, who had skippered Chelsea to their league championship as recently as 1955. His release from Stamford Bridge had come as a major surprise. His signature was obtained the night before the Rotherham game.

At least Haynes now had someone to share the responsibility. He would often cite Roy Bentley as Fulham's best buy, and the best player he ever played with in a Fulham shirt. Thirty-two-year-old Bentley would start his career in the inside forward position, but would gravitate to the centre half slot as his pace slowed.

Bentley scored on his debut as early as the seventeenth minute, and made the other two goals during a rather fortuitous 3–1 win over rock-bottom Rotherham United at Craven Cottage. It was considered that he would form a formidable partnership with Haynes in the forward line.

Bentley said on television after the game: "There was not much difference between First and Second Division football, just a couple more seconds to control the ball." He added, "I am sure I shall be happy at Fulham and will enjoy my football." Asked why he had picked Fulham, he responded, "I have seen them play, and that forward line with Johnny Haynes in it would make anyone pleased with them!"

Roy reminisced later: "Fulham were an ageing side at the time, but they had a number of excellent players, international players, and with John doing his stuff, they were a good side in the making and looked a really good bet for promotion. You don't become an international player without being a good player, and within just a few weeks of arriving I knew I'd made the right decision."

Haynes made a tentative comeback in a London Challenge Cup tie against Brigg Sports. There was major concern when he fell in a tackle and was carried off yet again three minutes before the end of extra time. Fortunately the problem was just cramp in the good leg, which disappeared once he was back in the dressing room. During his absence, Fulham had won both home games, but lost both away fixtures.

October

Still not fully fit, Haynes returned to league action halfway through the month at home to Grimsby Town. He eased his way back slowly, but his class was evident. He was tripped when closing in on goal during an impressive solo manoeuvre, and Arthur Stevens converted from the spot. Stevens grabbed a hat trick, including two penalties, in a 3–1 win. It was the first time Roy Bentley and Haynes had figured together in the forward line.

The following week was not so good, with Fulham losing 3–4 to Liverpool at Anfield. It was a fine contest with Fulham succumbing to a deciding goal from Jimmy Melia ten minutes from the end. Trevor Chamberlain had given Fulham an early lead but the team were pegged back. Soon Fulham were ahead again, Haynes splitting the defence with a gem of a pass for Chamberlain to score again.

After conceding twice more, Haynes made it 3–3 midway through the second half with a fine header from a Trevor Chamberlain corner. It looked as if Bentley had given Fulham the lead from another exquisite Haynes pass, but he was ruled offside in a very marginal decision. Two minutes later, Liverpool struck their winner. Haynes' goal was his first of the campaign—and a third of the season had already elapsed.

The injury still gives problems

The following Saturday, Fulham earned another victory, rounding the month off with a fine 1–0 win over second-place Stoke City, thanks to a first-minute goal from Stevens, although it was said that Haynes and Bentley struggled as an attacking force, and that the two stars didn't gel immediately. Haynes struggled again with his injury and showed poor control and distribution, so much so that his frustrations with himself were clearly evident and some of the Cottage crowd actually barracked him.

Fulham were up to ninth, the best position they would hold that season. Haynes somehow found the grit to return to the international arena in midweek, when he played for the Football League against the

On November 13th, Haynes joined his England colleagues at a Hendon hotel prior to the British Championship match at Wembley against Wales. Amongst those in this line-up are Johnny Haynes (left), Stanley Matthews (second left), Billy Wright (fourth left), Jimmy Dickinson (centre), Tom Finney (third right) and Ronnie Clayton (second right).

Irish League at St James' Park, Newcastle, returning with the third goal from a Matthews corner in a 3–2 victory. He had also made the second for Grainger and sprayed around a few passes, but was clearly not at the peak of his game, fading out of the action for long periods.

At the end of the month, Fulham had fifteen players, including Haynes, with injury problems, many having serious, long-term issues. Their squad was not the strongest at the best of times, and this spate of injuries meant that they failed to make any significant impression on the Second Division leaders. In just three months, Haynes' rosy future for both club and country had all gone horribly wrong. The young skipper was at a very low ebb.

November

At Middlesbrough, Fulham were quickly three first-half goals down to some super football, finally losing 1–3. Haynes scraped the post with one tremendous drive, and with another in the second half hit the keeper's legs, when in truth he didn't know where the ball was.

During this second half, Haynes gave evidence of his England form, and after shooting just wide following a clever run, he made another fine advance and combined with Eddie Lowe to present Jimmy Hill with the gift of a well-taken goal. After a fine move late in the game and a headed knock-down by Roy Bentley, Haynes grazed the post yet again.

The following week he showed his form at home to top-of-the-table Leicester City, a match which ended as a 2–2 draw. He was seemingly back to his best, but was tightly and sometimes unfairly marked by Leicester defenders. It was Fulham's first drawn game in sixteen league matches.

Haynes almost made a goal in the first few seconds, setting the tempo for the match. He also hit the Leicester bar himself when it looked easier to score. The home team should have won, but Roy Dwight and Bentley missed simple chances from exquisite Haynes passes to win the match.

Haynes won his ninth international cap in midweek playing in a 3–1 victory in the British Championship against Wales at Wembley. The Welsh goalkeeper, Arsenal's Jack Kelsey, was injured early on in the game, and replaced by an outfield player. After England had gone behind to a John Charles goal, Haynes found the net early in the second half for England's equalising goal. Matthews' corner kick was headed on twice for Haynes to volley into the net from close in. However, the win under these circumstances was not particularly satisfying.

He picked up an ankle knock in that game, as did many players from both sides, but substitutes were still a long way off, so he struggled on, limping during the last thirty minutes; the injury required an x-ray the following day. His goal was his fifth in just nine

Johnny Haynes grimaces as he is carried from the Wembley pitch by Beara, the Yugoslav goalkeeper. He suffered a leg injury after just half an hour, and took no further part in the England match.

full international appearances, a very decent record indeed.

After the ankle had given further trouble following the international game, he dropped out of Saturday's match with Bristol Rovers. The team returned to their bad old defensive habits at Eastville and were soundly beaten 0–4. Haynes was badly missed, the press' caustic comment being: "No Haynes—no Fulham."

The next week Fulham beat a struggling rock-bottom Notts County 5–1. Haynes on his return played gingerly, and from the start it was obvious he was not risking further injury to the leg, only occasionally splitting the defence with long passes. He did provide the pass for the second goal for Dwight, and also had three near misses himself, two flicking off bar and post.

It was clear he was nursing the injury and keeping out of the fray in view of the following Wednesday's England game against Yugoslavia. Certainly it was a comparatively easy game for Fulham, with Dwight claiming another league hat trick, his third in twenty league games.

Haynes is hurt playing for England

The joy of Haynes' tenth England cap was short-lived, as in the match against Yugoslavia at Wembley, he lasted barely half an hour. He was playing well, priming the England attack that looked capable of scoring at will. But he was then heavily tackled by the Yugoslavian full back Bruno Belin, and had to leave the field; he was actually carried from the pitch by the Yugoslavian goalkeeper, Vladimer Beara.

He had already provided the first goal with a super pass to Johnny Brooks to fire high into the net in the twelfth minute, and also had a snap shot brilliantly held by the goalkeeper. This was a rare match inasmuch as it allowed substitutes, and to make matters worse for Haynes, his replacement, Manchester United's Tommy Taylor, scored twice in the 3–0 win. Once more following an England match, Haynes' leg would require an x-ray the next day.

To add to Haynes's misfortunes, Taylor shone even brighter in his absence the following week by recording a hat trick, the first three goals in the 5–2 demolition of Denmark in the World Cup preliminary at Molineux. It was also of concern to Haynes that the 'play-anywhere' young genius Duncan Edwards of Manchester United scored the other two goals, both cracking shots. On this form Edwards was another competitor for Haynes' shirt. It didn't look good; he had to get fit quickly.

December

Amazingly, after missing just one match, he made a miraculous recovery from the injury, as he always seemed to do, and was back in the side for the visit of Leyton Orient who were on good form, undefeated in eight games. He duly came up trumps.

One press headline read: "Now Haynes fires the big guns." He was back to form, and was the architect of the strong second-half revival for the Cottagers. Fulham were a goal down at half-time, but the reliable Dwight had them level near the hour. Johnny Haynes' passes always had the visitors in trouble, and with fifteen minutes to go, he scored a great goal. Roy Dwight slipped the ball back to him and from more than twenty-five yards he rocketed it into goal. The force of the shot sent the ball rebounding back into play from the stanchion at the back of the net; the goalkeeper didn't move until it was over the line. The club programme described it as "a paralysing shot".

Then, just a couple of minutes from the end, he scored the third, pushing the ball home first time after Roy Bentley had made it easy for him with a downward header. Haynes agreed that the second goal was one of his most powerful shots. He added, referring to the previous England game: "See what happens when I watch Duncan Edwards on television!"

The following match was another fairly ferocious London derby against West Ham at Upton Park. The Hammers knew all too well about Haynes' current weaknesses in the leg and duly 'hammered it'. In this era, the club programme attempted to give its opinion diplomatically: "It was, of course, a coincidence that Johnny Haynes should be badly injured when we played West Ham in the opening league game of the season and injured again in the replay [return match]. On this occasion Johnny raised his right leg to bring down a high ball just after half-time when he received a kick on the calf muscle—the same muscle that has been giving him so much trouble and worry in recent weeks."

Fulham lost 1–2 and it didn't help matters that Haynes had to spend the greater part of this particular encounter as little more than a limping passenger on the wing. Fulham scored first, but were rocked by a freakish wind-assisted forty-yard free kick by John Bond that sailed straight in, and they never really recovered. Haynes had a golden opportunity to level the scores near the end, but unfortunately he had to put all his weight on his injured leg and sliced the ball wide.

After the game, he said he was suffering from nerve trouble in his right leg. The press suggested that it would be wise to take a rest over the festive period until it was fully cured. The *Fulham Chronicle* was worried: "Too often lately, he has finished up a passenger."

Due to this recurring injury, he missed the 0–1 defeat at home to third-placed Nottingham Forest the following week, the team looking devoid of attacking ideas. The trouble was that the young Haynes put the needs of the Fulham team above England and even above his own wellbeing. Even after this nasty knock, he only confined himself to barracks for a week, and returned for duty in a 0–2 defeat at Blackburn Rovers on Christmas Day.

Revenge was sweet, however, and he revelled in a 7–2 victory in the return match the following day. As it was Christmas there was little reported nationally. Seven of the game's goals came in the second half. Chamberlain scored a hat trick, and Bentley and Dwight two goals each. Little was mentioned regarding Haynes, the newspapers saying that he strolled ineffectively for sixty-five minutes, when the 'golden boy' who had recently become a 'problem boy' suddenly snapped into his zestful mood, and Fulham promptly scored five goals in the space of twenty-five minutes.

Fulham closed the year with a 1–1 draw at Huddersfield Town. They were mainly on the defensive, and there were few passes from the half-fit Haynes, but

Christmas cheer for Haynes as he receives a turkey from general manager Frank Osborne—one of the few times that Haynes 'got the bird' at Fulham!

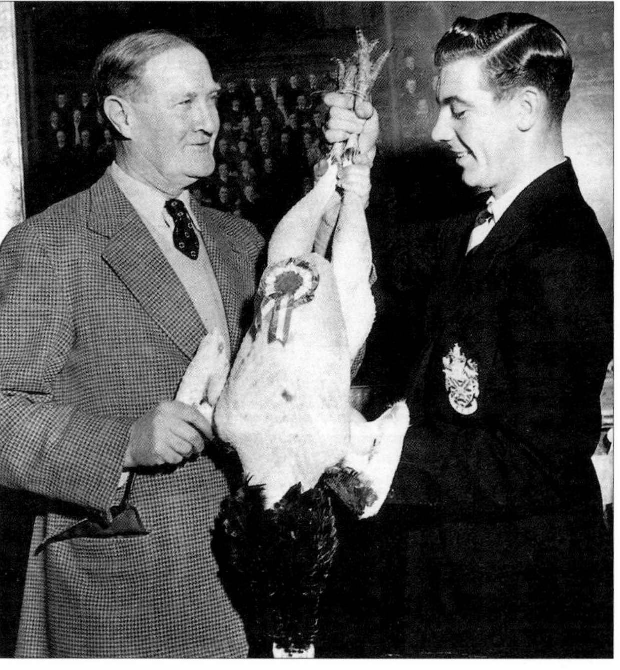

one defence-splitting pass led to the equaliser. Jimmy Hill, anticipating it, raced through on the wing, and his accurate centre was tapped in by Roy Dwight. Fulham had slipped to just below mid-table at the end of the year.

January

Early in the month Fulham made progress in the FA Cup with a 3–2 win at Ipswich Town. Ipswich were champions of the Third Division (South) that year, but Fulham should have won easily. Ipswich had only recently been formed, and it was the first time Fulham had ever played them.

However, it ended up being anything but an easy game. After going ahead in fifteen minutes, Fulham were pegged back five minutes before the interval, but right on half-time good work by Johnny Haynes and Roy Bentley on the wing presented Arthur Stevens with a beautiful square pass for the second goal. Plucky Ipswich fought back again and levelled, but just five minutes from the end, Haynes with quick thinking provided a first-time bouncing ball through the middle upfield to Roy Dwight, who breasted it down, beat two bewildered defenders and then the goalkeeper.

There was a sensational finish to the match when Ipswich clearly believed they had equalised with the last kick, but the referee indicated that he had blown for time before the ball hit the net (shades of Clive Thomas and Brazil…!). The home crowd were cheering so loudly that the players had not heard the whistle. Many of the reporters were not sure what had happened, and Ipswich manager Alf Ramsey had to check in the dressing room with the referee before admitting that Fulham had won.

Captain Haynes, though, was clear: "The whistle blew whilst the ball was in flight and I was actually walking off the pitch when the ball went in our net. I didn't even see whether or not our defence did anything to try and keep the ball out. I was expecting the whistle any time because I had seen both linesmen give the referee the full-time signal."

Haynes tried as a goalscoring forward

Aware of his lack of goals, Haynes tried to push further up the field to add to the firepower in Jezzard's absence, but this was at the expense of his linking and defensive work. Fulham beat Swansea 5–4 at the Vetch Field but Haynes did not score. It was a remarkable double over the Welsh side.

Fulham scored twelve goals against Swansea that season, with Dwight claiming a hat trick in both matches. Dwight's tally now stood at a truly amazing twenty-six goals in twenty-eight matches. Fulham, fortunately, seemed to have found another Bedford Jezzard from within their own ranks.

Johnny Haynes didn't get much of a mention. Fulham were 5–1 up at one stage, but an injury to full back John Chenhall saw Fulham hanging on by just a single goal at the end.

The following week a startlingly unpredictable Fulham lost at home to unfancied Lincoln 0–1. The press criticised Haynes for going too far into the forward line saying, "Without Jezzard, Haynes is trying to take on a double role, the forwards were deprived of those long through passes on which they thrive."

They did, however, stick to the formation in the fourth-round cup-tie in Blackpool. The match ended in a disastrous 2–6 defeat and a cup exit for another year. Little went right for Fulham or Haynes. Fulham were two goals down in the opening three minutes, but recovered. Haynes set up the equaliser to make it two apiece with a short pass to Bentley.

Unfortunately he then conceded a penalty for 'hands' which was, however, missed. He was tightly marked by Blackpool's Kelly, failed to score and again looked out of place in a disjointed attack. After fighting hard to get back on level terms, the defence collapsed completely and Fulham were a well-beaten side at the end. Jackie Mudie scored four for Blackpool and Derek Lampe put through his own goal—a day to forget.

February

Still Fulham persevered in keeping Haynes up front, but they lost again in a seven-goal thriller 3–4 to fellow-strugglers Rotherham United the following week, exposing once again the fact that Haynes' defensive covering duties were being neglected with another four goals conceded. Fulham had done all the hard work, tamely throwing away a draw just two minutes from the end.

Haynes scored the first after taking a pass from Arthur Stevens. The ball was heading for goal, but took a deflection off a Rotherham defender. However, in some statistics it is credited as an own goal. After an equaliser, a four-man move involving Eddie Lowe, Trevor Chamberlain and, inevitably, Haynes led to Roy Bentley putting Fulham ahead again.

Rotherham then scored twice either side of the interval, leaving Fulham with another hill to climb. However, they did, and Haynes' quick pass allowed Roy Dwight to level the scores once more. Haynes showed his England class with a hand in all three goals, but on a very muddy pitch the match was somewhat of a lottery.

The following week Fulham took on the hapless Port Vale side. They won at a canter 6–3, but even against this feeble defence, Haynes failed to find the net, despite hat tricks from both Dwight and Bentley. It was worrying that yet again Fulham conceded three goals.

Nevertheless, it was going to be a good day from the first couple of minutes when Haynes' first-time shot was finger-tipped over the bar. Two minutes later the first goal arrived when Robin Lawler, Trevor Chamberlain and then Haynes with a nod forward put Dwight through to score. Bentley made it two before the interval. Although Vale pulled one back, Haynes and Chamberlain from a wing movement assisted Bentley to set up Dwight again.

Bentley took his second before Vale stormed back with two goals, leaving them just one behind. Bentley then completed his hat trick, and with the crowd roaring, the usual trio of Chamberlain, Haynes and Bentley put together another move from which Dwight also completed his hat trick.

The press said: "Fulham proved once again that they are the best attacking side in the division, but also were playing against the worst defence in the division. Haynes was in top form, harnessing an attack which looked like it could and should have scored a dozen!" The Craven Cottage pitch was a quagmire, and although Haynes' scheming split the defence time and time again, the pitch often conspired to make these passes less effective.

Dwight was now breaking records; this hat trick was his fourth treble of the season, and his fifth in thirty-two games. He had registered thirty goals in those thirty-two games. Haynes was still concerned by his own form, and was contemplating whether he should be so far forward, but it looked as if he would have to stay in that position, as Bedford Jezzard's ankle was showing little sign of recovery.

Fulham sliding down the table, but Jim Langley arrives

Fulham hoped that the arrival of classy full back Jimmy Langley from Brighton would at least cut down the number of goals conceded. However, the following Saturday they went down again, this time to Bury 1–3 at the Cottage. The away side tried to mark Haynes out; the plan worked and he made a shaky start. After Fulham had gone behind, Haynes equalised with a good snapshot effort, following a throw-in from Langley right into the goalmouth.

Fulham had again conceded three goals, and this unpleasant dose of medicine was repeated the next week with the same 1–3 scoreline at Grimsby. In the driving snow and rain Haynes created a few openings, but in truth little went right. This time he did have a poor game, and hardly received a mention in the papers. The only positive note was a good goal from Fulham junior Trevor Watson on his debut. By this time Fulham had dropped to a precarious sixteenth position in the table.

In midweek, Haynes made another return to international football on a frosty and foggy evening in front of only 14,000 for his fifth England Under-23 match, against Scotland at Rangers' Ibrox ground, which ended 1–1.

March

The club stubbornly stuck to the 'Haynes up front' formation, but results were still not forthcoming. They gave it one last try at the Cottage but again Fulham lost, 1–2 against Liverpool, in a match that marked the debut of a fledgling George Cohen.

Fulham and Johnny Haynes both looked in poor form, and one report said, "Haynes seems to have deserted his role of chief provider and is now wasting his time up front waiting for the odd scoring chance." Another said that he looked a shadow of his former self.

The goal against Liverpool was provided, almost inevitably, by Haynes with a super through ball to Roy Dwight, who shot across the goal and just inside a post. International goalkeeper Tommy Younger made a number of fine saves for Liverpool. But Fulham had now lost five of the last six league matches, conceding sixteen goals in the process, and were just five places off the bottom.

After this latest reverse, the side was immediately restructured, with Haynes dropping back further into the middle of the field. The change had an immediate positive effect, and third-placed Stoke City were beaten 2–0 on their own ground, where they had only dropped two points all season and where they were unbeaten.

Fulham at last had a number of players returning after long-term injury. It was a typical enigmatic Fulham performance and result. One report said: "Haynes was straight back on international form, and kept the Stoke defence in bewilderment with his long and accurate passes—it was a grand through ball from Haynes which sent Bentley through for the first goal." Another report talked of Haynes and Hill playing their passes splendidly. It was the first time that Stoke had failed to score at home all season.

Unexpectedly, however, a capricious Fulham lost at home again the following week, this time 1–2 against an overly defensive Middlesbrough. After a Brian Clough goal in the first five minutes, Trevor Chamberlain netted Fulham's equaliser following a smart Haynes-Hill move, but it wasn't enough.

However, from this nadir, Fulham cruised through unbeaten until the end of the season. The run started with a 3–1 victory over Leicester at Filbert Street, who were, like Stoke City, unbeaten at home, at the top of the table and seven points ahead of their nearest rival. What followed was another Fulhamish performance. Haynes was back to form, and finding his touch.

The win looked unlikely initially, and Fulham were a goal down at half-time, thanks to master marksman Arthur Rowley, but then Haynes inspired Fulham's first and second goals with shrewd passes to Chamberlain and Bentley. Bentley scored the first, whilst Chamberlain slipped the ball to Hill for an easy second. Finally, a goal-bound pile-driver from Haynes was going in until a defender fisted the ball over the bar, and Jim Langley completed the win with his first goal for Fulham from the penalty spot.

A happier Haynes was on his travels again in midweek and played in the fourth and final group stage match of the Inter-Cities Fairs Cup, the match being the return leg in Frankfurt. The London XI lost in Germany 0–1 but remained on top of the group and thus qualified for the semi-finals.

In the final league game of the month, Fulham defeated Bristol Rovers 3–2 at the Cottage, only their second win at home since Christmas. After going a goal down, they quickly equalised. A gem of a Haynes pass found Chamberlain, who netted with a well-placed cross-shot. For the second goal, Haynes made a quick pass through to Bentley; he looked offside, but as the Rovers defence stopped, Bentley quickly squared the ball to Hill, who scored. Rovers came back again to equalise, but they were finally beaten by a rare goal from Fulham centre half Joe Stapleton just five minutes from time.

Haynes breaks records in London five-a-side

April

In midweek, Fulham travelled over to Harringay to try and recapture the *Evening Standard* five-a-side trophy they had won two seasons previously. It was a night when Fulham and Johnny Haynes broke all records. Fulham had been finalists the year before, but had not lifted the trophy.

This year there were twelve London sides competing, including all the First Division sides, and well over 8,000 spectators watched the event. Fulham won the competition easily, and to emphasise their superiority, they netted eighteen goals, whilst the other eleven sides mustered only seventeen between them!

Three of the side—Ian Black (goal), Jimmy Hill and Haynes—had played in the other finals; this time Roy Bentley replaced the departed Bobby Robson, and Jimmy Langley deputised for Eddie Lowe, who would have played had it not been for a toe injury.

The games went as follows: first round versus Queens Park Rangers 7–1 (Haynes 4, Bentley 3); second round versus Brentford 2–0 (Haynes, Bentley); third round versus Chelsea 6–0 (Haynes 3, Hill 2 and Bentley) and the final versus West Ham 3–2 (Haynes 2, Langley). Haynes scored in every match and on the night put away ten goals himself—a tournament record unlikely to be broken.

Haynes shot with tremendous power and formed a dream partnership with Bentley. He was a brilliant technician throughout the evening. The thrashing of the team from up the road in the semi-final was the highlight, and the final win over West Ham was sweet revenge over the physical team that had done the double over Fulham in the league that season. Haynes had his second Fulham medal.

Dropped by England

Being out of the FA Cup and with Fulham not pulling up any trees in the league, Johnny Haynes was a little bit out of the national limelight, and this had the effect he feared most, as he was sensationally omitted from the England team to play Scotland for the British Championship decider. Haynes' pride was hurt again, even though the England selectors stressed that the reshuffle was just an experiment.

Although he had been injured, he was now fully fit, and he was *always* selected for England when he was fit. He considered himself a far better player than the footballer who replaced him, Derek Kevan of West Bromwich Albion. Haynes was bitterly angry and very disappointed.

In the event, England played poorly at Wembley, and were thankful for Duncan Edwards' late goal six minutes from time, which enabled them to squeeze a 2–1 result. The team badly missed Haynes' guile and craft. The result would limit his exile to just this one match, and ensure that, when fit, he would remain a permanent fixture in the national side for the next five years.

Haynes instead played against Notts County in a 0–0 draw, only the second clean sheet in twenty-four games. He was described as quiet, but one of his shots, tipped on to the crossbar, deserved a goal. Fulham managed to hit the post twice with an empty goal gaping.

County were one from bottom, so Fulham should really have taken both points. Perhaps Haynes was ruminating on being overlooked by England. In the absence of an FA Cup run, Fulham and Haynes maintained their sharpness with a 4–0 victory in a friendly over Raith Rovers at the Cottage the following Monday.

The following week, Fulham punished Doncaster Rovers 3–0. The media quotes were emphatic: "In England form was Johnny Haynes who had the Rovers defence in a whirl in the first half. His brilliant through pass to Hill brought the first goal in the first minute."

Haynes was in total control and only Harry Gregg in the Doncaster goal stopped him adding at least two more. In the second half, Chamberlain fed Haynes again and with Gregg hopelessly beaten the ball thudded against the post and out. Five minutes later Haynes had his head in his hands again when Gregg saved an absolute certainty after he had hooked the ball towards goal from close in.

After Fulham had gone in three up through Stevens and Bentley they lost Hill to an injury, but still won comfortably with ten men. The club programme confirmed: "If Johnny ever really lost his England form, he found it again on this occasion with a vengeance!"

On Good Friday against Barnsley at Craven Cottage, Fulham won 2–0. Haynes took charge and he was winning tackles, and always looking for the ball. He was supplying opportunities galore, but they were all missed by an out of sorts forward line.

It wasn't until the last ten minutes that he finally put Fulham on the road to victory with a through pass to Chamberlain who stumbled his way forward and crashed the ball home from close range. Two minutes later, Haynes saw a chance and sent a long curling pass to Stevens, who shot through the keeper's legs as he attempted to smother the ball.

The season's job was done, and there was little to be added; a win at Leyton Orient, where "headmaster Haynes, riddling the Orient defence" was involved in the first goal in a 2–0 result, and a draw at the Cottage against Barnsley concluded Fulham's season. For a welcome change, the team conceded only four goals in the last eight matches.

All aboard for a trip behind the Iron Curtain. Haynes (front) joins (from left) Duncan Edwards, Ronnie Clayton, Geoff Pegg, Alan Hodgkinson and Manager Walter Winterbottom on an England Under-23 tour of Bulgaria, Romania and Czechoslovakia. The plane was involved in an incident near Bucharest when it was buzzed by a Soviet MIG fighter for straying out of the proper airspace, and a few warning shots were fired. Thankfully the plane arrived safely, and in the second match of the tour, against Romania, Haynes played superbly, scoring the only goal of the game.

To round off the season, German Premier champions Blauweiss visited Fulham for a friendly and the home side won 6–0. The Germans gave Haynes too much room, and he cut the visitors' defence to ribbons with his incisive play, opening the scoring himself with a pile-driver from twenty yards.

Some had said that Haynes was too young at twenty-two to take on the responsibility of captaincy. Manager Dugald Livingstone disagreed, saying: "The job takes time to learn. You can count the real captains of football on the fingers of one hand. Haynes has now had a season at it and I think he will make a very good captain."

Yet another mediocre season

Fulham ended the season where they had started it, smack in the middle, in eleventh place, their form in the last two months bringing them back to a respectable level. Ninety-one goals had been scored but eighty-four conceded. Although he had made a hatful of goals, Haynes' personal contribution had been just four.

Fulham had been very fortunate to have found Roy Dwight to replace Jezzard, his twenty-six goals from thirty-six starts being the most significant contribution by far. Without his friends Jezzard and Robson, Haynes had struggled for goals. He had scored just once after the turn of the year. He knew he would have to improve on that. The injuries to his ankle and calf meant that he had shown his true form only during the last two months of the season.

Recalled by England

May

After his omission against Scotland in the British Championship in April, Haynes was immediately recalled for the next three 1958 World Cup preliminary matches, against the Republic of Ireland (twice), and the return match against Denmark. He knew he had to grasp this opportunity, and responded with three scintillating displays.

England started off with a 5–1 destruction of the Republic of Ireland in front of 52,000 at Wembley. They were extremely comfortable, and were four goals to the good at half-time.

A week later the England team travelled to Denmark. Despite an early scare and going a goal down in Copenhagen after twenty-seven minutes, Haynes brought England back into the match with a neat right-footed equaliser a minute later. He continued to orchestrate the proceedings, apparently playing his best-ever game for England, but the Danes held out stubbornly until the last fifteen minutes, with play remarkably even.

Fitness and an injury to a key defender eventually told and England piled in with three late goals to register a 4–1 victory. The third goal in the seventy-fifth minute was scored by John Atyeo, who rose at the far post to head in a Johnny Haynes centre. Haynes almost scored his second a minute later, and it was only a defender's outstretched foot on the line that prevented a goal.

Then, amazingly, Haynes played his third World Cup preliminary in twelve days, tackling the Irish again in the return leg in Dublin. England, needing just a draw, started casually and conceded after just three minutes. Forty-seven thousand fervent Irishmen almost yelled them to victory, but England somehow survived, and a scrambled headed goal by Atyeo from Tom Finney's cross in the last seconds secured them a 1–1 draw and the point they needed for qualification. Haynes had played a fair game but was targeted by scything tackles from defender Nolan, and his influence then waned.

'Old head' Haynes helps the younger ones

As a thank you, Haynes, now the 'old head' in the England Under-23 side, was invited by the FA to help out the younger players in a tour behind the Iron Curtain. The team had already lost 1–2 to Bulgaria. Haynes readily agreed and flew out immediately, less than a week after completing the three World Cup matches.

He had a scare before he even reached the ground when a MIG fighter buzzed the plane in which he was travelling as it drifted out of the correct airspace. Relations were more strained than they are now, and a few warning shots were fired. Haynes was thankful that he got the chance to play at all.

What followed was his best display in an England shirt so far. On the field of play against Romania in Bucharest, he felt he could do no wrong. In front of a crowd of 100,000, masterful Haynes capped a superb display when he ran on to a Duncan Edwards free kick and hit a cracking thirty-yard shot that streaked home a couple of minutes from the end; it proved to be the only goal of the game. This win was followed by another success four days later, a 2–0 win over Czechoslovakia. Victory for this Haynes-inspired team arrived thanks to two goals from the mercurial Duncan Edwards.

Summer rest

After all this, Haynes was grateful to have the opportunity of a complete rest from football, and a chance to let his ankle heal fully. He did, however, play a few wicket-keeping games again for Winchmore Hill, but was now coming under a "little pressure" from Fulham directors Tommy Trinder and Chappie D'Amato to quit playing regular cricket league matches. The club's medical staff thought that the continual bending might have an adverse effect on his thigh muscles; this was considered particularly damaging to forwards who were expected to be extra nippy.

At least, after a topsy-turvy year, he was back in the England reckoning, but his chances of playing in the First Division appeared to be as far away as ever. He was concerned about Fulham's lack of progress, especially in defence, and the wholesale deterioration in the state of the Craven Cottage pitch, which was preventing him from showing his very best form.

12: So near, yet so far 1957–58

OFFICIAL PROGRAMME

THE FOOTBALL ASSOCIATION
CHALLENGE CUP

SEMI-FINAL TIE

Photograph by A. Wilkes & Son, West Bromwich.

MANCHESTER UNITED

v.

FULHAM

VILLA PARK, BIRMINGHAM
SATURDAY, MARCH, 22nd, 1958

KICK-OFF 3-0 p.m.

PRICE - 6D. ISSUED BY ASTON VILLA F.C.

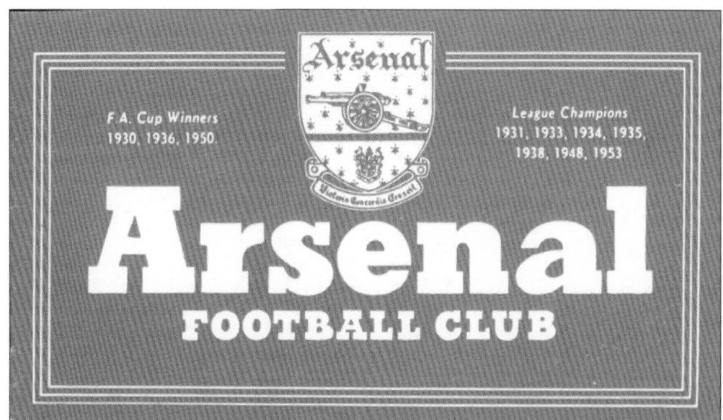

F.A. Cup Winners
1930, 1936, 1950.

Arsenal

League Champions
1931, 1933, 1934, 1935,
1938, 1948, 1953

Arsenal
FOOTBALL CLUB

Season 1957-8

F.A. Cup Semi-Final Replay — Wednesday, 26th March

MANCHESTER UNITED v. FULHAM

KICK-OFF 3 p.m.

OFFICIAL 6d PROGRAMME

12: So near, yet so far 1957–58

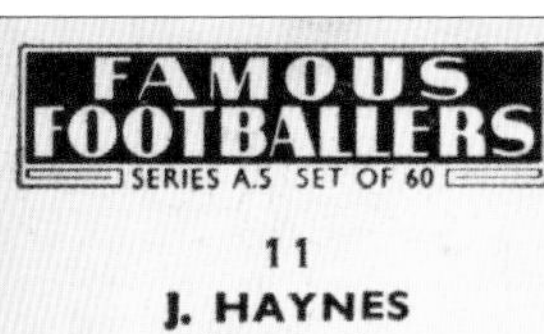

11

J. HAYNES

(FULHAM)

Johnny Haynes, ex-schoolboy international from Edmonton, first appeared for Fulham during the 1952-53 season. Was capped for England against Ireland, October, 1954, at the age of 19. During the 1956-57 season he added several more England caps to his collection, and scored the winning goal for Young England against Rumania.

Issued by

BARRATT & CO.LTD

LONDON - - - ENGLAND

PRINTED IN ENGLAND

With typical honesty in his assessment of his previous season's form, Haynes admitted that he had never been able to achieve peak fitness. Returning on the boat from South Africa with the stricken Bedford Jezzard had reduced his pre-season training, and subsequent injuries had kept him out early on. However, this year there was plenty of early pre-season training. Despite his hectic post-season schedule with the two England teams, Haynes returned early to Craven Cottage to put in one full day's strenuous workout per week.

Bedford Jezzard's career is over

In the annual Whites v Colours trial match, the Whites won 9–4, with Johnny Haynes and Roy Bentley each notching hat tricks for the Whites. Things looked good, but events turned sour quickly. Bedford Jezzard fell and turned his ankle in his attempted comeback match; it wasn't serious but he realised he would never be fit enough to play competitive first-class football again and immediately announced his retirement.

Despite the intensive treatment, the injury had never properly healed, and Jezzard's Fulham and two-cap England career was over. He was immediately taken in by the Fulham family and given a coaching and training position within the club.

August

Fulham made a fine start to the season, remaining unbeaten in the first eight games, and Haynes contributed another four goals, equivalent to his total for the whole of the previous season.

At home to Derby County on opening day, Fulham won 2–0. Johnny Haynes, in a new role as goal-snatcher, scored a fine goal after just twenty minutes of the first half. The whole of the Derby defence retreated, expecting him to pass, but he darted on to a Jim Langley throw-in from the left, sold a dummy by sweeping into the middle across the field, and beat three defenders before scoring with a sizzling right-foot shot into the corner of the net from twenty yards. He was on brilliant form, but his passes were wasted by colleagues. He was trying extra hard to do all the scoring and the creating. In the end he became very tired, and missed a sitter from five yards in the second half.

On the Thursday, Fulham travelled to Notts County and won 5–1. The team were immaculate, and Haynes was an inspiration. He opened the scoring with another beauty after just three minutes, exchanging passes with Jimmy Hill before scoring with a typical twenty-five-yard shot. County secured an equaliser three minutes later. Chamberlain scored on the stroke of half-time when Bentley and Haynes fashioned the opening.

Early in the second half, goalkeeper Black's clearance was moved forward by Chamberlain and Haynes for Dwight to score again. With twenty minutes left, Dwight made it four, and in the last seconds, following an excellent ball from Dwight, Haynes played an accurate first-time centre to Chamberlain and the winger rammed home an unstoppable shot past County's Linton. It was a magnificent goal, a length-of-the-field move that even drew applause from the shattered home crowd. Haynes had scored one goal and made three. Notts County were never in the hunt, the headline reading, "Haynes sparks off the Fulham fury."

At Swansea, Fulham drew 4–4. They attacked with gay abandon, neglecting some of the finer points of defending, and really handed Swansea a point. They were frequently two goals in front, and Haynes was the best forward on the field, creating the second Fulham goal with a beautiful pass to Dwight. Fulham's first two away games of the season had seen them score nine goals.

September

Against Liverpool in a 2–2 draw at home, the first goal was scored by Trevor Chamberlain. Johnny Haynes and Roy Bentley spreadeagled the Liverpool defence for Chamberlain to score with a low shot into the corner from ten yards after Haynes smashed the ball across the goalmouth. Fulham and Haynes could have had three more goals, but the ball didn't run all that kindly.

With Fulham behind at the interval, Chamberlain was badly injured. Captain Haynes rallied his flagging side and put in a forceful header to win a corner; from the flag-kick, Bentley challenged Liverpool goalkeeper Tommy Younger for the ball and the Scottish keeper dropped it. In a flash, Haynes seized Bentley's pass and converted the opportunity, crashing a first-time beauty off a post into the top corner of the net through a crowd of players. The game had been a spectacular

Where did he go? A classic picture shows Haynes leading the Liverpool defence a merry dance during the 2–2 draw at the Cottage.

affair, good enough for the higher echelons of the First Division.

Fifteen games unbeaten

Fulham were finding their exhilarating start difficult to maintain, and could only draw with Barnsley 1–1 in the next home game. One newspaper report was critical of the team: "The attack has lost its incisiveness. I exempt Johnny Haynes from the feeble attack. He scored the only Fulham goal, and looked the only one in attack who had any real purpose."

Haynes had one shot in the first half from fully forty-five yards that the goalkeeper just managed to fingertip to safety. He was marked by three defenders, but did wriggle free once, with twenty minutes to go, to receive the ball from a corner and lob Fulham in front. Fulham threw away a point with the usual defensive blunder, allowing Barnsley to equalise from a corner with just seconds left.

Two days later, Haynes wasn't selected for the first leg of the semi-final of the Inter-Cities Fairs Cup against Lausanne Sports, and the London XI surprisingly lost the encounter 1–2.

After a dull 0–0 midweek draw with Ipswich, Fulham had achieved fifteen games without defeat, including matches at the end of the previous season.

They then faced their usual brutal encounter with West Ham. Andy Malcolm, performing with more muscle than skill, was told to follow Haynes. Fulham already had significant injuries; in addition, an Asian flu virus had spread through the club. Fulham were forced to make seven changes, with Haynes, unusually for him, switching to the inside right shirt (No 8).

In yet another bruising clash at Upton Park, where two Fulham defenders sustained facial injuries, Haynes only once wriggled clear, linking cleverly with Trevor Watson to inspire a goal for Dwight. Fulham were at one stage in the lead, but West Ham fought back in the second half, and with just nine fit men Fulham finally lost their unbeaten record in a 2–3 defeat.

Final game for England Under-23s

During midweek, due to age restrictions, the 'veteran' Haynes waved goodbye to the England Under-23 side on a night of mixed emotions, when he was made captain of the side again for his eighth cap. He responded in typical fashion, contributing two goals as England slammed in six against Bulgaria at Stamford Bridge. In the 6–2 win were two goals for seventeen-year-old Jimmy Greaves making his international debut. He was unlucky not to secure a hat trick, missing a last-minute penalty.

Although home star Greaves was playing, the crowd at the Bridge was still an astonishing 56,000. Greaves scored his first goal after a Haynes rocket had been blocked five minutes before half-time, and just a minute later came the goal of the match. Alan A'Court beat three men in a tight space and fed the ball inside to Haynes who raced thirty yards leaving four Bulgarians flat-footed, before slamming the ball in. Chelsea's Peter Brabrook then added a third before the interval.

Bulgaria cut the lead immediately after the restart, but A'Court made it four, and then in the space of four minutes, Haynes created a goal for Greaves, and Greaves returned the compliment for Haynes to net the sixth. Bulgaria added a little respectability to the scoreline in the last minute.

Haynes left the under-23 arena having never been on the losing side. His eight caps and performances had produced eight goals. The Haynes and Greaves partnership would be rekindled four years later just as successfully at senior level.

Fulham signed off the month by hammering Sheffield United 6–3. Haynes was again on brilliant form, and made goalscoring simple for Dwight, who scored a career-best four goals. The attack showed some top-grade football. Haynes hit the bar with one of the hardest shots seen at Craven Cottage for years.

Due to severe injuries and sickness, Fulham had signed the Arsenal veteran Alex Forbes, who made his debut in the match. The defensive problems were still apparent, however, and at one stage, with the score at 4–3, the match was a close-run thing; only two goals in the last five minutes made the score look as if it had been easy.

October

With a number of absences and several players playing out of position, Fulham earned a very creditable point by holding promotion hopefuls Blackburn Rovers 1–1 at Ewood. Johnny Haynes had a very thin time of it. He was well held by his England colleague Ronnie Clayton, one of just a handful of players who could close down the England man when in this kind of form.

Then, away at Middlesbrough, Fulham lost 0–2 to two goals from Brian Clough. Haynes missed a sitter in the second half from under ten yards, shooting straight at Peter Taylor as the goalkeeper came out; Middlesbrough's goals came in the last minute of each half.

A four-goal trouncing of Wales

Haynes won his fourteenth England cap on the following Saturday, and played on a wet surface at Ninian Park, Cardiff, in a comfortable 4–0 victory over a poor Welsh side. England were aided by an early own goal by Spurs full back Mel Hopkins after only six minutes. Haynes' pass then almost made the second goal for Derek Kevan. Haynes had a field day, and the press wrote: "In addition to directing the forward line in superb style, Haynes shot two of the most brilliant goals one could wish to see."

His two goals—both magnificent right-footed shots—came just before half-time and midway through the second half. For the first, United's Taylor breasted down to Haynes who let go a first-time shot no goalkeeper in the world would have saved. The second, on seventy-two minutes, completed the rout and was a belting twenty-five-yard special that skidded past Arsenal's Jack Kelsey.

It was a match where Johnny's performance, described by one reporter as "near genius", once again caught the eye of Stanley Matthews. He said: "He'd been intermittent up to that point, and looked like he was a little short on confidence; this was his fourteenth cap and he looked a real all-round player." Some said that he had played the "game of his life so far" for England on that day. A total of eight England goals to date was also a very pleasing tally for a goal-maker.

This was a more settled England side, not the perfect mix yet, but looking good. Preston's Tom Finney had guided and nurtured Haynes through the game, and John, ever the gentleman, felt that he had to thank Tom, and said that he 'owed him.' Finney, known as 'The Preston Plumber' because of his business in the town, said, "OK, come and see me tomorrow afternoon. I'm putting a bathroom in a house in Preston and my labourer has gone sick!"

It was an excellent all-round team performance, and England were now unbeaten in two years and sixteen international matches. In Haynes' absence, Fulham still managed to beat Leyton Orient 3–1, but made hard work of it, and the local reporter was quick to point out: "To say they missed his [Haynes'] craft was the understatement of the year."

A cup final (of sorts)

Four days later there was further success. Haynes played in a team including Roy Dwight and Arsenal's Bill Dodgin in the second leg of the Inter-Cities Fairs Cup semi-final at Highbury. The London XI, captained by Haynes on this occasion, won 2–0 against Lausanne Sports and by so doing qualified for the final on a 3–2 aggregate.

London were poor and disjointed overall, but it was only wayward finishing that prevented the team getting double figures. Haynes as skipper was the hardest-working player on the pitch, and put the forwards through time and again but they fluffed every chance. He was driving the team on, but some players couldn't hear the whip. Greaves was particularly guilty, having a poor night, although he did score in the first ten minutes. Cliff Holton scored the decisive second London goal with just under a quarter of an hour remaining, chipping in following a fine cross from Haynes on the right to clinch a final place.

At Charlton on the Saturday, Fulham looked dead and buried at half-time at two down, but they were rallied superbly by Haynes in the manner of a great captain, and he inspired the equalising goals for Arthur Stevens and Jim Langley. The papers said: "Fulham resumed in fine style with Johnny Haynes showing what a fine strategist he is, spraying accurate passes inside the full backs with perfect distribution." The first goal was a classic; Haynes stroked the ball through to Roy Bentley, who guided it to Stevens for the winger to score with a glorious shot from the centre forward's position.

Then, from a hotly disputed free kick given for a foul on himself, Haynes showed quick thinking. He took the kick immediately to full back Langley who was moving swiftly into the penalty box. Langley was brought down in the area and lifted himself up to equalise from the penalty spot.

Fulham could have won the match in the last minute when Haynes' telling pass released Jimmy Hill, but his shot was fractionally the wrong side of the post. Fulham settled for the 2–2 draw. By the end of the month, things were looking very good indeed. Fulham had lost only twice, and were lying in fifth place in the Second Division, tucked in just a point behind the leading side.

Busy Haynes jetted off again in midweek, winning his seventh cap for the Football League against the Irish League again in Belfast, captaining the side but only flashing into the game at irregular intervals. He did however score the first goal for the League in the twelfth minute in a 4–2 victory. He started the move and finished it with a headed goal.

November

Against bottom-of-the-table Doncaster Rovers, Fulham won emphatically 4–1. Johnny Haynes was once again the driving force, and his genius led to goals. It was, however, clear that he was trying hard to avoid injury before the following week's international match against Ireland.

The Cottagers were aided by an own goal from Doncaster defender (and, later, comedian) Charlie ('Now, me ol' flower') Williams as early as the ninth minute. Haynes escaped the clutches of the defenders to make the second; he took a swift free kick that dropped the ball on to the foot of Jimmy Hill, who was running through virtually unchallenged, and he hit a beautiful goal from twenty yards.

Then Haynes added the third himself on the hour, although there was an element of luck about it. He took a long pass, went to the dead ball line on a solo run, but slipped as he was about to shoot. Harry Gregg, the Doncaster keeper, also slipped as he came out to challenge him and the ball just rolled over the line between the goalkeeper and near post. The press called it an audacious goal, but in truth it was a fortunate one.

First defeat in an England shirt

Haynes' first setback when playing for England arrived when Northern Ireland won 2–3 at Wembley the following Wednesday. It was his first defeat whilst playing in an England shirt, and he didn't enjoy the experience. It was a match that on any other day England would have won easily.

Ireland were awarded a very soft penalty, and scored another goal that was blatantly offside. All the while goalkeeper Harry Gregg, who had conceded four at Fulham on the Saturday, was in inspired form. Everything hit him, and what he didn't stop hit defenders on the line; what they didn't stop cannoned back off post and bar.

Danny Blanchflower's side had all the four-leaved clovers on the day, fondly remembered as 'Gregg's match'. It was the first time Ireland had beaten England for thirty years, and it was Haynes' fifteenth game before tasting a loss. He had faded after a brilliant start to the match, but was unconcerned afterwards, calling it just a blip.

At Rotherham on the Saturday, Fulham surprisingly went down 1–3. The press were blunt: "Unless Fulham stop totally relying on Haynes, the chance of promotion will disappear like chaff before an east wind. The attack has so far relied on the brilliance of Haynes—who has faded." The score wasn't surprising. The Rotherham team worked tirelessly and concentrated solely on stopping Haynes from playing effectively after he'd had a difficult midweek match—and the tactic worked.

George Cohen arrives

The Huddersfield Town game saw George Cohen come in for his second game and claim the right back position which he would retain. Overall, there was too much pretty stuff, with few ideas on how to put the ball into the net. The outstanding exception was Haynes, who worked untiringly and scored two great goals in a 2–1 victory.

He demonstrated his intent early in the game with two great shots in the first ten minutes, saved by a very able goalkeeper. Of that first shot Johnny said: "He did well to keep that one out." His first goal came in the twenty-seventh minute following Jim Langley's fine run; he made a cross to Haynes who hit a fine cross-shot from twenty yards low into the corner of the net.

Haynes continued to menace, and his second on the hour was a thunderbolt from the edge of the area after Jimmy Hill had laid the ball back to him. He began to tire and in the end Fulham were fortunate to hold on after conceding a goal ten minutes from the end. The press said, "There is still too much reliance on Haynes to make and score the goals."

In the 1–3 defeat at Grimsby, Haynes was still at his best, but was unable to charm the ball into the goal. He tried every trick he knew to spur the team on, and Grimsby didn't know where the next pass was going to go. Tony Barton tapped in a goal after a Haynes shot

This brave dive by the French goalkeeper Abbes to thwart Haynes at Wembley in November prevented a goal, but England ran out 4–0 winners.

had hit the post. Perhaps Haynes was trying to save himself a little for the next midweek international.

Reunited with Bobby Robson in England colours

Memories of the England performance three weeks previously were firmly shrugged off when France came to Wembley for a friendly. England cruised to an inspired 4–0 victory. The Haynes partnership with Bobby Robson at inside right was rekindled, and Robson scored twice on his international debut. England were out of sight three goals ahead before half-time.

Haynes' delicate pass sent Bryan Douglas away for the second goal, and he then crafted the third for Taylor's head with a glorious floated cross. Haynes was also involved in the four-man move that gave Robson one of his goals. Haynes' shooting on the night had been not up to scratch, but his passes had delighted the crowd. England certainly looked as if they were gunning for honours in the forthcoming World Cup. It must have been a fair performance, as later France would finish third in the 1958 tournament.

In spite of two consecutive away defeats, Fulham's first home defeat of the season, 3–4 against fourth-placed Stoke, came as a complete shock. Despite his midweek exertions, effervescent Haynes was virtually a one-man attack; Fulham managed just three first-half shots, all from him. The home defence let Fulham down badly again, and conceded as early as the second minute.

Fulham's second-half revival after a wretched first half was solely down to the spadework of Haynes, but it was not enough. The forwards were described as weak, and Haynes couldn't vitalise them.

The display was so poor that very unusually the club programme made little mention of the match. Instead, it chose to carry an impassioned plea from captain Haynes to supporters to stop the barracking and get behind the team, making it clear that a number of players preferred to play away from home. After twelve matches at home without defeat, this had been the unlucky thirteenth.

December

Fulham's response to this reverse was to produce a memorable 5–0 victory in Bristol over the City side. Using the 'H' plan—Haynes and Hill—Fulham and Johnny Haynes put in a lesson of controlled attacking football. Haynes was described as magical, and having the Bristol defence running in circles.

He scored the first of the five goals in the thirteenth minute with a snorting shot that ripped into the net, and had a hand in three of the other first-half goals. Fulham were four up at the interval and hardly needed to exert themselves in the second half. The game also marked the debut of Elio (Tony) Macedo in goal, not that he had much to do.

Next week Fulham beat Cardiff 2–0, in a match in which they hit the woodwork three times. Haynes also hit the foot of a post early on but was generally subdued, eventually missing a sitter mainly due to the churned-up conditions in the Cottage goalmouths.

He was well shackled, but even like this he still supplied some delightful touches. It was his shot, which was eventually poked into his own net by Cardiff's

Malloy, that saw Fulham take the lead. Finally, he escaped late in the second half and his pass put Jimmy Hill through. Hill's first shot hit the goalkeeper, but he was able to tuck away the rebound for the second and clinching goal.

The 3–3 draw at Derby County the following Saturday saw 'Johnny the Great' Haynes at his best away from home, and Fulham had him to thank for earning a point. After conceding a very early goal, Haynes' through pass to Roy Dwight levelled the scores in the ninth minute.

Exactly the same move was repeated in the twenty-eighth minute for Dwight to grab his second. To cap it off, Haynes provided the perfect corner from the left for Roy Bentley to head the third goal four minutes from half-time.

It was a very volatile match with Derby rallying strongly to equalise. The Fulham defence for once stood firm against late onslaughts, becoming notably physical in their play. The match ended in a chorus of boos, especially as the referee had denied the home side three late penalty appeals. The official was assaulted by a Derby supporter on leaving the field.

A very merry Christmas then ensued. Fulham won 1–0 at now-bottom Lincoln City on Christmas Day. In an unfestive physical game, Tony Barton and Dwight sustained injuries that ensured they took no further part in the festivities, and Jim Langley cut his head badly. Dwight was on the field long enough to get the winner.

On Boxing Day, it got even better, and Haynes, in the form of his life, destroyed Lincoln on his own at the Cottage. As early as the tenth minute, his clever pass found Trevor Chamberlain, and Fulham were on their way. After a Lincoln equaliser, he scored twice in the space of fourteen minutes with his famous snorting shots to put Fulham in the clear at half-time.

Jimmy Hill's goal fifteen minutes from time was the icing on the Christmas cake, and the 4–1 win was a picture of attacking football. Haynes was denied two further goals by cynical fouls just outside the box, after his consummate skill had taken him clean through.

In a second home match forty-eight hours later, Haynes undid Swansea Town, who were having a poor season and sitting just one off the basement place. Fulham won a hard game 2–0. Haynes led the Swansea defence a merry dance, although he always had two men on him. He split the defence time and time again, and Fulham ought to have scored five.

George Cohen and Jim Langley had the dangerous Cliff Jones and Len Allchurch buttoned up, and the Swans rarely looked like scoring. However, it took Fulham almost seventy minutes to break down the Swansea rearguard, before Haynes helped craft the first-ever goal for young John Doherty. The result looked in doubt until six minutes from the end, when the maestro settled the issue, beating the unsighted goalkeeper with a low shot following an intelligent pass from Chamberlain.

Top of the pile at Christmas

Haynes was inspired, and events were improving by the month at the Cottage. Tony Macedo and Cohen were now playing regularly, Jim Langley was playing superbly and Roy Bentley had moved into the half back line, where his experience and class calmed the back five.

Thanks to the super league run this month, when Fulham had taken five wins and a draw from their six league matches, they sat firmly on top of the Second Division at the turn of the year. Haynes had continued with his scoring run, being already in double figures with eleven goals.

January

The new year started with the usual third-round FA Cup game and Fulham's opponents were non-league Yeovil Town. The *Fulham Chronicle* said quite clearly that Fulham's eyes were set on league honours, and they were not expected to make a long cup run. Nobody told the players that!

Fulham disposed of the renowned giant-killers Yeovil 4–0 at the Cottage but not without a few scares and a tough fight. A headline summed it up: "Key the debutant, Hill the marksman, Haynes the star!" In the first half, Fulham were lucky and it was only a marginal offside decision that robbed Yeovil's Robshaw when he netted via a post.

Johnny Key scored on his debut, and both Jimmy Hill's goals were made by Haynes. Initially a Haynes and Jim Langley move ended with a shot that hit the post, and Jimmy Hill scored from the rebound. A glorious pass from Haynes put Hill through for the second two minutes later. Just three minutes after that came Key's goal. Four minutes from time it looked as if Haynes would add the fourth as he went through the defence on a solo run, but he was off balance and so instead set the ball up for young Doherty to score for the second successive match.

At Liverpool in a 1–2 reverse, Haynes was seldom seen; he was obviously suffering from a heavy flu-like cold. He really shouldn't have played, but with Liverpool in third place it was an important league game, and he felt that he had to be there. Despite Trevor Chamberlain's equaliser, goalkeeper Younger had another excellent game and with Fulham pressing, Liverpool scored the winner. A bad day for Haynes became worse when his poor pass was intercepted by Alan A'Court, who scored Liverpool's winner in front of 51,000 roaring Anfield fans. The press described Haynes as looking out of touch.

Normally Fulham would have thrown Haynes on to the pitch if he could walk, but the club could see he was not well or fully recovered, and for the following week's long trip to Yorkshire to face Barnsley, he was left out of the side in order to get over the remaining effects of the influenza and laryngitis that plagued him. Predictably, Fulham played poorly without him, and lost without scoring a goal. Barnsley were adjacent to

Fulham in the table so it was another frustrating defeat in a wind-affected game.

The following week it was the cup again, against Charlton Athletic in the fourth round. In front of a huge Cottage crowd of 40,000 and after Jimmy Hill had given Fulham the lead, a lax Fulham conceded an equaliser to Charlton's Ryan with the last kick of the game that ended 1–1. Haynes was still groggy following his illness and was out of the game for much of the first half, but he was considerably brighter in the second, having one twenty-yarder bound for the top corner clawed away at the last minute.

Fulham won the replay 2–0 in midweek in front of a massive 43,000 crowd at the Valley. They started at a fast tempo and Haynes was unlucky not to score twice in the first ten minutes from a shot and a header. They won the enthralling encounter with second-half goals from Bentley and Arthur Stevens, already knowing that were going to face next week's league opponents, West Ham, in the fifth round. Haynes, in scintillating form, played himself into the ground. He provided the pass to Trevor Chamberlain for the winger to shoot, and the rebound from the goalkeeper fell to the ice-cool Bentley who slotted home the first goal.

February

Fulham, seeking to add extra impetus to the attack, unveiled Maurice Cook, a 'battering ram' reinforcement centre forward signed from Watford, to aid them in their quest. Mullery says of Cook: "He was Johnny's whipping boy really, dear old Maurice, but he loved him [Haynes], he took everything he threw at him, and he'd honestly go out and do his best next game. But his best could never be good enough. Johnny was a perfectionist, and he wanted to see perfection, and nine times out of ten at that time he was perfection, but most of the others were below that."

West Ham were fortunate to come away with a point in a 2–2 draw. Haynes worked hard and scored Fulham's first equaliser with a clever hook shot just before half-time, following a corner from Trevor Chamberlain. He had his back to goal, but brought the ball immediately under control, swivelled around with defenders closing in and hooked the ball first time into the net.

Jim Langley had given Fulham the lead with a penalty after Haynes' shot had been handled with just five minutes left on the clock, but Fulham were robbed of a point by a freak, speculative thirty-five-yard shot in the dying seconds that went in off the crossbar. Fulham's centre half Derek Lampe was a limping passenger for most of the game and he was actually off the field for eight minutes, leaving Fulham with ten men.

The Munich air disaster

On February 6th, the news broke of a tragedy that the football community and the world would still recall half a century later, when a number of the Manchester United team and respected goalkeeper and journalist Frank Swift were among those who lost their lives in the Munich air disaster. This terrible event would not only rob Manchester of the backbone and heart of their side, but would also disrupt the England team that Haynes was pinning his hopes on for Gothenburg.

Tommy Taylor, Pegg, Byrne, Whelan and the man-mountain boy wonder Duncan Edwards were amongst those killed. Like many, Haynes was devastated. He had lost friends as well as playing colleagues and was deeply affected for some time.

The World Cup draw came out soon after the disaster. Three teams were pinpointed as those most likely to get the honours: England, Brazil and Russia. England were drawn in a group that contained the two other favourites, together with Austria.

The impetus that Fulham were building up in the league was halted as the following game at Bramall Lane was postponed due to bad weather. But things were certainly warming up at Craven Cottage, where tickets for the fifth-round cup tie at West Ham were on sale. The demand was breathtaking. Eight thousand people queued for three hours in the cold to get their hands on a precious ticket. The queue was reported at one stage as being six deep and a mile long.

The tie with West Ham a fortnight later was a tense, physical and intimidating match in front of another massive 40,000 crowd. Andy Malcolm shadowed, shackled and kicked Haynes in the first half, but the maestro emerged in the second half to escape and plot West Ham's downfall with a superb personal display.

Fulham had fallen behind to a gift goal scored by Grice after just ninety seconds following a disastrous error from Langley, but had fought back strongly to lead with goals from Dwight and Hill before John Bond had levelled things with a dubious and twice-taken penalty after sixty-five minutes.

Then, fifteen minutes from time, Haynes took Chamberlain's accurate cross in the inside left position before slipping the ball under goalkeeper Gregory from inside the corner of the penalty area as John Bond prepared to tackle, to notch the final goal in a 3–2 scoreline. The press enthused: "Haynes had a wonderful day, the complete tactician, backed up by Roy Bentley." This left Fulham as the only London club in the last eight.

Success generated success, and the following week's league game saw an emphatic 6–0 thrashing of Grimsby Town. Hill was superb, playing all over the pitch. An immaculate Haynes scored one of the goals, and Fulham looked the complete team.

Dwight hit the post in the first couple of minutes and Haynes was inches wide with a drive. Fulham then proceeded to score five in the space of twenty-three minutes in the first half, with Haynes netting the second goal, smashing in Hill's centre. Less than a minute later, a Haynes solo run created the third with a blockbuster from Chamberlain. Six minutes after that Haynes and Cook combined to give Hill a richly deserved fourth.

Johnny Haynes celebrates with Trevor Chamberlain, as West Ham's John Bond lies prostrate on the ground. Haynes has just scored the late winner at Upton Park, and the 3–2 victory swept Fulham into the FA Cup quarter-finals.

With next week's FA Cup quarter-final in mind, Fulham took it comparatively easy in the second half. Johnny's final contribution was to set up Dwight for the sixth goal ten minutes from the end. On a great day, all five forwards scored.

Roy Bentley recalls that happy time: "We used to go off to train in Worthing prior to a number of the cup games; we used to train very hard, but used to eat and drink very well as well [at the Warnes Hotel]. We all used to come back a lot heavier than when we had left, but I recall that every time we came back from Worthing we usually played a good game!"

March

With Fulham spirits soaring, Second Division opponents again came calling in the FA Cup quarter-final, when Bristol Rovers were beaten in front of another enormous 42,000 crowd at the Cottage. Rovers had disposed of a strong First Division Burnley side in the fourth round at Turf Moor, and had knocked neighbours City out in a seven-goal thriller in the fifth.

Fulham stormed into a three-goal lead before half-time, and then took their foot off the gas, allowing Bristol a consolation goal in a 3–1 win. Johnny Haynes' accurate pass and Arthur Stevens' cross in the tenth minute had paved the way for the first goal for Jimmy Hill who had been a doubtful starter, and he scored with a tremendous drive.

Three minutes later, Haynes combined with Hill and Trevor Chamberlain for Stevens to score. Haynes' through pass generated the third for thirty-seven-year-old veteran Stevens, allowing him a simple push-in goal. Haynes also turned defender in the second half, kicking a certain goal off the line with goalkeeper Macedo beaten.

One reporter observed: "This was match-winner Haynes at his brilliant best." Another said: "The accuracy of his passing in the first half was uncanny." Two days later, Second Division Fulham found out that they had been drawn to play First Division Manchester United at Villa Park in the semi-final.

On that same Monday, Johnny Haynes and Jim Langley played in the first leg of the drawn-out two-legged final of the Inter-Cities Fairs Cup at Stamford Bridge against CF Barcelona. After Jimmy Greaves had opened the scoring in the tenth minute, the London XI were only saved by a Langley penalty converted just two minutes from time, which made the score 2–2. Tony Macedo had also originally been selected, but was needed by the RAF for an important game and so couldn't register his first representative honour.

In their third consecutive home fixture, Fulham emerged victorious in a clear-cut 3–1 win over beaten fourth-round opponents Charlton. Haynes had never played better, with the energetic Hill turning his elegant

Alongside Barcelona's Enrique Ribelles, Haynes leads out the London XI at Stamford Bridge in March for the first leg of the Inter-Cities Fairs Cup final. This picture of Haynes wearing an unfamiliar badge on his chest was dug out from a Fleet Street archive where the print had suffered water damage resulting in some distortion.

passes into goals. High-flying Charlton did in fact score first. Then Maurice Cook veered away to the left taking a defender with him to provide an opening from which Haynes equalised. After Hill had put Fulham ahead, a frustrated Hewie fouled Haynes, which led to a free kick and a ferocious shot from Chamberlain that claimed the third and clinching goal.

With league fixtures piling up, Fulham beat Leyton Orient 3–1 at Brisbane Road on the following Thursday evening. Leyton held out until two minutes before the interval, when Roy Dwight scored from Haynes' pass. Although Orient levelled just after the break, Fulham won comfortably, and then had to play again two days later. Tired? Not a bit of it!

Five for Jimmy Hill at Doncaster

Just forty-eight hours later, Fulham took part in an amazing 6–1 win at now bottom Doncaster Rovers. Haynes didn't score, but as master tactician he certainly helped all the other players. He ripped the defence to shreds and had a hand in most of the goals.

It was a role reversal, Haynes cleverly trailing defenders with him out to the wings, leaving large gaps in the middle for others (especially Jimmy Hill) to exploit. The press said that Haynes' prompting was a big factor in the victory. After Cook had scored the first, Hill scored an amazing five consecutive goals to put himself firmly in the record book alongside such Fulham luminaries as Bedford Jezzard and Ronnie Rooke. It was a marvellous warm-up for the semi-final, and the headlines roared, "Watch out, United!"

Roy Bentley recalls the match well: "I think the coloured comedian Charlie Williams was centre half that day, and Johnny had a hand in every goal; some of them may have been tap-ins but they all counted. People very much undervalued Jimmy Hill's role in the side and he was one of the main reasons that Johnny Haynes could 'do his stuff'. He often took a lot of stick, but he never let it get to him. 'Give it to the Rabbi'—it would only spur him on; he would look at the crowd, stick out his chin and get on with it.

"They used to call Jimmy 'The Rover'. Jimmy was the best decoy you could have. He was very fit and could run all day. At times he was unbelievable and would run all over the place. He had a fantastic work rate and would often pull two defenders out of position. Even though he wasn't the most naturally gifted footballer, he created a lot of space on the field for Johnny Haynes to push those passes through."

Jimmy Hill (The Rover) was the man in form. Five goals at Doncaster were followed by a fine goal in the FA Cup semi-final at Villa Park.

The 1958 FA Cup semi-final

Villa Park

The semi-final was bound to be an emotional occasion, coming so soon after the Munich disaster, with the neutrals hoping for a First Division Manchester United victory. Survivor and England colleague Bobby Charlton played, as did Mark Pearson, later to become a Fulham player. There was a 70,000 crowd packed into Villa Park, and Fulham had a lot of backing, too, as underdogs. Villa Park seemed to be draped almost exclusively in black and white. Haynes won the toss and chose to play into a bitingly cold, strong wind, figuring that if Fulham could hold United until half-time, then they would take advantage in the second half.

Haynes was in his best form that day, playing truly superbly, breaking up United's attacks and setting his own forwards on the move. Charlton gave United the lead against the run of play. George Cohen takes up the story: "Johnny was stupendous that day both as a player and a leader; although we went a goal down, with players like him in the side there was no way we were going to roll over."

Stevens equalised for Fulham just a minute later with a lovely flick from Jim Langley's cunning run and centre. Then, in the thirty-eighth minute, Haynes began a movement from his own penalty area that found Dwight with a pass on the right. Dwight's cross led to Jimmy Hill gaining possession and riding a couple of tackles before sweeping the ball past Harry Gregg to put Fulham 2–1 into the lead. At this stage Haynes was sweeping passes everywhere. He and Hill were just dictating the game.

United became more physical, and some of their tackling was diplomatically described as unnecessarily heavy. In one bone-crunching encounter, left back Jim Langley was crippled by Alex Dawson. This was still before the era of substitutes, and it was clear that Langley was seriously hurt. Many considered this the turning-point in the game. Before Langley had even reached the dressing room for treatment, Charlton, during the period of disorganisation, again took advantage of a lucky defensive rebound from the unfortunate Cohen to score with a trademark rocket-like shot, levelling the scores.

In the second half, as no substitutes were permitted, Fulham's half back dropped to full back, and Johnny Haynes moved to left half, with Langley a makeshift 'nuisance' forward hanging out on the wing. Even in this position, Haynes excelled as a sharp-tackling wing half, but this limited his attacking abilities to a degree and some of the Fulham forward play lost its bite.

There were no further goals in the 2–2 game, although Tony Macedo made two brilliant saves from hotshot Charlton to deny him a hat trick, and Charlton also hit the bar; but Fulham's ten fit warriors attacked incessantly, and it was only the brilliance of Gregg in the United goal that ultimately denied Fulham a win.

Off to battle, from Euston to Birmingham for the cup semi-final at Villa Park. All smiles at their carriage window are Haynes, Hill and Bentley.

Roy Bentley said of that match: "Macedo was absolutely magnificent at Villa Park, diving parallel to the ground and just plucking balls out of the air. We really thought we had enough to beat them; in the end we were very unlucky."

A determined Haynes said after the match, "With a full strength team, we'll make the final." Fulham felt that they were unbeatable, unstoppable. They had remained in the capital for their entire FA Cup run up to then. The cup seemed to have their name on it, as it was back to London and Highbury for the replay. Fulham were now unbeaten in eleven matches.

Haynes and Langley had been selected for the Football League against the Scottish League, but as the international match coincided with the replay date, both players had to withdraw from the representative fixture.

Highbury

So it was off to Highbury on the Wednesday, and a crowd less than half the size of the one at Villa Park. Fulham sensed that it just might be their day. However, they were instantly uneasy on a heavy, wet, grassless pitch. Tony Macedo made a magnificent save in the first couple of minutes, but nineteen-year-old Alex Dawson scored an early goal for United, and Fulham's cause was further undermined when Roy Bentley took an early knock which limited his mobility.

Haynes then made a fine tackle and put through a superb pass for Arthur Stevens to score Fulham's equaliser. But gradually it appeared that it wasn't going to be Fulham's day, and Macedo, who had played so brilliantly to get Fulham to the semi-final, began to have a match to forget.

He failed to play in gloves and was responsible for the fumble which led to Dawson netting his and United's second, the ball just trickling in. Back came Fulham again, another foray, another goal, this time from Chamberlain. United looked stunned. Fulham began to gain the upper hand, but were shocked just seconds before half-time when Macedo inexplicably dropped the ball again, handing defender Shay Brennan the easiest of goals.

It looked all up for Fulham when Dawson completed his hat trick midway through the second half to give United a two-goal cushion. Far from it. Dwight pulled it back to a one-goal deficit in a slick move that involved Haynes, Stevens and Chamberlain, and Fulham were pushing United all the way.

Jim Langley was now feeling the effects of his recent injury but was playing on through gritted teeth. The defining moment came close to time. Haynes, from a move he started, breasted down the final cross and rammed the ball home. The referee wrongly penalised him for a handball that only he saw.

Whilst the arguments were still raging at one end, United broke away and Bobby Charlton galloped through in the last minute to seal the match with the final goal at the other. What would have been 4–4 a minute earlier, with the expectation of further drama, was now 3–5. Fulham were out and the ravaged Manchester United side were at Wembley. Even in Fulham's defeat, Haynes was the most influential player on the field.

Still promotion to go for

Despite the massive disappointment of the semi-final defeat, there was still promotion to fight for. Fulham were poised at fourth and had games in hand, but the backlog of games gave them a mountain to climb. Initially, they showed few signs of despair after the semi-final heartbreak, beating Huddersfield away from home in a 3–0 win. From Dwight's run and centre after twelve minutes, Haynes' well-taken shot went into the net off a post for the first goal. Haynes and Hill were adept at swinging the ball about. Fulham's surge had continued. The victory was their fifth consecutive league win and their fourth 'double' of the season.

April

But maybe tiredness and pressure were starting to tell. The encounter at Bristol Rovers on Good Friday marked Johnny Haynes' 200th league game for Fulham. In a game dominated by the wind, Fulham were two down in just nine minutes, but managed to get back to 2–2, with goals from Jimmy Hill and Roy Dwight. However, both Hill and Haynes fell below their normal high standards.

Fulham's backlog became worse, as the home game with Middlesbrough on Easter Saturday was postponed following a freak spell of weather including snow, sleet and rain. On Easter Monday, however, they looked revitalised with a comprehensive 3–0 win over the same mid-table Bristol Rovers at the Cottage.

Somehow surviving on pure willpower, Fulham kept it up the following week, winning at Stoke 2–1. Trevor Chamberlain scored one in only the third minute and made one, with Haynes conceding a penalty rather than winning one. The experience of Alex Forbes, making a rare appearance, nursed Fulham through defensively. Worrying, though, was the report that Haynes was very subdued, looking plainly tired.

But the facts didn't lie. Fulham had achieved seven wins and a draw in their last eight league matches, and had amassed twelve wins and suffered just two defeats in the last seventeen league games. The cup had been a bitter disappointment but promotion was now definitely on.

An optimistic Haynes left the Fulham team for a week whilst they contemplated a final promotion push. He joined the England squad alongside Jim Langley, called into the team for the first time, at left back; Bobby Charlton was also making his England debut.

England beat Scotland comprehensively 4–0 at Hampden Park, their biggest victory margin in Scotland for seventy years. It seemed that the team might just be able to overcome the emotions and traumas of Munich. Debutant Charlton combined well with Haynes and Finney to create the fourth goal for Derek Kevan a quarter of an hour from the end. Langley's debut was even more impressive, the press saying, "Langley—here to stay."

With Haynes and Langley away on international duty, Fulham looked completely impotent in the home match against lowly Bristol City; the team played disastrously and found themselves four goals down at home at half-time. The Fulham two on England duty heard the half-time score and couldn't believe it. Fulham were really out of sorts against the Bristol club and missing inspiration.

Tony Macedo was charged into the net with the ball in the first minute and that set the tone. Atyeo doubled the lead on just four minutes, and City's Tindill completed his hat trick before half-time. Somehow, in the second half Fulham pulled the game back to 3–4, but to no avail. The team just didn't look as if they had their heart in it when faced with spoiling tactics from the away side.

The rearranged fixture with Middlesbrough came just two days after this shock result. Fulham lost 0–1 thanks to an early goal by, inevitably, Brian Clough, again following a defensive mix-up. Roy Bentley was back but far from match fit, as was Jim Langley. The whole team looked tired and off-key and the stress was clearly showing on the faces of the players, who were very tense. Haynes, however, was still fighting every inch of the way.

The Cottagers were desperately unlucky not to get at least a point. Five times in the second half Haynes hammered in shots, all of which looked like goals. Each time Peter Taylor in the away goal got his long, lithe body across and in the way of the ball. Ten minutes from the end came controversy, when Chamberlain's goal-bound shot was deflected by an arm into the crowd by Middlesbrough full back Stonehouse. The Fulham players immediately surrounded referee Buckle demanding a penalty for hands which it was. Infuriatingly, the referee shook his head and awarded a corner, failing even to consult his on-the-spot linesman. The papers said: "Johnny Haynes just lost heart after seeing so many of his passes go astray."

Haynes is booked

Unbelievably, just forty-eight hours after that game, Fulham faced promotion rivals Blackburn Rovers in front of 32,000. This was the big one, the third home fixture in just five days. The tense and tired team, saddled with even more changes due to injury, cracked when the tension became simply too much.

The whole season hinged on this home fixture with fellow promotion chasers Blackburn. Rovers were five points in front, but Fulham had two games in hand. As feared, Fulham were without Bentley, Langley and Lowe. Fulham led with a twenty-fourth-minute Trevor Chamberlain goal, but seemed increasingly as if they were trying to protect their one-goal advantage—not in Fulham's style at all. Despite this approach they were ahead until the final five seconds, when the visiting centre forward, Johnston, charged keeper Macedo illegally and the ball flew from his arms for Blackburn's MacLeod to touch into the net. It looked a late challenge and an obvious foul. The linesman flagged for an offence, but the referee signalled a goal.

A furious captain Haynes asked the referee to consult the linesman, and it looked after a long discussion as if he had changed his mind, because the linesman confirmed that Macedo had been fouled, and the referee pointed towards the Fulham goalmouth for a free kick. A delighted Fulham broke away, and from Jimmy Hill's free kick almost increased their lead, but the place turned into utter confusion when the Fulham team suddenly realised that the referee had whistled again and that the goal still stood.

The press called it an extraordinary decision. The award of the goal provoked a near riot in the ground. Fulham players mobbed the referee and refused to restart the game, and three times the ball was knocked off the centre spot. Haynes, with an exemplary conduct sheet over several years, was now bitterly angry, and was finally booked by the referee for his sustained protests.

The match finished 1–1 and the result virtually guaranteed Blackburn's promotion at Fulham's expense. Haynes said afterwards, "Yes, he took my name and deservedly so. I was so mad that I was entitled to be sent off!" The referee, Smith of Newport, was smuggled out of the ground by a police escort to avoid an angry, baying mob massed at the main entrance of Craven Cottage.

Coming as it did just before the World Cup, the booking was seized on by the press, which had sometimes accused Haynes of being a football academic and purist but lacking fight. He replied, "Newspapermen are entitled to their own opinions, but I play every game to win, though it may not always look like that." He added ruefully, but with a smile, "I expect they'll now be saying I do too much fighting now—what with arguments with referees and what not."

Haynes misses out on promotion

Fulham knew that it was virtually all over, and at the end of an insane week, they travelled to Cardiff, to play their fourth league match in eight days. They lost 0–3 without putting up a great deal of fight after conceding two early goals. Haynes was described as still scintillating but the verdict on the whole Fulham team was "jaded".

Still they played on. Just two days after the long trip to Wales, Fulham embarked on another long haul to Bramall Lane. Fulham managed a 1–1 draw against Sheffield United on the Monday, thanks to an excellent Hill goal created by a centre from Stevens and a great ball down the line from—guess who?—Johnny Haynes. Unfortunately it wasn't enough.

May

Fulham played out their final game, against Rotherham United at Craven Cottage, in front of a meagre crowd of just 7,700 on a Thursday evening. They managed a comfortable 3–1 victory, but Haynes was omitted from the Fulham side, possibly in preparation for England's forthcoming World Cup campaign.

Haynes wasn't in the side for the second leg of the Inter-Cities Fairs Cup final either, this being played on the same day as the Rotherham match. Without him, the London XI were hammered 0–6 by CF Barcelona (all the Barcelona players reputedly being from the same club), and lost the final comprehensively 2–8 on aggregate.

After 1958, the Inter-Cities Fairs Cup was fought out amongst league sides, rather than sides made up from many teams constituting a city. The competition became the UEFA Cup in 1971. Haynes didn't particularly like the original set-up of players from many different teams, calling the inaugural competition "daft".

Close, but no cigar

Fulham had been forced to play their final nine vital league games (over 20% of the season's fixtures) in the space of just twenty-five days, and the last six in thirteen days, a match virtually every other day. It proved too much, and Haynes failed to find the net at all during those nine games.

"So, you've got here at last!" Is that what Fulham's skipper Haynes is thinking as he welcomes Scottish international winger Graham Leggat to his first Craven Cottage training session? After extended negotiations, Leggat left Aberdeen for Fulham at a reported fee of £17,000.

Fulham won only one of their last six vital matches, finishing fifth. The second of Haynes' dreams for the season had now bitten the dust. George Cohen said, "We finished four points short of promotion; the squad just didn't have the depth to cope with such a schedule."

Haynes, trying to contend with the international, representative and prolonged cup run matches, was clearly exhausted, and this Second Division scrap had not been, in his own words, ideal preparation for the World Cup tournament lying ahead—now only a few weeks away. His goal tally in the league since the New Year had been just four.

In terms of statistics, it seemed that this had been another 'groundhog day' season, a disappointment after promising so much early on. Haynes, pushing through a conveyor-belt of passes, had inspired his side to a massive 115 league and cup goals, but they had still managed to concede 70. At least the difference between 'for' and 'against' had been greater this year!

Despite all these disappointments it was clear that things were on the move at Craven Cottage, and perhaps the bitter experiences of this season could be turned into a positive weapon for the next one.

Graham Leggat arrives

Roy Dwight had scored fifty goals for Fulham in just two seasons, so Fulham did what they usually did—and promptly sold him to First Division Nottingham Forest for a paltry £4,000, although some reports said that it was for a significant fee. The following year, Dwight played in the FA Cup final that had eluded him in 1958, and scored the first goal in Forest's 2–1 victory over Luton Town. However, after thirty-three minutes he broke his leg in a tackle and was never fully the same player again.

Dwight's replacement at Fulham, Scotsman Graham Leggat, would prove a significant addition. After "protracted enquiries" and several refusals, Fulham finally got their man for £17,000. The Aberdeen manager said privately that Fulham had secured themselves a real bargain.

How right he was!

13: The 1958 World Cup

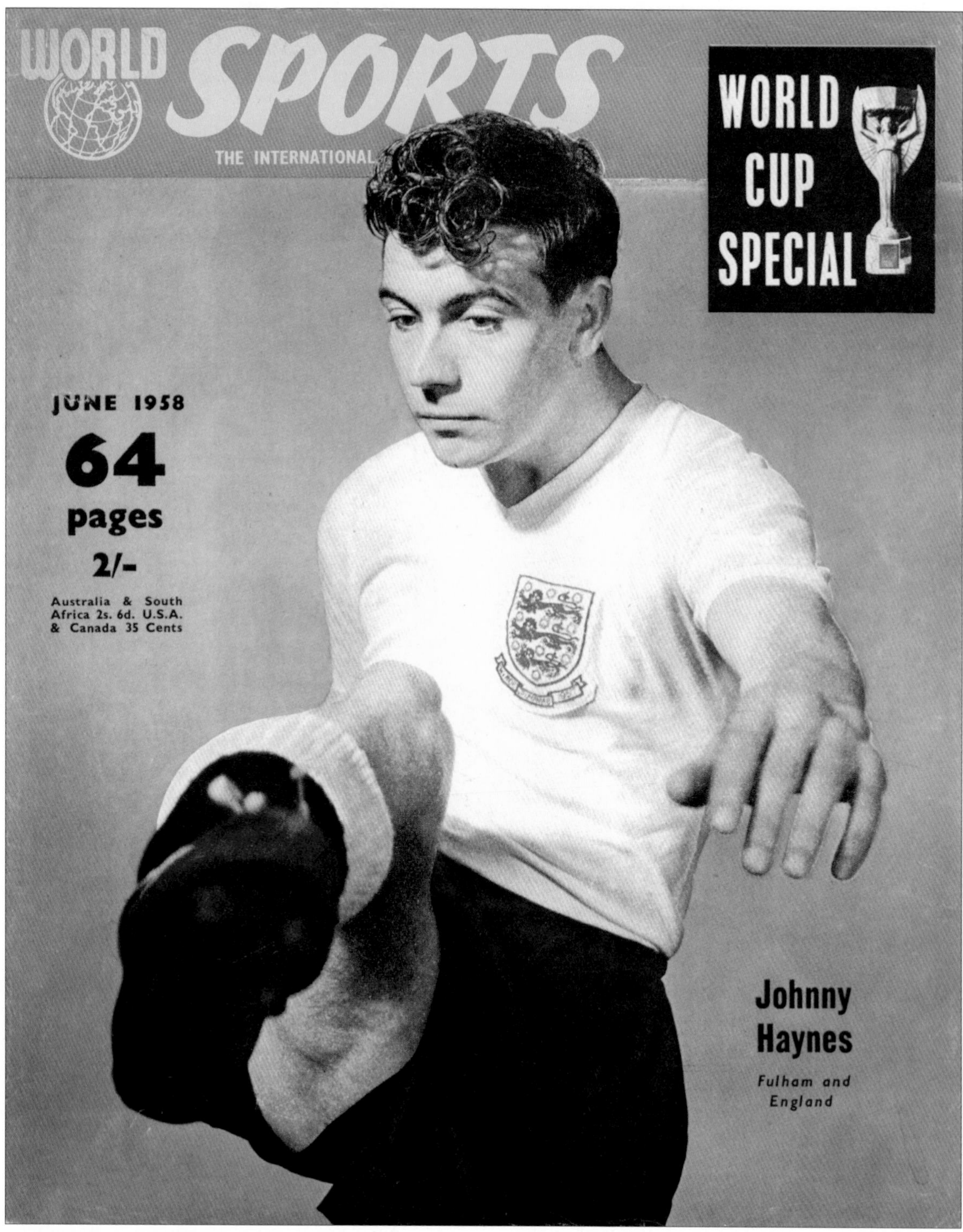

13: The 1958 World Cup

The spark that had been building in the England team seemed to disappear completely from their play during three pre-World Cup summer matches.

May

Johnny Haynes and Jim Langley played in the first two. First, England scraped home 2–1 against a mediocre Portugal side at Wembley, where they played very poorly and were extremely lucky to get a result. England's goals were scored by Bobby Charlton, who would repeat the feat and score in a far more important encounter eight years later. Only Portugal's reluctance to shoot saved England's blushes. A jaded Haynes was pretty inconspicuous, but he did rattle the bar with one thunderbolt. Jim Langley had an excellent game, kicking efforts off the line, but blotted his copybook a little by missing a second-half penalty.

England were then thrashed 0–5 by Yugoslavia. They were only one goal behind at half-time, but the Yugoslavians had already hit the bar, seen three goals disallowed for offside, and witnessed goalkeeper Eddie Hopkinson make several good saves. The home side also managed to miss a host of chances.

Fulham's Jim Langley was surprisingly made a scapegoat for this defeat, as the player he was marking, a difficult winger named Petakovic, claimed a second-half hat trick in only twenty-seven minutes, and Langley never played for England again.

The England performance was savaged by the press, but Haynes said: "We played on the hottest day on which I have ever played anywhere at any time, and that includes South America and Mexico. I cannot recall experiencing such playing conditions ever before or since. On such a day of heat and humidity thirty minutes play could drain you of all physical energy."

Yugoslavia reduced the game to walking pace and England were embarrassed trying to stop the hosts playing keep-ball. With the temperature at ninety in the shade, three Yugoslavian goals came in the last twelve minutes but that statistic wasn't good enough to satisfy the England critics. An exhausted Haynes looked ordinary, and barely merited a mention. Winterbottom candidly admitted, "We were outclassed."

England then put in a far better performance against the Russians in a third friendly a week later in Moscow but slipped to a 1–1 draw. Russian forward Ivanov clearly handled before scoring Russia's goal. Derek Kevan gave England the lead just before half-time, and it looked like being good enough until the handled goal. The linesman instantly flagged for the offence, but the referee, forty yards behind the play, over-ruled him. England captain Billy Wright chased the official and registered a strong verbal protest, but the referee had his ears firmly closed to any arguments. England also hit the woodwork twice through Robson and Finney. Once again, Haynes had a very quiet game.

Haynes could feel his form starting to dip, and admitted that he had played poorly on a hard, bumpy surface. The results from this tour would prove hard to shake off. Surprisingly, the England squad then returned to England and remained at home right to the last minute before travelling to Sweden.

England had qualified for the World Cup at the expense of Denmark and the Republic of Ireland and had to face two of the favourites, but they were fairly confident of turning over both Russia and Austria. The quickly rebuilt post-Munich team was thrown to the lions, but in Haynes' words, they "gave it all they had."

The group matches

June

The 1958 World Cup in Sweden saw the tournament receive international TV coverage for the first time, and Pelé made his bow on the global stage.

England's first World Cup game against the Soviet Union on June 8th proved a physical battle and ended in a creditable draw. The Russians, who had over thirty fouls awarded against them, had made many changes to the team that had drawn with England in the friendly three weeks previously. Soviet captain Nikita Simonian put his side ahead, Alexander Ivanov made it 2–0 after the break, and with only twenty minutes left England looked to be in real trouble.

However, Derek Kevan began England's fightback with a fine headed goal, and then Haynes got into the act, inducing an injudicious tackle from full back Voinov that he "made the most of." The flop into the area earned England a dubious penalty that allowed Tom Finney, a doubtful starter, to coolly level the scores from the penalty spot with six minutes remaining. Russian goalkeeper Yashin clearly manhandled the referee following the penalty decision and was lucky to remain on the field.

It wasn't all good fortune for England, however, as Bobby Robson had what looked like a perfectly good goal ruled out for a foul by Kevan on Yashin. Johnny Haynes had not been particularly effective. However, England had taken a point in a 2–2 draw. Fate conspired against England, and the match proved to be Finney's last contribution, as he was ruled out of the rest of the tournament with a knee injury.

Some papers suggested that Haynes had been totally ineffective, and a split in the selectors seemed to be emerging. The papers even suggested that his place for the next game might be in jeopardy, and there were arguments against him playing. In the end, a strong-willed Winterbottom got his way, and Haynes played.

The next group game, against a Pelé-less Brazil, ended as a 0–0 stalemate and was the first goalless draw ever in World Cup history. The game was televised on Eurovision. Haynes did produce one memorable through pass in the twentieth minute which might have decided the game, but it was not to be. The ball found Kevan and he was hauled back in the area with a two-armed grab. The referee, poorly positioned, saw no foul and awarded no penalty. Haynes also had a shot brilliantly pushed out by the Brazilian goalkeeper after Kevan had chipped the ball back to him.

By the end of the tournament England were the only team that Brazil failed to score against or beat. It was another creditable result, but it meant that England needed to win their final group game against Austria to be absolutely sure of progressing to the quarter-finals.

Haynes had a much improved game in the match against Brazil, though he picked up a leg injury late in the game. But the improvement wasn't enough for some. A brave, nameless England selector called for Haynes to be dropped for the final group game, saying, "If I have my way, Haynes goes." Other selectors dropped thinly veiled hints purporting to be the general mood of the selection panel. One described Haynes as stale; another said, "He has played too much football lately—he is played out." The general consensus was that the forward line was just not clicking, and that the passing and shooting were not up to standard. Nevertheless, Haynes took his place against Austria.

Haynes' only World Cup goal

The Austrians, who had failed to score in their previous two games, got off to a great start with Karl Koller's lucky strike early on when a shot rebounded to him off Billy Wright. Haynes replied with a goal just before the hour: A'Court's shot, following a quick free kick from Wolves' Bill Slater, bounced off the goalkeeper, leaving him to smash the ball into an empty net. Alfred Korner then restored the lead for Austria with another untidy, scrambled goal from a corner, which crept in off a post with just seventeen minutes to go. Fortunately Kevan equalised a minute later. Haynes bored through and from his excellent pass, Kevan hammered in off the goalkeeper's body to make the score 2–2 and send Walter Winterbottom's side into a play-off with the Soviet Union.

Even then the result had been a travesty. England had played well, and had the vast majority of the possession but none of the luck. Haynes alone had sent in four shots in the second half, two brilliantly saved. Five minutes from time Bobby Robson was denied yet again when he breasted down a cross and thundered the ball home only to be penalised, once again incorrectly, by the Dutch referee for handball. Haynes' goal was to be his only one in a World Cup tournament.

A play-off—and out

England were eventually beaten 0–1 by Russia after being forced to play their fourth game in ten days. Haynes was now running on empty, and he was shackled from the start by tight and sometimes unfair marking. He hardly contributed, and admitted later that "for all the use I was, I might as well have stayed in the dressing room."

Even in this game Lady Luck turned firmly away from Haynes and England. England debutant Peter Brabrook hit the post twice, and both times the ball contrived to stay out. In one Russian breakaway twenty minutes from the end, they, too, hit the post, but this time the ball went in. That was the solitary difference. Brabrook also had a goal ruled out, the third time in four World Cup matches when England had been penalised in this way. Even when England did break through, they found Lev 'The Lion' Yashin in the Russian goal in unbeatable form. England were out of the competition without losing a group stage match.

Haynes felt a great deal of sympathy for the England manager. It was his view for a long time afterwards that England could, and possibly should, have won the World Cup in 1958, but for the loss in Munich earlier that year of the three crucial players: left back Roger Byrne, the peerless Duncan Edwards in midfield, and centre forward Tommy Taylor. Later in life he reflected, "If we hadn't lost those three, I'm sure we would have gone at least very close, quite probably have won."

The first criticisms emerge

Since so much of the England team's game flowed through Haynes, when he struggled, the side in general also toiled. He thought the players had done the best they could, and considering everything, he thought he himself had played 'reasonably well', but below his imperious best. He had suffered from badly blistered feet caused by the bone-hard pitches in Sweden, and had been in great pain; it certainly had limited his effectiveness. He did, however, have the honesty to admit after the competition that he hadn't been on the best form of his life.

There was another side to that opinion waiting for him on his return. The press hammered the England team's performances, labelling Haynes ('Winterbottom's favourite') and Blackburn's Bryan Douglas, who had also endured a marathon league season, as the "failures of the trip".

A barrage of criticism was aimed at the selectors, and Winterbottom was personally criticised for the inflexibilities and inadequacies of the forward line and his apparent unwillingness to make changes (especially his reluctance to include Bobby Charlton), when it was pretty obvious where the problems were. There was significant tension between Winterbottom and the press corps. It was a difficult time for him, but later in life he had the courage to say, "Basically, if Johnny was fit during my time in charge, he played."

Haynes was the established inside left around whom England's attack had been built over the last two years, yet he had rarely been able to impress his personality upon this World Cup. Often he was to be found deep among his own defenders and, indeed, old newspaper photographs of most goals scored against England in Sweden show him working almost as a wing half back.

This positional play particularly surprised the Brazilians, who rated him as England's most dangerous

A welcome break away from the rigours of football. A relaxed Haynes is photographed on holiday in Jersey in July with girlfriend Eileen Farmer. Even though on holiday, Haynes still found time to take part in an inter-hotel sports event at St Helier's Springfield ground.

forward after his show against them at Wembley in 1956. Logically, there could be no possible excuse for stationing the brain of the attack almost permanently in the defence.

Following Finney's enforced departure, this wasn't the best England team technically, especially in the forward line, and Haynes had been forced to indulge in a lot of short passing and speculative shooting because of the forwards' failure to pull away from the massed ranks of defenders or to find the right space to receive the killer pass.

The rockets from the press surprised and upset Haynes, who felt the media had little sympathy for the hastily assembled line-up following Munich. It wouldn't be the last World Cup post mortem.

He realised that with a fraction of luck against Russia in the play-off match, it might have been a totally different story. He inveighed against "those in the TV booths" who considered themselves experts. He withstood all the accusations of the English media, but he said, "If you [England] win, faults are forgiven and forgotten; if you lose, faults are magnified and hammered at you relentlessly." As a professional player, he was asking himself what sporting qualifications you needed to become a TV sports commentator.

Even today, decades later, little appears to have changed, and his comments still seem entirely appropriate for the modern press and TV pundits.

Haynes was not yet twenty-four, and for the first time he was feeling a backlash at the highest level. He was concerned that the press seemed to think that the England team should win every game, despite the significant improvement in world football that had taken place over the past twenty to thirty years.

The three great hopes that Haynes had cherished for the season—promotion to the First Division, the FA Cup final and England success—had all tantalisingly slipped like sand through his fingers at the final hour. There was no doubt that a long rest was needed. He did just this, and allowed himself nearly a full month of self-imposed solitude in Jersey.

However, during the World Cup he was being watched and tracked, and the first Italian scouts and money-men were filtering into Britain awash with funds to lure English players to Italy, as it was widely rumoured that the laws restricting entry of 'foreign players' into that country were soon to be relaxed.

Haynes realised, without any doubt, that as a celebrity, a player with his own newspaper column (which upset a number of journalists!), and his face on the billboards, he was there to be shot at. Fame had come at a price and any indiscretions on or off the field were fair game for the journalists. By now there were two distinct camps; he had his fans as well as his detractors. There seemed to be no middle ground: you either liked him, or you didn't.

14: Balls, Brylcreem and breakfast

14: Balls, Brylcreem and breakfast

It has to be made clear that, unlike today's football agents, Bagenal Harvey was Johnny Haynes' agent only for his peripheral, commercial activities. Any serious footballing contract dealings with Fulham FC were negotiated by Haynes himself.

Haynes was very much the prototype of the modern footballer; he had 100% trust in his agent, who had represented him since 1956. It was a friendly relationship, and Harvey didn't adopt the airs of a *monstre sacré* and wasn't seen as the power or driving force behind his client. Haynes admitted that Harvey had put countless opportunities his way and led him through "an intricate maze of business offers and contracts." Harvey was an early exponent of image rights; he knew the value of Haynes' name, signature and picture.

Haynes' friend and agent, Bagenal Harvey, was a genial man who successfully negotiated Johnny's off-field commercial activities.

Haynes readily admitted that worrying over all the business details could have affected his playing form, so he was happy to leave matters to an expert. He candidly admitted, "We all want to make as much money as we can, while we can—can you blame us?" Bagenal Harvey also represented Denis Compton, Haynes' cricketer hero, and Haynes used his celebrity status to invade the world of advertising.

The Brylcreem Boy

In his words: "One of the most lucrative deals Harvey ever clinched for me was succeeding Compo as the Brylcreem Boy." Haynes became the nationally recognisable face of the hair-grooming product in the late 1950s. As the Brylcreem Boy pin-up with his glossy hairstyle, his face adorned newspapers, advertising hoardings, the flanks of buses and the London Underground.

The Brylcreem promotions also made their way on to television, and it was common to see Haynes combing his hair to an overdubbed commentary during those days of 405-line TV. His smoothly-oiled hair became the mark of the smart young man of the day. He said, "Frankly, it embarrassed me. I didn't own a car so travelling around by Underground and bus I was always seeing those pictures of myself."

What a sheen! Johnny Haynes, the new Brylcreem boy—and not a hair out of place. The contract earned him 50% more than his annual salary—for just three days' work!

Who can forget the Fifties jingle: "*Brylcreem—a little dab'll do ya; Brylcreem—you'll look so debonair. Brylcreem—the girls will all pursue ya; they'll love to run their fingers through your hair*"?

He was ribbed mercilessly in the dressing room by his Fulham colleagues, including Jimmy Hill and Bobby Robson. He went on to say, "I got plenty of stick from my fellow players, as you can imagine but, yes, my bank manager and me, we laughed all the way."

He could afford to laugh, since at the time of the maximum wage he could earn 50% more than his annual salary for a three-day photo shoot. He described it as amazing and confirmed: "Where I made the big money was doing ads for Brylcreem—I succeeded cricket's illustrious Denis Compton selling the hair cream with my picture on the billboards and in the papers. For three hours of photography for those posters I'd get £1,500 and I did them for three years."

"After training, or a hard match, nothing replaces energy so well as a long drink of milk." If you say so, Johnny! His contract with the Milk Marketing Board was another lucrative sideline.

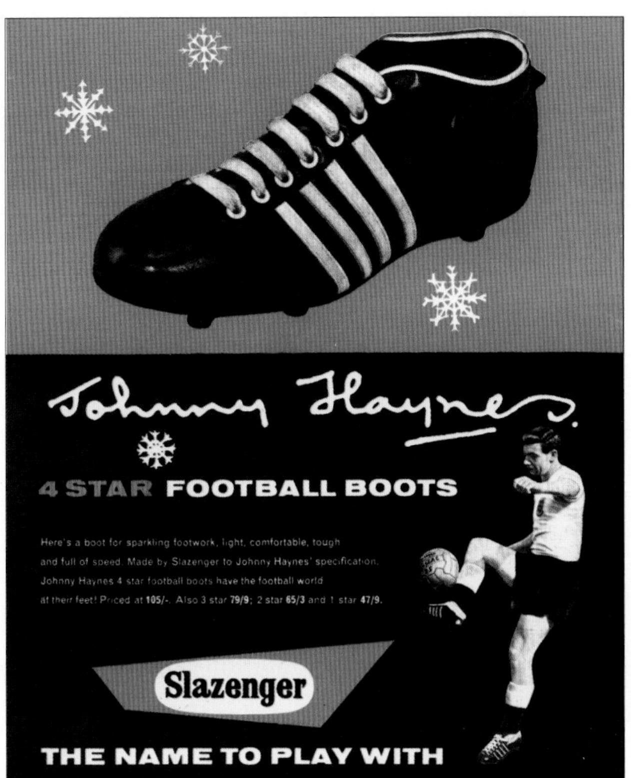

Boots were yet another of Haynes' endorsements.

Johnny and his parents had now left north London and settled in leafy Epsom in Surrey. Here he returns from training to Mum's home cooking.

Fulham fan Freddie Walker recalls the occasion when, as captain of the football team at Sir John Lilley primary school in Fulham, he was taken, with three other lads, to Craven Cottage to take part in a Brylcreem commercial. The four boys were filmed running up to Haynes as he emerged from the players' entrance after training. The commercial appeared many times on television. Freddie's 'payment' for the filming was an autograph from the great man—a souvenir which he still has, of course. Freddie remembers Haynes as taking it all in his stride, but being "a little aloof."

Haynes wasn't alone, of course, as a personality in advertising; Spurs' Danny Blanchflower extolled Shredded Wheat, and Wolves' Billy Wright waxed

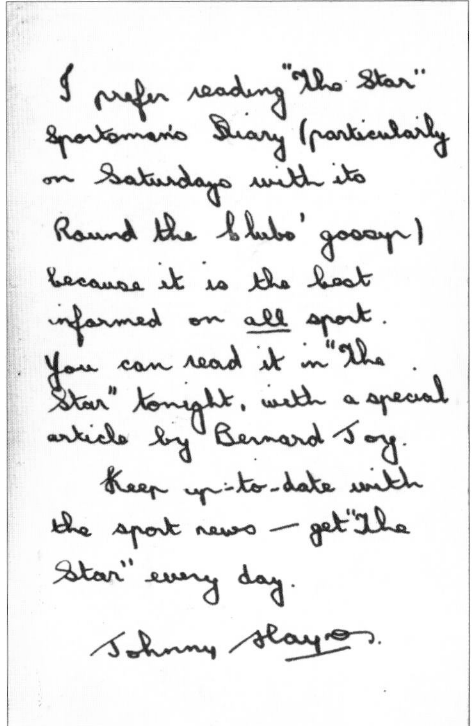

I prefer reading "The Star" Sportsman's Diary (particularly on Saturdays with its Round the Clubs' gossip) because it is the best informed on all sport. You can read it in "The Star" tonight, with a special article by Bernard Joy.

Keep up-to-date with the sport news — get "The Star" every day.

Johnny Haynes.

This postcard type of advertising was distributed outside the Craven Cottage ground in the early 1960s.

Haynes had a healthy regimen, which was closely monitored by his pet budgerigar.

lyrical over Lucozade. Haynes also had a lucrative promotional contract with the Milk Marketing Board.

Home comforts

The cash was rolling in, and later in life Haynes said, "I was pretty rich. For God's sake, I had a decent car!" Rumours abound that it took him three attempts to pass his driving test, but when he finally did, he became the owner of a brand new red MG Midget car, and it was his pride and joy. Although he was no mechanic, he was certainly interested in the car's exterior and was only too happy to turn up at functions or at the Winchmore Hill Cricket Club social evenings to show it off.

He didn't abuse his commercial contracts as some do nowadays. He never actually maximised his promotional earnings, and at his peak frequently turned down appearances, endorsements and articles. He said at the time, "My agent keeps me busy, and I could be busier, but I will not take on too much or I will never have any spare time."

With money flowing in from promotions and endorsements, he had moved away from north London and settled in Woodcote Park Road in Epsom, a pleasant suburb in leafy Surrey. He was a twenty-three-year-old bachelor with a comfortable home and a nice car. He made sure that he repaid his parents, who had done everything for him and had assisted him in every move throughout his career. He bought the house, apparently with the club's assistance, and his parents moved in with him.

Haynes' only extravagance was a pet budgerigar, which before long had learned to say "Good old Fulham!" His mum looked after his daily diet, which usually consisted of boiled eggs, toast, marmalade and—lemonade. After a day's work, John's motto was that home cooking's the best, and he couldn't wait to return for his favourite meal—Rose's steak and kidney pudding.

Roy Bentley recalls the young starlet: "John loved the crooners, and loved Frank Sinatra, and his dress and hairstyle were modelled on that of Sinatra. In fact he was often mistaken for him—and he loved that. He used to enjoy himself and was a very good looking lad, but he was never really aware of it.

"He never thought of himself as a pin-up. He would listen to the exploits of others, but certainly wasn't, even at the height of his fame, a ladies' man. In South Africa he probably made up for lost time a bit and discovered what he'd missed when devoting himself so much to football!"

"METTOY WEMBLEY VINYL FOOTBALLS

ARE IDEAL FOR TRAINING AND PRACTICE GAMES"

says Johnny Haynes

THEY ARE RE-INFLATABLE, REPAIRABLE, TOUGH AND WILL STAND UP TO ANY CONDITIONS AND TREATMENT, AND OF COURSE ARE IDEAL FOR YOUNGSTERS

Wembley Official size* 7/3** *in plastic net bag; in poly bag,* ***6/9.
Wembley Regulation *(Correct Football Weight)* ***10/6;*** *in tan or white.*

SEE THE VAST RANGE OF ***METTOY PLAYBALLS*** AT YOUR SPORTS SHOP ***NOW***

FULHAM

White Shirts, Black Shorts.

R **Tony Macedo** L

2 **George Cohen** 3 **Jim Langley**

This advertisement in which Haynes endorsed Mettoy footballs was a regular and familiar feature on the centre pages of the club programme for many years.

15: Hat tricks and promotion 1958–59

15: Hat tricks and promotion — 1958–59

Bedford Jezzard is the new manager

Bedford Jezzard at thirty was promoted and appointed as team manager after Dugald Livingstone returned to his native north to manage Chesterfield. His wife had failed to settle in the south, and was already back there. Fulham now boasted their youngest-ever manager and their youngest-ever captain. However, this move had not been a natural progression.

Roy Bentley describes how it came about: "Beddy hesitated in taking the job initially with so many having been his team-mates and with players older and more experienced than he was still playing in the team, like Eddie Lowe. So the senior pros got together, and we all said we need to let him know, tell him, so I went to inform him that all the squad were right behind him and we wanted him to take the job!"

In the Whites versus Colours pre-season trial, Haynes looked in good trim, and even more determined to achieve success. As usual the first team won, this time 3–1. Haynes did most of the shooting, as if he had mentally prepared himself to score more goals that season. He equalised an early Colours goal with a low shot underneath the reserve goalkeeper Ken Hewkins.

Jezzard wouldn't be drawn on promotion, saying simply, "I don't like prophesying. I only hope the boys play as well this season as they did last term. We had about our best season ever then. I can only say that I hope we do as well this time."

What a start for Fulham!

August

The season started in spectacular fashion for Fulham, and the club went on to lose only one of their first seventeen league matches. Stoke City were let off lightly in the opening match, with just a 6–1 score against them. Johnny Haynes scored probably the fastest opening goal of the season, finding the net in under forty-five seconds. A strong run by Jim Langley produced a corner, which he took himself. The corner led to a Jimmy Hill knockdown and a sweet Haynes volley, a hard shot all along the ground into the net.

Haynes was still receiving some stick following the 1958 World Cup, cynics alleging that he was unable to draw out or beat defenders; it was almost as if he had something to prove. His repeated mazy runs had the Stoke defenders on the wrong foot

Previous page: Ready for the new season. Back row: Lowe, Cohen, Bentley, Macedo, Stapleton, Langley; front: Leggat, Hill, Cook, Haynes, Chamberlain.

JOHNNY HAYNES

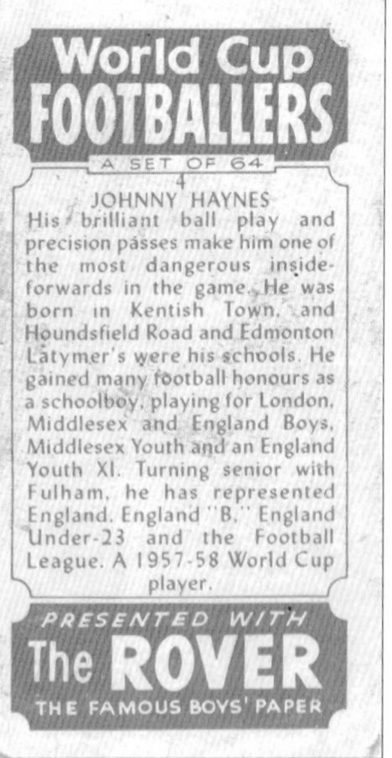

World Cup
FOOTBALLERS
A SET OF 64
4
JOHNNY HAYNES
His brilliant ball play and precision passes make him one of the most dangerous inside-forwards in the game. He was born in Kentish Town, and Houndsfield Road and Edmonton Latymer's were his schools. He gained many football honours as a schoolboy, playing for London, Middlesex and England Boys, Middlesex Youth and an England Youth XI. Turning senior with Fulham, he has represented England, England "B," England Under-23 and the Football League. A 1957-58 World Cup player.
PRESENTED WITH
The ROVER
THE FAMOUS BOYS' PAPER

throughout and totally demoralised. The national press remarked that Stoke had no answer to his scheming.

The much-criticised Maurice Cook scored a hat trick, his second goal from a Haynes pass and his third after combined work from debutant Graham Leggat and Haynes. Fulham were six up before an hour had passed. Haynes had a superb match, and gave direct answers to those who said that he was not world class; many had never seen him have a better game. The local press observed, "His passing was so accurate, that you could have plotted a ship's course by it!"

This was followed in midweek by a 2–1 win at Sunderland. A Haynes shot was charged down and the follow-up was converted by Leggat for the first goal, and an excellent Haynes pass out to the wing secured the winner for Trevor Chamberlain.

Leggat returned the compliment in a 2–1 win at Swansea, where Haynes set Fulham on the road to victory in the eighth minute, cracking the ball in from six yards after Swans goalkeeper King had parried a Leggat corner. The headline was, "Haynes unlocks the door." Fulham were already the only Second Division team with a 100% record.

A hat trick and Haynes approaches his zenith

September

This sensational start blossomed even further in the return midweek match with Sunderland at Craven Cottage. Fulham were behind to an early goal, and were still trailing for almost half an hour before Haynes levelled. Graham Leggat and Jimmy Hill combined and when the defender failed to control the centre, Haynes stepped in to beat goalkeeper Fraser from close range. Immediately Fulham went behind again, and they trailed at the interval.

In the second half, Fulham scored three in the first fifteen minutes; Trevor Chamberlain capitalised on a defensive blunder and then Haynes grabbed two to complete his hat trick. First he back-heeled Leggat's centre past the goalkeeper with a classy flick, and then he scored the best goal of the night.

He surged through on a forty-yard run, took a return pass from Cook and fired home a blistering cross-shot. A Leggat goal and a Jim Langley penalty in the last five minutes produced Fulham's second successive six-goal haul at the Cottage. Haynes was magnificent on the night, an evening where everything went right, and he couldn't put a foot wrong. The press reported: "Sunderland taken by storm—Haynes reaches his zenith."

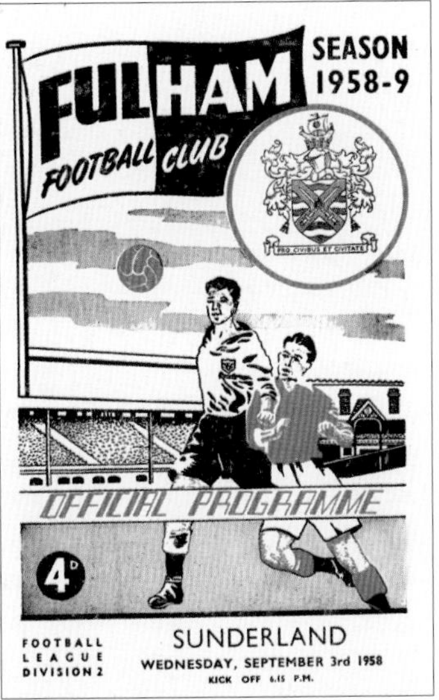

An early-season 'golden match', where Haynes could do no wrong.

He described the encounter as a golden match, and said: "I felt that I could do exactly as I pleased with the Sunderland defence. Three goals came my way and I walked off with that indescribable inner glow that lights up a man when he knows he has done his job to the absolute maximum of his capacity. These moments do not come so often in life."

He then recorded another goal, the first in a 3–2 home win over Ipswich Town. The game was played in sweltering conditions and even Haynes was, for once, badly affected by the heat. In truth, it was a tired performance and a lucky win.

Fulham went a goal behind in the twelfth minute, but equalised straight from the kick-off. Hill's square free kick-cum-pass was beautifully directed into the net by Haynes with a crashing shot that went in off a post past goalkeeper Bailey. Ipswich forced the lead for a second time but Maurice Cook levelled. Finally, another slick move between Hill and Haynes saw the ball swung into the middle for Leggat to score a winner with only three minutes remaining.

Haynes posted another goal in the 4–2 win at bottom club Lincoln City in midweek. Surprisingly, Fulham were two down at the interval, but after an astute change of tactics from manager Jezzard, they were rampant in the second half. Haynes created the first for Leggat with a lovely pass just on the hour, and scored the equaliser ten minutes later after solid work from Hill.

It was Haynes again who repeated the movement for Leggat to put Fulham into the lead for the first time with eight minutes to go, and Chamberlain's solo run and shot in the last seconds confirmed the win.

Bristol Rovers finally managed to stop the Fulham goal-machine with a 0–0 draw, despite Haynes hitting the bar. Fulham also failed with a twice-taken penalty. Langley successfully converted the first, only for the referee to rule against Leggat for encroachment. When Langley re-took the spot-kick, he hit the post.

Haynes hits four in a match

Haynes' golden boots were very much in evidence when Fulham played the return match against struggling Lincoln City at Craven Cottage. He netted

Johnny Haynes gives the Lincoln goalkeeper Thompson no chance with a shot from a narrow angle. It was the first of four that the Fulham star scored that day, in another convincing personal and team performance. Fulham won the encounter 4–2.

his first in the seventh minute following a one-two with Maurice Cook, with a first-time low shot from an acute angle, and then doubled the lead on the half-hour from a Leggat and Chamberlain move. Lincoln somehow clawed their way back to level terms, but Haynes was unruffled, and midway through the second half he collected his hat trick. Seven minutes from the end he claimed an individual fourth goal after Chamberlain's shot had hit the post, producing a final score of 4–2. It was the first time Haynes had ever scored four goals in a senior match, and it put his name in the record books.

He scores goals of the season against Derby

Still it continued, although things looked bleak at home to Derby County at 1–2, with just over thirty minutes remaining. Star striker Leggat was injured after just ten minutes, and Fulham were playing with ten men after half-time. It was left to Haynes to show his colleagues how to turn defeat into victory.

Alongside a goal for Cook, he contrived to net two of the best goals he had ever scored; goals that were talked about for a considerable time afterwards. Ten minutes after the interval, he chased a forlorn pass from Hill and caught it, then took the ball virtually half the length of the field through the left in a dazzling run, leaving three lunging defenders trailing in his wake, before slotting past the advancing keeper into the corner of the net from an impossible position. Two minutes later, Fulham had the lead from Jim Langley.

Haynes' second just eight minutes from time, which gave Fulham a 4–2 victory, was almost a carbon copy of his first. Receiving another through pass from Hill, he left several defenders on their backsides in a swerving run, this time waltzing around the goalkeeper to score the clincher from the acutest of angles. The goal was described as amazing, and was already being hailed as the goal of the season. It inspired an almost unprecedented headline: "Ten men and a genius."

To bring the month to a close, Leyton Orient were beaten 2–0 on their own ground in another first-class Fulham performance. Haynes had already amassed *thirteen* goals, and many centre forwards would have been happy with that total for their entire season. Fulham were clear at the top of the table, with an amazing nineteen points out of twenty.

Haynes wins his 25th England cap

October

Johnny Haynes was much in the news, and this month he reached the next milestone in his career when he was awarded his twenty-fifth cap for England, which, like his first and second, came in a match against Northern Ireland. A pulsating and exhilarating game, played in appalling conditions in Belfast on a virtually waterlogged pitch, ended 3–3.

England hauled themselves back three times from being a goal behind to force the draw. Bobby Charlton scored their first and third goals that day, both from stunning passes by Haynes. The media were quick to point out that Haynes had done enough to quieten his critics with a sound display.

Amazingly, despite this game and his consistently stunning performances in the league, there remained some shaking of heads in other quarters. After the recent World Cup, some of the nine England selectors were definitely anti-Haynes.

They were genuinely upset that the England team was seemingly being built around him. The 'Haynes factor' was also being discussed in boardrooms by the game's petty-minded *éminences grises*, mostly First Division chairmen, directors and managers. Many of them were pushing the opinion that he shouldn't play in the forthcoming match against the Russians.

A fair amount of abuse was being directed his way. He was, amongst other things: over-rated, not in the same class as some of the England inside forwards of the past, and not a ninety-minute worker, and he was attracting the limelight solely because he was with a London club. There were further signs of northern influence as there were calls for a regular place for Bobby Charlton and Brian Clough instead of Haynes.

Haynes the journalist upsets the FA

Then, as usual, something had to come up. Haynes wrote about the recent England versus Northern Ireland international game in his column for the *Daily Express*. The comments were all complimentary, and he discussed individual players and tactics. Yet even this apparently fell foul of the FA rules, which stipulated that a player couldn't comment on matches in which he had taken part. He was given a mild rebuke by the FA. His detractors in the media decided to home in on this punishment, some absurdly suggesting that he had talked his way out of the forthcoming Russian match and should be dropped.

More controversy followed. The BBC *Sportsview* commentary team, in a stunt aimed at the men at the top, omitted Haynes from their team, rehashing the brickbats thrown at him after the World Cup in Gothenburg.

They boldly expressed the view that England were a better team without him, and that he was not much of a player. This assault was led by the cheesy Kenneth ("They think it's all over") Wolstenholme who, in Haynes' opinion, knew little about football and was someone he never particularly warmed to.

Whilst Haynes was away with England, Fulham had entertained Scunthorpe United. In a lacklustre performance, Graham Leggat's goal salvaged a 1–1 draw, Fulham losing their 100% home record. The press were very unkind to the Cottagers, suggesting that Fulham without Haynes resembled a flock of sheep without their shepherd; he was missed as a forager, sharpshooter and link man. They said: "To say he was missed generally was the understatement of the year. His shadow haunted the game!"

FOOTBALL ASSOCIATION INTERNATIONAL
ENGLAND
V
U.S.S.R.
WEDNESDAY, OCTOBER 22nd, 1958 KICK-OFF 2.30 pm
EMPIRE STADIUM
WEMBLEY
OFFICIAL PROGRAMME - ONE SHILLING

Haynes answers the critics in fine style, as he cracks home one of his three goals against the Russians at Wembley. The 5–0 victory was sweet revenge for the World Cup play-off defeat.

Fulham forced another draw the following week, 2–2 with Grimsby at Blundell Park. Fulham were quickly two goals down. Jim Langley pulled one back, and then a Haynes, Robin Lawler and Roy Bentley move was expertly finished off by Trevor Chamberlain. Fulham then took command, with Haynes showing how he could dictate the pace of the game; he was in top form again.

After nine wins and three draws in their opening twelve games, Fulham finally lost their unbeaten record at Craven Cottage in their unlucky thirteenth game of the season to a very physical Liverpool side by a 0–1 score. A dogged Liverpool were repeatedly lectured by the referee on foul play, but somehow managed to plunder a breakaway goal in the last five minutes.

Haynes had two scorching drives, and Arthur Stevens had a goal wrongly disallowed. In the last seconds, Haynes struck another shot with the keeper helpless on the ground. The ball was bound for the net but was miraculously headed off the line. Only Haynes had shown much confidence, and the tension had been building up a little in the team. Haynes had worked untiringly to get his forward line going, but on this particular day received little response.

Hat trick against the Russians

On a depressing run, England had not won in seven games, and some sports editors jumped on the bandwagon, brazenly stating that Haynes lacked sparkle during that period. They earnestly pleaded for him to be dropped before the Russia game. Fortunately the real England selectors paid little heed to the baying, and picked him for the friendly against Russia, the team that had knocked them out of the World Cup just four months previously.

Roy Bentley remembers the time well: "Around this time the press and critics were having a real go—Haynes was selfish, greedy and hard to get on with on the field. They just couldn't see it: Johnny was so advanced that he was ahead of the England players. The other England players were just not taking up the right positions. They considered that it wasn't possible to receive the ball from that distance; well, you could if Johnny Haynes was there, whether it was a chipped pass or a driven ball."

The match was one of Haynes' finest days at Wembley, in front of 100,000 fans. He and England wreaked revenge on the USSR, thrashing them with five goals, three of them fiercely struck left-foot shots from Haynes. The Russian side included more than half the team that had beaten England in the play-off.

Haynes was back to his mercurial best. Despite being tightly marked by a very classy wing half, Voinov, he scored with a low shot just before half-time, receiving Douglas' pass and shaking off the attentions of the centre half. There wasn't even time to restart the game. Then, in the second half, he revelled in an advanced role. He pounced on a partially saved Nat Lofthouse header and deflected clearance midway through the second half to make it 2–0. Finally he burst through into the penalty area, after working a short corner and return pass with Tom Finney, to claim his real hat-trick—three consecutive goals—nine minutes from the end. By full-time it was 5–0 to England, with Bobby

A smiling and highly satisfied Haynes leaves the field behind Nat Lofthouse and the blitzed Russian goalkeeper Belyayev at the end of England's comprehensive victory.

Charlton scoring a penalty five minutes from time, and Nat Lofthouse netting a last-minute ferocious volley to equal Tom Finney's record of thirty England goals.

The game totally silenced Haynes' critics. Alan Mullery recalls: "The first international match I ever saw him play in was when Frank Osborne was the general manager at Fulham back in 1958. On the day he came up to us and said, 'We're all going over on the coach to Wembley this afternoon to watch England.'

"England were playing Russia and on the way there, Frank told me that I was going to see one of the greatest footballers ever to live. I didn't know who he was talking about. Johnny Haynes led the England team out, they won 5–0 and he scored a hat trick.

"It was a magnificent performance in front of 100,000 people. Frank Osborne said to me afterwards, 'Now who's the greatest player in the world?' and I said, 'Johnny Haynes.' If I had to pick an all-time World XI, Haynes would easily make the team. He's in my top five all-time greatest ever players."

It may be apocryphal, but the story goes that in amongst the stunned Russian contingent that day was a young Mikhail Gorbachev. After seeing Haynes' performance he became a huge fan. During the Thatcher years, visiting politicians would be puzzled when asked by the architect of perestroika and glasnost: "And how is Johnny Haynes these days?"

Even after this stunning performance, there were still some within the press who could not recognise the quality of his performance or England's, and described the Russians as weak. Again, Haynes was furious with the press, and wondered what he really needed to do to win some people over.

He was also angry when he found out that the earlier BBC *Sportsview* team selection escapade had only been a spoof. Despite a sackcloth-and-ashes apology and retraction, he found the whole escapade childish, irresponsible and unprofessional.

A wound-up Haynes then took part in a tough, physical match at Middlesbrough. Fulham were back with a bang, and Haynes carved out all three magnificent goals for Leggat in a 3–2 win. He and Leggat were a dream combination and were described as pure class.

A sublime pass in the ninth minute, and a one-two with Johnny Key in the eleventh, brought the first two goals that Leggat devoured greedily. Finally, in the thirty-fourth minute, a free kick from Haynes brought the third with a glorious header. All this in spite of Jim Langley being a passenger.

Due to Langley's injury, Haynes dropped back to left half to mastermind both attack and defence. Two goals from Brian Clough and a rough-house last thirty minutes were not enough to save Middlesbrough. The press talked incessantly of the genius of Johnny Haynes and the opportunism of Graham Leggat.

November

The following week, Haynes brought Fulham back from the brink against Sheffield United, who had at that time the best defence in the league. It was going to be a difficult game without Jimmy Hill or Trevor Chamberlain. For forty-five minutes Haynes worked himself into the ground holding together a ragged forward line. His accurate passes and lobs cried out for goals, but the forwards couldn't cash in.

However, he scored a key goal on the hour mark with Fulham level. The press said, "Haynes turned the tide, by scoring a brilliant goal with his head from a Lowe free kick." It was only the genius of Haynes that put Fulham on the winning path. They were fortunate to win 4–2 with two late goals by Maurice Cook and Graham Leggat, who was set up by a Haynes and Tony Barton move. Haynes was described as brilliant throughout the game and could not be blamed for his obvious sighs as his colleagues missed chance after chance.

The most important aspect was his work rate. One headline read, "Haynes the worker silences critics." In one match summary, barbed comments were aimed at the doubting England selectors: "Haynes gave the 'anti-Haynes' brigade another kick in the pants by steering and inspiring Fulham to victory."

Fulham's draw the following Saturday against Bristol City at Ashton Gate was a fine achievement. Again it was the incomparable Haynes who provided the spur. To score a headed goal in successive matches was very rare for Johnny Haynes but he managed it in the 1–1 draw, keeping Fulham's unbeaten away record intact.

It was already his sixteenth goal of the season, scored from several yards out and was described as, "another brilliant header connecting powerfully with Johnny Key's accurate centre." It came after Bristol City had taken the lead four minutes earlier with a penalty.

He was unlucky not to give Fulham the win when he scampered through, but his final drive was just an inch or two outside the post. Another report pointed out how Haynes the schemer had "fed his forwards beautifully."

A big injury scare

A major hiccup occurred when he was injured in midweek playing in his eighth game for the Football League against the Irish League at Anfield. Fifteen minutes from the end, Irish goalkeeper Rea accidentally fell on Haynes' leg, again injuring knee ligaments. After attention he carried on, trying to score more goals, even though obviously injured.

England were already five up at the time, including a Haynes goal. Being slowed by the injury, he was further hurt in a last-minute midfield tackle that badly bruised his knee, and had to be carried from the field. After the game, skipper Haynes received a rare, almighty blast from Fulham general manager Osborne for prejudicing his own fitness for the sake of a fairly meaningless representative game which was already won.

The Football League eventually won 5–2. Haynes had been in devastating form on the night, scoring the first goal after just eight minutes following a Len White header. He then hit the crossbar, and flashed a header just wide of goal—all in the first fifteen minutes. He also made the third England goal for White with a perfect pass. He was described as masterful, and his play drew long and loud cheers from the Anfield faithful.

It was confirmed that Haynes had injured internal ligaments and would be out for some weeks. In fact he missed six vital league games, and Fulham lost three of them, relinquishing their top-of-the-table spot. With Haynes in the side, they had been unbeaten away from home up to that point in the season; without him they lost all their next three away games.

Fulham promised that to protect their promotion bid, Haynes could not and would not be rushed back. The injury he had received ruled him out of England's 2–2 draw with Wales at Villa Park in the British Championship.

Initially the ball ran kindly for Fulham in the first game during Haynes' absence. They managed a 2–1 home win against Cardiff City, which kept the team on track, but the following week, without Leggat as well, they lost 1–2 at Huddersfield Town. They then proceeded to put five past a very poor Barnsley side in a 5–2 victory at the Cottage.

December

The Barnsley result may have induced some complacency, as a major shock occurred the following week, when Fulham crashed 0–4 to bottom-of-the-table Rotherham United. It was a dire performance, the defence being described as all at sea, and the first rumblings regarding Haynes' absence were heard.

Fortunately, debutant Mike Johnson's two goals the following week and the resultant 2–1 win over London rivals Charlton Athletic kept those concerns temporarily muted. The next match, however, saw the worries erupt again as Fulham were truly hammered 1–4 at the Victoria Ground by Stoke City. After three successive away defeats, the club needed Haynes back—as soon as possible.

Haynes returns after six matches

Against their better judgement, the Fulham management pitched Haynes back into the fray, and he returned gingerly against Brighton at the Cottage on Boxing Day. In one incident in the Brighton goalmouth, he took another kick on the knee and split his eye, coming up with a real 'shiner'. The crowd were hushed as he couldn't rise from the deck without assistance from the Fulham trainer. It looked as if the knee had gone again, but thankfully it wasn't as bad as first thought.

He played on, but his form was very quiet. At least he came through relatively unscathed. Fulham thankfully won 3–1, and the press commented that his fine generalship had led to a marked improvement in the play of the forward line.

He and Tony Barton had constructed the first goal for Johnson, but victory was only achieved by a rare event, goals from both full backs in the same match—George Cohen and Jimmy Langley (not a penalty goal). It was Cohen's first ever league goal, and Langley's goal came from a short corner by Haynes. All that was missing was a goal from the maestro, but he hit the bar close to time. He said afterwards, "I know I was a bit slower than I like to be, and that I wasn't hitting the ball quite as hard with my right as I can, but at least I didn't feel any pain."

Two games in two days proved too much for him, and Fulham's patchy away form continued to cause concern with a 0–3 defeat at Brighton. The match produced a record attendance of 36,747 for the Goldstone ground. Haynes had a quiet afternoon, and the heavy mud and very close marking defeated his best attempts at skilful football. Graham Leggat couldn't escape the chains, either, and Brighton won easily. Fulham were, however, still in second place in the league.

The *Fulham Chronicle*'s end-of-year summary said that the injury for Haynes had "come at the most unfortunate time, as he had produced the best football of his career. His peak form has coincided with everything he learned from the 1958 World Cup. It is undeniable that Johnny's 'one-man' shows have carried the team to victory many times." The national papers at this stage of the season seemed to agree, almost all calling for Johnny Haynes to be crowned as Footballer of the Year.

January

The New Year started badly for Fulham. In the initial match they had little luck, and they lost 1–2 at home to Swansea Town, further denting their promotion prospects. Haynes was described as very disappointing and looking only half fit. However, Fulham would drop no more points at home that season.

They received some good luck when they unconvincingly scraped home 1–0 in the second of two poor displays against then non-league Peterborough United in the third round of the FA Cup.

Haynes should not really have taken part in the first game against the 'Posh'. The pitch was frozen solid, being reported as more suitable for ice hockey. Despite the poor pitch and his lack of fitness, Haynes could have won the game. Clear through in the box he was hauled down—an obvious penalty. However, in the true spirit of the FA Cup, the referee declined the award.

Haynes somehow managed to put in two sizzling shots that might have gone in on another day, but an inspired visiting goalkeeper kept them out and gave underdogs Peterborough a second bite of the cherry after a goalless draw.

Before the replay Fulham visited Ipswich, where they had their backs to the wall despite playing against ten men in the second half, during which the home side equalised an early goal from Maurice Cook. Then, in the last thirty seconds of the game, the Ipswich goalkeeper was harshly adjudged by the referee to have handled outside the penalty area.

The free kick award was heavily disputed by all the Ipswich players. After the rumpus had died down, Haynes cleverly scored with a powerful free kick through the wall; the shot barely rose above the ground and flew past the unsighted and luckless goalkeeper Bailey, after a Cook dummy had drawn defenders out of position. Unsurprisingly, his first goal in two months proved to be the deciding one in a 2–1 victory.

In the Peterborough replay, young Mike Johnson came to the rescue with the only goal after just seventeen minutes. Unusually, the replayed game was on a Saturday, two weeks after the first encounter. A bad injury to Jim Langley after ten minutes meant that Fulham played with ten men for the whole of the second period.

Centre forward Maurice Cook dropped to the half back line following the injury and played with some merit. Haynes played himself into a state of exhaustion to obtain the required result. The press called Fulham's display very creditable. They were lucky, however, as the Posh hit the bar three times with Tony Macedo beaten, and other shots were deflected wide off Fulham defenders, but the ball just wouldn't go in for the home team!

Four days later, Fulham played the fourth-round tie against First Division Birmingham City at a fog-shrouded St Andrews. They played well and emerged with a creditable 1–1 draw, following a good goal from Jimmy Hill on the half hour, after an excellent passing movement between Haynes and Cook.

This was followed by another league win, against Bristol Rovers, the home side squeezing through 1–0 with Cook's goal. He shot in from a Roy Bentley pass following a pinpoint free kick by Haynes.

Haynes' passing was as accurate as ever, but once again many of the chances he created went begging. It was an unlucky day for Cook, who had a goal disallowed and hit the post. He should have scored when put clean through by a 'straight down the middle' pass by Haynes, but he dallied and was robbed by the goalkeeper.

February

In the midweek fourth-round replay at the Cottage, Fulham were dumped out of the FA Cup by Birmingham City 2–3, despite a brilliant display by Haynes, who crafted both goals. They were handicapped by an injury to winger Johnny Key when the match was just a couple of minutes old, which left them with only ten fit men.

Despite this, Fulham went in front in the eighth minute when, from a re-taken free kick by Haynes, Graham Leggat rose highest to plant a fine header beyond goalkeeper Merrick. After Larkin's equaliser for Birmingham, Fulham somehow went in front again when a fine Haynes, Maurice Cook and Jimmy Hill move led to Key setting up Hill. Leggat came within a whisker of making it three just before half-time, but unluckily hit the goalkeeper.

Birmingham broke away immediately and made the match all square. A tough and sometimes crude First Division Birmingham, handing out a lot of stick to the Second Division side, finally won through with a spectacular long shot from Harry Hooper midway through the second half.

On the Saturday, Fulham lost 0–2 at Derby where Haynes had started out brightly, but faded completely in the latter stages of the game. He provided a chance for Tony Barton with a brilliant pass early on, but his shot was turned over by the Derby goalkeeper. This latest reverse meant that it was now five away defeats in the last six attempts, nothing like promotion form.

Certainly Haynes wasn't at his best, and was taking a considerable time to get over his latest injury. The team had other injuries, too, and was also struggling with a flu epidemic that was ravaging the club. In some games, Fulham had been without six first-team players.

During this month, and after playing so well against Russia, Haynes was shocked to hear that his England place was once again under threat. This time, however, it was through no fault of his own.

Five years earlier Fulham had had a golden inside forward trio; now it was Manchester United who had one, home-grown Bobby Charlton and Dennis Viollet being augmented by the brilliant Albert Quixall, recently signed from Sheffield Wednesday. The three were turning in brilliant displays at Old Trafford bordering almost on the telepathic, and for the sake of continuity it was being suggested that all three should play for England. If this proposal were adopted, Haynes would be ruled out of the running.

Alan Mullery arrives, and another hat trick for Haynes

Typically, after this short period in the doldrums, Haynes selected Leyton Orient to be the next victims of his own inimitable classy act. Fulham were two up within eight minutes. Leggat was the initial star, scoring the first with a thirty-yard shot, and a minute later setting up Doherty who scored from a similar distance.

Then Haynes hit the headlines. He scored his first in the twenty-first minute, taking the ball on the volley, after Leggat's centre dropped right on his foot. Leyton managed to pull a goal back just before the interval.

Haynes added his second ten minutes after half-time with a long-range shot, following Leggat's corner, that trickled into the goal off a post after being deflected by a defender. He then completed a real hat trick with a brilliant header, following a corner from Tony Barton, which flew into the net via the underside of the crossbar. Fulham eventually ran out easy winners by 5–2. It was Haynes' second hat trick of the season.

The match also marked Alan Mullery's debut. Like Haynes before his first match, Alan didn't know he was playing until an hour before the kick off. He played well from the start, and very quickly cemented his place at right half, adding even more strength to Fulham's defensive back row; perhaps he was the final piece in the jigsaw. Although he didn't openly say so, Haynes was pleased Mullery was put in the side. Mullery instantly became "a Haynes fan for life."

Alan recalls: "I used to play against Johnny as a sixteen-year-old in training matches where the first team played against the reserves, and I kicked a few lumps out of him, which he wasn't too happy about; and the language…! But once I got into the side as a seventeen-year-old, he'd already seen that side of me and the image I was going to project when I got in the team."

The following week against Scunthorpe United, Fulham were missing seven regular first-team players with either injuries or flu. Fortunately they had Haynes to supply the magic touch, and he won the game for them with a second-half goal in the 2–1 victory.

Fulham were truly hammered in the first half, and were lucky not to go in at half-time at least three behind, but after Jimmy Langley had scored with a penalty following a foul on Leggat, Haynes took command. Just two minutes from the end of the game, and with the score at 1–1, his exquisite pass out on the left found Doherty. Haynes ran into the goalmouth and positioned himself for the return cross. His first volley was pushed out by the Scunthorpe goalkeeper, but he dived full-length to head home the winner off the goalkeeper.

In the last match of the month, Leggat's goal was enough to beat Bristol City 1–0, Haynes being involved in the build-up with young Doherty. City employed quite a rough-house tactical game and Haynes tended to stay out on the wing to protect himself. In this game he was strangely quiet, although he did send a screamer into the net in the last seconds, but the effort was mysteriously disallowed by the referee for an alleged foul on the goalkeeper. Fulham were happily still in the two promotion slots.

March

The following Saturday, Fulham garnered a well-earned point in a goalless draw at promotion rivals and third-placed Liverpool. It was a backs-to-the-wall performance in the wind. Fulham ground out the draw mainly thanks to Haynes' control and distribution on a very difficult playing surface. His ferocious shot in the last minutes was scrambled away by the home goalkeeper.

Before Ken Coton became Fulham's photographer he was following the club around the grounds. He remembers the windy match at Anfield where he stood in the middle of the Kop. On Liverpool's Lime Street station after the match, he spotted the Fulham players and managed to get his programme signed by the maestro himself.

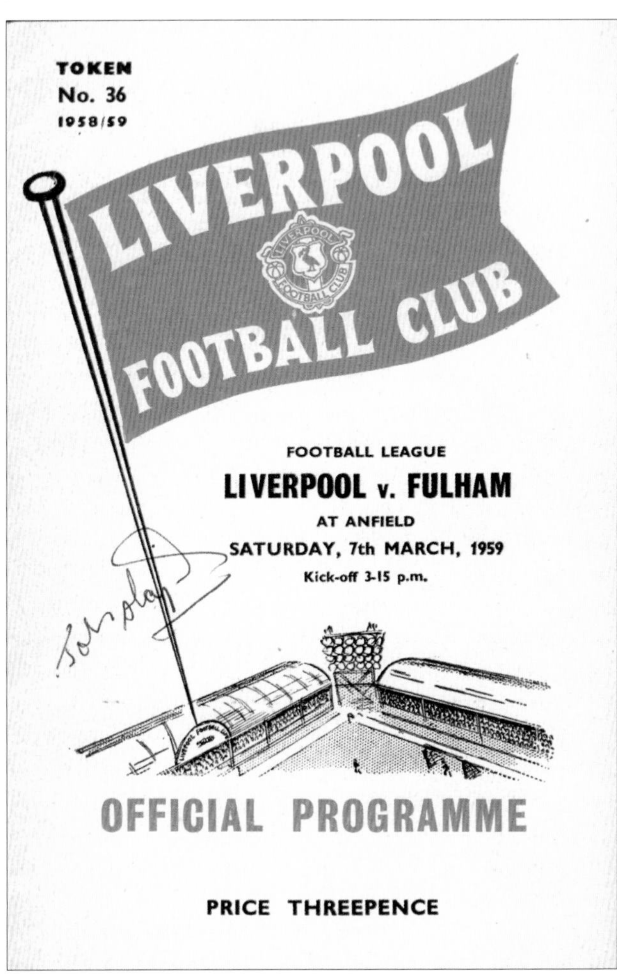

The 3–2 victory over Middlesbrough the following week saw Haynes quiet for most of the match, and Fulham in unpredictable form. After going ahead through Graham Leggat, they conceded two soft goals immediately after half-time. But Haynes came into the game late on and rescued the match for Fulham.

Leggat grafted the equaliser on seventy-two minutes with a fine chip to Haynes, which he shot home. This broke the northern side's stubborn resistance, and turned the tide in the home side's favour, and Tony Barton headed a winner just two minutes later.

In midweek, Haynes hurried away to represent the Football League against the League of Ireland at Dalymount. The match in Dublin was his ninth appearance and in view of all the goals scored during the previous encounters between the two sides, the match produced a surprising goalless draw.

Fulham proved at Bramall Lane on the Saturday that they still had some way to go to achieve their desired promotion. Fulham and Haynes, possibly tired after his midweek international match, were equally disappointing; their performance being described as rock bottom.

Sheffield United, in the promotion hunt themselves, had Haynes safely locked up, and he was marked out of the game, surrounded by a phalanx of defenders. Although Fulham hit the bar and were victims of a very questionable penalty for handball against Alan Mullery, the 0–2 defeat was probably deserved. This was Fulham's sixth defeat in nine away matches and they were now conceding an average of two goals a game away from home. Promotion was in the balance.

Three headed goals for Jimmy Hill

However, cometh the hour, cometh the Rabbi, when Good Friday saw table-toppers and promotion favourites Sheffield Wednesday visit the Cottage. During Fulham's indifferent form, no-one had suffered more than Jimmy Hill from the press and the supporters—and probably from Haynes the skipper as well. Nothing would go right for the bearded trier, and the booing had reduced his confidence to a very low point, although he kept gamely plugging away. Inside right Hill had failed to find the net in his twenty-four league matches that season, so was due a goal.

This was the big one. It was a tense game at one stage, and although Fulham went ahead Wednesday had little trouble in equalising. Fulham led at half-time via a Langley penalty, but Wednesday looked ominously dangerous and well capable of winning the match. They notched an equaliser immediately after half-time, to make it two-all, before Fulham edged ahead again through Maurice Cook.

This still wasn't enough for some in the crowd, who were continuing to barrack Jimmy Hill. It was vicious stuff, too, until Haynes finally snapped, openly remonstrating with the crowd and telling them to pack it up and get behind his colleague. It was a vociferous rant that stunned those in attendance, but it had the desired effect. Jimmy Hill went on to complete a hat trick in just twelve minutes—all headers.

Fulham finally destroyed Wednesday 6–2. Hill would score six in those last eight league matches. Although he was not on the scoresheet, Haynes was in the form of his life, tearing the Wednesday defence to shreds.

He bagged yet another goal the following day with a seventeenth-minute power drive, the first for Fulham away at struggling Grimsby Town in an easy 3–0 win. The Grimsby goalkeeper could only parry a shot from Hill, allowing Haynes to slash home a right-footed shot. By rights, Fulham should have scored a dozen, and they won without really breaking sweat. Goals from Leggat and a Langley penalty completed the rout. Fulham could even afford the luxury of missing a penalty in the last minute.

Ultimately, Fulham made it a very happy five points out of six over Easter, with the toughest match of the lot, the return game against Sheffield Wednesday at Hillsborough on Easter Monday. They won a point thanks to two smash-and-grab goals from Maurice Cook, the first from a brilliant through ball from Haynes. Aided by some superb goalkeeping from Tony Macedo, Fulham snaffled a 2–2 draw. The Cottagers were almost there.

April

There was still some work to do. At Cardiff on the Saturday, Fulham went a goal behind after forty-five seconds, and it could have been worse, with only Tony Macedo and Jim Langley keeping the score down.

In the second half Johnny Haynes led a recovery. Just fifteen minutes from time he burst through and smashed the ball across the goalmouth, his fierce cross-shot being deflected in by Leggat through a forest of legs. He finally settled the issue with another text-book pile-driver eight minutes from time for a 2–1 win. The goal had an element of luck about it, as a defender tried to stop the shot but only managed to deflect the ball on to the shoulder of another Cardiff player and into the net—some good fortune at last!

Haynes missed the next game during the promotion run-in when he played for England in a 1–0 win over Scotland at Wembley in the British Championship. Graham Leggat played for Scotland. Even this wasn't simple for Haynes, as he broke a finger on his left hand following a fierce tackle from Tottenham's Dave Mackay.

On that Saturday the weakened Fulham side still managed to eke out a single-goal win at home to Huddersfield Town. They looked a shadow of a side, but out of all the missed chances they managed to take the one that mattered, when Cook converted Trevor Chamberlain's centre a minute before half-time.

Fulham promoted to Division One

Fulham then visited Barnsley, who were fighting for their lives at the other end of the table. The relegation-threatened side fought back strongly to make it two-all with twenty minutes to go, after Jimmy Hill and Cook had given Fulham daylight.

Happily, Fulham edged ahead again straight from the restart, when Haynes broke Barnsley's heart with another hard shot that was cruelly deflected into the net by the outstretched leg of Barnsley defender Bartlett. Barnsley now had to come back at the away side, but this left gaps for Leggat to score Fulham's fourth goal. After the 4–2 victory, the press commented that Haynes had no peer at inside left. Fulham were back in the First Division.

Fulham had never been out of the top two positions all season, but probably relinquished any chance they had of winning the Second Division championship by losing in a tired performance on the following Thursday 1–2 at Charlton in their last away match of the season.

To finish off, another hat trick for Haynes

In the final home match of the season, with promotion already won, Johnny Haynes rounded off the season in style with his third three-goal haul of the campaign, against Rotherham United. Despite an early goal, Fulham didn't have it all their own way; Rotherham hit the post, and a second shot hit the upright but rolled along the goal-line without going in.

However, it's goals that count, and Fulham did the scoring. In the fifth minute Haynes finished off Hill's approach work with a neatly placed shot from the edge of the penalty area. The second goal was an excellent move involving Cook, Hill and Leggat, which was finally converted by Haynes. The goals were scored with that "lazy ease which delights his admirers and irritates his rivals."

Two goals ahead with just ten minutes to play, Fulham were awarded a penalty for handling. Captain Haynes gave the ball straight away to regular penalty-taker Jim Langley. His playing colleagues urged Haynes to complete his hat trick, but as usual he wanted to put the club and team first. Reluctantly, he eventually agreed and slid the spot kick home. This was yet another real hat trick—three consecutive goals.

Cook's pass then put Hill through to slot the final goal just two minutes later putting the icing on the cake in a 4–0 win. The press exclaimed, "Haynes played world class football and dictated the play to the team's requirements." At the end of the match, Haynes was applauded from the field by the opposition players.

It had been a great day for him, and a personal triumph for 'captain courageous.' Tommy Trinder said: "He is one of the world's greats. I think he will challenge Billy Wright's record of 100 caps." Fulham had won twelve of their last seventeen matches to clinch promotion.

Fulham's top goalscorer

Ten years after their last promotion, Fulham were back in the top flight at the first attempt under the stewardship of Jezzard and the captaincy of Haynes. They finished two points behind Sheffield Wednesday but seven points better off than any of the chasing pack.

Haynes had become the club's leading scorer, with twenty-six goals in thirty-four league games, including one four-goal haul and three three-goal hauls. He had also created most of the other Fulham goals. His strategy and skills had been the chief factor in bringing First Division football back to the club.

Leggat and Haynes had scored just under fifty goals between them. This was the only season in his entire eighteen-year playing career when Johnny Haynes finished as Fulham's leading scorer. There is a story, purportedly true, that Jimmy Bowie had laid a bet at the start of the season with fellow-Scot Leggat as to who would score the most goals that season, and that Johnny did it just to prove a point.

Despite being able to field their 'first choice' eleven in only fourteen league games (a third of the season), Fulham had registered exactly 100 goals in both league and cup (three figures yet again), but importantly they had conceded far fewer this year. The team had scored in all but seven league games, and in every home league game except one.

Haynes, at just twenty-four, had achieved one of his prime objectives, which was to play in the First Division—and "with little Fulham, the riverside club with the quaintly named ground!"

He was relishing the prospect of testing his skills against the best, and although he had supreme confidence in his own ability, he spent the summer asking himself whether he and the team would be able to succeed in the top flight. He was immensely proud of the fact that he had won twenty-seven England caps (almost half his final tally) as a Second Division footballer.

To build on this domestic success, Haynes was looking forward to the England summer tour of 1959, but as often happened in his life, as soon as he had reached one peak, he began to slide down from another.

FULHAM

Football and Athletic Co., Ltd.

Registered Office: Craven Cottage, Stevenage Road, Fulham, S.W.6

L.P.T.B. Trolley 'Buses—630 from Tooting & Harrow Road. 628, 626, 655 from Clapham Jct. & Hammersmith. **'Buses**—30, 74, 93, pass near the ground. **Underground**—Putney Bridge & Hammersmith. **Southern Railway**—Putney Station.

President—Sir LESLIE BOWKER, K.C.V.O., O.B.E., M.C. Chairman—T. TRINDER
Directors—N. A. D'AMATO (Vice-Chairman). R. A. DEAN
J. G. WALSH. C. B. DEAN (Jun.).
Medical Officer—Dr. W. R. D. WIGGINS, M.R.C.S., D.A., R.C.P. and S. (England)
Secretary and General Manager—F. R. OSBORNE. Team Manager—B. JEZZARD.
Telephone—RENOWN 5621 Telegrams—" FULHAMISH, WALGREEN, LONDON "

Saturday, 25th April, 1959 Kick off 3.15 p.m.

Chairman's Congratulations

NO chairman could possibly have a more pleasant job in his first year of office than to congratulate everyone at Fulham for attaining First Division status. It is a wonderful achievement for Bedford Jezzard, also in his first year as team manager.

When one realises than on 14 occasions only this season were we able to play our recognised first team, and in one match had to rely on six reserves, then the heartiest congratulations of the Board are due to General Manager Frank Osborne, Bedford and Frank Penn, our trainer.

To all our supporters I say: "Thank you for your support. You have my assurance that the Board will do all in their power to keep real First Division football at Craven Cottage."
T. TRINDER.

BEDFORD JEZZARD

INSIDE THE COTTAGE

ANY anxieties we had about returning to the First Division at the end of this season were set at rest with a certain amount of ease at Barnsley last Saturday. But what a bizarre situation this was.

There we were battling for points which we knew would assure us of promotion, while Barnsley were all out for a win to help them stem the tide of threatened relegation. Obviously someone had to be disappointed, and it is no use trying to hide the fact that we were glad it wasn't us.

So today we wind up a highly successful season. For the second time in exactly ten years we have gained promotion. No doubt all our supporters are looking forward again to Division I football at the Cottage as much as we are. There are some wonderful games in store.

But now let us make it clear that Barnsley did not go down without a struggle. Twice they levelled the scores

JOHNNY HAYNES
Congratulations !

From the club's programme for the final match of the season, and promotion is celebrated.

16: England trouble and FA trouble 1959

16: England trouble and FA trouble 1959

The summer of 1959 was a worrying time for England, as the selectors were once again chopping the side around trying to find that elusive winning formula. This was doubly hard for Haynes, who had observed the benefits of playing with a settled team during Fulham's promotion from Division Two.

The first game of the close season showed all of England's weaknesses. They played against Italy in a friendly at Wembley at the beginning of May, and threw away a comfortable 2–0 first-half lead to be finally pegged back to 2–2.

The England tour disaster

May

Following this uncertain start, England embarked on an arduous tour of South America. It had been a long and hard season for many of the players and most of them were jaded, but the next World Cup was to be in Chile, and Haynes thought that now would be a good opportunity to become acclimatised to the high temperatures and high humidity, and to try out the different ways in which it might be possible to play in such conditions. The England team trained at noon, the hottest part of the day, and the locals thought they were insane; you could almost hear the dulcet tones of Noel Coward.

Haynes loved the training and seemed to be one of the few players who actually relished the heat. He always admitted that he was a sun-worshipper, and never conceded that the England team could be over-training, insisting instead that variety of the routines was the key.

For the first match, there was a massive, noisy crowd of 150,000 at the Maracanã Stadium when the World Champions Brazil played England. It was maybe an understandable defeat, because England lost two early goals and never really got back into the match. Haynes played fairly well, and experimented by using oxygen at half-time to aid his breathing. He and Bobby Charlton managed to rap shots against the Brazilian posts, but England lost 0–2. The tour then began to disintegrate.

England played the unfashionable and somewhat unknown Peru just four days later and were soundly beaten 1–4. There were no excuses at all. The match was played in perfect conditions on a perfect pitch. England's defeat was simply down to four horrendous defensive lapses. Privately Haynes fumed at the casual way in which England had performed, but, since he was not the captain of the side, he decided that a discreet silence was the order of the day. Unknown winger Seminario was able to claim a hat trick.

England arrived in Mexico travel weary; they were forced into terrible accommodation with three or four sharing a room, and the general atmosphere was made worse by the fact that the English press were also there.

The match kicked off in the intense heat of the mad-dog midday sun on a badly damaged pitch that had been used for a gymkhana only two days previously. It was played at midday at the insistence of the Mexican officials, who claimed that rain had been forecast for the afternoon, which would have adversely affected the attendance.

England actually took the lead through Derek Kevan, and were totally in control. However, despite a week's rest, they were 'shot' after an hour in the torturous conditions, and couldn't get their game going again. The forward play was poor and they failed to maintain possession well enough.

Even so, the Mexicans had just three efforts on goal in the entire match; two went in, due once again to easily preventable defensive blunders, and one hit the crossbar. Goalkeeper Hopkinson missed an easy cross for the first goal.

These latest mix-ups in defence left Haynes incandescent with rage. He had grafted well enough but his hard work had been frittered away. He didn't accept that he had done well, saying, "My passing game was useless on that lottery of a pitch; my passes were just as likely to find an opponent as a colleague."

With all their problems, England still managed to get the ball into the Mexican net three more times during the game. Each time, the goal was suspiciously disallowed for a dubious offside decision. Certainly the referee was going to ensure that this friendly ended as a home win, and England lost 1–2.

At this stage the England team, at a low ebb, had won only two of their last fourteen games. The tour was completed by an 8–1 rout of the novice USA. The team flew to Los Angeles and found that the welcome, accommodation and western style of living made them feel far more at home. Again, however, they were forced to play, just four days after the Mexico game, on an unsatisfactory surface—a baseball pitch, complete with sandy running lanes.

Initially, England made heavy weather of it. The part-time USA team had a goal disallowed and then scored first inside ten minutes. It looked like being a repeat of the 1950 World Cup disaster, and England were falling over themselves in the sand and booting chances high and wide.

Haynes' view was that you could almost see the steam rising off the typewriters in the press gallery.

Previous page: For many years the FA's address of 22 Lancaster Gate was well known throughout the football world, though Haynes rarely had occasion to visit there for disciplinary purposes.

England were still a goal down ten minutes before half-time, but went in level.

Fortunately England, now attacking the grassier end of the pitch, found their shooting boots in the second half, scoring from all distances and angles. Haynes provided the icing on the cake with the final eighth goal three minutes from time.

It had, however, been a poor tour all round and Haynes returned to more gloom and doom from the press, something he was beginning to get used to. The England team had rubbed shoulders with the press for the majority of the tour, but Haynes and the squad were flummoxed by the negative reporting.

It seemed that the hangovers from the World Cup in Gothenburg were stubbornly refusing to go away. Rumours abounded of too many late nights, too much socialising and too little heart. Some even suggested that England had *deliberately* played badly.

Haynes was hurt by the performances and the defeats, but kept a solid sense of perspective; it had been a good learning curve with priceless experience for the younger players like Charlton, Greaves and himself in advance of the next World Cup. He remarked that he was not going to pull down the shutters, go into mourning and live a monastic lifestyle just because England had lost a game.

Roy Bentley recalls this time well: "The papers were writing all sorts of silly stuff, but John would never give them the satisfaction of letting it get to him. He wasn't upset or distracted from his game; he just let it fly right over his head. He was so confident that his game was the right one."

Even the FA were moved this time and complained to the Press Council about the style and factual correctness of some of the reporting. Although there was no formal apology or retraction, the Press Council did admit that some reported events never actually took place. The vitriolic criticism angered Winterbottom and the relationship between the press and the England management team definitely deteriorated further.

Haynes was now experienced enough to know that off-the-cuff comments and throwaway lines could be twisted and contorted by the media, and this undoubtedly formed his guarded stance with the press in later years.

Although hardly any England player escaped blame, Haynes was once again in the thick of things. He recalled one particular comment in *The Daily Telegraph* written by his arch-enemy Kenneth Wolstenholme: "Haynes will have to learn that he is not the be-all and end-all of the England team. Too often he has erred and then shown petulance in blaming others who

WAGs Fifties-style! Here, wives and girlfriends join in a team picture during the club's relaxing two-week tour of Italy. In the centre of the middle row are Johnny Haynes, Jimmy Hill and George Cohen. Standing centre is Robin Lawler; next to him is Jim Langley, and standing at far right is long-time club servant Frank Penn.

have not been slow to comment. Haynes has done his reputation harm, and although he has been a fixture in the England team for years, he can no longer remain a certainty after the dismal showing of the forward line he is supposed to control."

Common post-match verdicts on this tour were: "Not too good," and "Haynes had a quiet game." The northern press were particularly harsh. When the England team as a whole had played badly and Haynes had played well, praise for him had been rare. When other England players were greater failures the fact often passed without comment. But when Haynes played badly it *never* did.

Wolstenholme and the BBC cronies once again removed Haynes from their *Sportsview* team of 1960, but again the real England selection committee paid no heed to television. Walter Winterbottom was firmly behind his man and would be using him as the lynchpin for the foreseeable future.

After an exhilarating but tough promotion season, it had been another exhausting close season where Haynes had seen the other side of the world, whilst playing five games for England in the space of just twenty-three days. Happily this was followed by a two-week relaxing Fulham tour to Italy.

Although Haynes hadn't been mortally wounded by the criticisms, even he was glad to escape the sustained and vitriolic fallout following the tour. The few games with Fulham were ideal. He even found time to take himself off to Germany for a few days fairly solitary confinement.

Haynes the 'smuggler' upsets the FA (and Customs)

During the short holiday in Germany, a friend of Haynes was given a mini-camera, and took some shots. He had to return home before John, and asked him to get the prints developed for him, which he duly did, placing them at the top inside his baggage. Haynes liked the look of the easy-to-use camera and bought one himself at the airport on the way back, taking a few pictures. Absent-mindedly, he put the camera in his top pocket.

On showing the contents of his luggage at London Airport at midnight, a tired Haynes was questioned about the prints and replied truthfully that they were for a friend, taken with *his* camera. He forgot to declare his own camera, and he was held and lectured regarding the dire penalties for trying to evade duty. The camera was confiscated. It was hardly an incident to compare with the three 'B's (Bobby's Bogota bracelet), but it was serious enough at the time.

Haynes needed all of this like a hole in the head. It would mean more publicity—more adverse publicity. The fine could be anything up to £250, a massive sum in those days. His legal team were confident that they could keep the fuss to a minimum. Nevertheless, England's midfield general was forced to appear at Uxbridge Crown Court, and was eventually fined £35, still a significant sum.

He drove away feeling like a reprieved man, hoping for damage limitation. However, when he switched on his car radio for the midday news all he could hear was: "Johnny Haynes fined for smuggling"—another bombshell. The case was all over the national papers the next day. The incident scarred him quite deeply, although it had been a genuine error. He hoped that the FA would not let it damage his prospects of playing for England.

In trouble again as Haynes the bookmaker upsets the FA

Haynes' former team-mate Jimmy Bowie had to retire following a broken leg in 1956, and found himself with nothing to do. Bowie had great knowledge and connections in the bookmaking industry but no capital. Haynes, on the other hand, had spare capital but no experience.

It was an ideal match and the Glen Commission Agency was formed in the Fulham Palace Road. There were rumours that Bowie was in trouble financially, but, even in business early on, Haynes was incapable of selfish action, and went out of his way to help a seemingly less fortunate colleague. After a while, however, *The Sunday Pictorial* splashed the headline: "Haynes—the Bookmaker."

Fulham were surprised at the frenzy that broke out, as an ever-honest Haynes had made his intentions completely clear to the club at the start and they had raised no objection. They had, however, not provided him with some necessary and important advice. Specifically, Football Association rule 37 said that being a bookmaker or being associated with betting amounted to—misconduct!

The fact that Haynes' business was based on horses and greyhounds and had nothing to do with football was deemed immaterial. The newspaper story had been well researched, but got one important fact wrong when it claimed that the enterprise was floundering and losing a great deal of money. Exactly the opposite was true, and Haynes was doing rather well out of it. He had to smile, as it wasn't a major scoop anyway; most of the journalists already knew about it and many were his best customers.

His newspaper employers, *The Daily Express*, threw their weight behind him, pointing out the absurdity that he was able to place a £100 wager, but not allowed to receive one. Haynes was arraigned by the FA, and, despite his pleas, was formally told to disassociate himself from the enterprise within seven days.

He was informed of this by a letter that was delayed in the weekend post. It infuriated him when this letter was injudiciously leaked to a journalist who asked him about the contents before he even knew about its existence. Haynes maintained a dignified silence.

However, the FA got their way, and he withdrew from the business, allowing his father to take his place in the day-to-day operation.

17: The First Division and captain of England 1959–60

17: The First Division and captain of England — 1959–60

Johnny Haynes was in a quiet mood in the pre-season trial match, in which the Whites duly beat the Colours 2–0. He still showed he was a master footballer and hit the post with one scorcher. The First Division held its breath for the arrival of what some had sarcastically dubbed 'Haynes United'. Haynes said that he would be quite content if Fulham could maintain a position somewhere in the middle of the table.

First game in the First Division

August

Haynes proudly led his Fulham team on to the pitch at Ewood Park for their opening match of the season in the First Division against Blackburn and England colleague Ronnie Clayton, but after starting the match well, they finished on the receiving end of a 0–4 scoreline.

Haynes was pretty well shackled and shut out by his England colleague playing at his uncompromising best, and had to wander all over the pitch to try and escape his attentions. The press admitted that he had little chance to shine. Fulham made it easy for the home side with many defensive errors.

They were undone by a great display from Derek Dougan making his Blackburn debut; he put the skids under Fulham with the first two goals. The Lancashire press had a field day, wasting no time in reporting that spoilt Haynes and his 'southern softies' were going to be First Division makeweights, and that there were far better inside forwards in the First Division than Johnny Haynes, especially up north.

Haynes' first goals in the First Division

Those critics were forced to eat their words, however, as in midweek northerners Manchester City were hit for five at the Cottage. Haynes, who had allegedly said "I'll show them we're good enough" before the game, was in inspired form, scoring twice in a 5–2 thumping. He plundered the first two goals himself; Chamberlain beat two startled defenders in the fifteenth minute and presented Haynes with an easy opening, then young John Doherty supplied the pass for his second in the First Division.

The irrepressible Haynes masterminded the win by setting up the third for Alan Mullery's first-ever league goal and then creating the fourth for Graham Leggat. Fulham were four up with less than forty minutes played. Despite a slight City comeback, Leggat completed the rout eight minutes from time. A reporter boldly stated, "As long as there is Haynes, there will be First Division football at Craven Cottage."

Haynes crocked

In just the third match of the season, at home to Blackpool, Haynes received a fairly late but seemingly fair tackle in the second minute, when his left leg was relaxed. He had aggravated his left knee ligament with another strain. He carried on as best he could as a nuisance value passenger.

Fulham won 1–0, thanks to a Leggat goal following a move started by Haynes and carried on by Trevor Chamberlain and Roy Bentley. The team finished with only eight fit players on the pitch. They should have won more comfortably but erratic finishing let them down. Haynes saw a specialist in the evening after the game and received some initial injections. He made a second visit the following day.

Out for six weeks

September

Initially it was expected that Haynes would be out for no more than two or three matches, but in fact the injury was far worse than originally envisaged and Haynes would be out for six weeks, missing the next *nine* matches, more than 20% of the season's fixtures.

Despite the injury to their skipper, Fulham worked their way through the fixtures picking up points regularly. They achieved a point in a 0–0 draw at Everton without Haynes, Graham Leggat and Jimmy Hill and despite having Alan Mullery carried off twenty minutes from the end. Fortunately this injury proved to be less severe than thought and he returned for the following match.

The highlight of this period was a 3–1 midweek win over reigning league champions Wolverhampton Wanderers at Craven Cottage. Wolves, however, were able to avenge that defeat comprehensively a week later winning 0–9 at Molineux, Fulham's biggest ever defeat in a league match.

Trouble seemed to be piling up for Fulham; they had no luck at Bolton, where they went down by the odd goal in five. Derek Lampe in a rare appearance at centre half netted an own goal, Jimmy Langley suffered a rare penalty miss and Tony Macedo was hurt bravely diving at the feet of a forward.

The bad luck seemed to reach an all-time low in the 1–3 defeat by neighbours Chelsea at the Cottage the following Saturday. Fulham hit the woodwork twice, and there were innumerable scrambles in a Chelsea penalty area that led a charmed existence. To cap it all Chelsea had the benefit of an extremely dubious penalty decision, given for handball against George Cohen. The result was described as a travesty for Fulham. At this stage, they had won just twice in the

Previous page: England 1959–60. Back row: Armfield, Robson, Swan, Springett, Flowers, McNeill; front: Douglas, Greaves, Smith, Haynes and Charlton.

seven matches of their captain's absence, and one of these victories was against Luton Town, a side already struggling badly.

October

However, all things change, and the following week Fulham had nothing but good luck when fortune smiled on them in a 3–1 win over Nottingham Forest, mainly thanks to two goals from Alf Stokes, a summer signing from Spurs.

Then, at the Hawthorns, Fulham played superbly against Bobby Robson's West Bromwich Albion. Fulham scored in the first minute, and at one stage they were four goals clear. Only a little lax defending near the end allowed Albion to add an air of respectability to the 4–2 scoreline.

It proved one important fact—that Fulham could score goals and win matches even away from home in the top flight without their magical skipper. Trevor Chamberlain, having an extended run in the side, scored twice that afternoon. Haynes played for the reserves on the same day, testing the knee and making a goal in a 2–1 win over Watford reserves.

He worked like a demon to get fit, and having felt no effects following the reserve match, was ready to return. The injury had caused him to miss the opening international match of the season, England drawing 1–1 in the British Championship match with Wales at Ninian Park.

He returned to the Fulham fold in a thrill-a-minute home match against Newcastle United, marking his recovery with a goal in a 4–3 win. Haynes' return added even more punch to the forward line.

Newcastle were by far the more cultured side, and playing better football, but were hit by a three-goal burst. Johnny Key and Maurice Cook gave Fulham daylight following defensive blunders, and Haynes then took the third goal himself.

Chamberlain beat two players and gave the ball to Haynes, who turned at an angle that seemed far too narrow but drove a magnificent right-footed shot into the far corner of the goal all along the ground. The press said that this goal crowned fine work and was a scorcher from twenty yards. Fulham led by three goals at one stage but had to hang on gamely to finally secure a victory as Newcastle stormed back with two late strikes.

Surprisingly, the England selection panel considered that Haynes would *not* be fit enough for the Sweden game so soon after returning from a two-month injury, and omitted him. Instead, to prove a point and although he didn't score himself, Haynes inspired the Cottagers' attack in a diamond-studded 4–2 win at St Andrews. After Cook had put Fulham two ahead inside fifteen minutes, Birmingham were never able to get back into the game. This result made it fifteen league goals in just four games. Haynes' contribution was described as inspirational and his influence as tremendous.

Ultimately, the England result was a very disappointing one, a 2–3 friendly defeat against the

Concentration against Newcastle in a thrilling 4–3 victory.

unfancied Swedes at Wembley. Haynes had to laugh about the post-match comments, coming so quickly on the heels of the criticisms. "No Haynes—no schemer" was the cry. Haynes considered that England should always have ten outfield schemers anyway, but was inwardly perplexed as to how such an openly critical press could so soon be relishing his return.

The following week Haynes had to cope once more with the stopping techniques, a quaint analogy for foul play, from his personal Moriarty, Andy Malcolm of West Ham. He had to drop back and graft as the older inside forwards had done in the past. He never really turned on the class, however, and was irritated by a combination of his lack of full fitness and Malcolm's close marking.

For once, though, Haynes had the last laugh, and his quick thinking gave Fulham their goal and victory. During what was for him a quiet performance, he virtually jumped over a Johnny Key cross and the dummy or slightest of touches bamboozled Malcolm completely, allowing Stokes to poach the only goal out of nothing.

England manager Walter Winterbottom had been present to monitor Haynes' progress following the injury, but went home probably enthusing more about the performance of the young Alan Mullery. The 1–0 victory made this five league wins in a row for Fulham, and by the end of the month the Cottagers were lying an impressive sixth in the table. The Hammers were lying second at the time, so it was an important victory.

Haynes thrills Old Trafford

November

For the next encounter, it was back to Lancashire and a trip to Old Trafford, a game that Haynes had no intention of missing. He gave it all he had, from early tricks with the ball to superb timing and passing. The 'Lion's Den' Manchester United crowd of 44,000 were very fair, loudly applauding the maestro's finesse and delightful skills.

His constructive play helped Fulham to secure a 3–3 draw, with winger Graham Leggat delivering a hat trick from a very unfamiliar centre forward's position. It was the first time that the Scotsman had ever played with a number nine on his back.

Dennis Viollet put United ahead early on, but Leggat scored twice before half-time. Manchester United equalised just after the interval, but another blistering shot from a Haynes opening secured Leggat his hat trick. United were saved only by a typical Bobby Charlton thunderbolt goal just nine minutes from time.

The game absolutely delighted Haynes as he was up against Charlton, Quixall and Viollet, all potential challengers for the inside forward role for England. By a clear consensus he outshone them all on the day! The press said, "The honours went to Haynes; his tactical intelligence was stamped on the game." It was a display that really had supporters buzzing, and happy days were truly back at the Cottage.

He was pleased to see the next day's papers which trumpeted: "Johnny Haynes, the target of northern critics for so long, had them wildly cheering him at Old Trafford. Any 'Haynes for England' move now has 44,000 new supporters. The match proved this—there is room in this England team for both Haynes the goal-maker *and* Charlton the goal-taker."

The next match was a Fulhamish disappointment. It was home to a Preston North End team who were lying third in the table and which included Tom Finney. The match was tremendous, full of artistry and thrills, and there was a fantastic contrast of styles with Haynes using the long passes and Finney showing his superb ball control. Haynes shone as usual, and looked likely to score every time he received the ball. He did eventually score with an opportunist effort fifteen minutes from time, with the match seemingly heading for a goalless draw.

It was a piece of quick thinking when he snapped up the ball after goalkeeper Else had beaten down a header from Jimmy Hill. Preston, however, turned the tables with two late goals; the winner four minutes from time was a rare goalkeeping blunder from Tony Macedo, who allowed a greasy ball to slip through his arms and legs after looking to have the shot well covered. Preston escaped with a 1–2 win.

On the basis of his current performances and fitness level, Haynes was returned to the England fold, and took part in a 2–1 victory over Northern Ireland in the British Championship, England netting the winner just two minutes from full time. He took a nasty knock on the ankle in this game, and was a doubtful starter for the next league game against Leicester City right up to the last minute.

He insisted on playing in the Fulham side, but he was undoubtedly restricted. However he still managed, fifteen minutes from time, to draw the Leicester defence out and slip the perfect long, flighted pass that gave Trevor Chamberlain the opportunity to secure a 1–0 Fulham victory. Trevor duly obliged by veering inside and cracking a beauty into the top left-hand corner of the net. It was probably the best goal seen at Filbert Street that season. The papers said that Haynes supplied a constant service of the kind of passes that centre forwards dream about.

The statisticians raved about his passes. During the match he made forty-four passes, almost one every other minute; in the entire match only five failed to reach their target, an 89% success rate.

To show how eager and willing he was to play for the cause and improve his fitness, he turned out for a 'Fulham XI' taking part in a minor competition, the Southern Floodlit Cup, against Luton Town.

The next match, at home to fourth-placed Burnley, was a fascinating game, as it pitched Irishman Jimmy McIlroy against Haynes. Even when he might be overshadowed by the performance from the opposing playmaker, Haynes had the last laugh. As one paper put it, "One never knows when Haynes may produce the master stroke that will beat any defence."

In the thirty-third minute with no serious danger threatening, his quick thinking, with a perfectly timed run and immaculately lobbed cross, put Hill through to head the only goal; the ball was in the net before Burnley keeper Blacklaw could move. Goalkeeper Macedo was in fine form and Burnley should have won but they missed vital chances. Instead Fulham annexed the spoils with another 1–0 win.

Both teams received a roaring, standing ovation at the end of the match because of its quality. It was a great result for Fulham, seeing that Burnley had put eight past Nottingham Forest the previous weekend! Once again Haynes was under the watchful eye of Walter Winterbottom.

December

At the start of the month, Leeds scored an early goal in the twelfth minute at Elland Road. Alan Mullery had his one well-documented run-in on the pitch with Johnny Haynes that day. He remembers it well: "In the first five minutes, I knocked him a pass that was only about half a yard wide of him, but a Leeds player clattered him, and he started giving me the biggest rollicking … but I went over and grabbed him by the throat and I said to him, 'Don't you talk to me like that' and from that day I never got another rollicking from him." It was true; from that day the pair maintained a considerable mutual respect for each other.

After the row, a wound-up Haynes provided an equaliser himself with a sharp turn and a well-placed shot just inside a post. It proved to be a springboard. Fulham settled it with three goals in the last quarter of the match. Trevor Chamberlain gave Fulham the lead and then Haynes helped set up Graham Leggat to score two goals in the last five minutes, which saw Fulham run out comfortable 4–1 winners.

The scoreline flattered Fulham somewhat, and Haynes was not as busy or energetic as he normally was, but he wasted no ball, and everything he did was dangerous. Fulham were again grateful to goalkeeper Tony Macedo who at times waged a one-man war against the Leeds forward line. In this sequence of ten league matches into early December, Fulham had won eight, drawn one and lost just one, picking up a very impressive seventeen points out of twenty.

A cracker against Tottenham

It was as if Haynes had been saving himself a little at Leeds for the following match, when second-placed Spurs came to the Cottage. After Cliff Jones, seemingly well offside, was brought down and had given Tottenham the lead with a dubious early penalty, Fulham quickly levelled. From Macedo's throw in the sixteenth minute, Haynes, at the top of his game, hit a superb long, low raking pass from forty yards through the entire Spurs defence to craft the equaliser for Jimmy Hill. The pass was described as 'a gem.'

The match was pacey from start to finish with vigorous tackling, but played in a good spirit, and provided superb entertainment for the crowd of 37,000. Haynes was again unlucky not to score himself, and had two full-blooded shots saved by goalkeeper Brown.

Once again Fulham were robbed of victory when the blond Spurs full back Peter Baker (later to play in South Africa with Haynes) clearly palmed out Hill's deflected shot as the ball was entering the net, but referee Mr T Cooper (probably Tommy!) magically decreed that it was not a penalty, forcing Fulham to settle for a 1–1 draw. The crowd were so incensed that they refused to return the ball.

The Spurs skipper Danny Blanchflower had given Haynes too little respect and too much room to play in. One reporter agreed, saying that Spurs had no tactician to compare with him. Another produced a marvellous analogy, saying that "Haynes sprayed passes around as if the ball was on a piece of string." Another commented: "Haynes had a great match, his passes at times were sheer perfection, and his dedicated inspiration affected the whole team." One newspaper gave him a very rare ten out of ten mark for his display, saying, "He gets a 100 per cent certificate from me for his performance in this match."

Fulham and Haynes hit a grey patch

Johnny Haynes then hit a bit of a grey patch. He was strangled by tight marking again by England's Ronnie Clayton as Blackburn Rovers came to the Cottage and secured a dour, defensive 0–1 win by an effective use of a blatant, blanket offside trap, and thereby accomplished the double over Fulham.

Blackburn knew that this Fulham side could play, and in appalling weather conditions set out to stifle the home side however they could. The match was pitted with petty fouls and unsavoury incidents and at one stage players were openly fighting on the pitch. Haynes was eventually caught up in the violence as much as anybody and failed to control his side's fraying tempers.

In a galling match, Leggat was twice crudely chopped down in the box, but the official saw no foul. Typically, in a match of this kind, Fulham lost this unedifying spectacle to a first-half breakaway goal on the half-hour to Irish international Derek Dougan. Typically, an inept referee awarded Blackburn a penalty which they missed. The official was forced to run the gauntlet of angry fans at the end of the match and received a police escort.

The two matches against Sheffield Wednesday over Christmas were barely better. Wednesday, probably still smarting from the last season's six-goal thrashing, won 1–2 at the Cottage, after Fulham had secured a creditable 1–1 draw on Boxing Day at Hillsborough where Haynes and Leggat always looked a danger.

Haynes received a kick at Hillsborough and the injury was exacerbated with two more nasty tackles in the return match at the Cottage, where he was reported to be playing in the first half-hour almost at his best.

The second of these tackles rendered him almost totally ineffective, and he played the second half of this match with his right leg heavily strapped. At the turn of the year, and despite picking up just two points from the last four fixtures, Fulham were still surprisingly eighth in the table.

January

The knocks were enough to force Johnny Haynes to miss the next league game at Blackpool. There always seemed to be some bogey whenever the words Haynes and Blackpool were put together! Fulham, forced to play several reserves due to injury and illness, played poorly, and lost 1–3. The only memorable statistic was a goal on his debut for promising youngster Brian 'Doc' Sullivan, who went on to play just one further game for the Cottagers.

The FA Cup and lower level opposition provided some light relief and Fulham went nap with a 5–0 haul at the Cottage against Hull City. Haynes inspired four of the goals. Not for the first time, he was heralded as the master craftsman.

Haynes' sliced shot from Graham Leggat's pass was charged down for Trevor Chamberlain to open the scoring, and he was then involved in the move for the second goal. A Chamberlain and Haynes combination gave Leggat a simple third.

Haynes put the seal on this particular show with a magnificent forty-five-yard pass. Standing with his back to the Hull goal in his own half, he turned on his heel and swept the perfect chance to Leggat, which allowed the Scottish winger to run in on goal and score easily, shooting on the run into the top corner. A late Maurice Cook headed goal completed the scoring.

The club ran an article on Haynes in the programme and must have had a crystal ball when they wrote, "Yes, this is the Haynes era in the history of Fulham FC, an era which ought to last well into the 1970s."

The following week Fulham returned to the winning league trail at last and rather fortunately disposed of struggling Everton 2–0 at Craven Cottage on a dangerously icy 'skating rink' pitch. Fulham were kept out until midway through the second half by magnificent goalkeeping from the Everton number one, but Haynes finally beat him with a magnificent, sizzling cross-shot. He then inspired the move for Mullery to shoot home from close range through tangled legs to settle the match. It wasn't a great display and once more Haynes was linked with Leggat as the only ones looking certain of themselves or capable of shooting on target.

Fulham's season began to become bogged down in the winter mud after that. They picked up just two draws in the next four league games, which included an embarrassing 1–4 defeat at Luton Town who were bottom and were eventually relegated. Fulham lost a one-goal advantage and capitulated easily.

On this kind of dangerous pitch, Haynes didn't appear to be up for the game. Jimmy Hill put Fulham ahead on the muddy ground after just seven minutes but minutes later was carried from the field after being sent sprawling in a late tackle.

This forced Fulham, not for the first time that season, to play with ten men. This time, unexpectedly, the usually resilient Fulham side collapsed, after holding out until five minutes before half-time; they folded completely in a one-sided second half.

Haynes did not receive any credit. One reporter said, "I criticise Haynes, as captain he should have inspired greater efforts once Hill went; but this was one of Johnny's bad days. He looked unhappy, and frequently looked round as though blaming colleagues for bad passes or missed opportunities." Hill would be out for six weeks.

The Londoners also made a disappointing exit from the FA Cup 1–2 on an absolute morass of a pitch at Filbert Street where they had won in the league as recently as November. Haynes tried to park himself out on the drier touchlines in an attempt to have some influence, but was out of the reckoning for most of the game. Even Fulham's goal that day was an own goal created by both full backs. A timid Fulham side fell away badly after the interval after turning round at half-time all square.

February

In another anonymous game, Fulham snatched a 1–1 draw at home to Bolton Wanderers, the only worthwhile recordable statistic being a goal for Fulham from the young Allan Jones on his debut after just thirty-five seconds, following a neat interchange with Alf Stokes. Already without Jimmy Hill and Graham Leggat, Fulham were further handicapped by the loss of Alan Mullery, forcing Johnny Haynes to play most of the match in the right half defensive role.

Fulham were then out of luck against rivals Chelsea at the Bridge. On a pitch of cloying mud, Roy Bentley returning for the first time to his old ground was injured early on, and despite a goal from Johnny Haynes converting Leggat's centre, Fulham were well beaten 2–4, being four behind before an hour had been played.

Haynes was even criticised for trying to play too much football on a pitch that was suitable only for long ball tactics. It was obvious that he hated these surfaces as the conditions brought an unfair parity to teams with far less ability than Fulham. When it became obvious Fulham were going to lose, Haynes appeared to fade from the game.

The Cottagers' form improved in the next match with Nottingham Forest, and Haynes again split open the defence for Leggat's equaliser in the 2–2 draw. In the first half, to assist a hard-pressed defence that was beginning to leak goals, he played like an additional wing half.

In the second half he ventured further forward, and "exploited ball manipulation." In the end, however, it was only another magical performance in the Fulham goal from Tony Macedo that earned Fulham their point. The press hailed Macedo, who had never played better.

Finally some momentum returned, and Fulham recorded a crushing 5–0 win over relegation-haunted Leeds United at the Cottage. Leggat contributed an individual four consecutive goals, three in a devastating ten-minute spell. Most of Leggat's goals came from opportunist finishing, and none was really crafted by the master.

Haynes showed a lot of artistry but again a number of chances went begging. All the Fulham goals came in the second half, and a very poor Leeds side were relegated at the end of the season. So this five-goal win couldn't really be construed as an upturn in form. Unfortunately the season sagged again from here and Fulham went another seven matches without recording a win.

March

Newcastle gained revenge for their defeat earlier in the season by polishing off Fulham 1–3 at St James's Park. In this game Johnny Haynes was vying with George

Eastham of Newcastle for the England inside forward spot, and both these talented players pulled out all the stops.

Fulham made an ideal start to the match, when, in the fourth minute, Haynes combined with Johnny Key to put the ball on Roy Bentley's foot, and he had an easy lob over the goalkeeper, Bentley once again scoring against one of his previous clubs. Haynes continued to toil away, but for once in this super season he was overshadowed.

Eastham was, like Haynes, a pioneer in the game, and would work closely with Jimmy Hill to smash the 'retain and transfer' system, the subject of a bitter dispute that was already in progress with Newcastle, and which ultimately precipitated High Court action.

The following week saw Fulham pull a draw out of the fire against bottom-placed Birmingham City. Two goals down at home and staring defeat in the face once again, captain Haynes pulled Graham Leggat back into the centre during the game, and proceeded to provide him with two perfectly weighted passes to bring Fulham level, one before half-time and one after.

Concerted training soon got Haynes back to fitness after his injury at Preston, though it ruled him out of the British Championship match against Scotland.

Leggat was unlucky not to complete a hat trick, shooting straight at the keeper following a bad back-pass. But apart from Haynes and Leggat far too many players in the 2–2 draw were off form and the attack looked disjointed.

Another cracker against Tottenham

Included in this winless run, however, was a trip to Spurs. Haynes' return to White Hart Lane was an emotional one, and gave him time to reflect on the training and work he had put in there as a very young schoolboy from Edmonton. On the other side of the coin, it was the first time he had played there since losing 1–9 to Spurs in a combination game at the age of eighteen. Tottenham, leaders and title favourites at the time, were rocked as Fulham put in a fine display, and few neutrals would have disputed that Fulham were the far better side.

Haynes put on another special show against Spurs, in front of a bumper, atmospheric crowd of over 52,000. He was in top form and he baffled the Spurs defence with his foraging and probing passes. Fulham, with Langley on the wing in place of flu-victim Leggat, were unlucky not to be three up in the first half-hour, each effort being fractionally wide.

Haynes scored a brilliant goal in the thirty-fourth minute to give Fulham the lead. Jim Langley and Bentley fashioned the move, Hill then dummied the ball, allowing Haynes to pick it up, and in the same movement sweep the ball into the far corner of the net with a dipping volley.

Fulham, giving one of their best displays of the season, were unlucky as Bentley rounded Spurs centre half Maurice Norman and then, with an open goal, hit the angle of post and bar, but the ball bounced out. Dave Mackay galloped through for a Tottenham equaliser from Blanchflower's pass with only five minutes left. The dangerous Spurs winger Cliff Jones was completely snuffed out and blunted by the brilliant George Cohen, and it was the Spurs players and their supporters who were relieved to hear the final whistle in a 1–1 draw.

Haynes often reserved his very best displays for Tottenham, and on this day according to one journalist he had played Spurs virtually on his own. Again he was closely watched by England selector Colonel Gerry Mitchell.

The effort Fulham and Haynes put into the match must have drained them, as they were firmly flattened 0–5 at the Cottage by Manchester United the following week! Fulham were already without three or four forwards, including Cook and Chamberlain, and then suffered the kind of luck of which nightmares are made.

Goalkeeper Tony Macedo was rendered lame early on, which made it an impossibly difficult match. Johnny Haynes had already hit a post, and forced Harry Gregg into another super save from a superb drive, but it was not to be his day. Fulham found themselves two down at the interval to goals from Viollet, against a United side playing superbly.

Later in the game, pivot Derek Lampe sustained a head injury and had to leave the field, and then Hill was crocked by a knee injury. Hill hobbled over to the wing and played little further part, and the injury would rule him out for the remainder of the season. Effectively Fulham were down to eight fit players on the pitch. The mercurial Cohen was often up against three classy United players—Pearson, Charlton and Viollet. In direct contrast to the previous week, it was the Fulham team that were relieved to gain the sanctuary of the dressing room at the end.

April

Fulham's much weakened side struggled at Preston too, and, despite an early Haynes shot that was deflected away by a defender, they were three goals down before Haynes' goal soon after the interval, a simple shot that trickled over the line off a post. Eventually Fulham lost 1–4.

Haynes took another bang on the knee that had been repeatedly targeted all season. The wrench forced him to play a cameo role on the wing. He was very subdued by the injury, and the Fulham attack never ran smoothly from that point. The Cottagers were just plain unlucky. Alf Stokes hit a post and John Doherty hit the underside of the bar, but again it wasn't their day, finally undone by two skilful goals from veteran Tom Finney, who had a superb game.

The knee injury caused Haynes to miss Fulham's next league match, against Leicester. If fit, he would have been selected for the England versus Scotland game in the British Championship that ended 1–1. However, Graham Leggat did play for Scotland and netted his side's goal. Haynes from this point would miss only one of the next twenty-three England matches.

In the next match, Fulham squeezed a point out of Leicester City in a 1–1 draw at the Cottage. Without Haynes' guile, the match was labelled a poor excuse for a First Division match. Fulham were severely hit by injuries and call-ups, and fielded a ghost forward line including Mike Johnson, Doc Sullivan, John Doherty and Brian O'Connell, and scrambled a goal from Johnson following a lucky rebound.

Johnny Haynes stored up a cameo for the end of the season. Although Fulham lost 0–2 at Highbury on Good Friday, the result was yet another travesty of justice, as Arsenal were also a decidedly average bunch at the time. On this day the papers recorded "a return at last to England form for Haynes." In this game, however, Haynes appeared to pick up a thigh injury.

At this stage Fulham had won just two league matches in the four-month span between the middle of December and the middle of April and had ominously dropped into the bottom half of the table.

The following day, Easter Saturday, the headlines proclaimed once again that Haynes turned on his England form in a 2–1 success at West Ham. Despite the usual terrier-like attentions from Andy Malcolm, Haynes was the architect of the win.

He didn't score but was here, there and everywhere in the Fulham attack. He tantalised the Hammers' defence unmercifully. Trevor Chamberlain, back after a long injury, cracked in a beauty to give Fulham the lead, and, despite an equaliser, Fulham grabbed the winner in the next minute, Brian O'Connell in only his third game heading in Chamberlain's corner for his first league goal.

On Easter Monday in the return match against a poor Arsenal side, Haynes was superb throughout; the Fulham programme testified that he had dictated the tempo of the game, created so many openings, and stamped his personality on to the match.

Fulham waltzed home 3–0. Haynes was magnificent in both attack and defence and all three goals stemmed from his educated feet. He sent Johnny Key away on the wing for the first goal, slipped the ball through nicely to Allan Jones for the second, and provided the final pass in a move for Brian O'Connell to slam home the third. Haynes was unlucky not to score himself when set up by Chamberlain.

The last home game saw Haynes score the winning goal in a 2–1 win over fifth-placed West Bromwich Albion at Craven Cottage. Although it was an unimportant end-of-season encounter, it was a classic match, one for the purists—clean and sporting.

He again proved himself the master footballer, and the crowd witnessed some fascinating duels between him and his friend and England colleague Bobby Robson, playing against him at Craven Cottage for the first time. Haynes also made the first goal for Allan Jones, sliding an accurate pass down the middle for the unmarked youngster to make no mistake in front of goal two minutes before the interval.

Haynes' winning goal came after the Albion keeper had pushed out Chamberlain's flowing centre, and he ran on to the ball and scored with a first-time low ground shot.

To round off the season, Haynes showed his rarely seen defensive class as well in a hard-fought 0–0 draw at eventual champions Burnley. The press said that Fulham overall were fabulous, and that Haynes himself earned fresh laurels in the north in a display that Turf Moor fans expect to see only from Jimmy McIlroy. Fulham might even have won, Johnny Key hitting the post from a Haynes cross. Seven points out of eight constituted an excellent end to the first season back in the top flight.

A satisfactory finish

At the end of the season, Fulham had attained a very respectable tenth position. They had, just, surpassed

Seconds before the end of the Wembley international against Yugoslavia, Haynes is on hand to head in the equaliser in a fortunate 3–3 draw, after a Joe Baker shot rebounds from the bar.

Johnny Haynes' pre-season expectation for a mid-table finish. The number of goals scored was expectedly down against far superior opposition, and again they conceded eighty! Away from home, only two clubs had conceded more than Fulham's fifty-two, one of those being the cavalier West Ham team.

Fulham, with a small squad, had been forced to survive their annual injury crisis, which normally occurred between the beginning of January and the end of February. During the season, Jimmy Hill missed three months through injury, and Leggat, like Chamberlain, played in only two matches out of three.

Haynes' own scoring return had been ten league goals from just thirty-one games, so he could call the first season he had played in the First Division a considerable success. Fulham had finished only five points behind fourth place, and had beaten both champions Burnley and runners-up Wolves at the Cottage, drawn twice with third-placed Spurs, and completed the double over fourth-placed West Bromwich Albion.

A happy Haynes had seen nothing in the end to terrorise him, and was quietly confident that soon little

A proud moment for Johnny Haynes as he captains England for the first time. The match was on May 15th, against Spain in Madrid.

A solid display from the new England captain in the match against Spain in Madrid couldn't prevent a 0–3 victory by the home side.

Fulham would be competing amongst the cream of the crop for the league title. Although he didn't know it then, his next career high was just around the corner.

Johnny Haynes – captain of England!

May

Matters on the pitch hadn't been going that well for England for some time. The last twelve months had seen the national team win just two out of their nine matches. Both those wins had come against mediocre opposition—Northern Ireland and the USA beginners.

The first match of the close season for England was against their regular opponents, Yugoslavia, at Wembley. England would be looking for some revenge following the five-goal mauling they had received before the World Cup in 1958. It turned out to be anything but, with England delivering another poor, clumsy performance, and fortunate indeed to secure a 3–3 draw, thanks to a Johnny Haynes equaliser just ninety seconds from the end, when he turned in a rebound after Joe Baker's header had hit the bar. Haynes, however, played well, and was described as the strong man of the attack.

The press, the selectors and Walter Winterbottom all felt that a change was necessary, and now that Haynes had proved himself in the top flight, they turned to him for captain. England were training at the Bernabau stadium, when manager Walter Winterbottom took time out after a strenuous ninety-minute training session to say, "Congratulations Johnny, it's been decided that you should take over as skipper against Spain on Sunday."

Haynes succeeded Ronnie Clayton, his tight-marking Blackburn opponent but close friend. Clayton took the news well, and was the first to congratulate Haynes. It was a very proud moment for Haynes and the culmination, in his eyes, of eleven years of hard work. As soon as the honour fully dawned on him, Haynes was planning; he knew that the position would be short-lived if he failed to deliver.

It was a surprising break with tradition, as up to then England captains had tended to be defenders. It was the first time such an honour had been bestowed on a Fulham player.

Haynes, at just twenty-five, would be a popular captain within the squad, and would show leadership and character on the field as well as tact and diplomacy off it.

He couldn't weave his magic immediately on the England side, and they lost the first two matches under his captaincy, 0–3 against Spain in Madrid, and 0–2 against Hungary in Budapest. By most accounts, both of those defeats were scarcely deserved.

Against Spain on a decidedly muddy pitch, Haynes worked to his last breath with the new responsibility on his broad shoulders. The Spanish were a good side, with their clever covering, and their tackling was powerful, tight and—yes, ruthless. Haynes made two clear-cut chances that could well have made a difference. In one of these he put Jimmy Greaves clean through but the Spurs forward over-ran the ball and the fleeting opportunity was gone.

The scoreline somewhat flattered Spain, who netted two late goals. Haynes was already beginning to influence the way England played, and the team, more settled in its line-up and adopting a 4-2-4 formation, was definitely showing signs of improvement. Even though scoring chances were tossed away against the Hungarians, the midfield approach work had looked decidedly better.

Haynes could have been excused a poor match against the Hungarians, as during a pre-match meal a fishbone became trapped in his throat. In acute discomfort, he endured a thirty-five mile drive in a thirty-seater team coach to the nearest hospital. On arrival, the matter was hastily resolved and nothing was found, so the offending material must have been eventually swallowed. The incident, however, left Haynes with a badly scratched throat.

The overall opinion was that Haynes, in his first stint as captain, had had a great tour.

18: Lure of the lira
1960–61

18: Lure of the lira 1960–61

In the pre-season trial match, the Whites beat the Colours 6–2 and Johnny Haynes was amongst the scorers for the Whites. He looked "every inch a skipper and an England player."

Four goals in the first four games

August

The season started off with a home fixture against newly-promoted Cardiff City, and Fulham managed a 2–2 draw. They were fortunate; for the first half-hour they were extremely jittery and were two goals down in eleven minutes. In the second half a Johnny Key cross following a Johnny Haynes pass made the first for Graham Leggat; this put some pep into the side. In one move, Haynes tipped the ball over the head of a Cardiff defender, turned and then beat three men on the run in a dribble worthy of continental supermen.

Haynes himself salvaged the draw for Fulham just four minutes from the end, walking round the goalkeeper to slot the equaliser; the goal was born out of sheer desperation. His final shot into goal was deflected by a Cardiff defender. It was a fine solo effort, and he was so exhausted in the summer sun that he could only lie on the ground and signify his delight by beating his hands on the turf. The press said that he had played like two men, and showed all the old magic. It was another one-man show, and rather ominously the press said: "He was *well* overworked."

Fulham visited Newcastle United in midweek. Newcastle, managed by Johnny's former wing partner Charlie Mitten, had a number of injuries, and Fulham were expected to do well. Haynes' bright play in the first quarter of an hour set up Johnny Key to give Fulham the lead, but unfortunately the Cottagers then disappeared underneath an avalanche of first-half goals, conceding five in the space of twenty-two minutes; a couple of them just comical.

Haynes was totally exasperated, as he was providing "the only sparks". He sparked off a number of incidents with the referee as well, and was seriously threatened with the dressing room if he persisted with his talking. Fulham eventually lost 2–7 due to two further late goals. It was not the script that Haynes had written or envisaged.

Fulham and Haynes found themselves two down at half-time against West Bromwich Albion at the Hawthorns the following Saturday; they were under heavy pressure, and it should have been three but one shot hit the bar and stayed out. However, under Haynes' inspiration, the passes suddenly began to come good.

Fulham produced an amazing *four* goals in thirteen minutes. Haynes' pass to Key in the fifty-fifth minute set up the first for Leggat. After two further quick goals from Leggat and Maurice Cook, the win was sealed by Haynes who "completed Albion's discomfiture."

Haynes picked up a faulty Albion clearance and hit a blistering thirty-yard drive through a narrow gap that only he spotted. The ball was covered by keeper Wallace but the sheer power of the shot took the ball through his hands. Haynes' contribution to the 4–2 victory was described as a pure captain's example. It was acknowledged that whilst Haynes expected a lot from his team-mates, he was not slow to lead by example.

Haynes proceeded to improve on his display in midweek, when Fulham exacted some revenge on Newcastle with a 4–3 victory at the Cottage. In a super display, Haynes netted the first two goals inside the first twenty-five minutes.

He was stopped illegally by Newcastle's Woods, and from the indirect free kick Jimmy Hill flicked the ball to Haynes for him to ram into the net. Then Leggat picked up Tony Macedo's long throw, and from his run and cross Haynes netted his and Fulham's second from fifteen yards. He was denied a real hat trick when his third storming effort of the half hit the outside of the post and bounced away.

Later, Newcastle goalkeeper Harvey fisted out another piledriver from Haynes, only for the maestro to back-heel the ball from twenty yards only an inch or two wide of goal. Reporters said that it would have been the goal of the season. In a furious fightback in the second half, there were several niggling incidents, and Haynes and Allchurch were, as captains, called to the referee and told to cool things down. Haynes' goal tally was now four in his opening four games.

September

Next up were Birmingham City at the Cottage, and Fulham won 2–1. Johnny Haynes didn't score and at times was shown such respect that he was marked by three men! But the space left by this tactic was exploited with goals from Brian O'Connell and Maurice Cook. Johnny Key and Graham Leggat sparkled on the wings due to the passes from Johnny.

After O'Connell's goal, Cook hit a post and Fulham were unlucky not to be three ahead. Birmingham managed an equaliser, but Cook put Fulham ahead again before half-time. Fulham were slightly fortunate to take the points when Hooper's weak penalty for hands against George Cohen three minutes from time was easily saved by Tony Macedo.

Fulham picked up some injuries before and during the following Sheffield Wednesday game. They went down to ten men, with Tony Macedo off the field and full back Jim Langley playing in goal. Haynes dropped back to help out playing left half (No 6). The papers defined his performance as an outstanding defensive display. Haynes was applauded in the north for the

---

Previous page: Looking good—an England blazer and an MG car.

quality of his passing. In the game overall, Fulham were unlucky and deserved a draw, but instead received a 0–2 defeat for their toils.

Two days later, a busy Haynes flew to Manchester to help put Young England through their paces before returning the next day to prepare for the midweek game against the current bottom team, Nottingham Forest, which Fulham won 1–0.

Fulham were lucky to win and only two acrobatic saves from Macedo kept Forest out. Haynes was involved in every move from full back to forward line. His clever early pass to O'Connell was cracked home, but the goal was ruled out for offside. The Fulham forwards clumsily wasted almost every opportunity. It was a night where Haynes exhibited many tiresome tantrums, and these were hardly encouraging to his nervous colleagues. Forest were contributing little to the match and their constant negative offside tactics had the maestro seething.

Luckily Fulham took the one chance on the hour; Haynes plucked a headed clearance out of the air and touched the ball to Leggat, who blasted the ball home.

Haynes comes away with the ball following a tackle from his England colleague and friend Jimmy Greaves. Haynes scored in Fulham's 3–2 win over Chelsea. Greaves would be playing in Italy in the near future.

Haynes had spent a significant part of the evening with hands on hips delivering icy stares, and the press could not help but comment, "Fulham can seldom have looked such a one-man band."

The following weekend, in front of 37,000, Haynes hit the all-important goal after half-time to defeat the neighbours from down the road, Chelsea. The papers said that Haynes always had the beating of the Chelsea defence with his manoeuvres, and he was in magnificent form. After Leggat had put Fulham ahead in the nineteenth minute, Haynes had a hand in the second goal four minutes later. A clever one-two with Leggat enabled him to put in a blistering shot from the wing. Peter Bonetti could only parry the drive, and O'Connell easily netted the rebound.

For his goal, four minutes into the second half, Haynes picked up a pass from full back Langley, darted cleverly between two defenders and held off a third before sliding the ball under Bonetti as he came out and tried to dive at his feet. This was described as one of his finest goals, a typical effort stamped with the hallmark of international class. He was then just wide with another shot and would probably have won himself a penalty if he had gone down under a challenge from full back Peter Sillett. However, he sportingly tried to recover and the chance was gone.

In this thrilling clash, Chelsea pulled back two late goals, one of which looked very doubtful as it appeared not to have crossed the line, Langley seemingly chesting the ball out. Fulham held on to win 3–2 with something to spare. With the Haynes genius at the helm Fulham's forward line played with precision and method. One reporter said, "He is in such commanding form."

Fulham's defence didn't play well at Nottingham Forest in the middle of the following week, and the team found themselves on the wrong end of a 2–4 scoreline. Forest were still bottom, but victory over this average Fulham side lifted them from the base.

Fulham even had the impetus of scoring in the fifth minute when, in their first raid, Haynes laid on a goal for Cook, but just five minutes later they were trailing, and they lost a further sloppy goal before the interval. Haynes again passed a beauty through a gaping defence for O'Connell to make it just one goal in arrears, but Forest's Geoff Vowden completed his hat trick with a clearly 'handled' goal soon after, and Fulham offered little resistance after that.

They shook that defeat off and returned to winning ways against Preston North End on the Saturday. In the first ten minutes Fulham and Haynes passed their way all over Preston and looked likely to score a dozen. Haynes inspired both goals in this victory as well, slipping the ball through for Cook to score an easy first, and then doing his bit just one minute later.

In a fine run he wriggled right through and was about to pull the trigger, when he was floored in the box. Langley made no mistake with the resulting penalty. It was, however, a dull game all round and "Haynes shook his head in disbelief at some of his colleagues' misses." It wasn't his best game either, as he managed only one shot in the entire ninety minutes. Still, the 2–0 win was very welcome.

Two days later, Haynes also made a modicum of history by taking part in the first-ever League Cup (Carling Cup) match. Predictably, Fulham lost 1–2 away to lower league opposition in Bristol Rovers. Cook at least had the honour of scoring the first-ever goal in the inaugural competition, because the match kicked off fifteen minutes earlier than all the other matches that evening—and Cook scored in that quarter of an hour! The reporter said the home crowd took delight in watching Haynes' passes, but also tut-tutted at his tantrums, and loved it every time he was beaten to the ball.

October

The following week, Fulham took a 0–5 humbling from league champions Burnley at Turf Moor. Burnley were excellent on the day, and Fulham were without Tony Macedo and Alan Mullery. For once, Haynes was shackled, being ruthlessly marked out of the game by a young Walter Joyce making his home debut. Haynes was truly put in the shade by his opposite number and playmaker, Jimmy McIlroy. Irish international McIlroy made three of the Burnley goals, which included a hat trick for Jimmy Robson.

Haynes missed Fulham's bright 5–2 away victory at struggling Blackpool due to international duty. It was described as an easy day for Fulham, who plundered five goals easily with Johnny Key and Graham Leggat running riot on the wings.

Haynes becomes Fulham's most capped player

Following England's two defeats under Haynes, the critics were already sharpening their pencils to pass judgment on what they considered was the worst England team ever selected. However, England's form under Haynes began to take off with an emphatic 5–2 victory over Northern Ireland in Belfast. The German manager watching the performance purred at the brilliance of the positive and incisive breaks. The cap for Haynes (his thirty-seventh) established another record, as it was the highest number of caps any Fulham player had *ever* received.

Tottenham's Bobby Smith scored with his second kick in international football after Haynes had rolled a short free kick into his path in the sixteenth minute. After Ireland's equaliser, their goalkeeper Harry Gregg could only palm out Haynes' cunning centre, and Jimmy Greaves put England ahead again. Haynes had a decent match, and worked hard and used the ball well. Just when it had seemed that the English team had hit crisis point, they had, thankfully, embarked on a winning streak.

Before the next international match, Haynes had time to return to the Fulham side to create goals for Johnny Key and Jimmy Langley in an unlucky 2–3 home defeat by third-placed Everton. After playing a grand first half and establishing a lead, Fulham were weak and listless in the second, conceding two avoidable goals.

Key's goal came from a low drive following a Haynes pass, and despite an Everton equaliser, full back Langley gave Fulham the lead when roving upfield, taking Haynes' chipped free kick and blasting the ball home.

It seemed that Haynes was beginning to feel frustrated with his domestic colleagues after playing for England. He provided many chances for his team in the first half, only to see them nearly all wasted. In the end he lost heart. So disgruntled was he that he perpetrated the worst miss himself; when clear through, he failed to beat the goalkeeper from close range.

After this disappointment, Haynes returned to the England fold in midweek to take part in the 9–0 win (walkover) against minnows Luxembourg in a World Cup preliminary. He scored one on the hour; it was the goal of the game, a thundering shot. The victory was England's biggest win for thirteen years. Haynes had another brilliant game, creating chances galore. One sports writer referred to England as "The Johnny Haynes eleven".

Fulham's topsy-turvy league form continued. The following week at Burnden Park saw Haynes produce a masterly powerhouse performance, creating chances that allowed Leggat to grab a hat trick in a fine 3–0 win against Bolton.

The England goal has been scored by Tottenham's Bobby Smith, but Haynes can't resist a joyous secondary celebration in the 4–2 victory over Spain.

Unbelievably, the hat trick came in the space of just twelve minutes. For the second goal, Haynes swept through on his own and laid on a fine pass for Leggat to crash in from fifteen yards. In a match that marked amateur Bobby Brown's debut, Haynes had to move back once again to the number six position when Jim Langley was injured.

The press acknowledged that Haynes was the driving force behind this improved showing, bolstering up a jittery defence to find time to set up attacks. One report said that Haynes gave Bolton umpteen lessons in link-manship, turning defence into attack with a delicate wave of the boot.

This win was followed by Haynes disappearing to report for England duty once again in midweek to compete in a fine 4–2 friendly victory over Spain on a rain-soaked Wembley pitch. It was the third England match in nineteen days. England played well, and scored early on through Jimmy Greaves.

The classy Spaniards drew level and overpowered England for a while, threatening to take the lead, but it was England who drew next blood shortly before half-time. A further two goals put the match beyond doubt. Haynes showed his respect for his opponents, and proved he was the boss, when a few England players started to take the mickey by playing 'keep ball' in their own half towards the end of the match. The crowd loved it, but Haynes was upset by the showboating, immediately running back to pick up the ball and launch it forward for another attack.

At last after nearly forty caps, Haynes seemed to have won over the doubters, even Tom Finney. Prior to the start of the season, Finney had offered the opinion that England's poor form was due to the forwards having been chopped and changed around, with the exception of Haynes who had been left alone.

Given those poor results, he suspected that Haynes himself might be the problem, and so suggested that he should stand down as a team member for a while. All this was washed away with the rain that evening. England had kept the same team for the last few matches and the blend and subsequent results were beginning to appear.

After the game Finney admitted: "Haynes is not only a must, he is our number one priority. Against Spain he played like a man inspired. He was prompting, urging and calling his boys to greater effort all the time, a leader with a field-marshal's command of the soccer situations. It was one of the finest displays of captaincy I've seen on a football field for years."

This win didn't diminish Haynes' appetite for the domestic game, and in a 1–1 draw with West Ham, he was described as being here, there and everywhere. This was a fascinating struggle between Haynes and his play-making counterpart at West Ham, Welsh international Phil Woosnam. The heavy rain during the week had made it a muddy pitch.

Fulham snatched a point thanks to a Leggat and Haynes combination goal. It should have been a win and two points, when Haynes slipped a perfect through pass right to the feet of Bobby Brown making his home debut. Unfortunately the youngster lost his composure and delayed his shot, allowing the goalkeeper to smother the effort.

Fulham in truth were rather lucky to take a point. The defence appeared to have large gaps in it and West Ham, without an away victory for almost a year, missed several clear-cut chances. At the end of the month, an impressive Fulham had already notched up eight wins and were lying, like last season, in a very creditable sixth position in the table.

A tentative approach from Italy

November

Three days after this league match Johnny Haynes was invited to captain the Football League XI versus the Italian League XI on his tenth appearance for the side in the San Siro stadium in Milan. A tough and tetchy inter-league game, very short-tempered at one point, ended 2–4 to the Italians—much to Haynes' relief as he feared a lynching.

After the match, a surprised Haynes was formally approached for the first time by a representative of Milan. He was asked straight out, "Would you like to play for Milan?" A thousand thoughts flashed through his mind—money, lifestyle and sunshine. Without hesitation he said that he would *have* to be interested if the laws on foreign players in Italian football were relaxed.

On sober reflection, Haynes insisted, correctly, that all formal lines of communication should go through Fulham Football Club. Milan respected this, and approached Fulham, but no bid was forthcoming at the time.

This was a strange up and down month for Haynes. Initially Fulham were beaten 1–5 by Tottenham, thrashed out of sight by the eventual champions. Spurs sped off like a train and built up an early two-goal lead. Graham Leggat reduced the arrears and for the best part of an hour it looked as if Fulham would equalise, as they had as much of the game as Tottenham.

The press pointed out that every time Haynes had the ball, an equaliser looked a probability. But in the end, Spurs found an extra reserve of power, switched to a higher gear in the last fifteen minutes and netted three times to waltz away with the match.

On the day Fulham were outclassed by a better side, as they had been at Turf Moor. Haynes had tried to inject some life into the patched-up attack, but it only functioned in fits and starts. Considering that two of the Spurs goals had come in the last four minutes and that it was Tottenham's fifteenth victory in sixteen games, it maybe wasn't too bad a result.

Haynes the defender

Due to the injuries affecting Alan Mullery and George Cohen, Haynes was then forced to start in the number six shirt, one of only two very short spells at Fulham when he wore a shirt outside the forward line numbers. It looked like a good move in the first instance, as, lying deeper and in a semi-defensive role, he produced an inspirational display, with a stream of precision passes, assisting Leggat to score his second hat trick in four games to dispose of Leicester City 4–2 at the Cottage.

It didn't seem so good early in the game when Fulham found themselves two goals down after just sixteen minutes, but Haynes was "one minute in defence and then in attack" and eventually he mastered the Leicester side. One report described him as the essence of perpetual motion, which stamped him as a fine player in any position.

However, the move didn't work out so well in the next two games, with two losses sustained against Midland clubs—1–2 at Aston Villa and 1–3 at home to the mighty Wolves. Against Villa, after a good start which produced a first-minute goal for Leggat, Haynes was too far back and had too many defensive duties which forced him to mix it with the firm-tackling Villa wing halves, limiting his attacking flair and ultimately forcing him out of the game.

However, he did contribute a goal, a fine drive, in the Wolves defeat at Craven Cottage; it was his first scoring effort in ten games. He started in the experimental role, but it was now plainly not working. Two Tony Macedo errors had Fulham reeling inside ten minutes and Mason gave Wolves a third on twenty-five minutes. Haynes was non-existent, and Fulham only came back into the game at all when he moved up the field. One newspaper headline summed it up: "So easy Wolves—Haynes despairs."

In between those last two fixtures, Wales were the next victims of England in the British Championship, on the receiving end of a 5–1 hammering at Wembley. Haynes provided yet another goal on the hour mark, running on to the ball, taking it inside, and shooting for England's fourth. Once again, England scored early on in each half to put a stranglehold on the game.

Haynes was delighted that the improvement in England's form was coinciding with the return of his old team-mate Bobby Robson, who had been moved by Vic Buckingham, later to manage Fulham, from the inside forward position to the half back line. This had been so much of a success that his form had taken him from Albion's reserve team to the England side!

December

Whether the initial tap-up discussions from Milan had distracted Haynes was never known, but his domestic form certainly began to dip. As he lost his form, predictably Fulham lost theirs too.

At Blackburn on a cold day and a slippery, muddy pitch, Haynes never really mastered the ground conditions, and in the end was totally eclipsed. Blackburn's first two goals were both penalties inside the first half-hour and Brian O'Connell's effort just before half-time was scant consolation in a 1–5 defeat, the defence wilting again in the last twenty-five minutes when Blackburn scored three times.

Fulham were again without Tony Macedo, Jimmy Hill and Maurice Cook. The inspirational Roy Bentley also sustained an injury in this game through an accidental collision with centre forward Derek Dougan, and never played for Fulham again; this further de-stabilised the jittery defence.

The home game against Manchester United produced a marvellous spectacle for the neutrals, a 4–4 draw, but this was down to the defensive inadequacies of both sides rather than any inspired forward line play. Reserve goalkeeper Ken Hewkins and reserve centre half Derek Lampe made mistakes that no-one could get away with against the likes of Bobby Charlton, and Fulham were two goals down inside eight minutes.

Bobby Brown's first league goal was a brilliant header from a Haynes free kick after the maestro himself had been fouled. In a whirlwind game, from being two behind, Fulham went three-two up with three goals in seven minutes, then three-four down, before settling for an eight-goal draw. The eighth goal of the game went in with twenty-five minutes still to go!

Fulham were also without Graham Leggat at Cardiff, and their bad luck with injuries became worse when once again Haynes had to drop to the half back line when full back Jim Langley sustained yet another injury, leaving him as an immobile winger.

One report said that despite the re-shuffle it was still Haynes who produced the only real threat. Another said: "There were several classic passes and also several planned and cleverly co-ordinated moves of which Haynes was the architect." At the end of the day, however, the result was the same, a goal in each half and a 0–2 defeat. After obtaining just one point from five games, it was obvious that too much was falling on Johnny Haynes' shoulders.

A close shave in a car

Just before Christmas there was more trouble. Haynes, Bentley and Chamberlain were all injured when Haynes' car, driven by Johnny, was in collision with a huge coal lorry while returning from training at the Harrods sports ground.

The collision occurred near the Cottage, where the lorry had gone through a brick wall and the accident was a near catastrophe. Haynes' MG lay thirty yards away from the lorry, a complete write-off. All three players were taken to hospital as a precaution.

Bentley was actually detained in hospital overnight with concussion. Haynes broke a bone in his hand, and had four stitches put in a head wound. He also sustained several cuts and bruises. He afterwards recalled: "We were lucky to come out of it without being worse off!"

Frank Osborne winced as he recalled the incident: "I rushed out of the office when they told me that Johnny was in a car smash just up the road. ... Tosh Chamberlain and Roy Bentley sat on the pavement cut and shaken. And there was Johnny, blood pouring down his face from a head wound, telling me: 'Don't worry, I'll be all right for Saturday. I never head the ball much anyway!'"

He declared himself fit enough to play in the 2–3 defeat at Maine Road on Christmas Eve, City were two up in the first six minutes, Fulham now seemingly making a habit of giving two goals away in the first ten minutes in league games. Ironically it was Haynes' bad pass in a defensive position that gifted the ball to City's Gerry Baker to score the first, in the second minute.

He then picked his side up off the floor almost on his own with a magnificent display in which his passes were a model of control and accuracy. Despite two more goals from the mercurial Leggat, Fulham lost again, although they had the better of the play. Two days later, a scrambled goal by Trevor Chamberlain provided some much-needed relief and his effort was enough to beat Manchester City 1–0 in the return Boxing Day fixture.

Even during the season of goodwill, Haynes received another snub. The club's directors had wanted to present him with a £50 gold watch, or a present of equivalent value, in recognition of his service to the game. They had to apply to the Football League for permission—just a formality, so they thought. The league management committee came back with a resounding "no". The press thought that Fulham should have thought up a phoney milestone like his 10,000th through pass, and then maybe the committee would have seen the matter differently.

Haynes did manage another goal on New Year's Eve against struggling West Bromwich Albion in a 1–2 defeat at the Cottage. Fulham looked in the right mood for this match, and Haynes' goal came as early as the fourth minute. It was described as another wonder goal. As the ball came over from a corner, Johnny blasted it straight into the net with a full-blooded volley from twenty yards.

It was unfortunately downhill from there. Bobby Robson fashioned an equaliser for England forward Derek Kevan just four minutes later. Fulham put in another listless performance and Bobby Robson, still a Cottage favourite, policed his old friend out of the rest of the game with the help of the two other Albion half backs. Albion scored again moments before the interval. Haynes strove valiantly to put some vitality into the Fulham attack but what passes he was able to squeeze through were wasted by his profligate colleagues.

In this month Fulham had won just one of six matches and had conceded sixteen goals. To be fair, they were having a very rough time with injuries, and reserves Ken Hewkins (goal), Trevor Watson (wing), Bobby Brown (centre forward) and Dai Edwards (half back) all played in a number of games. By the year end, Fulham had slipped dramatically from sixth to mid-table.

January

Things didn't improve at the start of the New Year either. Johnny Haynes tried desperately to lift Fulham out of the doldrums and inspire them in the FA Cup third round, but they were buried again away at Newcastle United 0–5. A twenty-year-old Duncan Neale playing right half for Newcastle scored three of the goals, and Fulham were really beaten before half-time.

The press said that Haynes had tried so hard, but it would have taken a superman to turn this game around. The result was bad news; Mitten's Newcastle were at best a mediocre side at the time, and another crack at the FA Cup had been swiftly snuffed out for captain Haynes. The media reported that even Johnny Haynes seemed content merely to work hard without seeking any personal glory. The scoreline meant that twelve goals had been conceded in just two trips to the same ground that season.

Haynes seemed back to his meticulous best the following Saturday when a Sunday paper gave him the rare maximum ten out of ten mark for a masterly display with slide-rule passes. Fulham still lost 0–1, however, against Birmingham at St Andrews.

The home side missed a host of chances including a penalty, and Fulham were saved from total mediocrity by the class of Haynes. One frustrated journalist said, "It was amazing how the forwards contrived to make such a muddle of the openings created by Haynes."

The inexperienced forwards hardly created a worthwhile chance, and the match descended into a hot-tempered brawl towards the end. Haynes had the only real chance, but his shot was superbly saved by Withers in the Birmingham goal. The final headline read: "Haynes art is wasted."

The abolition of the maximum wage

Whilst Britain according to Harold Macmillan had 'never had it so good,' the maximum wage for footballers had been in existence for seventy years, set up before the turn of the century. There was almost a feudal 'master and serf' relationship. Fulham player and future Coventry manager Jimmy Hill was head of the Players' Union. Although football was classified as a sport, most football clubs were businesses, often limited companies with directors, shareholders and assets. While most clubs did not make massive profits, most had capital.

Many very good aspiring footballers were turning their backs on a full-time career in football, as they could earn more doing a 'normal' job augmented by playing football on the side. Footballers were more intelligent and ambitious than ever before and better craftsmen. They were beginning to rail against Victorian attitudes and Dickensian contracts. They had to mount a serious challenge to the autocratic hegemony which the Football League had sought to maintain over the game since the war. Jimmy Hill was fighting for fairness, and recalls: "Nearly all of the professional footballers of that time, some 2,500, were enrolled into the union. The clubs should have been able to pay players what they could afford and not have a cap of £20 per week."

Roy Bentley remembers the time: "It was a tribute to Jimmy Hill, he was often away at weekends working on this task, and often involved in meetings. But he always returned for training on Monday, raring to go."

Haynes said: "I was proud of what we did, we *had* to do it. Jimmy was a Fulham player at the time, and in the end he was more interested in our case than he was about playing. He got us all involved and had meetings all over the country."

Haynes wanted more money brought in from the local industries booming in Britain in the Fifties. With more cash injected, football clubs could afford better facilities, pitches and pay good players appropriately.

The Edwardian feeling prevailing in football at the time was that everyone should be paid the same, regardless of ability, as it was a team game and anything else would have shattered morale.

Haynes argued that under this rubric there was never any incentive to improve, and that football's wasters and vagrants would be treated and paid the same as the game's top artistes. He had seen that overseas teams hammering English teams in the European matches had no such thinking or restrictions. Despite these pay inequalities he had observed no loss of team spirit abroad.

Footballers at that time were not supposed to have opinions, but the rumblings started in 1959. Denis Viollet, the Manchester United captain, began to comment that low-morale English league teams lagged behind and would be exposed for their shortcomings in European football.

Sure enough, Wolves in a cup quarter-final against Barcelona conceded *nine* goals over the two legs. Viollet was rebuked by the FA and his comments brought far-reaching damnation, but all he was expressing was an honestly-held personal opinion.

After England's 2–3 defeat against lowly Sweden the previous November and Real Madrid's 6–1 victory in a friendly at Old Trafford, things began to change, and a dismantling period emerged.

League secretary Alan Hardaker's initial responses to the players' overtures late in 1959 were stony and predictable: "Train harder, work harder, play better, don't ask too many questions and you *might* get more money at a later date." These few crumbs from the masters' table infuriated the players; it was too feudal, too patronising and just not good enough.

The players politely chipped away at the granite stance proffered by the Football Association. During 1960, they continued to negotiate, working skilfully in contract talks, always taking legal advice and never stepping out of line. Over time this began to frustrate the football powers, and at one stage the league committee even stated that discussions with the players' representatives would cease. The players, led by Jimmy Hill, reported an 'industrial dispute' in January.

However, during the spring and summer, both sides met again to resume hostilities and were assisted in arbitration by an early form of ACAS. In November, the league spluttered out a few incentives, but the meeting descended into total chaos.

The players' representatives, meeting in three separate locations in the country, were hanging out for two principal changes: the abolition of the maximum wage, and an end to the loathed 'retain and transfer' system. The players gave full backing to their representatives, and instructed them to go to *any* lengths to obtain these rights.

Early in December, the clubs' chairmen met and adamantly refused to accede to the demands of the players or their representatives. This inflamed the players as never before, and after holding further regional discussions, they gave a formal one month's notice of their decision to strike—to totally withdraw their 'labour'; this date was 21st January 1961. The minister for labour, John Hare, interrupted a tour of the north-east to become involved at this point.

The clubs tried to call the bluff of the players, saying that they would field amateur sides to complete fixtures and to satisfy the contracts they had with the football pools companies. The public were alarmed and stuck in the middle. They did not want to see their beloved game disappear, but neither did they want to accept the quality of amateur football. Over Christmas 1960, a truce was declared in all areas.

In a meeting on 9th January 1961, the clubs agreed to scrap the maximum wage, but would keep the 'retain and transfer' system. The players thought only half the job was done and held out, and on January 18th, three days before the scheduled strike, the clubs capitulated and freedom of contract was included. The strike was averted, and the game continued uninterrupted. It was said that the shackles were off the shekels.

Even this wasn't the end of the story. Further rumblings began to emerge, this time from the clubs, who were very concerned over the players' new-found freedom, saying that somewhere there had been a misunderstanding and that their representatives had never offered freedom of contract. In March of 1961, the clubs reneged on that aspect of the agreement, despite the fact than an eminent QC had stated that the clubs' case would never stand up in court.

The TUC remarked that the change of stance had been the most diabolical double-cross in the history of industrial relations. George Eastham would eventually win a historic battle in the courts over the 'retain and transfer' issue but this would not happen for more than two years, in the summer of 1963.

After the abolition of the maximum wage, many in the country expected Johnny Haynes to move to a more fashionable and successful club almost immediately. Haynes, however, was far more loyal than people realised. With the 'glass half-full' attitude, Haynes mused that if 'lesser' teams such as Leicester City and Luton Town could reach the cup final, and Nottingham Forest could actually win it, then a team like Fulham must have a chance.

Also if teams like Burnley could play in Europe, then Fulham could well be in there pitching. Fulham had progressed to the FA Cup semi-final already under Haynes' control as a Second Division team—why not again? Haynes made an astute observation: "A player can pick a new team every year and still never pick up a championship medal."

Tommy Trinder heard of the lifting of the maximum wage whilst appearing in pantomime at Golders Green, and amongst the greasepaint and powder, he was asked delicately how he would handle the financial ramifications. A master of the ad-lib, Tommy was a little stunned; he said: "Obviously, we must find out what lolly Johnny is hoping to pick up. This figure will then have to be balanced against what we should pay other top players to strike a fair comparison in ability and effort. There is also the small question of how much we have in the kitty.

"He deserves all we can give...but there is a level where taxation would mean merely making another handsome donation to Her Majesty's government."

Even in this wages victory, a modest Haynes did not want to exploit Fulham. He said of the potential £100 per week: "Of course I won't hold them to that, it would hardly be fair or fitting." When asked what his demands might be, he said politely, "That's a little delicate; naturally I want to pick up as much as I can. I'll see what they offer first and then we can negotiate."

Back to league action

Black January ended with a dark 1–6 home defeat at the hands of Sheffield Wednesday, although Haynes missed the match through injury. His absence led to Stan Brown's debut. Fulham hit rock bottom, the makeshift team looking untalented and demoralised, with little or no co-ordination between attack and defence.

The tone was set by stand-in captain Alan Mullery's own goal in the very first minute. Tony Macedo, asleep and kicking the mud off his boots against the post, failed to spot Mullery's over-hit and lax back pass and Fulham were a goal down. Somehow Brian O'Connell contrived to conjure a headed equaliser, but the first forty-five minutes were one long agony for the fans, as the team found itself three goals behind at the interval. It was a little better in the second half, but two more late goals had everyone begging for the final whistle.

The local papers were already calling this a crisis year; with no reserve strength, the pressure was on a few good players. The last comment from the press was: "To say that Fulham missed the Johnny Haynes touch and the services of Graham Leggat is putting it mildly—this was surely the poorest Fulham side fielded this season."

February

Events became worse the following month with three more consecutive defeats in the league against Chelsea, Preston and Burnley. Against Chelsea, although Jimmy Hill was fit enough to return to combine with Johnny Haynes to produce a few purple patches, Fulham were poor again, and loose marking and a sprung offside trap gave Jimmy Greaves the winner shortly before half-time. Haynes had not played well at the Bridge, received no mentions and had appeared distracted. Ominously Chelsea were on poor form as well and this was their first victory in *ten* matches!

A dressing room bust-up?

Somehow the press got hold of a story of unrest in the Fulham dressing room, and reported that Haynes had demanded a transfer. This scoop was based on an overheard bust-up at Stamford Bridge following the 1–2 defeat. The story went to press, and Haynes admitted that there had been a fairly heated row.

He was away with England taking part in an early form of get-together at Anfield, where the England team played a Liverpool XI in a training match. On hearing the story, he phoned general manager Frank Osborne, who was able to put his mind at rest, confirming that he had the full support of the team. Again Haynes was miffed at the press for falsely putting out allegations that were without foundation and this further fuelled his distrust of some of the media.

It was the same story but worse at Deepdale where Fulham lost 0–2. It was bottom-of-the-table Preston's first win for four months and *fifteen* matches, and Haynes just wasn't in it. He had another off-day, failing to colour the game at all, and the whole team appeared to sag and had little appetite on the mud-filled pitch. Fulham were in the match up to the last minute, when Preston's second goal went in. The press said that Fulham's key man Johnny Haynes was lost in the mud.

The weekend match against Burnley was delayed and instead Fulham played a friendly against West Ham at the Cottage on the Saturday and won 2–1. Haynes had a very quiet game, although he looked as if he could have upped the pace if league points had been at stake. Young Mike Johnson scored both Fulham goals.

Champions Burnley arrived in midweek but Fulham's league form continued to nosedive with a 0–1 home loss. Fulham were right out of luck once again against the fourth-placed team. Haynes went close on several occasions, Trevor Watson hit a post and when Haynes put Maurice Cook through with a beauty he also hit the post. Fulham had the lion's share of the play, but, almost inevitably, Burnley broke away to score the winner just fourteen minutes from the end. Young reserve forward Mike Johnson was the latest to be forced to play his first match of the season due to the continuing injury crisis.

Johnny Haynes is unsettled as Fulham struggle

By this point, Fulham had won just *one* of their last *fourteen* league matches, which included eleven defeats, and the team had plummeted down the league

A muddied Haynes in the thick of the battle, a crucial relegation fixture against Blackpool. Responding to the skipper's pleas, the team reacted positively, defeating the Seasiders 4–3.

to sixteenth place, now looking like firm candidates for relegation.

Haynes' mind was definitely on his possible Italian move; he hadn't been sleeping well for the last couple of months, and the stress was beginning to eat into his football. This second season in the top flight was proving a very tough one for the Fulham and England captain.

He spelt out to his team what relegation might mean. Fulham's next match was at the Cottage against Blackpool who were themselves in desperate need of points, bottom of the table. They contained the evergreen Stanley Matthews in their ranks, still playing on strongly at the age of forty-six.

Fulham responded to their captain's request in style and took an early two-goal lead through Hill and Cook; Blackpool pulled that back to one goal. Fortunately, despite the transcendent artistry of Matthews, Fulham broke away twice whilst under Blackpool pressure in the second half to build up an unassailable lead, Haynes making the third goal for young Johnson with the perfect opening.

Although wingers Matthews and Perry were being blunted by George Cohen and Jim Langley, Blackpool wouldn't lie down and due to casual marking they pulled the game around with two goals of their own in the last eight minutes. Fulham managed to hang on grimly in a nervous finish to register a 4–3 win.

Haynes was praised in the match for his cunning and the series of crisp, precise passes. He was, however, still shocked by some of the defensive lapses going on around him. The only real plus was that Fulham had scored four good goals, and had given themselves a glimmer of hope.

March

At the start of the month, Fulham didn't improve immediately, and they lost 0–1 at Everton. But this time it was down to bad luck rather than bad play, and the winning goal came just four minutes from the end. Goalkeeper Tony Macedo protested that as Gabriel's cross floated in over his head, he had been clearly impeded by Everton forward Alex Young, but the referee waved aside his protests.

Fulham had made and missed some good chances, and the watching press surmised that Fulham would not be relegated if they continued to play like this. Johnny Haynes' own play was still pretty much in the doldrums and little was said about his performance. Fulham also picked up further injuries with centre half Derek Lampe a hobbling passenger at centre forward for most of the match.

Fulham, in financial difficulties, were further destabilised when a mystery bidder attempted to purchase the freehold of Craven Cottage from the Church Commissioners. Trinder was shocked and so began negotiations offering a five-figure sum in an attempt to secure the freehold interest for the club.

At the same time, thirty-four-year-old Jim Gregory, a tycoon car dealer, made an offer to put £50,000 on the table to enable Fulham to buy reinforcements to help stave off relegation. Gregory said, "This has nothing to do with my business, but I cannot deny that I have an ambition to get on to the Fulham board." Gregory ultimately made his name as chairman of Queens Park Rangers in the Sixties.

Fulham then managed a 2–2 draw at home against Bolton Wanderers, Haynes making the second goal for Graham Leggat with a quick, accurate corner seconds before half-time. Haynes was praised for the usual supply of precision passes. But the team did nothing to alleviate the pressure on their hard-working skipper, and they still looked booked for a rapid return to Division Two. Fulham were twice in the lead, but consistent defensive laxity cost them yet another valuable point.

Confidence was significantly raised by a morale-boosting 2–1 win at relegation-threatened West Ham. This result seemed to enable the Cottagers to turn the corner. Injury-hit Fulham were bolstered by the return of Bill Dodgin from Arsenal, who came back at centre half for the match, and played a significant role.

Fulham rode their luck at times, but won in the end, as the press said, "largely due to the skill of captain Johnny Haynes. He took matters into his own hands. He played inside left, left half and even centre half; he finished in defence to ensure that West Ham didn't get an equaliser."

Haynes was described by the papers as being involved in the move of the season. He came down the wing, shoulders bunched, head down, dribbled thirty yards, exchanged passes with Cook, stopped dead, sidestepped a defender, looked up and fired in a shot—narrowly wide. After Maurice Cook had equalised a West Ham opener, Bobby Moore of all people gifted Fulham victory with a needless handball in the penalty area on the hour that enabled Jim Langley to win the match for Fulham from the resultant penalty.

Fulham followed this result with what was probably their best performance of the season, a 0–0 draw at home to a top-of-the-table Tottenham side steaming towards the double. Fulham had to be at their very best to match them. It was a helter-skelter game played at furious speed. It was full of marvellous shooting from both sets of forwards, matched by inspired goalkeeping

In the first minute, Haynes had a shot punched away. His masterly play won more praise and was described as "a sort of confidence that's a sign of greatness. He was master of the midfield manoeuvres. His passing had uncanny accuracy." It was a classic match, with Spurs in the end hanging on to salvage a point from rampant Fulham.

Alan Mullery was dominant in the match, blotting out wingers Cliff Jones and Terry Dyson. Spurs would not have a harder match all season. Despite all this, neither side produced a goal. Even the watching reporters were impressed: "Fulham will *not* go down."

The following Good Friday saw Arsenal come to the Cottage. Arsenal were not a great side but they were on good form. They plundered a two-goal lead, and Fulham heads went down; at this stage they looked like a well-beaten side.

Haynes was the exception, and he turned the tables with two thumping, right-footed goals in the last eight minutes, the second in injury time, to scrape a point in a 2–2 draw. For the first, he took possession, broke through the middle, manoeuvred himself into position, and fired home a sliding shot.

The second, also from the edge of the penalty area, followed a typical Haynes swivel that masked the ball from a defender in the tightest of spaces and foxed the entire defence. This was followed by a searing shot into the opposite corner of the net.

Both efforts gave Welsh international Jack Kelsey in the Arsenal goal no chance at all. Haynes' celebrations were a restrained jump for joy, not quite letting go. They were his first goals of the year. Although the press were pleased for Fulham, and expected the point gained to keep them in the First Division, most conceded that Fulham expected too much from their captain. Another said: "The policy of persistently playing the ball to Haynes has landed the club in its current serious predicament. The forwards all seem to want to pass the ball back to Haynes as soon as they receive it!"

Planning Scotland's downfall with Bobby Smith and Jimmy Greaves during pre-match training at a muddy, grassless Stamford Bridge.

April

Fulham then did themselves no favours at all with two early defeats in the month over Easter. The first was at Old Trafford where they lost 1–3 and the cultured play of Haynes seemed futile, for his colleagues gave him little support. Fulham scored first early on, goalkeeper Tony Macedo was magnificent throughout, but in the end the pressure told with inevitable consequences.

At Highbury two days later, despite losing 2–4, Fulham played very well, coming from two goals down to get back to level terms, with Johnny Haynes' brilliantly judged chip putting the equaliser on to Leggat's head, the Scot providing a beautiful finish.

Two of England's nine goals against Scotland, both scored by Haynes. In the top picture he turns away in triumph after beating goalkeeper Haffey for the sixth goal; in the lower photograph, Haynes (out of picture) nets the seventh just four minutes later.

Fulham fell to two fairly late goals, the match finally being decided in the last minute. Two of Arsenal's goals came from penalties and two were scored by veteran Scot Jackie Henderson, who would join Fulham the following season.

Relegation beckons

However, the drop was edging ever nearer and the dark relegation trapdoor was opening up. Fulham were very fortunate at this stage that other teams around them were likewise failing. The Highbury match was followed by a 1–1 home draw with lowly Aston Villa that kept Fulham perilously close to the relegation zone, as they dropped to eighteenth.

The draw with Villa was another dour affair, the attack being described as a thing of rags and tatters, with the exception of Haynes. He struggled to bring some cohesion into the attack, and their scrappy work gave the impression of a side that *was* going to be relegated. In this game Fulham were once again thankful for a superb equaliser from the classy Leggat, who rounded three defenders before beating the onrushing goalkeeper.

Haynes missed the next Fulham match at Leicester with good reason—a certain encounter with the Scots at Wembley. He left his colleagues behind with a very heavy heart; Leicester City were playing strongly, were the cup finalists and had not lost at home since the early

The triumphant captain is carried aloft by his England colleagues at Wembley after England 9, Scotland 3. Receiving the championship trophy from the Queen was his proudest moment.

days of the season way back in September. Haynes was none too optimistic about the team's chances.

The pinnacle of Johnny Haynes' career, a 9–3 victory over Scotland

If you hadn't seen or heard much of Haynes at three o'clock at Wembley on 15th April 1961, by five o'clock you knew all about him. Eleven years (to the actual day) after annihilating the Scottish schoolboys, Haynes scored two more at Wembley against Scotland but mostly spent that heady afternoon passing the loaded revolver to Jimmy Greaves, who scored three, and the others in that memorable forward line who inflicted the 9–3 pasting. The Scots were no mean side, but their defence was repeatedly ripped to tatters by Haynes' rapier-like passing.

England scored early on and were three up at half-time. Bobby Robson scored the first with a twenty-yard shot after just nine minutes. This was followed by two goals from Jimmy Greaves, applying the finishing touches to superb Haynes passes, firstly with an ice-cool finish and a delightful lob in the twentieth minute, and then from a rebound.

England then took their foot off the gas and Scotland, playing well, brought the score back to three-two within six minutes of the second half. Just as they were pressing hard for the equaliser, everything went right for England. Haynes used a quick free kick to give Bryan Douglas the fourth, the Scots not being ready for it, and then Bobby Smith scored number five in the seventy-fourth minute. Still the Scots wouldn't give it up and pulled the score back to five-three.

There wasn't much to choose between the attacks, both were excellent, but Haynes finally wrested control of midfield, and from then on it was one-way traffic. He scored goal number six when through on his own in the seventy-eighth minute and goal number seven just four minutes later. The Scots just didn't have the quality in defence and sometimes only Celtic defender Billy McNeill and goalkeeper Frank Haffey stood between the goal and a host of marauding English forwards.

There followed an exhibition goal from Greaves for his hat trick and the eighth a minute after that, and then Smith wrapped it up with the ninth, and his second, four minutes from time. England had managed to score five in the space of just thirteen minutes. At the time it was the highest number of goals ever scored in a match at Wembley stadium. It was also Scotland's heaviest ever defeat at the time. Frank Haffey, the Scots keeper that day, fled to Australia, and by emigrating hoped to escape the memories.

Haynes was described variously by the national press as: "king of the giants", "a player extraordinary" and his performance as "his greatest display—ever!" It was summed up by: "He truly has become the golden boy of soccer." The England team overall was praised, the press saying: "Great to belong to the soccer nation that has bred men like Jimmy Greaves and Johnny Haynes, and great to watch this team, and realise that finally England have the men to challenge the world again."

Sir Bobby Robson recalled: "He was brilliant, absolutely dominated the game; he was untouchable on the day. And it wasn't a bad Scotland side either—Denis Law, Ian St John and Dave Mackay played. But make no mistake, just look at the goalscorers; we had a *very* good England team indeed at the time."

Hat trick hero Greaves said of this England side: "The fact that England enjoyed such an amazing sequence and scored so many goals was in no little part down to Johnny Haynes. In the 9–3 victory over Scotland he produced a performance that surely ensures his place in the pantheon of football gods. Bobby Smith and Johnny each scored twice. Bobby Robson and Bryan Douglas got a goal apiece and I managed a hat trick, but it was Johnny Haynes at his merciless best who was the provider. Johnny controlled the slaughter, pulling the Scottish defence apart with a procession of precision passes that created countless openings."

It was certainly a red-letter day for Haynes and also the pinnacle of his career. After receiving the British Championship trophy from Her Majesty the Queen, Haynes was cheered off the pitch on the shoulders of his colleagues Jimmy Armfield and Peter Swan.

He knew it had been the biggest day of his career: "I, as captain, collected the trophy from the Queen; before I knew what was happening, the lads had me up in the air. We were all feeling nine feet tall anyway. You can't ask for a better day than that."

Later in life he admitted: "That's the moment I live over and over again, the one which makes everything worthwhile. I can tell you there was none prouder than England's captain that day. There are hard times in football—but this was not one of them!"

The day after the game, Haynes declared: "This is the best team I have ever captained; the main thing is we are scoring goals. Things didn't look too good when Scotland pulled up to 3–2, but I thought that if we kept on playing our kind of football, goals would come. They did!

"After the fourth goal went in, everything we hit ended up in the back of the net. Players from teams like Manchester United and West Brom had to leave Wembley straight away to catch their trains, but a few of the London lads gathered to have a bit of a party. Bobby Smith and Jimmy Greaves of Spurs came out with me; it was quite a night."

Very much later in life, Haynes confessed: "But seriously, can I come clean after all these years? That 9–3 was a bit of a travesty really. On the hour it was only 3–2 and still anybody's game. Scotland had a terrific attack and might just as easily have got a grip on us, but in those last twenty-odd minutes we just couldn't do anything wrong, almost supernatural, everything we tried ended up in the back of the net. We'd have beaten any team in history in that last half-hour."

Final goals in an England shirt

Haynes wouldn't know it on this day of triumph, but those two goals would be his last in an England shirt. For those interested in statistics, during the Scotland game Haynes made fifty-one passes, ranging from six yards to forty yards, of which only five failed to reach their intended target—a 90% accuracy rate. His prospective Italian employers must have been salivating.

Fulham general manager Frank Osborne was quick to acknowledge Haynes at the peak of his game: "It's almost as if he has a radio antenna which receives signals, telling him what to do with the ball. Most first class players run with the ball and then pause momentarily to get their bearings and decide where to pass it, but not Johnny Haynes. He sprays out passes as quick as a flash where they will do most good—and few go astray."

The match had meant a great deal to Haynes, and he readily admitted: "If I was asked to choose between any of the game's honours I would take that of being the captain of England as the greatest of all. I prize the honour above all others. I am jealous of England's international reputation, I want it to be of the highest while I lead her, but then so does any player taking part, be he the captain or the newest boy in the international side."

However, being a typical club man, and even after his greatest triumph, his first question on leaving the Wembley pitch was, "How did Fulham get on?" Haynes' greatest day was then further embellished with the fantastic news that even in his absence, Fulham had *won* their vital league match 2–1 at high-flying Leicester. They had ridden their luck a little at Filbert Street, and two uncharacteristic slips by goalkeeper Gordon Banks led to the Fulham goals. Graham Leggat once again scored the winner; he always did well against Leicester City! Haynes' day was complete.

Is it Haynes' last game for Fulham?

It now emerged that during the past three months Johnny Haynes *had* been conducting further serious negotiations with representatives from Milan, with the full consent and knowledge of the Fulham board of directors. During this period of discussion, the maximum wage in England had been abolished. The negotiations had come to a head in April prior to the game between England and Scotland.

News was leaking out that Jimmy Greaves had already been secured on a 'heads of terms' agreement with Milan, and the Italian shopping list was plastered across the back pages of virtually every national paper

A solemn Haynes trudges off the muddy Craven Cottage pitch after the 1–1 draw against Blackburn that meant Fulham were safe from relegation. But would he ever play for Fulham again? He should have been happy but here was a man with a lot on his mind.

on almost a daily basis. All the top British talents were up for grabs: Joe Baker, Denis Law, Bobby Charlton and of course England captain Johnny Haynes. The press appeared to have the inside track too, as Milan was Haynes' quoted destination.

Blackburn Rovers then arrived at the Cottage for another vital crunch match. Rovers were doing very well in the division, and Fulham had won just four league fixtures since mid-November. It was virtually the same date in the season as it had been in 1958 against Rovers, but this time it was a relegation struggle for Fulham rather than a promotion battle. There was also the question: Would the Craven Cottage faithful ever again see Johnny Haynes play in a Fulham shirt?

Haynes clearly struggled throughout the very tense match; uncharacteristically he appeared worried and was well below his usual form. The fans were desperately trying to keep him at Fulham by applauding their skipper every time he touched the ball.

Fulham went a goal behind, and luck was running with them when Blackburn should have increased their lead, but didn't. Eventually Haynes cleared the cobwebs from his mind just enough to send Graham Leggat through the Blackburn defence with an exquisite pass just nine minutes from the end to level the match.

With his back to goal, he screwed the ball through the middle to Leggat who dribbled round a defender and the goalkeeper to score. The crowd were delirious, as the 1–1 draw was enough to see Fulham safe from relegation. Immediately after the whistle many didn't know whether that one point would be enough, but it was; Preston had lost at home and ultimately Newcastle United were also pushed into the relegation furnace. Fulham's next step was to secure Haynes.

Johnny Haynes off to Italy?

The news came through that Italy's ban on imported players had indeed been relaxed, as was expected, and the whole deal for Haynes to move abroad appeared to be gathering pace. Although Haynes never got to see the bid, it is almost certain that Milan tabled an offer of £100,000 for him, an astronomical sum that staggered all of football and Fleet Street. Both Milan and Roma now wanted Haynes.

A Roma emissary, Collaluci, came to London to find out what it would take to get Haynes out to Rome, knowing that he would have to outstrip his salary and his income from endorsements and his bookmaking business.

Originally the Milan bid was shrouded in secrecy, and the Italians actually denied making a £100,000 offer, stating that the bid had come from a freelance talent scout. An irritated Tommy Trinder said, "If their bid wasn't genuine, then why did Milan officials telephone me at the Fulham ground last night? Why did they insist on making a separate phone call to talk with Haynes?" After a period of cat and mouse, both clubs agreed that there were negotiations in progress. The *News of the World* exclusively printed a copy of the telegram sent to Trinder from Milan officials outlining their offer.

Haynes was reputedly offered a £15,000 signing-on fee payable over three years, and inside this initial incentive, a three-year contract, with bonuses and wages, up to £9,000 per year. These wages were around ten times that of the working man, and double that of a cabinet minister! He would also be given a car, villa and servants—he would have been set up for life.

The lower cost of living and lower income tax were another great attraction. There would also be the possibility of playing alongside the world's greatest players; this was a window of opportunity to test his skills against the best and of course play in European cup football. He knew in his heart that, on current wages, Fulham would never stand in his way.

The telephone rang incessantly in the Haynes household, and he felt under real pressure. He had truly never considered moving abroad before, but since the approach the matter now occupied all of his waking time. He needed some quick answers from the club. He said at the time, "Normally I would look about a week ahead, now I was having to plan my whole future."

The clash: "Should I stay or should I go?"

Johnny Haynes had to weigh up the plusses and the minuses without emotion. He was certainly not an impetuous man, and would deliberate soberly on the merits of both sides of the case. On the *plus* side for Italy, apart from the remunerative aspects, were the sunshine and living in that beautiful country.

Then he looked at the *plus* signs for staying at home—and there were many.

Firstly, he was a Londoner and, make no mistake, he loved London. His parents were with him, his non-footballing associates and friends were in London, his playing colleagues were in London and he had a number of very close friends in the team, who mixed well socially at clubs and shows. Jim Langley, Jimmy Hill, Graham Leggat, Maurice Cook and of course Trevor Chamberlain were all there. Haynes readily admitted, "We were a really happy bunch at Craven Cottage."

He was also the commanding figure of the Fulham team. He liked to have things his way and in Italy, and also maybe at other league clubs in England, it might not have been the same. He was given free rein by his manager and close friend Bedford Jezzard. He maintained an admirable fealty towards the club. He considered that loyalty was very important, and that he owed Fulham something for giving him his big chance.

On the wider front, he was also captain of England, and he was playing in an England team on excellent form and heading for the 1962 World Cup; he thought he owed the team in particular something, as well as owing something to the English game in general.

As for the money, Haynes' business associates were in London, and he had a number of lucrative commercial contracts, already earning him as much as £100 per week. The most important factor of all was that Jimmy Hill had succeeded in forcing the abandonment of the dreaded maximum wage in January.

There were also some *minuses* in joining an Italian club. Haynes didn't live the high life and wasn't really one for the bright lights. As a bachelor, he didn't really relish living alone in a new land with a new culture and a new language; professionally he knew it could make playing difficult if he had trouble translating what his team-mates said. Perhaps he lacked a little self-confidence when he said, "Imagine me sitting in an Italian dressing room with ten other blokes whose language I couldn't understand—I'd feel a proper Charlie."

Haynes would have only moved to Milan, not Roma, because "Jimmy Greaves was also there," but he would have still thought of himself as a foreigner. Also being a fairly shy guy away from the pitch, he didn't really fancy the goldfish bowl existence in Italy.

Haynes started working on the figures. Being commercially very astute, he worked out pretty quickly that his potential 'new' salary at home, augmented by his endorsements, investments and other commercial activities, could possibly earn him as much money as playing in Italy. For three years, however, he could probably survive Italy. Although his heart was saying Fulham and England, his head was saying "Go for the cash and the lure of the lira in Italy."

Now that the maximum wage in Britain had been scrapped, Haynes *had* to test the water with Fulham and Tommy Trinder. It was just two businessmen with an issue to resolve, and the outcome would probably depend on a logical gut feeling. He knew that Fulham could never offer or even approach the fabulous figures being touted by Italy, but he evaluated and fixed a figure in his head.

Typically, Haynes would never have wanted the discussions to be a public spectacle, and he was unable to contact Tommy Trinder on the Saturday evening after the Blackburn match. Tommy was, however, cornered by journalists on that evening, and said emotionally: "It's impossible to put a figure on Johnny's head. Right now I feel that £100,000 is not enough. It's either £100,000 or a kick in the face for us, but I'll offer Johnny £5,000 a year to keep him. Let the other clubs bellyache. They didn't ask me when they were tossing around cheques for £40,000 and £50,000!

"Maybe it will break us, I don't know, but Johnny is worth more than £100,000 to us, or anyone else. I'd like to say to him, this place is yours, you pay the other ten!

"This boy has been with us for eleven years. He's been maligned and misunderstood, but by heavens he's done us proud. It's up to him now—a yes or a no. We can wrap it all up in ten minutes."

After the Blackburn match Haynes said of the Milan offer: "I don't know exactly what's in it for me. If it's a fantastic offer, and things don't go well for me here, I'll have to think it over. But I am a Londoner and I don't want to leave. Fulham is a big part of my life, and would I be able to play for England if I left? Even if I put a clause in my contract, the Italian League could rule the other way."

High noon in leafy Surrey

On Sunday 23rd April, after helping to secure Fulham's place in the First Division, Haynes phoned chairman Tommy Trinder at home. He always trusted Tommy Trinder, and respected his position in show business. Trinder was at home entertaining friends, but immediately invited him over.

Haynes discussed what wage he would like over a gentlemanly Sunday afternoon cup of tea in leafy-green Surrey. Trinder put Fulham's position and proposed a salary in the space of three minutes. Haynes' response inside two minutes was just as emphatic: "I'm happy to stay at Fulham." The whole verbal side of the

It may have been raining when this picture was taken at his Epsom home, but for Haynes the sun was shining. He'd just agreed to stay at Fulham, where Trinder had kept his word by offering him £100 a week. The new deal had been concluded between the two men in just five minutes over a cup of tea.

transaction was concluded in less than five minutes!

Trinder had been as good as his word and Rose Haynes was delighted and thanked Trinder for keeping her son at home. Most of the press were also pleased that the England captain was staying within these shores. Although Haynes never spoke of £100 per week, he did little to deny it either when questioned later by journalists. The true values would emerge when contracts were renewed on July 1st.

I'm staying with Fulham

After the dust had settled, Haynes said: "I am staying with Fulham and England next season instead of going to Italy. I have never yearned for the high life, the highly paid life, the sunshine or the soccer of Italy. All I have wanted is to stay at home with my mother and father, my girlfriend Eileen Farmer, my old dog Chum, my friends and *my* club Fulham. ... The gap between the salary Fulham offered me and the sums I might have earned from Italy will be partly filled by my income from my outside interests."

He had done his sums, and he knew that by accepting Trinder's offer he would be earning probably a third in basic salary terms of what he could have earned in Italy, but the true Haynes shone through. He knew and understood that Fulham as a smaller club were paying the absolute maximum they could afford, and in the end the pull of London, the familiar surroundings of Craven Cottage and his team-mates kept him in the country. He was also very pleased that Fulham wanted him to stay so much.

He said later in life: "I lost money by staying at Fulham, but they had been very good to me and on the contract I secured, I preferred to stay there. I would not have gone to any other [English] club on those terms."

As he prized his England international career so highly, Haynes stipulated in the contract that he would *always* be released for any England commitment; Trinder readily agreed to that. Trinder had also been fairly astute in this deal, as he knew that he would have had to fork out a similar sum to replace a player of Haynes' calibre, assuming of course that lowly Fulham could entice another player of Haynes' ability to join them! Also he reckoned that the club would have probably been taxed highly on Haynes' transfer fee, if they had accepted the Italians' massive offer.

Ultimately Haynes may have been right to stay as many of the English stars who went to Italy, apart maybe from John Charles, returned to these shores after just one or two years. Londoner Jimmy Greaves was one player who missed the capital badly and despite being one of football's hottest stars in England, returned home very quickly.

Haynes would often say publicly that although later times with Fulham had their frustrations, he never had any regrets about staying with them. For him it was "peace of mind at last—and for me it's rainy old England!"

George Cohen remembers: "It was amazing, really. I mean, he could have gone to any club in the world, and Milan offered £100,000 for him which was an enormous amount of money, and even though he was an Englishman going abroad, you'd have to say about the salary…just a minute, that's really attractive. But like me he was a big fish in a small pond and there was a great family atmosphere."

Following the retention of Haynes, the Fulham team rejoiced and relaxed completely, finishing the season in fine style with a thumping 4–2 victory over third-placed Wolves at Molineux. In closing this season, Haynes showed exactly how valuable he was to the team. Fulham were two up in the first four minutes through Cook and O'Connell and in each case Haynes was the brains behind the goal.

After Wolves had replied, another great cross from Haynes in the fifty-third minute gave Cook his second. Then Haynes made a rare boob; in trying to lob the ball back he gave it away to a Wolves winger, who streaked away and scored!

Naturally he redeemed himself; in the sixty-eighth minute he rammed in a shot which was pushed behind for a corner. He took the corner himself and Maurice Cook completed his hat trick. The papers just marvelled at the brilliance of Johnny Haynes.

Summary

Fulham finished the season in seventeenth place, a poor final position. In all competitions, Fulham had gone back to their bad old ways and conceded over 100 goals, whilst the goals scored were thirty short of that figure.

Newcastle, who had scored fifteen goals against Fulham in three encounters that season, were relegated. A bad crop of injuries was partly responsible for the poor showing, but a lack of quality and experience in the reserve side, especially in the forward line, had cost Fulham dear.

There was no doubt at all that Haynes' domestic form had been poor in the four months of 1961, and some thought his mind was elsewhere. After five goals in the opening eight games, sharpshooter Haynes finished the season with just nine, scoring in only three other matches after the middle of September. He had still continued to put in the occasional excellent display, but some were not up to his gold standard.

Fulham were thankful for the super Scot Graham Leggat's twenty-three goals in thirty-six games, and Maurice Cook's twelve. In this particular season, these two probably did more to keep Fulham in the First Division than Haynes did. Even so, many described it as Haynes' greatest season so far, having played his heart out for Fulham and England.

Around this time, Haynes opened his heart a little admitting some of his faults, but also taking time to have his first real digs back at the press, especially those northern papers that had never taken to him. He had always harboured the thought that northern fans resented him because the England selectors were all based cosily in London and believed that matches north of Watford were unimportant.

He said: "From time to time it's been reported that I am demanding and over demonstrative, over-rated, over-publicised, with small talent and a big opinion of myself. I like to think my role as England captain has helped modify some of those views, because I don't honestly believe they are all true."

To finish the season on a near perfect note, Johnny Haynes was voted runner-up in the Footballer of the Year poll, coming second to the exceptional skipper of Tottenham Hotspur's double-winning side, Danny Blanchflower. He was also voted one of the runners-up to boxer Terry Downes by the Sports Journalists Association; this prize was rarely given to a footballer.

The maximum wage fallout

Haynes' potential salary caused shockwaves throughout the football world, many claiming it had set a very dangerous precedent. Many clubs thought they would be ruined if they were forced to pay similar wages to their own star players—even though they had been making money for years by keeping players' wages down. Members of Parliament referred to the Johnny Haynes affair, and the matter was discussed at the highest levels.

Criticisms were directed at Fulham from other club chairmen from the First and Second Division regarding Haynes' potential wages. This cut no ice with Frank Osborne, who defended the club saying: "They have no grouse. They voted to remove the maximum wage. It's no good trying to arrange an artificial ceiling, which is what some clubs would like now!"

Senior clubs met in an attempt to form a cartel in order to agree an under-the-counter maximum wage as there was no longer an official maximum. On the other side of the coin, the top players met in London to swap ideas on their plans, and for the first time they were employing accountants to assist them in their deliberations. Many senior players were now saying that £50 per week was the lowest weekly figure that they were prepared to entertain.

Clubs cut back and pruned their staff to compensate for the larger salaries paid to their star first-team players, and ironically this led to Jimmy Hill, who had fought so hard and helped negotiate Haynes' contract, being one of the first to feel the axe at Fulham, and he was given a free transfer in the summer of 1961. Roy Bentley was also released alongside several other junior players. It was rumoured initially that Fulham's playing staff would have to be drastically cut from thirty-three to twenty to accommodate the Haynes wage and other players' higher salaries!

This was again something that general manager Frank Osborne had predicted: "The players were warned when they wanted the wage restriction removed that a few would benefit and a lot would suffer."

In the end, the cuts did not take Fulham's playing staff down to the predicted level, but such was the outlay that it led to the suspension of other projects such as the plans for floodlights. This was because Fulham had confirmed that they were not going to raise season ticket or admission prices to supplement the increased wages.

It was very rough luck on Jimmy Hill who had worked so hard for everybody else. An injured Hill made no comment, except: "I am making no decision on my future, until I get my knee injury cleared up, and that will mean an operation in the summer." He never played league football again.

He quit football with a parting shot regarding clubs' sabre-rattling about future wholesale unemployment in the game, saying: "Clubs must still have some sort of reserve team in which to bring through their younger players and I think many of them are having second thoughts about mass clearouts. And remember, last year the PFA coped with 700 unwanted players last season, and most of them were fixed up."

Team group photographed during the get-together for the Mexico match. Standing: Robson, Armfield, Flowers, Springett, Swan, McNeill; in front: Douglas, Kevan, Smith, Haynes, Charlton.

Haynes also lost a mentor. Roy Bentley's release was another major surprise as, although he was thirty-six, he could still have helped the club as player/coach. He was still a quality player and servant, and still head and shoulders above some of the First Division defenders.

George Cohen and Alan Mullery both pleaded earnestly with the club to retain Bentley, as his own unofficial coaching of the youngsters had seen their personal standard of play improve dramatically. Roy Bentley went on to have two further very successful seasons down the road at Shepherd's Bush with Queens Park Rangers, eventually retiring at the age of thirty-eight.

Now eight goals against Mexico

May

Next up at Wembley were Mexico in a friendly, playing with virtually the same team that had beaten England two years before. England took a great revenge, winning 8–0. Johnny Haynes failed to score in the rout, but strangely the result gave him immense satisfaction.

Under Haynes' orchestration and captaincy, England had now scored *forty* goals in six matches in the space of just over six months. The team had been inspired by the vision and direction of Haynes, the prolific scoring form of Jimmy Greaves and Bobby Smith, the strength of Bryan Douglas and Bobby Charlton on the wings and, not least, the industry of Bobby Robson.

The England tour after this long season included a World Cup preliminary match and two friendlies, all three to be played in the space of seven days. Haynes considered that this bordered on madness, and he severely criticised the planning. The World Cup preliminary in Lisbon was played in immense heat in the high eighties. Haynes showed he was human when he plonked himself down in the centre circle on hearing the final whistle, immediately removing his boots, and walking off in stockinged feet. The match finished 1–1.

Beating Italy in their backyard

Three days later came a famous 3–2 friendly victory over Italy in Rome. The Italians were world famous for their *catenaccio,* a sweeper system that suffocated opposing teams. It was unheard of for Italy to concede three goals, especially at home. At one stage the Italians held a lead, but really squandered it.

Johnny Haynes accidentally injured the Italian goalkeeper Buffon, breaking his nose after he had dived at the Fulham man's feet to prevent a goal. The keeper was carried off, and this took some of the gloss off the game. Greaves laid on an equaliser and second goal for Gerry Hitchens, and then finally Haynes sent a superb penetrating pass through for Greaves to slot home the winner in the final minutes.

The Italians possessed a star in striker Enrique Sivori, who used to play with socks rolled down and did a celebration when he scored. Haynes, after the

A concerned Haynes helps bloodied Italian goalkeeper Buffon from the pitch after the accidental collision that resulted in a broken nose. A superb England performance in Italy ended in a 3–2 victory.

England winner, showed the lighter side of his nature, pulled down his socks and did a little jig mimicking the Italian's own celebrations; initially he was deluged by missiles thrown by infuriated Italians. The gifted Sivori was one of Haynes' top five favourite footballers of all time.

At the end of the game, Haynes drew all the England players together and led them on a lap of honour. The 100,000 crowd whistled and booed, then suddenly stopped. At first Haynes didn't know the reason for their sudden silence, then he realised the supporters had been showing their disapproval of the Italian team as they left the pitch. Once the last Italian player had disappeared down the tunnel, the England team continued their lap to polite applause.

England's unbeaten run finally came to an end with a 1–3 friendly defeat against Austria just four days later in Vienna. Two of the Austrian goals were scored late in the game when Haynes admitted the team were tiring fast in the last twenty minutes. However, he was confident about England's future, saying, "It was great to be in such a team, full of ideas, full of good football and full of goals."

For what remained of the close season following all the England matches, Haynes had committed himself to a contract to play for Toronto City in the Eastern Canada Professional League. The play was only third or fourth division standard at best, but he admitted that it kept him nicely tuned up.

He greatly enjoyed his time there and stayed for a further three weeks beyond his contract date. This left him only ten days in Majorca for a summer break. He said candidly, "Apart from the money I make, I prefer it that way. I always get fed up if I am out of the game for a few weeks." At the end of his stay in Canada, he commented, possibly to keep Fulham on their toes, "I like the people here. I would like to return and stay here permanently."

The first ever £100 a week player

July

At the start of this month, when his contract was renewed, Haynes became the very first English player to be paid £100 a week, a fortune back then, instantly becoming the highest paid footballer in England. He was the first player to take significant advantage of the freedom to negotiate contracts so brilliantly argued and astutely concluded by his Fulham team-mate Jimmy Hill.

Hill recalls: "When I got the wage limit scrapped, all Johnny had to do was knock on the door—and that's what he did." This financial breakthrough paved the way for the modern day football icon. Although his main love was playing, Haynes said at the time: "We professionals are in it for a living, and it's the money that matters. Don't let anyone kid you otherwise."

Fulham's chairman Tommy Trinder could not perhaps have imagined quite what a floodgate he was opening on that historic day in January 1961 when, as the first director to take advantage of the abolition of the maximum wage, he announced to the world, "Johnny Haynes is a top entertainer and will be paid as one from now on—I will give him £100 a week to play for Fulham." If this sum seems a far cry from the massive wages garnered by today's top players, it must be remembered that it was a huge amount then, and it was Trinder's recognition that the game's best players were not merely supreme sportsmen, but also stars of entertainment like himself.

Haynes' own recollection of that period was typically modest: "Looking back, I did not realise it would go the way it did. It was a bit of a hassle. We were threatening to go on strike at the time because we were on a maximum wage of £20 a week in the winter and £17 in summer. At the time at Fulham, we had a 'show business' type president in Tommy Trinder and he loved to be in the headlines.

"He opened his mouth and, not realising that the maximum wage was going to be abolished, said that if the maximum wage was abolished he would certainly pay me £100 a week. Of course, the maximum wage was abolished and he had to stick to it.

"To be fair to him, he did. I think he regretted it, but had to live with it; if the maximum wage hadn't been lifted I would definitely have gone abroad. It didn't change my life all that much; I put a few pounds

After England's victory over Italy in Rome, Jimmy Greaves and Johnny Haynes pause for a chat with an Italian fan, perhaps asking what life would be like if they ever decided to move to an Italian club.

in the bank. Having said that, I think I got a car soon afterwards. It was an S-type Jaguar and I think I paid £3,000 for a brand new one! Apart from that, I didn't go throwing my money around."

Haynes had apparently kept the press clipping in which Trinder had promised him the wage. Each year when the Fulham players had to re-negotiate their contracts, the players normally went in alphabetical order, but this time Haynes went in first. He was only in there for two minutes and when he came out he said, "That's me lads, £100 a week." He tore the press clipping up in the dressing room and let the pieces float to the floor.

Even at this magical time for him personally, Haynes still showed that he was in touch with the players whose careers had just finished or were almost finishing and who had missed the boat on the wage bonanza, players such as the great Jimmy Dickinson at Portsmouth, like Haynes a 'one-club' man for almost twenty years. Haynes said: "I have played for nine years under the shadow of the maximum wage; Jimmy will be retiring soon and will not have received the benefits of his great service."

The average working man's salary was then around £15 per week, so Haynes' new wage was almost seven times that of a man in the street. The increase made little difference to his lifestyle, as a third of his salary was lost in income tax alone. It was worked out that if Haynes' pay had gone up from £25 to £50, just *under* 50% of his total pay would have been lost to tax and other deductions. A rise from £50 to £100 per week would have seen the deductions *exceed* 50%. Certainly Haynes was in the hated 'super-tax' bracket.

Sir Bobby Robson pointed out that Haynes was acutely aware of the pay differentials between himself and his Fulham team-mates, and there was never a cheeseparing attitude from the great man: "He was generous with it; nobody else was allowed to pay for a drink or meal. He was a lovely man. I think he deserved to be the first £100 a week player, he worked so hard, and at the time he was the greatest player in the game." He recalled later in life: "I don't know anybody within Fulham Football Club at the time who begrudged him even £1 of that. He deserved it; he was the leader and the star. The remaining players got what was left. He was a true legend."

George Cohen concurs: "He was particularly generous, always first at the bar. It was amazing, we were never jealous of his £100 per week. Isn't it wonderful to think that his team-mates never felt they were being short-changed! I thought Fulham did the right thing, paying him the right money."

In some ways Haynes regretted being tarred with the epithet of the 'first £100 per week player', because as he said in his succinct way, "I think I had more to offer than that, to be honest with you."

What is truly amazing is that after the massive pay rise in 1961, Haynes is reputed *never to have received another pay rise from Fulham*, although, with inflation, the value of that weekly one hundred pounds was eroded significantly over the next decade. He said, "My wages didn't change from that moment on, so I was quite easy as far as the chairman was concerned!"

Haynes was now in a pleasant and self-contained world, happy to be a good host and entertain. Showing the convivial side of his nature, he held frequent parties at Epsom for his close friends, which were by all accounts fairly lively.

John's guests wouldn't necessarily be Fulham players or showbiz personalities, as he had a close

Johnny's girlfriend Eileen Farmer makes the papers! Here she is pictured in a film role, playing the part of a WRAF girl in the film 'On The Fiddle'.

circle of personal friends. His father Eddie was quiet but extremely hospitable, whilst his mother was an overt party-lover. The parties often went on until dawn, with many people ending up sleeping on the floor.

George Cohen recalls: "Rose and Eddie were terrific people, great hosts and what you consider a *real* mum and dad to be, and they were of course immensely proud of him. Often the parties went on very late; once I recall waking up on the stairs!"

Alan Mullery: "We was always there. June and I used to live at Worcester Park, just a few minutes down the road. Eddie and Rose were always at the parties. One night there was a knock at the door and there were Bobby Moore, Johnny Byrne, Alan Sealey and others from the West Ham side with their wives and girlfriends! Goodness knows how they knew there was a party at John's house, but we were all pals, did everything together."

Alan Mullery and Fred Callaghan both remember that Rose and Eddie weren't averse to helping out at the Cottage either. Alan Mullery recalls: "You never went straight home after a match. We used to stay possibly an hour or an hour and a half and congregate at the Cottage to talk about the game. John's Dad sometimes served behind the bar. He'd open up the cans of beer and Rose would go round with the sandwiches. There would be film stars there—great family times."

Haynes was more than happy to kick a ball around in his own back garden with friends or over on Epsom Downs. Like Bobby Robson, many players would come down for a round of golf at nearby Leatherhead. Yet superstar Haynes was still an intensely private man, and was reluctant to expose his parents or friends to the glare of publicity, and certainly ruled out any pictures of Rose and Eddie at his home.

Haynes the private celebrity

Johnny Haynes would occasionally let slip a few fragments of his personal life. He had a girlfriend by the name of Eileen Farmer although at the time they were rarely seen or photographed together (though they were pictured holidaying together after the 1958 World Cup—*see page 120*). Eileen was a dancer from Edinburgh living in Chelsea, and she was also trying to break into show business.

Haynes had also been linked in the newspapers to stunning starlet Janette Scott, daughter of actress Thora Hird. Sir Bobby Robson said: "I don't think there was a relationship, she was one of the up and coming young actresses, and because Fulham was a showbiz club, and through Tommy Trinder, Janette was invited to come to the games. Johnny met her and had his photograph taken with her, but I don't think there was any relationship at all. She was a very beautiful girl though."

Janette Scott wasn't really looking for a relationship either as she had one eye on Hollywood and a career. She would have probably been better off with Johnny Haynes as, despite marrying American singing star Mel Tormé, her career peaked in 1962 with the British sci-fi film *The Day of the Triffids*, later starring in 'B' movies.

Sir Bobby Robson recalls: "I socialised with Johnny very little in the early days. Initially I shared digs with Tom Wilson, but I was married by the time I was twenty-three and I went home to my family. I assume after training, if we weren't upstairs in the Cottage playing snooker, Johnny went home to his parents. He was a very homely boy. I certainly didn't socialise with him in the evening."

19: Top sportsman avoids relegation 1961–62

19: Top sportsman avoids relegation 1961–62

It was customary at the time for England to play pre-season matches against First Division club sides to put themselves through their paces. This season it was Fulham's turn to be England's opponents. 'Turncoat' Johnny Haynes (being captain) played for England, but in a well-fought match Fulham beat England 3–0 with goals from Brian O'Connell, Graham Leggat and Maurice Cook. Haynes was well marked by Alan Mullery.

Despite the close shave with relegation the previous season, Fulham had made no close season signings whatsoever, possibly partly because of their increased wage bill. For the first time in many seasons, Haynes missed the normal public trial match as the Whites beat the Colours 5–2.

Instead he was a member of the FA XI who competed against Tottenham for the Charity Shield at Wembley. Tottenham had secured 'the double', so couldn't play themselves in the League Champions versus Cup Winners pipe-opener. Therefore the FA put a team together to play Tottenham. Spurs won 3–2, but Haynes scored one of the FA XI's goals; the other was from Johnny Byrne who would later play for Fulham.

August

Fulham lost their opening game of the season 1–2 at Birmingham City after being reduced to ten men on the half-hour, Graham Leggat suffering an injury that would keep him out for some weeks. Initially there were fears of a broken leg, but these turned out to be unfounded. Johnny Haynes was quite out of touch in the first half, but found the missing magic and precision in the second half and combined cleverly with Jim Langley to set up the opening goal for Brian O'Connell.

At this point Haynes was dumbfounding the home side, who simply didn't know which way to turn once he had the ball. The handicap of having only ten men in the heat proved overwhelming, however, and Fulham eventually conceded the two goals that cost them the game. The press were dismayed by Fulham's performance: "Haynes showed he was worth his wages; with more support for the captain, Fulham could have won. He couldn't be everywhere with ten men. Fulham needed a centre forward."

One headline pointed out that Haynes couldn't do it alone, and another stated that he faced a tough struggle keeping Fulham in the First Division. It was an ominous remark and the next match, against Manchester City at Fulham, wasn't too clever either, for although Haynes was brought down in the box when through on goal to give Fulham and Langley their second goal from the penalty spot, Fulham squandered a three-goal half-time lead to lose in true Fulhamish manner 3–4, missing a second penalty in the process!

Previous page: Haynes receives his Daily Express Sportsman of the Year trophy during October at a luncheon at the Savoy Hotel in London.

INTERNATIONAL SOCCER STARS

A SERIES OF 12

No. 7

J. HAYNES

Fulham

Johnny Haynes is a born footballer who joined Fulham from school in 1950 and played his first League match two years later. In a career studded with Youth, Under-23 and, at the time of writing, 40 full international caps and the England captaincy, Haynes has proved himself one of the best inside forwards of all time. He assisted in Fulham's long Cup run to the semi-final in 1957/58 and in their promotion to Division I in 1958/59. Johnny's role in the England team is that of master-schemer, linking defence and attack. He passes the ball with pinpoint accuracy, and this, coupled with his brilliant ball-play, creates many scoring chances.

ISSUED BY

KELLOGG COMPANY OF GREAT BRITAIN LTD.

They did recover, however, to beat star-studded Everton at the Cottage 2–1 in the following game. Although not on the scoresheet, Haynes was given top honours by the press as the midfield master who dictated the play. The maestro kept the forward line moving, and he "shone like a beacon in a very average game." He looked the perfect footballer and captain as he swept pass after pass out to his hesitant colleagues whilst constantly shaking off close marking. He plagued the defence and from his superb free kick on fourteen minutes he accurately found the head of Maurice Cook, who put Fulham ahead.

A rare moment of joy in the 3–4 defeat at home to Manchester City, as Haynes congratulates scorer Brian O'Connell.

The next encounter was the re-match against Manchester City at Maine Road, and despite producing "fighting and intelligent football, under the guiding genius of Johnny Haynes" Fulham lost again 1–2, thus producing the double for City—and three defeats in the opening four games.

September

The month started in mediocre fashion with a dismal 0–0 draw at Chelsea in punishing heat. On Dave Metchick's debut during which he rattled the bar, and in stifling conditions, Haynes was still pushing through goal-making passes and foiling attacking forwards right up to the final whistle. The press said that, with the exception of a chap called Haynes, all skill had evaporated. Fulham again were virtually a ten-man side, as forward John Doherty with a swollen ankle was lifeless on the wing.

This was followed by a home draw against Bolton 2–2. Despite a lengthening injury list, Fulham then took a splendid point at league leaders Sheffield Wednesday 1–1, Haynes being described as spellbinding, and helping defensively when Fulham were under intense pressure. Fulham's equaliser from Metchick arrived in the very last minute. Even at this early stage of the season the press were worried that the Fulham side were again totally reliant on Haynes. Although he was in superb form, there was still too much of "Give it to Haynes."

The season started to take off soon after that with three straight league wins. The first victims were Leicester City, 2–1 at home. Haynes made both goals during a three-minute period after Fulham had gone behind. He laid on the pass for Graham Leggat to equalise, and then stroked the ball through for Trevor Chamberlain to score the winner.

Such was his play that the papers eulogised his performance. "What a truly great player is England's captain Johnny Haynes. It might be a slight exaggeration to say that he beat Leicester City on his own ... but the goals were laid on by the incomparable Haynes." Another report said: "The industry of Haynes was something to marvel at. He never gives himself a breather, his ball distribution was magnificent and no-one could rival his tactical control." The headline blazed: "Old, old story—Haynes does it again."

Fulham won away 3–2 at Bolton Wanderers in midweek, and then again on their travels with a fine 4–2 win over Ipswich Town, the season's eventual champions. Haynes scored Fulham's third goal in the match; it had taken him ten matches to get off the mark that season.

Fulham had been a goal down to Ipswich's Ray Crawford until close to the interval, when Cook levelled. Haynes was doing as much work in defence as in attack. George Cohen with a rare goal gave the Whites the lead.

Haynes then took control. Chamberlain's shot was headed out to him; he exchanged passes with Johnny Key, took the return, wheeled away from defenders on the wing and hammered the ball in from twenty yards from an incredible angle. It was a glorious effort.

His performance that day was one of his very best, described as a brilliant exhibition of master-craftsmanship. The press said that his passes were so accurate that even when Ipswich guessed their direction, they still couldn't prevent them from reaching their destination. One journalist said, "They [Ipswich] don't always run up against the genius of maestros like Haynes." He was making headlines every week, and on this day they read: "Haynes hits the peak." This was an eager young Fulham side full of stamina and energy.

There was, however, a problem ahead, as during a training session with England the following week (England v Chelsea) Haynes picked up a thigh injury. He said, "As soon as I made a quick turn, I felt the trouble again. I felt confident shooting and running, but when I made a quick turn, I realised it was no use." The injury forced him to miss the 4–1 England World Cup preliminary win over Luxembourg at Highbury.

He watched the game as a spectator. England stumbled and stuttered to a win, but the Highbury crowd booed and laughed at England's performance against the minnows, something Haynes considered a disgrace and shameful. The injury also put him out of Fulham's side for their League Cup replay with Sheffield United at Bramall Lane. A Haynes-less and lifeless Fulham bowed out meekly 0–4.

Fulham were unbeaten in the league that month until the last day, when they lost 3–5 at home to a crack Burnley side topping the table, a John Connelly hat trick doing the damage, though this included a very dubious penalty decision. On the day the ball didn't run kindly for either Haynes or the Fulham team.

Even the Fulham programme eulogised Haynes' performances with a paragraph saying: "Can anyone remember our Johnny having a greater start to the season, playing like a man inspired—intelligent, commanding football that dissects defences like a surgeon carrying out a major operation." The watching England selectors observed a magnificent match. Burnley had scored *twenty* goals in their last four *away* games!

The news of the superhuman standards that Haynes was setting was still filtering over to Italy. Milan sent their representative, trainer Rocco, back to England again to try and unsettle him with more praise. Rocco thought he might now have better luck as Jimmy Greaves had returned to England following his unhappy time there, and with money to burn he thought that he could still make Fulham an offer they could not refuse. He said, "He is your greatest [English] player; to my mind he is as good and complete a footballer as Alfredo Di Stefano."

October

Fulham next overcame Aston Villa at Craven Cottage. In the 3–1 victory, Haynes often had three men around him, but his guile and experience served him well. Watched by Walter Winterbottom he came through

Job well done—and West Ham are beaten 2–0. The Fulham players following behind Haynes are Maurice Cook (left) and Graham Leggat. West Ham's John Bond, later to manage Bournemouth and Norwich, looks duly deflated.

unscathed before the next England match. It was a game for defences, but Haynes helped to put Fulham ahead with a very quickly taken corner. Nearly everyone watched the ball except Graham Leggat who anticipated the move and scored. Haynes was back in top gear.

During the week he made his eleventh appearance for the Football League, scoring a goal against the League of Ireland in a comprehensive 5–2 victory in a match played at, of all places, Eastville, the home of Bristol Rovers.

Haynes missed Saturday's league game at Nottingham Forest whilst on England duty, taking part in an unsatisfactory 1–1 draw in the British Championship with Wales at Ninian Park.

In a rough encounter, he was involved in a tackle-cum-body check with West Bromwich full back Graham Williams and from that point on he was roundly booed every time he touched the ball; it was unnecessary as the game was never dirty, but both sides were keyed up, and Haynes only managed, by his standards, an average performance.

He returned to league action for the game against second-placed West Ham at the Cottage, and completely overshadowed his opposite number, Phil Woosnam. Fulham played classy football and Haynes stamped his personality on the game, raising the level to continental standard. George Cohen was Fulham's sixth attacker, giving Mullery the cross for the first goal. Then in another foray up the field the full back was brought down, and from the inevitable Haynes free kick, Leggat headed the perfect second in a 2–0 win.

The media said: "At twenty-seven, Haynes is a far more mature player than ever before. The lethal accuracy of his passes, the uncanny ability to find a colleague whatever the situation and his knack of changing the whole direction of attack puts him in the genius class."

He then took his England team out to secure their place in the 1962 World Cup with a 2–0 preliminary win over Portugal at Wembley, in front of 100,000. Again, it wasn't a classic England performance, and after taking an early two-goal lead England sat back and allowed Portugal to get back into the game. It became almost too lax, and the great young Eusebio twice hit the post for the visitors. However, in the end England successfully qualified without too much bother.

Fulham then salvaged another league point in a 2–2 draw at Bramall Lane. Sheffield United monopolised the play, and led twice, but Haynes with his cool head marshalled his troops, and inspired the rest of the team, causing Sheffield plenty of trouble all afternoon.

With two wins and two draws in the month, the table looked very much like the previous season, with Fulham lying fifth at the end of October, with six wins and five draws already under their belt; they had also beaten some quality teams in the process. In addition, England had qualified for the finals of the World Cup—it had been a very satisfactory month.

Daily Express Sportsman of the Year

In that month, Johnny Haynes was voted the *Daily Express* Sportsman of the Year in the national ballot. He was the first footballer to win the award since the

England captain Haynes shakes hands with his opposite number prior to the World Cup preliminary against Portugal at Wembley. England won 2–0 and qualified for the finals.

year of his debut, 1952. Basically what earned him the title was skill and sportsmanship, and he was applauded for his splendid service to England. He was also given the award on another important count—loyalty.

He recalled later: "Footballers rarely won the trophy at the time, but England had had a good year, and Haynes was the captain so … it seemed appropriate." He was described in a testimonial as an unspoilt chap with a quiet sense of humour and a great appetite for the challenges of the game. He received the award at a lunch at London's Savoy Hotel attended by all the sporting celebrities of the day. (*Photograph on page 173.*)

The skies begin to darken

November

After yet another sunny start to the season, the skies began to darken for Fulham during November with a home defeat by lowly Cardiff City 0–1. When the Welsh team came to London, they possessed six players under the age of nineteen. Fulham were expected to win easily, but played badly and it was a strangely hesitant performance, considering what had gone before.

It was Haynes' worst display of the season. He was very tightly marked by an unknown eighteen-year-old, Barrie Hole, and he tried too hard. He couldn't get a strategic influence on the game, and seldom had he been held in such subjection. Cardiff poached a first-half goal and returned victorious to Wales with the single-goal win. It was a very big shock for Fulham.

During the week Haynes departed to represent the Football League for the twelfth time, playing the reciprocal match against the Italian League at Old Trafford. Unfortunately the League were not able to avenge the defeat in Italy the previous year, and lost 0–2.

Fulham had to take on the mighty Spurs on the Saturday and suffered a predictable 2–4 defeat at White Hart Lane, where Haynes picked up his second goal of the season. It was a match of astonishing skill played in cloying mud. The score did not reflect the game, and Fulham were extremely unlucky not to take at least a point.

They hit the post twice through Alan Mullery, saw chances cleared from the goal line, and missed others through poor finishing. Fulham were quickly two goals down and fought back to two-all before half-time. Graham Leggat pulled one back after a defensive slip, and Haynes' equalising goal, a tremendous shot, was described as a gem. Cliff Jones edged Spurs ahead again just before the interval.

Mullery and Haynes were putting the talented Spurs side in the shade. A very late goal from Dave Mackay saw Spurs home, but it was Tottenham who were glad to hear the final whistle. The press said that Haynes was back to classic form and had carved out enough chances for a goal riot. The form of Mullery was making him the perfect linkman, and his ball-winning capabilities were enabling Haynes to have plenty of possession. With great foresight, journalists were already tipping Fulham as a good cup bet.

After the disappointment of the Tottenham defeat, the league form unexpectedly sagged again against Blackpool at the Cottage the following week and a single-goal defeat ensued. The young John Doherty played instead of Maurice Cook but was unable to 'read' Haynes' passes. The skipper was also guilty of an astonishing miss from just three yards. Despite the usual masterly promptings, Fulham lost for the second consecutive time at home 0–1.

The poor month continued for Haynes when he took part in England's very disappointing 1–1 draw with Northern Ireland in the British Championship at Wembley in front of scarcely 30,000 spectators. The result made their chances of retaining the championship unlikely.

Matters looked slightly rosier with a 2–0 victory over Blackburn Rovers at Ewood Park at the end of the month. This time Fulham had the luck; Blackburn played very poorly and Fulham, not significantly better, profited from their mistakes.

After taking the lead just after half-time, Fulham sealed the match three minutes later. Haynes sent Dave Metchick away and his hard cross was turned into his own net by Blackburn defender Matt Woods. Haynes was never prominent and his class was only seen in glimpses. It was a tough old game, with Mullery, George Cohen and Eddie Lowe all being booked by the referee in the space of five minutes. From this point in the season Fulham would not pick up another league point for *three months*.

December

Ominously, the season became very much darker for captain Haynes. Fulham lost all five league matches during the month, failing to register a single goal. At

A mid-December break from league struggles, as Haynes joins up for training with England hopefuls Johnny Byrne, Alan Mullery and Freddie Hill at Lilleshall.

the Cottage against sliding Wolves, Fulham looked as if they still needed a centre forward, but they had no luck at all. In one incident, Haynes was clear through but shot straight at the goalkeeper. Graham Leggat and Maurice Cook missed easy chances, and Leggat was then robbed of a goal by an incorrect offside decision.

As if things could not get worse, the side had to be re-jigged with Jim Langley in goal and goalkeeper Tony Macedo playing on the wing after an injury. Although they put up magnificent resistance, Fulham typically lost to a last-minute goal. It was their third consecutive 0–1 home defeat.

Crucially, Haynes also picked up an injury against the Wanderers, and both he and Macedo missed the important game at Old Trafford. Manchester United were only one place off the bottom of the table at the time. On the day, however, Fulham were no match and were well beaten 0–3.

Fulham tried to rush Haynes back into the side the following week for the visit of Birmingham City, but the idea backfired badly; he was obviously not match fit. He again tried to do too much for the team, but his lack of fitness saw him robbed of possession when trying to make one pass too many.

Although he produced several of his golden passes he seemed reluctant to shoot at goal. To make matters worse the injury hoodoo struck deeper, with Jim Langley being injured again, and just one early fatal defensive mistake gifted the points to the Midlands side. Almost unbelievably, it was the fourth consecutive 0–1 home defeat and only 12,000 had bothered to turn up.

The following week, the performance was as bleak as the winter weather that was closing in, and Fulham received a 0–3 pummelling at Everton. Haynes was restricted by the shackles of Jimmy Gabriel, and Fulham were relying too much on the captain. The icy conditions did no-one any favours, but Fulham never really got going.

On Boxing Day on a treacherous pitch at Highbury, despite a heroic display from goalkeeper Macedo, Fulham almost inevitably lost by a single goal. Haynes was now beginning to show despair at the lack of response from his colleagues, who had apparently all forgotten how to shoot. Fortunately bad weather came to Fulham's rescue and the final match of the year was frozen out.

There were reasons for the slump, since Fulham could never field the same team twice, and could never put out their best eleven players. Young forwards Doherty, Key, O'Connell and Metchick, together with second-team defenders Mealand, Edwards, Lampe and even the veteran Robin Lawler, were all forced to play throughout the period due to the crippling first-team injuries.

The current scenario spelt disaster for Haynes. The defeats at home to Blackpool, Wolves and Birmingham had been especially hard to take. Fulham had overrun their opponents for most of the matches, and completely outplayed them in terms of skilful football, but had no luck in front of goal.

In each match the away team had somehow contrived to produce one breakaway move where a forward managed to scramble the ball past Macedo in the Fulham goal. Haynes often stated, "At Fulham we were just not capable of handling injuries and illness, we weren't rich enough to have it any other way."

The alarming slump had seen a crisis emerge for the second consecutive season. From a high-flying and confident fifth place at the end of October, Fulham had tumbled right down the league, and sat precariously near the foot of the table in twentieth position at the turn of the year.

January

This was a month punctuated by bad weather and cup ties. Fulham lost both league matches, but whilst they were going through 'the perils of Pauline' in the league, they were having, surprisingly, better luck in the FA Cup. As in 1958, they were drawn at home in the third round and they disposed of Fourth Division basement team Hartlepools United (as they were then known) by 3–1. Johnny Haynes missed the game due to injury, but two Maurice Cook goals and one from Johnny Key saw Fulham ease through without too many problems.

The league match that hurt the most was at the Cottage to local rivals Chelsea, where ex-Arsenal forward Jackie Henderson made his Fulham debut. Barry Mealand presented Chelsea with a gift own goal to start the proceedings as early as the fourth minute.

Haynes was well off form, and only emerged in fleeting moments in the second half. These glimpses were enough to rally the side back to level terms, but lax defending allowed Chelsea to plunder the winner in the very last seconds—another home loss, 3–4, and the fifth consecutive home defeat in the league.

The following week saw the seventh consecutive league defeat, 0–2 against Sheffield Wednesday, again at the Cottage. This time it was Key who was hurt, as early as the ninth minute. Haynes had an instantly forgettable match, including an incredible miss from three yards out.

It was the sixth consecutive home defeat and people were beginning to look at the record books. It was rumoured that a totally fed-up Haynes was ready to jump from this sinking ship. To counter this slur, he emerged from the post-match shower and surprisingly issued a rallying call and statement which was a real confidence-booster for Fulham.

He said: "I will stay with Fulham even if we go down. There is no question of me wanting to play First Division football with any other club but this one. Remember I have played in the Second Division before and will do so again if it becomes necessary, but we are far from being dispirited and think we have a fighting chance of pulling out of trouble.

"Luck has been all against us with injuries. Last week we were short of two first-team players and had Jackie Henderson hurt in the first half against Chelsea. Today again we had to play two reserves and had Johnny Key hurt in the first few minutes.

"All we want is a break and a goal or two to revive our confidence. I was only about three yards out and Ron Springett had turned his back on me in the Wednesday goal thinking I was offside, but I still couldn't get the ball into the net. That's how it goes when you're struggling.

"But don't think we've thrown in the towel. The spirit among the boys is great and we'll be fighting every match to pull out.

"Our away record is useful, but I think the slide really started at Spurs when we might have had the match sewn up at half-time, but still lost. That game proved though that we can play well against the best.

"I know the fans have not had a lot to cheer since then, but believe me we need support now like never before."

BBC Junior Sportsview Personality of the Year for 1961

A modicum of light relief came during the month. Youngsters throughout the country voted for their Mr Sport for 1961, a sportsman of the year, and most had no doubt. Haynes won, and the BBC Junior Sportsview Personality of the Year award was presented to him at the Schoolboys' Exhibition at Olympia by grinning commentator Kenneth Wolstenholme, alongside BBC controller Stuart Hood.

The next match was another difficult encounter. Fulham were drawn at home again, this time against Second Division giant-killers Walsall, in the fourth round of the FA Cup. The first half saw Fulham concede a penalty and play like untrained amateurs, with Haynes chasing shadows and not being able to do anything right. He was petulant, and one reporter said, "There was far too much protesting without getting on with it!"

But in the second half Haynes got cracking straight away, and a better performance and two goals in two minutes saw the home team scrape to a draw. Fulham should have won in the end, but a shot from Brian O'Connell from a glorious Haynes pass hit the post with the goalkeeper beaten. Fulham won the replay at Fellows Park 2–0 four days later.

February

Unbelievably, Fulham contrived to lose *all four* of this month's league matches as well. The only bright spot for Haynes was that he scored his third goal of the season at Leicester in a 1–4 defeat. Midway during the first half he put Fulham ahead against the run of play. With Fulham's current luck, even this effort had to be deflected past the goalkeeper by the Leicester

More mid-season relief from the rigours of the football fixtures, as Haynes receives his BBC Junior Sportsview award.

full back! Like the fine captain he was, he tried to inspire his colleagues to greater effort, but the team again relied too much on him; he was tightly marked by Frank McLintock and it was not to be.

The following week, against an Ipswich team heading for the title, Haynes was hurt again. Alan Mullery shot Fulham ahead, but crucially Graham Leggat also picked up an injury and Haynes emerged for the second half with his thigh strapped, looking far from fit. Many considered that he should not have played at all. The injuries took their toll and Fulham eventually succumbed 1–2 in a match where little went right for the Cottagers, including a comical own goal by reserve goalkeeper Ken Hewkins who punched the ball into his net.

Fulham then drew lower league opposition again in the fifth round of the FA Cup. Once again they were drawn at home, prompting many to begin to make comparisons with the 1958 cup run. They squeezed past Third Division Port Vale via a single Jimmy Langley penalty goal. Haynes missed the game following the injury he had received the previous week. Nor did he make it back into the team for the midweek match against high-flyers Burnley at Turf Moor, where yet another frustrating 1–2 defeat ensued.

Fulham's bad luck reached new heights at Villa Park at the weekend, where they hit the bar and had shots scrambled off the line. Haynes did not play well, and at this stage even he thought it was all up for Fulham, and gave an ultimate shrug of resignation. After the 0–2 defeat a reporter wrote, "Haynes, back after injury, can rarely have had a more indifferent game. His play lacked urgency and the old accuracy was often missing." The press were openly talking about the inevitable writing of Fulham's relegation story, saying that they were psychologically conditioned to believe that they were the most jinx-ridden outfit in the league!

Relegation beckons again

By the end of February, Fulham had played fifteen league games in four months—and lost fourteen of them, *eleven in succession.* They had slipped from fifth place to bottom of the table, and were trailing the next relegation place by a clear four points. In those fifteen games they had scored just ten goals and conceded over thirty! They had lost seven consecutive home league games—the worst run in their entire history. Even the club programme called the team's position "far from healthy." Haynes knew that the situation required effort of herculean proportions.

Haynes rallies the troops

March

Typically, Fulham rallied during the next two months,

Fulham, in changed strip at home, are led out by Haynes for the sixth-round cup tie against Blackburn Rovers that finished 2–2. Fulham were saved by a headed goal from Haynes just two minutes from the end.

with only one defeat in their next eight matches. Haynes was now returning to fitness and, if not at his best, was playing better than of late with accurate distribution. A goal in the seventh minute by Jackie Henderson against lowly Nottingham Forest seemed to have halted the losing run, but a goal that looked suspiciously offside three minutes from the end lost Fulham yet another precious point. It seemed all over for Fulham now, and even the press talked about the Forest goal that must surely have sealed their fate as a First Division club.

Haynes keeps Fulham in the cup—just

At last it was First Division opposition in the FA Cup in the form of Blackburn Rovers, Fulham being drawn at home yet again in the quarter-final. It was all Fulham, but Blackburn maddeningly scored with their first attack on the half-hour, and then Jimmy Langley missed a penalty, sent yards wide, after Haynes' goal-bound shot appeared to be handled by Blackburn captain Ronnie Clayton.

Fulham had some good fortune after the interval when Blackburn conceded an own goal, once more donated by defender Matt Woods just as he had done in the league match four months earlier. Fulham frittered away further chances, but they were again very unlucky.

Fulham hearts were broken once more three minutes later when Bryan Douglas, looking offside, waltzed round Tony Macedo to score. The home side then hit the bar twice—and the post—and had numerous other efforts hacked away. Yet somehow Haynes managed to scramble a priceless equaliser with his head just two minutes from the end, keeping Fulham in the cup and taking the match to a replay 2–2.

In the replay, Fulham were outplayed for most of the match, surviving a torrid opening period. However,

Haynes makes it look easy against Sheffield United at the Cottage, as another slide-rule pass cuts the visitors' defence to ribbons. The skipper orchestrated a 5–2 victory, which included a Maurice Cook hat trick.

the hosts failed to score in that time, Maurice Cook poached a goal in a breakaway and Fulham were through 1–0. Haynes was a little embarrassed by the score, saying, "We were very lucky." The press opined that with form and luck like that, Fulham could win the FA Cup, the Boat Race and the Grand National!

Inspired by Haynes and the cup successes, Fulham finally notched up a league win at the Cottage, 5–2 against Sheffield United, who had shot up the league to fifth position, and provided tough opposition. Haynes did not score but was instrumental in the team's success. The Cottagers were three up at the interval, with Eddie Lowe claiming the third with a grand header following a Haynes free kick.

It was a fine day, too, for Maurice Cook who grabbed a hat trick. He was marked by debutant Reg Matthewson, who later joined Fulham. The papers hailed Haynes' performance: "Back to his best World Cup form. He passed out to the wings in majestic style and his defence-splitting moves had the United defence in a rare old tangle." Fulham owed a lot to Haynes, who had one of his best days.

Final game for the Football League

Haynes found time to slip out of the domestic turmoil and record his thirteenth and ultimately final appearance for the Football League, against the Scottish League at Villa Park, during the following week. It proved to be 'unlucky for some' for him as this last match ended in defeat in a seven-goal thriller, the Football League finally being edged out 3–4. He did, however, have the satisfaction of signing off with a goal, his seventh in thirteen representative appearances.

Just forty-eight hours later, with little time to recover, came a critical four-pointer against fellow strugglers Cardiff City at Ninian Park on a Friday evening, where Fulham played superbly and won 3–0. Once more Haynes was without a goal, but was in majestic form, inspiring the team, which led to incessant attacks on the Cardiff goal. The win reduced the gap on Cardiff to three points. Fulham could finally see a chink of survival light and the emphatic victory put them in confident mood for the cup semi-final.

The 1962 FA Cup semi-final

It was the other way round from the 1957–58 season. Last time Fulham were in the cup semi-final they were fighting for promotion; this time they were battling against relegation. In both seasons there was also a World Cup looming. Haynes was definitely thinking that it could be Fulham's year in the cup.

Villa Park

Haynes rallied his team in the semi-final against league leaders Burnley at Villa Park, the same venue as in 1958, telling the team: "We can do this." Twenty thousand Fulham supporters travelled to the Midlands. Haynes again had a superb game, and was at his best, linking with Eddie Lowe and Alan Mullery to blunt Burnley's attacks.

Fulham, under the captain's inspiration, were dominant for the whole match and it was only thanks to Burnley goalkeeper Adam Blacklaw making three

Semi-finals again! Haynes leaves Paddington Station for the tie against Burnley at Villa Park.

superb saves from Maurice Cook headers that the Clarets sneaked away with a replay. Graham Leggat deservedly put Fulham ahead, a lead they held until half-time. Haynes provided Leggat with the goal chance, and he slammed the ball home from twenty yards; Blacklaw never moved. Haynes also had shots blocked that made him raise his hands in despair.

Burnley came back with an undeserved equaliser through John Connelly, their first on-target shot of the match, and then Fulham had a penalty appeal turned down when Burnley captain Jimmy Adamson appeared to handle the ball on its way to the net.

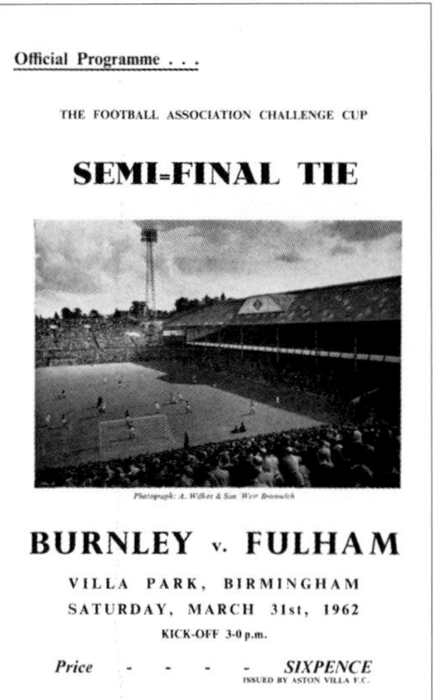

Official Programme . . .
THE FOOTBALL ASSOCIATION CHALLENGE CUP
SEMI-FINAL TIE
BURNLEY v. FULHAM
VILLA PARK, BIRMINGHAM
SATURDAY, MARCH 31st, 1962
KICK-OFF 3-0 p.m.
Price - - - - SIXPENCE
ISSUED BY ASTON VILLA F.C.

The turning-point, however, occurred just ten minutes from time. Centre forward Maurice Cook, clean through from a superb pass by Haynes, attempted to go round Blacklaw and was flattened by a flying feet-first hack from the Burnley goalkeeper. It was as clear a penalty as you could wish to see. As the crowd held its breath, the referee made a decision—no penalty. Haynes was amazed! Fulham had been clearly and cruelly robbed of a deserved victory. The match finished 1–1.

Fulham's fury was compounded when the referee sought out Cook after the game and confided to him that he had made the wrong decision—but it was too late. How Fulham had scored only one goal was amazing—they had ten chances to Burnley's two in the match. The press agreed that Burnley had never been more fortunate to escape defeat! It was one of Fulham's finest hours, the press headline proclaiming: "Salute Trinder's Tigers."

April

During the week, Haynes won his forty-ninth England cap, against Austria in a friendly at Wembley. England won 3–1, and Haynes played well—indeed 'superb' was not too strong a word for his display. England avenged the defeat in Vienna the previous year, thanks mainly to the midfield domination of Haynes, who kept picking holes in the massed Austrian defence with low, angled passes.

The only blip in the eight-match league run was the 1–2 defeat by Blackpool two days before the semi-final replay, when Haynes tucked away his fourth goal of the season. The defeat was a travesty of justice for Fulham, and Blackpool stole the points.

Fulham had taken the lead; Maurice Cook misjudged Langley's pass but recovered to hook the ball back from the by-line into the path of Haynes who hit a stinging half-volley past Seasiders' keeper Harvey. However, Blackpool equalised and then ran in an undeserved winner just six minutes from time. Fulham looked disgusted at the end of this barefaced robbery, and Tom Finney, writing up the match report, clearly stated that he couldn't understand for the life of him why the Fulham side were in danger of relegation!

Filbert Street

Just forty-eight hours after this league match, Fulham ventured north for the semi-final replay. Johnny Haynes had a sixth sense that the chance had gone and that Burnley would not play as poorly or be as subdued again; and so it proved. In the game, at Leicester's Filbert Street rather than Highbury, Fulham never really recaptured the form they had shown in the Midlands. Jim Langley's goal with seconds remaining was just a late consolation, as Fulham were already two down.

OFFICIAL PROGRAMME 6d.
LEICESTER CITY
FOOTBALL
CLUB
FOOTBALL ASSOCIATION
CHALLENGE CUP
COMPETITION
SEMI-FINAL REPLAY
Monday 9th April 1962
BURNLEY v FULHAM

In the second half, Haynes had thrust himself forward into a full attacking role, having two headers saved and putting a fierce shot into the side netting in the space of just five minutes. But it proved fruitless in a 1–2 defeat.

He felt desperately empty inside. No lush green Wembley turf again for himself or his little Fulham—how many years did he have left? The Fulham programme reflected that under the inspiration of Johnny Haynes, the lads had given all they had.

Although Haynes would not have known it, during the remainder of his time at Fulham the team never advanced beyond the fourth round again. After the game, a reporter noted that at the end of the match, Haynes smiled bravely, turned towards the dark tunnel at Filbert Street, and led fighting Fulham out of the headlines and into obscurity.

Somehow, though, Fulham exorcised the cup semi-final replay defeat of just forty-eight hours earlier from their systems with a magnificent 5–2 victory over Arsenal at Craven Cottage. In this second consecutive five-goal haul, Haynes again failed to find the net, and was the only forward not to do so, but Jackie Henderson did score against his previous colleagues. In a tough game, Arsenal had two players booked and Haynes took another kick on the ankle. He played on but said, "My foot has been badly bruised for some weeks and it was aggravated against Arsenal. It doesn't affect me once the game starts."

Johnny Haynes wins his 50th England cap

Haynes missed Fulham's vital league game against Blackburn Rovers with good reason. After being selected to captain the England side against Scotland, he became only the fourth person ever to receive fifty England caps, following in the illustrious footsteps of Billy Wright, Tom Finney and Stanley Matthews.

It wasn't the happiest of afternoons for Haynes, as England lost 0–2 to Scotland at Hampden Park. In front of an extremely partisan crowd, a massive 135,000 attendance, Scotland beat England for the first time in twenty-five years. With England a goal down, Haynes had a piledriver hit the underside of the bar and drop a clear foot over the goal line before McNeill headed the ball away, but the goal was not given.

Scotland's win was only confirmed very late in the game with a penalty, but although England badly wanted the victory, for the first time in fifteen games they failed to score. The victory gave Scotland the British Championship for the first time in eleven

Great technique from Haynes, and a special club tribute on the award of his fiftieth England cap—but neither could prevent a 1–2 home defeat inflicted by West Bromwich Albion.

years. Coming just before the World Cup it was a very poor showing by England, and only Haynes and goalkeeper Ron Springett came out of the match without criticism.

Haynes admitted afterwards: "No complaints; Scotland deserved their win. It would have been good to win that one as it would have been a nice build-up to the World Cup and Chile. We like to beat the Scots as much as they like to beat us." Sportingly he added, "I did not envy Eric Caldow [Scotland's captain] and his boys the wonderful ovation they received from that packed Hampden crowd when it was all over. Their feelings at Hampden then must have been similar to mine after that great day at Wembley a year earlier."

During the match at West Bromwich, a tense Haynes was out of sorts and out of focus, and Fulham lost 0–2, adding to their relegation worries.

Fortunately, Fulham proved that they could win in the league without Haynes when they beat sixth-round opponents Blackburn Rovers 2–0 at Craven Cottage. It was a very lacklustre performance from Blackburn and Fulham claimed the points easily. Importantly, it enabled Fulham to pull themselves one point in front of Cardiff City and out of the bottom two.

Three days later in this run of matches came a fine 1–1 draw with third-placed Spurs at Fulham, the third home game in seven days. Haynes made the Fulham goal. He collected the ball in the penalty area and could have scored himself, and maybe he ought to have shot, but instead he cleverly flicked a sideways pass to Brian O'Connell whose drive went in just under the bar.

It should have been two points, but for goalkeeper Bill Brown and some poor shooting. Haynes was at his greatest, delicately carving out a tracery of victory for his team-mates but only once was the pattern completed. Late in the game, in front of 43,000, Haynes tried for the winner with another powerful shot that seemed bound for the net, only for Brown in mid-air to leap and turn the ball aside.

Spurs captain Dave Mackay would say of Haynes later: "He was the most difficult player in the world to mark. I've tried close-marking him and getting in quick tackles, but it didn't stop him. Once, I decided to lay off to see if that worked, but he was even more deadly."

However, the relegation issue was still not fully resolved. Alan Mullery was injured in the 3–1 win at Wolves on Easter Saturday. Fulham made Wolves look second rate, and took the lead in the thirteenth minute. When Haynes received Cook's pass, Davies in the Wolves' goal could only parry the skipper's fierce shot, and the alert Leggat followed up to put Fulham ahead with ease.

After Broadbent's leveller for Wolves, Haynes provided a difficult cross which Davies could only push out and O'Connell scored from close in. Leggat confirmed Fulham's win with a fine solo goal in the second half. It looked as if Fulham were almost safe but news filtered through that Cardiff City had beaten Birmingham City, so there was still a great deal to do.

Fulham in true style then lost both Easter matches against West Bromwich Albion, throwing themselves firmly back into the relegation mire. The club's programme cover for the home match against West Bromwich was changed to show a picture of Haynes in honour of his fiftieth cap.

Haynes managed his fifth goal of the season, scoring six minutes after half-time firing in a back-heeled pass from O'Connell. The papers said that he was magnificent in the forward line and it must have broken his heart to see so many chances go to waste. He tried to save a point three minutes from time with a personal effort, a screaming shot bound for the top corner, but goalkeeper Tony Millington made the save of the match, and Albion won 1–2. The match was a disaster, the press berating the home team for their woeful shooting and mis-kicking.

Fulham lost 0–2 the following day at the Hawthorns, 'thanks' to two goals from Haynes' international colleague Derek Kevan. The press concluded that it was in many ways a performance typical of Fulham's hit-and-miss season. Haynes, playing his ninth match in nineteen days, couldn't for once find the energy to chase back, and his old colleague Bobby Robson had a big hand in both the goals that undid Fulham.

What was more of an issue was that Cardiff had overcome West Ham on the Monday, so Fulham were truly in the flames once more, ahead on goal average by just 0.25 of a goal. Haynes was furious, as in his mind Fulham were a far better side than their league position suggested, but here was the England captain facing the prospect of Second Division football once again.

Will it be Cardiff or Fulham?

Chelsea were already relegated, and it was now a straight fight between Fulham and Cardiff City for the other spot. Haynes told reporters before the next match, at home to Manchester United, that he would not be interviewed if Fulham lost, stating, "I would be too choked." The club doctor reported that many of the squad were feeling the effects of the punishing league and cup schedule but not Haynes. He carried the greatest burden, but had "abnormal resilience."

Fulham took on United in front of another 40,000 crowd, held their nerve and played well. They put together a 2–0 win with an early goal from Maurice Cook and a remarkable header from Graham Leggat, flying horizontally through the air just two feet from the ground to secure the win. This was all in the first twenty minutes.

United were no match for Fulham on the day, and Haynes was as usual the man of the match, looking in determined mood. The press said that all the Fulham forwards responded enthusiastically to the magnificent leadership of Johnny Haynes, who hardly put a foot wrong. Matt Busby paid tribute to Fulham's form saying, "Fulham's fine football puts them among the four best clubs in the division."

Cardiff City travelled to Goodison Park where Everton trounced them 8–3. Fulham had ultimately survived in the First Division by the skin of their teeth; Haynes recalled that it was far too close for comfort. Due to their FA Cup commitments Fulham had been forced to play their final nine league matches (almost a quarter of the season's fixtures) in the space of just twenty-four days, a game almost every three days! Not the greatest preparation for the forthcoming World Cup.

So Fulham survive again

Fulham had finished twentieth, just outside the relegation spots, and had survived by a single point. Although the defence had tightened up considerably, conceding five only once, the team had netted just sixty-six in the league, with only two players reaching double figures in goals. Johnny Haynes' contribution was a meagre five, just one better than his lowest-ever contribution. The forward line had had a very inexperienced look about it all season.

At the end of the season, Fulham youngsters Alan Mullery and George Cohen were both married, leaving Haynes at almost twenty-eight the only remaining bachelor in the senior squad.

At least the season ended on a fairly high note when Haynes was named in third place in the Footballer of the Year awards, being placed behind two Burnley players, Jimmy Adamson and Jimmy McIlroy.

He finally took part in the England versus Young England match which was played regularly on the eve of the cup final. The match took place in a thunderstorm and in incessant rain, and as Haynes tried to pass his way through the Highbury swamp he was wondering whether this was really the best preparation for an England team on the verge of the World Cup.

20: The 1962 World Cup

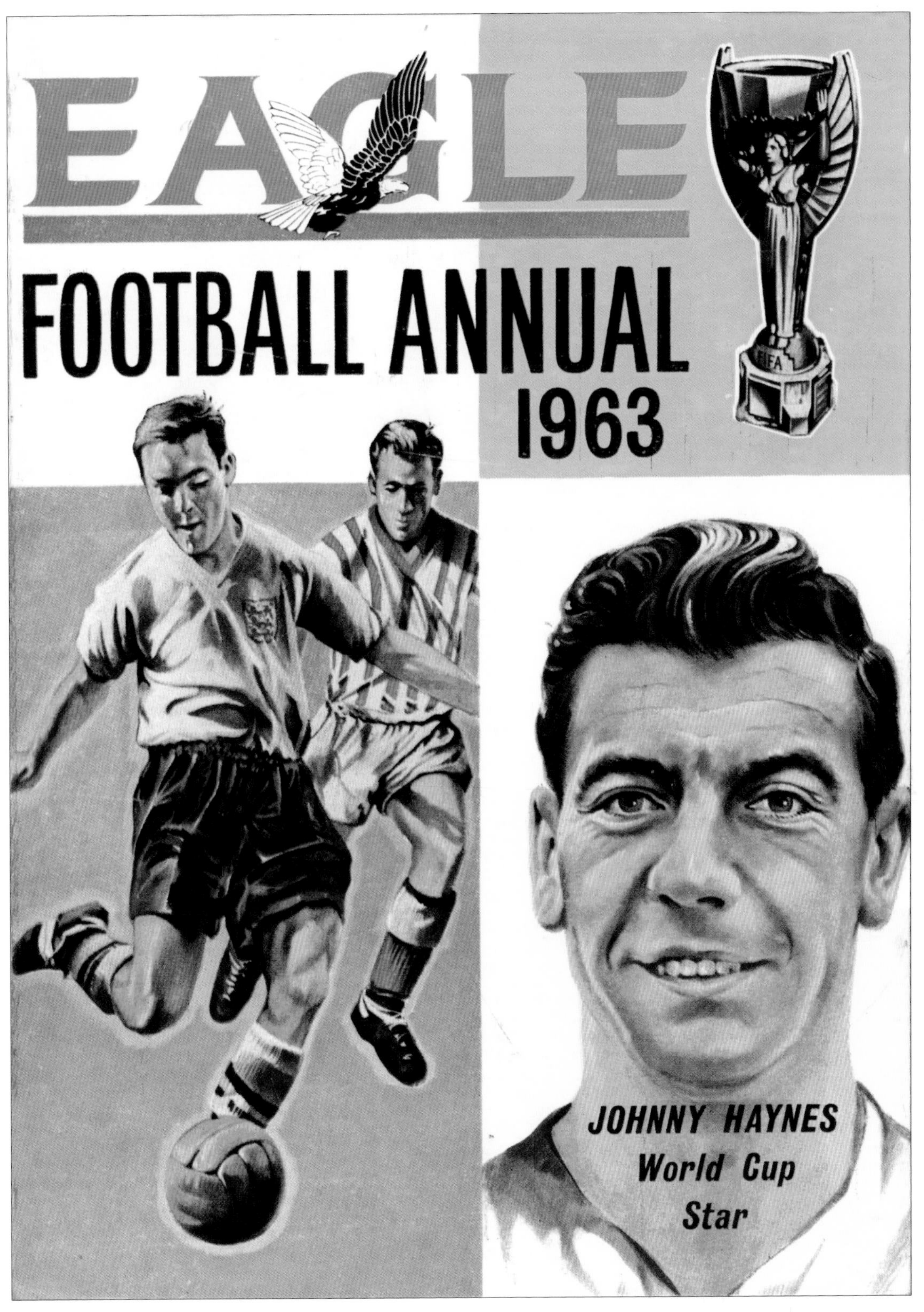

20: The 1962 World Cup

The World Cup preparations started just one week after the football league season ended. Haynes was openly critical about England's preparation in general, the lack of forward thinking by the FA about the tournament, the lack of time together and the number of league games and representative games played in a season.

Pre-World Cup

May

Before the World Cup there were yet more England warm-up games, a 3–1 win over Switzerland at Wembley, and a 4–0 win over Peru in Lima. Johnny Haynes played in both, winning his fifty-first and fifty-second caps. England played well at the start of the Switzerland match but then lapsed into mediocrity, a point not lost on the critics. Later in the game Switzerland missed many presentable opportunities, and only brave goalkeeping by Ron Springett kept England in front.

Haynes was starting to get concerned over England's form. There were the usual press suggestions that the 'Dynamic Duo' of Johnny Haynes and Bobby Robson had lost their powers of command. Suddenly, the shadow of the selectors' axe hung over Robson, with Bobby Moore waiting urgently in the wings.

The defensive faults seemed to be over when England played their second pre-World Cup game, which was against Peru eleven days later. Avenging the defeat of three years earlier, England this time played very well indeed, with Jimmy Greaves, now back at Spurs after a brief and unhappy period in Milan, scoring a magnificent hat trick. Haynes also played well, hitting the bar with a clever shot.

In the seventeen matches before the World Cup finals, England had lost only twice and were ready for the competition in Chile. Haynes and England were drawn in a much easier qualifying group than they were in the World Cup in Gothenburg.

It consisted of the Hungarians, who had slumped from their 1953 pinnacle, the unfancied Argentinians in the middle of political unrest, and the fairly unknown Bulgarians. Johnny Haynes arrived in Chile tired and jaded after having played around sixty competitive matches in the season.

Some maintain that the 1962 World Cup finals were the first that England really took seriously. Haynes liked the heat, but others failed to acclimatise or became sick. The England team were locked away in a mining community at Coya perched on the Andes at an altitude of 8,000 feet, home to the Braden Copper Company, and it took an absolute age to get to the training facilities and to the matches.

They were cooped up in barrack-style shacks with corrugated roofs and there was not a great deal to do. Often the rain thundered on to the roofs, making it difficult to sleep. Some privately described the arrangements as madness. The squad were away for a long time, and in the end many were desperate to get home. Walter Winterbottom had built this team around Haynes, and the manager said, "Haynes can pinpoint passes that destroy opposing defences. He can, by use of the ball, alter and dictate the tactics of a game. It's a natural ability."

England's World Cup squad preparing for the matches in Chile. Back row: Armfield, Norman, Robson, Swan, Hodgkinson, Springett, Howe, Flowers, Anderson, Wilson, Moore; front: Peacock, Hunt, Eastham, Connelly, Greaves, Hitchens, Haynes, Charlton, Douglas.

Haynes watches in frustration as the Hungarian goalkeeper, Grosics, makes a save in England's group stage 1–2 defeat. The weather is bleak, and no atmosphere is generated by the small crowd huddled together and spread thinly across the gaping terraces.

The World Cup matches

In the first game, against Hungary that they truly thought they could win comfortably, England very surprisingly lost 1–2, the match becoming more of a lottery due to the soaking wet pitch and the persistent drizzling rain. There was also little atmosphere from the sparse 10,000 crowd huddled under the grey sky. Haynes admitted he had worn the wrong footwear, and slithered and slipped around the pitch in the first half, not at all effective.

England fell behind when Haynes missed a tackle and keeper Ron Springett missed a shot he should have saved. England were back on terms through a Ron Flowers penalty, but then a lack of communication between Flowers and the luckless Springett, augmented by the appalling conditions, saw Hungary snatch a gifted and undeserved winner.

Privately skipper Haynes was seething about the two gift goals, and could see his England dream already starting to fade away. Certainly the massed defence employed by the Hungarians after they had taken an initial lead was a novelty to Haynes, who had expected an open, fluid game like those in the domestic league. Seeing queues of defenders lining up was quite alien to him.

The Hungarians had done their homework and contrived a plan for Haynes—tight marking, stifling his creativity. Their manager said: "The number ten takes corners, number ten takes the throw-ins, number ten does everything; so what do we do? We put a man tightly on number ten—goodbye England."

The press had some sympathy for the captain, saying that he battled hard, but couldn't find a way to alter the tactics. Winterbottom learned from this game, but insisted that the through pass which Haynes had mastered so well was more than ever the essential factor of victory against the square-lying defences of the foreign nations.

June

England had to put things right quickly, which they did in the following match against Argentina. Haynes played well, linking superbly with the forwards. One report said that he had worked up a spirit of anger that had exploded violently. England surged into a 3–0 lead through a Ron Flowers penalty, and goals from Bobby Charlton and Jimmy Greaves, before their customary late lapse allowed Argentina to pull back a goal, but England coasted home 3–1. Hungary had beaten the Bulgarians by a mighty 6–0, which left England needing just a draw in the next match to qualify.

The Bulgarian match turned out to be a tense and tetchy affair. The Bulgarians, hoping to avoid another pasting, posted nine men behind the ball, and skipper Haynes had to drop ever deeper and forage for the ball. He had, by his standards, a very average game.

As the time wore on without an early goal, England's play began to get edgy, and nerves got the better of them. Even England started to avoid throwing men forward for fear of being caught on the counter. The game finished a wholly disappointing 0–0, but they had qualified, and as Haynes quickly pointed out, that had been the sole objective.

But the performance did not please those at home, and the critics were swift to point out the shortcomings. One report described Haynes' play as slow and careless. Another wrote that he redeemed one of his worst performances by a gallant defence in the last heart-stopping minutes, and added: "He certainly couldn't plan a goal for the forwards." This aroused resentment in Haynes and other senior players, and the press were once again beginning to get under their skin.

As England had finished second, they had to face the winners of another group—Brazil again, the world champions, virtually in their own back yard. Yet England still thought they could win. They had met three times previously and each side had won one, drawn one and lost one, so this was deemed to be the 'decider'.

The match started well for England and Haynes, who was winning his fifty-sixth England cap. But then 'little bird' Garrincha netted with a perfectly timed header from a corner, beating centre half Norman to the ball with Springett again caught on his line. Although the goal was well executed, Haynes saw it as a defensive flaw, and muttered to himself, "Here we go again."

Fortunately England levelled quickly. A Johnny Haynes free kick was met beautifully by Jimmy Greaves, but his header bounced back from the intersection of post and crossbar; Gerry Hitchens, however, alert as always, tucked away the rebound, so it was one-all with everything to play for.

The second half, however, collapsed in on England in the first fifteen minutes. From a harshly awarded free kick for handball against Flowers, Garrincha sent in a wicked shot that Springett failed to hold and the rebound was crashed home. Minutes later and Garrincha's contribution was complete; he let fly with

Haynes and Jimmy Armfield cannot prevent Brazil's Zagallo firing in a shot on target in the 1–3 quarter-final defeat. Haynes is once again having to help out in the England defence, showing the shortcomings of the national team.

a dipping and swerving shot that Springett thought was going wide, and the goalkeeper moved too late to prevent the ball going in for the third goal.

After this, Brazil just kept possession in a parade of exhibition football, and all Haynes could do was stand and watch his World Cup dream go slowly down the plughole once again. The final whistle blew and England were out 1–3.

Apart from making the goal, there had been little to report about Haynes' play. One reporter was adamant that during the last twelve months he had not been an effective captain. Haynes knew that England had not been good enough and was further frustrated when the English squad and management returned home without watching the final stages of the competition. The overall view of the England selectors was: "We have nothing to learn," whilst most of the domestic press were now firmly describing English football as ten years behind.

The criticisms emerge again

Haynes had been really pent up and involved completely in the competition. When it all died down, and in his personal quietness before returning home, he realised in his disappointment that he might not have done quite enough: a good game against the Argentinians, a fairly good game against Brazil, an average one against Bulgaria and a poor one against the Hungarians. Two out of four as captain wasn't good enough for him; he didn't need to be told that. The television pundits this time round were quite civil, but the papers savaged England.

Alongside Walter Winterbottom, Haynes was targetted as the main reason for England's World Cup flop: too stereotypical, lacking in ideas, poor ball control, and under-performing as a captain; in fact everything. Haynes and Jimmy Greaves, on whom so much had depended, both had relatively poor championships. Haynes had, on occasions, been an abrasive and somewhat petulant captain. One vitriolic comment labelled him as a selfish captain who thought only of himself.

The competition had shown the first signs of a tightening in international defences with the additional centre half appearing in the first 4-2-4 formations. This had considerably cut down the options for through passes, especially those inside the full back. There were criticisms of Haynes for making England too predictable a team. Some said that he had been found out at this level, that teams could read his game and that he couldn't split the defence as he had done before. His style was easier to anticipate and counter. Some even doubted whether he had the will to compete at the highest level.

There were, however, others who had a great deal of sympathy for Haynes. Opponents knew very well that he was the focus of the England team, and were aware of the over-reliance placed on the captain for the team's creativity. In addition, the marking had been extremely tight. Haynes would also grumble *sotto voce* about the inadequacies of colleagues, and another very valid view was that he had once again merely exposed the national team's technical limitations.

To Haynes these criticisms were now nothing new. He had endured plenty of criticism from journalists in the past, especially newspapermen from the north, but this time even London-based journalists smelt blood, and there seemed to be an extra edge to the criticism and extra barbs in the words. He felt he couldn't win, and late summer 1962 saw him in a particularly disillusioned frame of mind. A depressed Haynes allegedly excoriated journalists on his return to the country, saying: "You want us to lose."

He later responded with what he considered was an open reply: "Let me say I respect everybody's right to criticise. I am a critic when I sit and watch a match, but I don't take a lot of notice of criticism. I am my own severest critic. I have been in the game long enough to know when and why things have gone wrong. I accept that we can all have our say, but I believe myself to be the best judge of what should be done."

Haynes' final England game

Although he would not have known it at the time of that Brazil quarter-final, Haynes would never play for England again. He had missed just eight of England's last sixty-three games.

He admitted privately afterwards that he had been neither mentally nor physically prepared for the tournament, and that the massive relegation struggle in a bloated domestic fixture list with Fulham and the long, long road to the FA Cup semi-final had again taken their toll on him.

After his first disappointment had subsided, he sincerely hoped that he would still be around and available for the next World Cup in 1966, although he would be then almost thirty-two. He really thought England, in their own garden, must have a good chance and that he would be able to contribute; fate, however, had other plans in store.

When he arrived home, an acquaintance asked whether it would be the end of the world if England never won the World Cup. His reply was unequivocal: "It matters very much. It may be just professional pride, but I am a professional footballer. It is my business and the World Cup is a major part of this."

Much later in life, he said of the 1962 experience: "That was one of the most disappointing experiences of my life. Chile weren't ready for the World Cup and our accommodation was out of the way, because Walter had been criticised for having stayed in Gothenburg city centre four years earlier. The crowds were tiny and after we lost the opening game to Hungary, the team were dispirited. Then we beat Argentina, but there was no strategic plan for the third game against Bulgaria. If we'd gone for the big win we'd have avoided Brazil in the quarter-finals. Instead we were content to qualify with a tame draw."

The World Cup quarter-final match against Brazil proved to be Haynes' last for England. In all he won 56 full caps for his country, and was the captain for 22 of these. Playing for England remained his proudest achievement, and a few years later he was delighted to pose for this picture with some of his England caps—and, of course, his parents, Rose and Eddie.

21: Car crash and dogfight 1962–63

21: Car crash and dogfight — 1962–63

At the start of the season, Johnny Haynes was presented by the mayor of Fulham with a framed address from the supporters' club to commemorate the winning of his fiftieth England cap. The directors, players and club officials awarded him a silver salver bearing the Fulham coat of arms.

Bobby Robson returns

Haynes played in the annual Whites v Colours trial and scored twice before half-time in a 4–2 win for the Whites, both fine opportunist efforts. Fulham and Haynes were boosted by the return to the Cottage of Bobby Robson, just over a year since starring for England in the big defeat of Scotland. Perhaps Fulham had finally realised that the squad needed strengthening. It was a surprise that West Bromwich Albion had released him, but the £20,000 fee was a large one for Fulham, and they had offered Robson a significantly better pay deal than the one proposed by Albion.

Whilst Haynes had done well following the abolition of the maximum wage, Albion had been far more reticent about passing on increases to their own England warrior. Robson was on around £25–30 at the Hawthorns, and Fulham effectively doubled his wages to around £50 per week.

Haynes hoped that this year Fulham would be a team going places. The Craven Cottage ground had been significantly re-vamped with flagpoles, tea bar, and electronic half-time scoreboard put in along the riverside terrace—and most of all with floodlights. Fulham had been the last club in the First Division to install floodlights.

August

The 2–1 home win over Leicester City that opened the season was in some ways unconvincing; there were a few flashes from Haynes and that was all. He did apply tireless energy, and carved out the opening for Graham Leggat to score his second goal and win the match. Haynes remained in the north after Fulham had lost 0–2 to Sheffield United at Bramall Lane in a colourless midweek performance. The rest of the Fulham team returned to London.

The car crash

Fulham were due to play a league game with Bolton on the Saturday, and the team had travelled up to stay close by at the Norbreck Hydro hotel in Blackpool. On the Friday evening, Haynes had been out with a lady, June Max, who was termed as a family friend, but who was cruelly described by some of the press as a local courtesan.

June Max, who lived in Hodgson Road Blackpool, was just twenty-five years old and already had a colourful background. She'd had a son at eighteen who now lived with her first husband. That marriage had been dissolved. She had lived for a year in Blackpool since separating from her second husband. She was driving a sports car with Johnny Haynes in the passenger seat when an accident occurred at around 11.20pm on the Friday evening. Whether the sports car belonged to Johnny or not was not chronicled, but reports say it was a red MG, so it is highly likely that it was his.

He had definitely broken curfew and should have been back in the hotel by 10pm. There are varying reports as to what happened, but what is clear is that it was a dreadful night of wind and heavy rain.

The accident occurred opposite a convalescent home on Blackpool North's Queen's promenade at Bispham. It appears that a strong gust of wind blew the car on to wet tramlines and caused a skid. June Max was unable to control the vehicle, and it spun across the road and slammed into an oncoming Ford Anglia.

Haynes had little recollection of the accident: "It all happened so quickly. We had gone out for a drive; it was raining hard and very windy. I was in the passenger seat; the next thing I knew we had hit something and were on the opposite side of the road. I was trapped by my legs, but someone managed to open the door and got me out. June's mother is a friend of the family and lives in Epsom. This was only the second time I have met June socially … we went out for a drive—and this has to happen."

Haynes had a few moments to lie in the car thinking what it might all mean, but he was quickly pulled from the crumpled wreck, though some reports say that he needed to be cut free. Both he and Mrs Max were taken straight to the Victoria Hospital in Blackpool; his condition was described as very dodgy and he was operated on immediately.

June Max had received a shoulder injury and was also operated on, remaining in the same hospital as Haynes but on a different ward. The three male passengers in the other car were also detained in hospital but were discharged the next day with only superficial injuries.

Both cars were towed to a garage in Harrowside near Blackpool. Next day a garage spokesman said: "Although we have not made a thorough examination it looks as if both cars could be written off—it was a

Previous page: The start of a new season, as Fulham take on Leicester City at Craven Cottage. But what would the season bring for the captain and the team?

The wrecked sports car. Haynes was sitting in the passenger seat and must have wondered if he'd ever play football again.

marvel nobody was killed. The side of the car on which Mr Haynes was sitting was extensively damaged." Haynes ruefully reflected later in life, "In those days, sports cars had fibre-glass bodies. There was no protection."

Haynes had broken bones in both legs and badly injured a cruciate ligament in his right knee which was stitched together, the normal procedure those days. There was a hairline fracture just above the right ankle and an injury to the left foot, possibly broken toes. All the injuries were remedied in an operation on the Friday night, and both legs were encased in plaster. Many predicted that the accident would signal the end of Fulham in the First Division.

However, his initial reaction the day after the crash was surprisingly upbeat: "It's a pretty frightening thing for a footballer to look down and see both his legs in plaster. But I know my injuries are not too serious and I'm determined to be back in the Fulham team just as soon as I can. … My boss, Beddy Jezzard, tells me I'll probably be taken home to London for specialist treatment this week. That's good, because the sooner it starts, the sooner I can get back to football."

The initial trite remark was followed by news of a different kind from the surgeons. The orthopaedic specialist's words were akin to a death sentence to the stricken Fulham star. "So sorry, but it's the end of the road, Johnny. It's a very bad fracture and you'll never be able to play football again." Haynes was devastated. "I had joined Fulham straight from school at the age of seventeen [*sic*] and now at the age of twenty-seven the doctor was telling me I would have to find a new job when football meant everything to me."

England's chief selector Joe Richards said: "No player is automatically chosen on his name and we have already been looking deeply for other inside forwards, but this is still very bad luck on the player and the country."

Many of the Fulham team did not know about the accident until the following day. Haynes' team-mates visited him in hospital early on the Saturday in twos and threes before departing for their match with Bolton Wanderers. Haynes' place in an already injury-hit side would be taken by eighteen-year-old Dave Metchick.

Apart from the normal England matches, the accident robbed Haynes of the opportunity of playing in the first-ever European qualification matches ahead of the 1964 tournament. Without Haynes, England were held 1–1 at Wembley by France and firmly trounced 2–5 in the second leg in Paris, hence failing to qualify for the tournament finals.

The farce getting Haynes home

Haynes remained in the Victoria Hospital for three days, and left on a stretcher the following Tuesday. Haynes shook hands with his doctor and ward sister

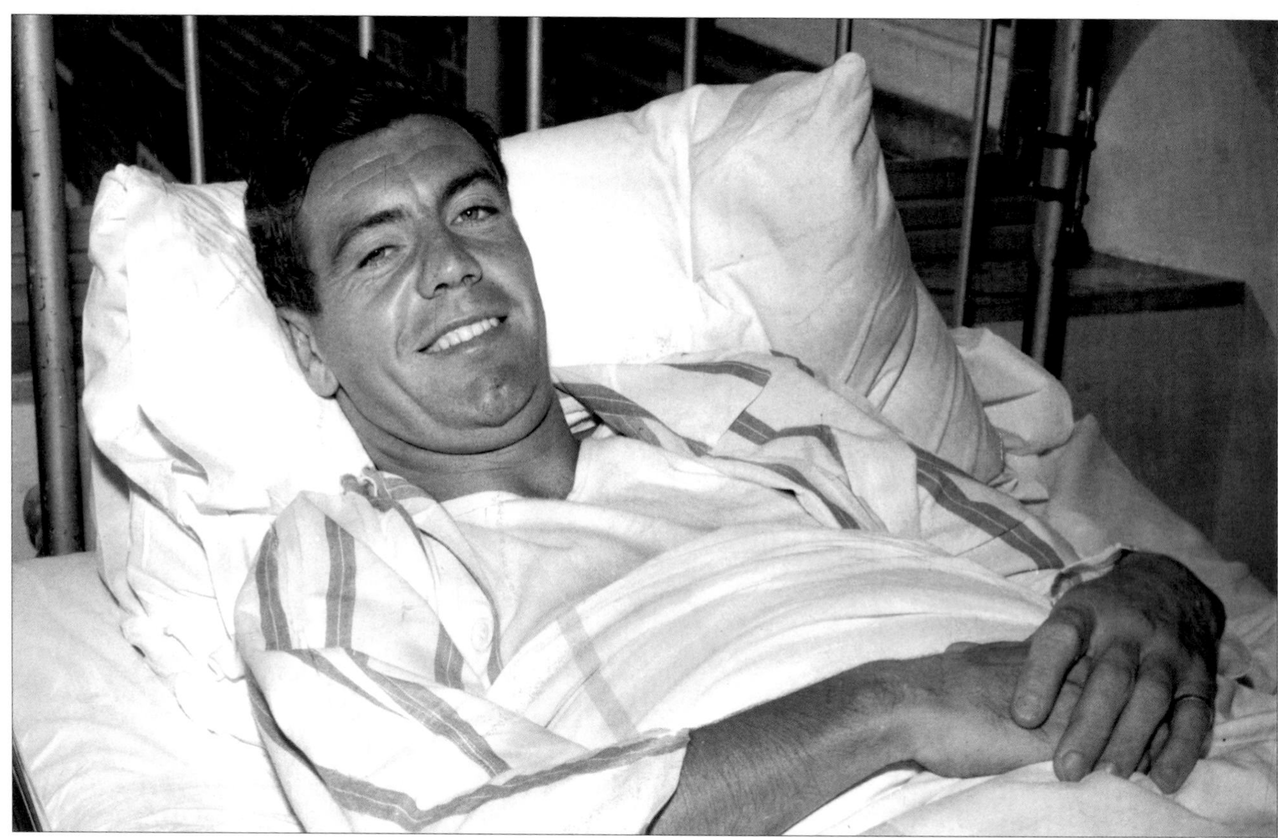

Still smiling in hospital in Blackpool and ready to go home, but Haynes' recovery was months away.

before departing. His doctor, Dr Chatterjee, said, "He has been a marvellous patient and has been given no special privileges." Ward sister Lilian Pitchford said, "He has been no trouble at all, and it has been a great thrill for the boys and teenagers here; he has signed lots of autographs."

Bringing Haynes home turned out be a fiasco in keeping with a Ben Travers farce or a Brian Rix play. After leaving the hospital, he was taken to Manchester's Ringway airport in good time for the 2.15 flight to London. He had been booked as a sitting passenger. A flustered BEA (British European Airways) representative said: "We cannot take him, we didn't expect a stretcher case." He explained: "Medical authorities advised us that he must travel as a full stretcher case—taking up four seats." He added, "Although there is room on the plane, a special stretcher and special equipment is needed." During this hiatus, there was the surreal sight of tailcoated waiters giving Johnny the VIP treatment by carrying his lunch out to him in the ambulance while he waited on the airport tarmac. The arguments raged for almost two hours.

A hurried call to British Railways brought the reply, "We will take him. Try to catch the 4.05 train." Haynes was whisked quickly across the city to Manchester Piccadilly railway station and his first class compartment—only to find that the stretcher couldn't go in first class. He was hurriedly put into a second class 'special stretcher-case' compartment and departed for London Euston. A car was organised to meet him there.

Fulham officials arrived at Euston and observed very quickly that the car provided would not be big enough and fumed: "That won't take his stretcher—we need an ambulance!" A forlorn Haynes waited patiently

Silver salver service for Haynes at Manchester's Ringway Airport.

Looking remarkably cheerful on the train taking him from Manchester back to London Euston.

in the train compartment whilst the officials phoned for an ambulance. Soon an LCC (London County Council) ambulance raced on to the platform with the red accident lights flashing.

The ambulance backed up to the carriage door and its crew alighted. Nothing happened and one of the ambulance crew returned to his cab, and radioed headquarters saying, "It's not an accident at all—it's Johnny Haynes." For more than twenty minutes the ambulance crew argued with Fulham general manager Frank Osborne and the club doctor Robert Wiggins, maintaining that this was a 'general removal' case which was not their job. Eventually a compromise was reached and the ambulance team reluctantly agreed to take Haynes to St Stephen's Hospital in Fulham and no further.

Haynes was then forced to wait on his stretcher inside the hospital entrance until a hired ambulance arrived to take him to his Epsom home. Frank Osborne explained: "We hired an ambulance to meet Johnny at London Airport but something went wrong with arrangements." At the end of a difficult day, a weary and clearly fed-up Haynes could only mutter, "All I want is to get to bed."

Ironically, a senior ambulance officer at Blackpool said: "If we had been asked to deliver Haynes to London ourselves it would have been done. We have made 323 similar deliveries without a hitch over the past two years—but the club took it upon their own shoulders and that's how the snags occurred."

During that fraught day, Haynes phoned his girlfriend Eileen Farmer to state the facts. "I phoned Eileen to explain that June [Max] was a friend of the family. She understood—there has been no rift." To finish the day on a dark note, Eileen was not there to meet him in Epsom, but she said, "I didn't arrange to meet him because I had a hard day filming. I am still very much his girlfriend and I shall go and see him as soon as I can."

Later Eileen commented: "It's rotten luck; we were together on Tuesday just before he went to Blackpool. I know June's parents well. They are friends of Johnny's mother and father. There was nothing more between Johnny and June than family friendship."

Haynes also felt that he had to defend his position, stating: "June's mother is a family friend. She [my mother] has often suggested that if I was ever in Blackpool to look up June, so I phoned her. There's no question of romance." Whilst he was on crutches, he would meet his third wife Avril for the first time.

Haynes had recovered sufficiently by mid-September to be a spectator at the Arsenal home game with both legs still in plaster, and on crutches, to witness a disappointing 1–3 home defeat. He reported that he had been touched by those who had written wishing him a speedy recovery. He added: "I very much appreciate the kind wishes; it's been a great consolation to know that I have so many friends." He had already decided to take absolutely no notice of the gloomy medical opinions and battle his way back to fitness.

At the Arsenal match, Haynes was determined to keep smiling and keep battling. After the match, he hobbled on to the pitch on his crutches.

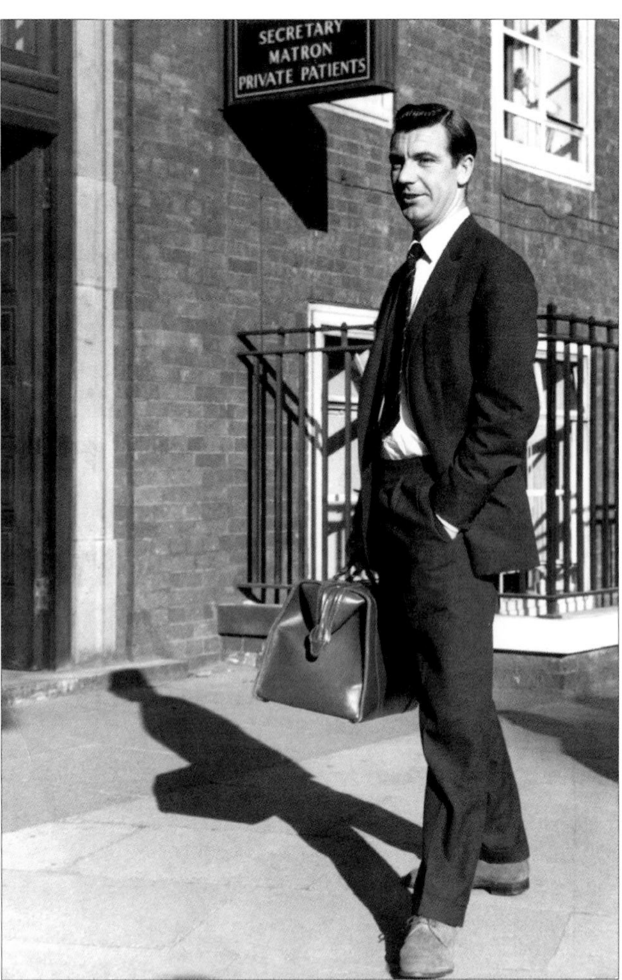

Ready for his rehabilitation 'torturers', on the way to fitness at Westminster Hospital.

Haynes back in six weeks?

September to January

People at the club were desperately trying to avoid predicting a comeback date. It was difficult to judge, but the guess was that it could be as much six weeks or a couple of months. After the Arsenal game, when the crowd had left, a depressed Haynes hobbled on to the green turf at Craven Cottage saying, "I think I will have a look at the ground for old time's sake."

In fact it was between two and three months even before the plaster was removed. Haynes spent most of that time at home in Epsom, playing cards with his father, watching television and dealing with a backlog of personal fan mail and correspondence.

The surgeons had told him that after the plaster had been removed, it could be just a month before playing could be resumed. With this in mind, Haynes had pencilled in the Manchester City game on the 24th of November as a comeback date.

However, this plan was immediately quashed by the surgeons after the removal of the plaster at the end of October. A cyst had formed on the cartilage, and once they had removed that, they weren't entirely happy with the condition of the ligaments. The surgeons categorically told him to think of nearer January instead.

During his rehabilitation, Haynes took a further blow when his staunchest ally and the man who had the utmost confidence in him, Walter Winterbottom, resigned as England manager following the World Cup failure. He was ultimately replaced, after serving a notice period, by former Tottenham player Alf Ramsey whose own England career had been terminated in that 3–6 defeat by the Hungarians at Wembley that Haynes had watched as a young man.

Six months of pain

To the astonishment of professional medics, and as a testimony to his resilient temperament, Haynes embarked on a gritty rehabilitation regime to return to professional football. He described this period as an agonising time both physically and mentally, but he was determined to play the game he loved so much again.

What followed the removal of the plaster was masses of medically supervised exercises, designed

Testing out the legs against the reserves on a snowy Leatherhead pitch. The tackle was hard, but Haynes came through unscathed, ready for the forthcoming relegation dogfight.

to strengthen the leg. Haynes described some of his supervisors as torturers. Following these tortures, he returned to jogging and light training on December 10th. He then took part in a practice match on Christmas Eve, an ideal present. He was still pinning his hopes on a return in early January and the FA Cup. The club however were more cautious. Manager Jezzard said, "If anything happens to the knee now, he might be out for the rest of the season."

Haynes said: "I feel quite fit, I have done no kicking, nor have I attempted to twist and turn, actions that would test the knee to the full. I am looking forward to getting back to training, but you can definitely write me out of the cup-tie at West Ham in January, and for some time after that."

A short time later Jezzard spoke again of the injured captain. "It takes players five weeks to get fit for the start of the season; Johnny has to start to all over again, and he cannot take any sort of risk as he would in pre-season training. We just cannot afford to take a chance. He will play when he is absolutely sure of himself; when that will be—nobody knows."

As predicted, Fulham struggled badly without Haynes. Also, for short periods when they were also without George Cohen and Graham Leggat, they *really* struggled. In fact during Haynes' enforced absence, Fulham won just *four* out of twenty-one league matches (half a season), and apart from a brief spell in October, they were in the relegation spots all that time. The Cottagers had also been dumped from the League Cup by Second Division Norwich City. It was not the ideal scenario for Haynes to return to.

However, by the time he was truly fit to resume playing he had missed only twenty-one league games solely on account of the winter of the 'Big Freeze'. After Boxing Day, Siberian heavy snow and arctic conditions enveloped the country, and put paid to any football being played in Britain for around *six* weeks. This removed the opportunity for Haynes to play in a proposed reserve comeback game against Birmingham City reserves on January 21st.

Manager Jezzard commented, "Johnny has had a tough time trying to strengthen the knee; he's been working extremely hard every day from 9am to 5pm." Haynes joined the first team squad for two days' light training in Worthing.

Haynes returns to another relegation dogfight

February

Right at the start of the month, Johnny Haynes took part in a friendly against the reserves at Leatherhead to test out the knee. Fulham won 2–1 and Haynes grunted and puffed his way through the ninety minutes but made two special passes that led to the two Fulham goals. He walked off that pitch a much happier man. Contemplating his return, he said: "I'm delighted with the way things went, and if the West Ham pitch were as good as this one at Leatherhead it would be a possible, but I am afraid it won't be. It would be too big a risk after such a long time. I'm hoping the tie will be off (postponed) again, for every extra day is a day on my side. What I did prove this morning is that my right knee is completely sound. There were times when I

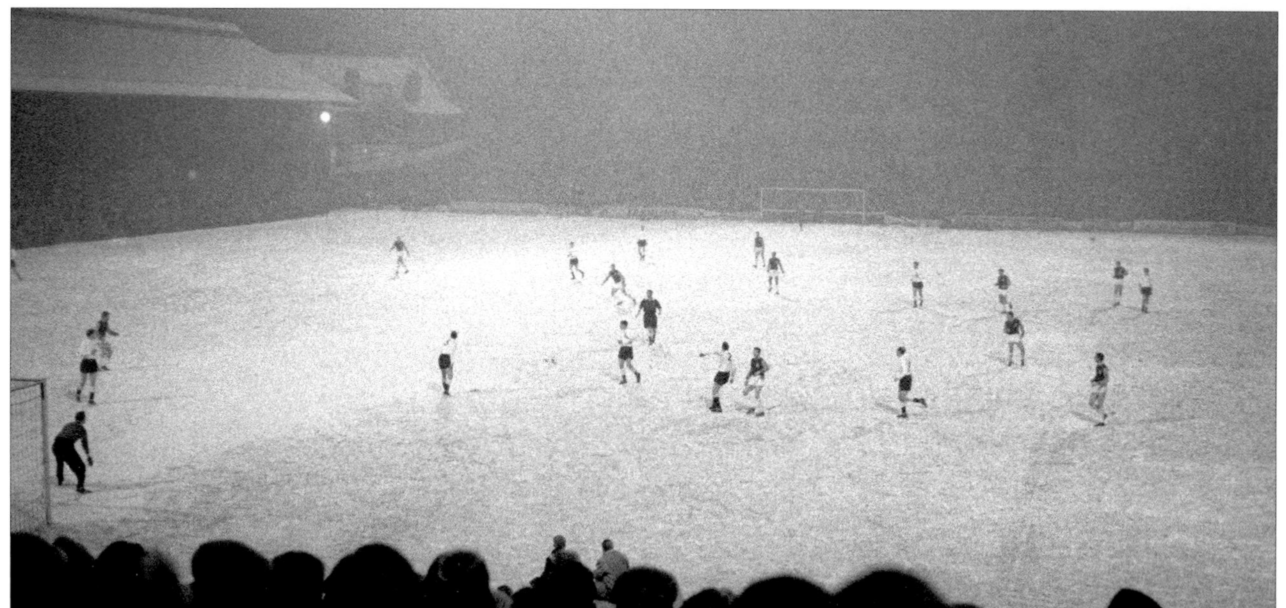

Spot the ball—and spot the maestro! For his first match at Craven Cottage after his car crash, Haynes took part in this snow-ravaged 1–2 defeat in the FA Cup third-round replay against West Ham.

thought I might not play again. Now I am sure it is 100 per cent. I need a month to get back to my best. I should be ready for England if they want me in a couple of months."

When the arctic conditions finally began to abate in mid-February, he returned to a standing ovation against struggling Leyton Orient at Brisbane Road on a muddy pitch that could scarcely have been more demanding, helping Fulham to secure a 1–1 draw. He had been missing for almost six months. It was Fulham's first league game since Boxing Day.

Both teams were in the mire, seemingly handcuffed together for relegation. Orient had not won a league game since beating Fulham way back in September. The press said: "The old roar of greeting must have been music to him, and he clearly was as eager as a young schoolboy to get moving again." With his first touch, Haynes put a beautiful through pass to reserve forward Reg Stratton who was robbed at the last moment. Observers thought that he had lost none of the accuracy, mobility and ball control and he made hardly any errors.

Easing his way back and taking no undue risks, Haynes faded in the second half due to lack of match practice. He was also carrying excess weight, albeit just half a stone; in his own words he was "carrying a little surplus." Already the papers said that his long passes bore the stamp of his old accuracy. He gave the thumbs up and came through unscathed.

He commented after the match: "I was very pleased with the way things went for me. Naturally I felt a little tired towards the end, but I didn't feel a thing with the injury. I got one kick on my left ankle but it was from one of my own players and so no damage was done. I received several hard tackles as one would expect in such a tussle, but there again I had nothing to worry about. I reckon I'll be back to top condition after three or four matches and I think Fulham will get out of trouble."

Fulham's third-round FA Cup tie with West Ham at Upton Park had been postponed a record *eight* times before a goalless draw was played out. In the replay, Fulham made a quick exit, losing 1–2. In front of 20,000 windswept souls braving a bitter snowstorm, Fulham were two down before Bobby Robson pulled one back three minutes from time.

One reporter said, "Haynes is coming back fast—and as a shooting star." He was extraordinarily unlucky, putting in five shots that stood out for sheer power and precision, and he almost made it all-square in the very last minute when a magnificent low, left-foot shot was fingertipped away. As the snowflakes fell there were many of the touches of his old self.

He captained Fulham to a 3–1 victory in the following game against Nottingham Forest. He said that he felt very rusty, but observers said that the magic still looked intact. Although it was not vintage Haynes, his all-round excellence on a stamina-sapping pitch made observers marvel at his resilience as well as his inborn artistry.

Fulham benefitted from a gift own goal as early as the third minute, and after Forest had equalised, a superb free kick from Robson restored Fulham's lead before Haynes got into the act shortly after half-time. His superb long through pass landed right at the feet of Johnny Key, who lobbed over the goalkeeper, the ball going in just under the bar. The papers said, "Undoubtedly, Haynes was the inspirational captain." Time and time again Robson and Haynes split the Forest defence.

George Cohen remembers the comeback. "I thought his first game back was totally unimpressive and I thought, 'Oh, God. What's it all about here?' But then the next game you wouldn't have thought he'd been away from it! He just needed a game to break himself back into it. I don't think he went back to the reserves even, which most of us would have had to do."

March

In his third game back, against relegation-threatened Ipswich Town, Haynes was unluckily injured again. Before the mishap he had proved to everyone at

Portman Road, not least the watching England manager Alf Ramsey, who had just taken over following Winterbottom's handover period, that he was already right back to peak form. In the sixteenth minute, his glorious pass down the middle split the defence. Maurice Cook received the ball and passed through for Graham Leggat to run on and score the winner.

However, in the thirty-third minute Haynes, back helping the defence and evading a tough tackle, twisted and fell heavily, lying on the ground in apparent agony. Trinder buried his head in his trilby and Jezzard held his head in his hands—not again.

The first thought was that the problem could have been a paralysed nerve, but it was soon decided that it could be something more serious and therefore Haynes was carried off by trainer Frank Penn and a member of the St John's team. Worryingly, it was the right knee again.

Despite this injury, Fulham battled on for almost an hour with ten men. Haynes' magical contribution whilst he was on the field had helped produce a convincing victory, Fulham winning 1–0. They had picked up five points out of six since Haynes' return and were unbeaten.

Out again after just three games

At least Tommy Trinder sounded more upbeat the following day: "We are now much more hopeful. We think that Johnny has merely fallen heavily on a nerve and temporarily paralysed it. We decided at half-time not to risk him any more because we'd rather lose two points than Johnny. The lads were marvellous, they said, 'Don't worry Guv'nor; we'll do it all right'—and they did.

"On the way back Johnny was in no pain as you would expect if ligaments had again been damaged. So it's fingers crossed until Monday when we will have a check from the doctor."

Haynes saw a specialist at St Stephen's Hospital on the Monday, and the verdict was encouraging. Haynes spoke with a sense of relief: "It could have been a whole lot worse. It's a bad wrench, but although there is fluid on my knee, my ligaments are not damaged. The doctors say I will be able to play again in two to three weeks. I won't be able to train until the swelling goes down, but I shall be doing some knee exercises. It's rotten luck, but at least we won 1–0!"

It was going to be another tough fight, and the expected two to three weeks turned out to be over two months and thirteen more missed matches.

Fulham survive without their captain

Fulham had a number of injuries, but shook off the cobwebs and realised that they *had* to make a fight of it without captain Haynes again. Including the games that Haynes played on his brief return, the team recorded a remarkable eight consecutive wins and a draw in nine games. This change of form saw them shooting up the table from rock bottom at the end of February to mid-table by the end of March.

They were the in-form team. Under Jim Langley's captaincy, although they didn't score many in Haynes' absence, the defence suddenly became watertight, conceding only four goals in those nine games, including, unusually for Fulham at the time, six clean sheets. Among these wins was a 1–0 victory over Aston Villa, where Rodney Marsh made a scoring debut, and a remarkable 2–0 victory at Old Trafford.

April

Haynes continued to battle on in the background. He tried to make an early comeback but, playing in a reserve match at Craven Cottage at the end of the month he was injured again ten minutes before the end. Once more he had to be helped from the pitch. Fulham were now reluctantly reporting that he might not play again that season. He then underwent special courses to strengthen the leg which had obviously not fully healed.

May

Through sheer determination and grit, he managed to make it back for the last three league games of the season, which had extended well into May because of the bad weather. He returned at Everton and according to the press looked remarkably fit, considering the circumstances. He provided a superb cross for Johnny Key to score. A reporter noted that the passes inside the full back were still there.

Despite his inclusion, Fulham lost 1–4, being one-three down before half an hour was up. Fulham kindly

More drama as Haynes is carried off at Ipswich after playing just two full games.

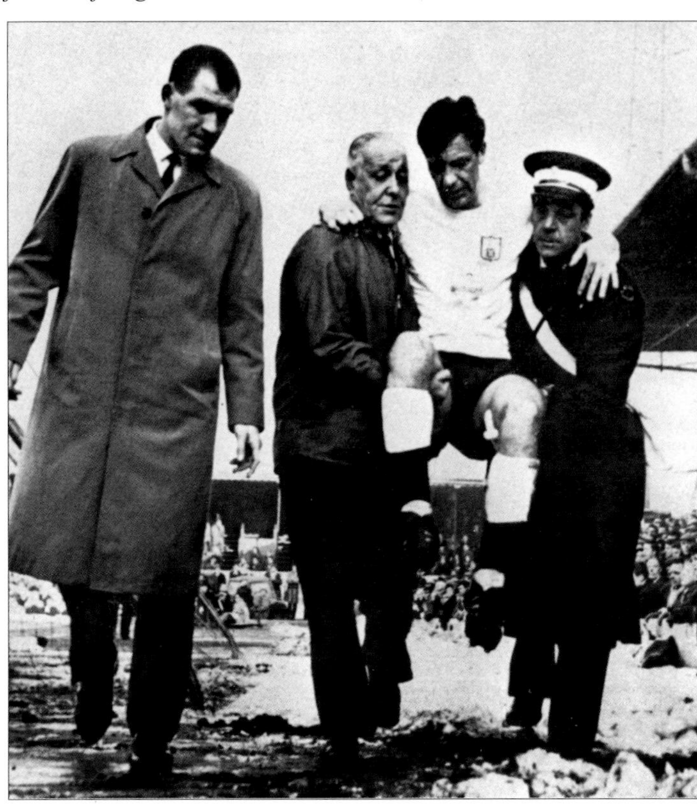

In the last match of the season, at home to West Bromwich Albion, Haynes looked tired and strained. The Fulham faithful were wondering whether the maestro could come back from his injuries and once again reproduce the glorious football that they had seem him play for the last ten years.

donated Everton the First Division championship, thanks to a Roy Vernon hat trick. They were also beaten convincingly at Arsenal 0–3 in the middle of the following week, this time falling to a Joe Baker hat trick.

The final home game of the season was against West Bromwich Albion and was played on a windy day and a bumpy pitch, with neither side having anything to play for. The match was poor, but for Haynes personally, matters looked worse. He was obviously still troubled by the leg injury, and continually shook his head—he knew it still wasn't right.

He was in a very subdued mood. After half-time, he surrendered the midfield completely to his former England colleague Albion's Don Howe, thus enabling the visitors to come away from the Cottage with a 1–2 victory. The question on some people's lips was, "Would Johnny Haynes come back again or was he finished totally as a top-class footballer?"

The end of a traumatic season

Fulham's last ten league games had proved remarkably difficult, with seven of them being against teams in the top eight of the First Division. Fulham had won one and drawn four. They finished a distinctly average sixteenth, but in the end retained their First Division status quite comfortably, being seven points clear of relegated Manchester City in twenty-first place. This probably put an end to the idea that Fulham without Haynes were a team without any hope of survival in Division One.

Although the team had conceded little more than seventy goals, without Haynes they scored only *fifty* league goals all season, and Maurice Cook's fifteen and Graham Leggat's ten accounted for half of those! The tally was the worst for fourteen years, the previous worst being in the 1949–50 season, long before Haynes set foot on the Cottage turf.

It was a drop of 25% on the previous season, and of over 30% on the season before that, showing just how much Haynes' passing, scheming and scoring skills had been missed. He had played in just eight league matches that season. It was his worst time for being absent from the side, but near the end of his career he would say, "I can't complain really, I've not been too unlucky with injuries."

Around this time the dapper Bobby Keetch was emerging at Fulham as a tough, no-nonsense but stylish centre half, both on and off the field. Haynes was Bobby Keetch's hero, and the two men remained firm friends.

Before Keetch's untimely death, he talked of the early days with Johnny and why he was amongst the best on and off the pitch. He said of his friend: "One of the truly greats; I was seventeen when I joined Fulham. John was captain of England. The first day we went to a pub for lunch and I sat apart from the others. I didn't dare speak. The team left and I asked for my bill. The landlord said that John had paid for me. Didn't have to, except he knew that as a young player I was likely to be broke and I was. It proved my theory that I never met a really great player who was a complete arsehole!"

22: Off! But to Spurs? 1963–64

22: Off! But to Spurs? 1963–64

Surprisingly, Johnny Haynes was named in the Fulham side that played the annual pre-season friendly cricket match against Putney, and came through well, scoring twenty runs. However, there were warning signs on the football field that things were not so good. He had come through two practice matches with no problems, but in a third he failed to appear after half-time.

He reported that his leg was aching and that there was a recurrence of pain in his knee. To test himself, he was part of the Fulham squad that flew to Bilbao to play two matches in Spain; a despondent Haynes said, "I hope to play in at least one." Many people privately considered that these early days would be make or break for Haynes.

He played in the first match, and for twenty minutes he seemed to be in peak form, almost scoring with a cracking shot that was deflected just wide by a defender. Then, slightly worryingly, he flicked at the leg several times indicating a problem, and in the twenty-fifth minute left the field to speak to manager Bedford Jezzard. Thankfully he was only concerned about stamina. Jezzard said afterwards, "I could see that he was short of stamina, and nearly called him off the field. I felt that if he could get through forty-five minutes, he would be OK for Everton on Saturday."

He returned to the pitch and stormed his way through ninety minutes, playing a captain's role and pulling his side out of trouble when necessary, although the final 3–4 result was of no real consequence. At the end, he was grinning like a man who had left a load of worries behind on the pitch. However he was not risked in the second match against Sporting Lisbon. Inside, he felt that he was almost ready for action.

As the game of football began to change following the 1962 World Cup, and as a result of the injury, Haynes' play changed too. He played a much deeper role but was still the hub around which every Fulham move turned. He could still size up a situation in an instant, and had complete mastery of the ball, with the cunning to veil his real intentions, and the patience to bide his time before releasing one of his defence-cutting passes.

He realised that the shorter pass and first touch were now more important than ever. Fans held their breath, anxious to see how he would perform in the new season after a full close season's rest, no cricket, no England, and a light Fulham tour in Spain. They didn't have long to wait.

Previous page: Cartoon strip fame for Haynes in the famous Charles Buchan football magazine.

PRESENTED WITH

TIGER

50 STAR FOOTBALLERS OF 1963

16. JOHNNY HAYNES
(Fulham)

Brilliant inside - forward. Born near Spurs' ground; won 5 England Schools caps (1949-50); joined Fulham ground-staff at 15. Won Youth cap; debut for Fulham 1952, aged 18; over 350 games; 56 England caps. Captained England in World Cup.

© FLEETWAY PUBLICATIONS LTD.

August

It would be a very tough first game back, away to star-studded champions Everton at Goodison. Ironically, Everton had been Haynes' first opponents when he made his return following a second lengthy lay-off the previous season. He played well, but disappointingly was overworked by his colleagues. Although he coped for a while, he was really short of match practice and was ultimately ushered out of the game by Everton's impressive Scottish international Jimmy Gabriel. Fairly predictably, Fulham lost 0–3.

His first goal for sixteen months

Fulham's first midweek home game of the season saw them post a 2–0 win over Sheffield Wednesday. Both goals came in the last seven minutes of the first half. Alan Mullery shot the first off a defender from Chamberlain's cross, and Haynes landed a typical second on the stroke of half-time. Following a dexterous move involving Johnny Key and Bobby Robson there came, from the edge of the box, a typical precision shot from Johnny Haynes. The strike was extremely accurate, beating Ron Springett's dive and going in just inside the far post.

The club programme reported that Haynes was back in command. The goal must have been particularly sweet for him, as it was the first time he had found the net in sixteen months.

The national press were even more impressed after the match, producing a banner headline "Haynes back to England form", and reporting: "Haynes indeed, proved himself the centre-piece, and if any England selector were there, he must surely have realised that Haynes has served notice of his intention to win back his place in the national side. It would certainly be hard to exclude him on this form. His pin-point passes, either first time or carefully thought-out as he drew the defence, were pitched to the last refined inch, creating situations which might have brought goals and nearly

In the match against Arsenal at Craven Cottage in September, Haynes displayed his usual style and artistry, but could not prevent a 1–4 defeat.

did, from Cook, Key, Brown and even the irrepressible and popular Chamberlain."

One swallow doesn't make a summer

Fulham then recorded a second win, 2–1 against Birmingham at the Cottage. Two great goals from veteran Trevor Chamberlain proved to be the highlight of the day. The win masked Haynes' problems. After the praise he had received in midweek, he now looked pretty despondent and seemed to be only playing at half pace. The press thought he was not yet back to top form. It was a full year since the original injury—it didn't look good.

September

Fulham then suffered two successive 0–3 reverses, one in the return match at Hillsborough against Sheffield Wednesday, and another at the Hawthorns against West Bromwich Albion. At Sheffield, the Fulham team were never in it, and although Haynes looked as fit as in his heyday, he failed to put any zip into a forward line that never moved with any purpose.

In the Midlands, his performance was said to be improving, and he put some chances on a plate for his colleagues but they missed them all. One reporter said that it was as if they had forgotten how to play with him in the side. The situation looked even more ominous when Fulham were trounced 1–4 at Burnley. They were overwhelmed and Haynes was "among the also-rans".

In the Arsenal match at the Cottage, although Fulham again lost 1–4, a superb floated free kick by Haynes gave Graham Leggat an equalising goal. Fulham lost mainly due to defensive errors and the lack of cover offered to seventeen-year-old Martin Townsend, Fulham's third choice goalkeeper, who only ever played two matches in league football. Again Haynes was over-used by his colleagues, and one paper said, "He is currently not the powerhouse he was, he just couldn't run the show." Another said that Haynes' ability to make an international comeback seemed very much in doubt.

Nevertheless, he increased his goal tally with Fulham's first goal in the 2–1 midweek win over Burnley. All the team raised their game to win this one, and Fulham came from a goal behind to secure the victory. Bobby Robson initially sent Haynes away. He carried the ball forward and after an interchange between Maurice Cook and Rodney Marsh, he ran through cleverly to equalise. George Cohen bisected the defence for Leggat to score the winner in the second half. Burnley had finished third last season and so this was a very important confidence-boosting win.

It was even better at the weekend against Leicester City at Filbert Street when, from Cohen's pass, Haynes produced a beautiful lob into the goalmouth

Exasperation from Haynes in the match against Bolton, but it was directed more at himself than at his colleagues. Happily this game resulted in a 3–1 win for the home side.

three minutes from time that allowed Marsh to head a superb winning goal. In doing so, Marsh collided with a defender and a post and was carried off unconscious, not knowing he had scored in the 1–0 win. The injury temporarily halted his promising career and left him partially deaf.

Is Johnny Haynes finished?

When Fulham drew struggling Third Division Colchester United in the League Cup it was perhaps a chance for a breather. It is rumoured that Haynes and Bobby Keetch thought it might be all right to have a drink (or two) *before* the game, and a mistake it turned out to be. A rampant Colchester were five-one up with twenty-five minutes still remaining, although some respectability was restored with two late goals. But the 3–5 score was an embarrassment to Fulham and captain Haynes, and the pre-match drink never occurred again.

Haynes scored the third goal in the next home match, a 3–1 win over a poor Bolton Wanderers side stranded at the foot of the table. It was a game to forget, and Haynes in his present form couldn't raise the standards. His goal in the second half was defined as a fine effort. He fastened on to Cook's pass and put the issue beyond doubt. However, he was still not playing to the old standard; most of the diehards could readily see that.

At least this gave Fulham three league wins in a row, which deflected concerns away from the captain's fitness. They then went on a winless streak again, first of all falling 0–1 to Blackpool at Bloomfield Road just two days after the Bolton win. Although Haynes was struggling with fitness and form, he had played *nine* matches in twenty-seven days, enough to test the resources and resilience of any player.

October

Fulham were defeated 0–2 at Ewood Park by Blackburn the following Saturday. Haynes' performances seemed to be getting him down; he was slow and described as erratic with his distribution. He had totally failed to lift the Fulham side. One caustic comment was that he had nothing to show.

The following week Fulham fought out a 0–0 draw with Nottingham Forest at the Cottage. Johnny was again well below his best, and major anxiety ensued when he spent the second half languishing on the left wing and totally out of the game. Without him there was no pilot and two inept forward lines failed to produce a decent encounter. It was almost a third of the way into the season, and many were now quietly asking themselves whether Haynes was finished as a top-class player.

It was obvious that in his current form he needed some quality support in terms of stamina and experience to help him out whilst he was trying to regain his form and fitness. Manager Bedford Jezzard then played a master card; he moved Graham Leggat to outside left and Bobby Robson temporarily over to left half to assist Haynes, and the changes paid off straight away at Stoke.

Leggat, knowing his friend and colleague was in trouble, was brilliant on the day, hitting the woodwork three times. Then he scored in the first half, and it was Haynes who crafted the opportunity for the Scot to sweep home a stunning shot from thirty yards. Haynes was beginning to raise his game, and Fulham earned a creditable point in a 1–1 draw. Bobby Robson also played very well, and the reporters were impressed, one saying that the left wing triangle of Leggat, skipper Johnny Haynes and Bobby Robson was the slickest combination he'd seen that season. Another noted that Haynes placed some nice passes and had poise and smartness.

Back to England form

The new left-side partnership was cruelly broken the following week, when it was feared that Leggat had broken his leg against Chelsea. Fortunately it turned out to be just badly bruised. Fulham were once again left with ten men for the whole of the second half. In a shadowy game, Haynes' play shone out like a beacon and his passes had the Chelsea defence groping.

Even with ten men Fulham should have won, but the forwards couldn't take advantage of Haynes' promptings. In the end an inferior Chelsea side escaped with a 0–1 victory, courtesy of a very fortuitous goal just a quarter of an hour from the end. The press recognised that the match might be the turning-point for Haynes with a headline proclaiming that he was again in top form.

They enthused: "Johnny came romping back with his best display for Fulham since he was injured in a car crash, and he is winning his fight to regain international recognition. He was undoubtedly Fulham's man-of-the-match always in the heart of the battle, a master of tactics and if the Cottagers had not been cut down to ten men for the whole of the second half it could have been a very different result."

Despite the plaudits, Fulham had started the season quite differently from the way they usually did. By the end of the month it was five games without a win, and already eight defeats. The team were sitting just three places off the bottom of the table—in relegation trouble.

November

It was the same story the following week against Spurs. Haynes worked very hard, created good opportunities and saw many chances wasted. This had been a good chance to beat the Spurs, as they were off form and hadn't won for a month. For Fulham there was the usual injury problem which necessitated several reserves playing in the forward line. Fulham lost to another late single goal, Jimmy Greaves' 199th, and the 0–1 defeat at White Hart Lane meant that it was now six games without success.

There was some joy the following Saturday with a 2–0 home win over Aston Villa. Fulham still had injuries to the forwards and their performance was inept; the attack was struggling to find any sort of quality. Fortunately for Fulham, Villa's key centre half, their centre forward and their half back were all hampered by injuries received during the match.

It took a very rare goal from George Cohen, actually a cross that the goalkeeper misjudged, and an opportunist effort from Johnny Key in the final minute after Haynes' fierce shot had been blocked, to secure the victory. Exempting Haynes, one critic said that four of the five Fulham forwards were so off form that they would be pushed to hold a place in a struggling Third Division side. The press acknowledged that in recent times they had come to expect a mixture of brilliance and bathos from Fulham.

However, Haynes' game definitely seemed on the way up. In this match, he produced a personal performance that could rarely have been bettered, and by the end he was back as a legitimate England candidate.

After the game at Anfield, where Fulham were unluckily undone 0–2 by two goals in the last four minutes, the media were saying that Haynes had showed the form which had made him captain of England. It was, however, another match of missed chances.

Fulham then took on Sheffield United at the Cottage. United were top of the table and had the tightest defence in the league, so, of course, Fulham won easily, 3–1. But the injury jinx was still active; full back Jim Langley was badly injured and spent the game on the wing, and striker Maurice Cook moved to left back. Haynes had to play deeper to assist the new formation but the rotation worked well, and gave the Blades a very unhappy afternoon.

Fulham's third goal was scored near the end by inside forward Bobby Howfield, signed from Watford to alleviate the injury crisis. Haynes did not score or make goals in this particular game, but the press headline left no doubt: "Back-to-form Haynes shows his old England class!"

The news that he was putting in some truly spectacular performances and was returning to top form prompted Alf Ramsey to run the eye over him in a 1–1 draw with West Ham at Upton Park. Haynes was in magnificent form, pushing passes all over the pitch, and although he didn't score himself or make the goal for Graham Leggat, one reporter wrote that his display must have left a deep impression. Another admitted that he was the outstanding forward on the field. Fulham were denied a victory only by a late Bobby Moore goal volleyed past the unsighted Macedo.

December

Haynes posted his fourth goal of the season in an emphatic 4–1 win over Wolves at Craven Cottage. Fulham played some majestic football at times, and Haynes reminded the watching England selectors that he was definitely still around.

He scored a brilliant goal in the fifth minute of the game, his blistering shot from thirty-five yards leaving Wolves goalkeeper Davies rooted. He led his side on the rampage in the second half, when Wolves were threatening an equaliser. Two goals in three minutes saw Fulham romp home easy winners.

After the game many critics admitted that there were few trios in the country to match Robson, Mullery and Haynes. One summed the situation up well: "Johnny Haynes, snubbed by England, masterminded Fulham to this decisive win. On this display he would be worth a place in *any* international team." There was now some significant campaigning by journalists to return him to the England fold, but no immediate news was forthcoming from the Ramsey camp.

After a 2–2 draw against Everton at the Cottage in the following game, there was even more praise: "Johnny Haynes was back to his brilliant best. He has been an inspiring figure in recent matches."

Haynes managed to wriggle clean through and had an early chance of a goal, but the ball was smothered at the last by the Everton keeper. Although Haynes was described as Fulham's mainspring, he could never quite escape the clutches of Everton right half Stevens to win the match for Fulham. Even so, it had been a very creditable display against the current league champions and a good comeback considering that the Fulham team were two goals down with only thirty minutes left.

Sent off!

Just before Christmas Fulham took part in a nasty, violent game at a freezing Birmingham City, where both teams had seemingly settled for a 0–0 draw. Although the icy pitch looked innocent enough from the press box, it was like a skating rink.

The referee had already spoken to players about minor skirmishes and numerous fouls. Haynes and Birmingham's transfer-listed Bertie Auld had been the best of the two sets of mediocre forwards. According to the local press, every pass made by Haynes was loaded with danger. Two of his shots before the break had brought excellent saves from the home goalkeeper.

Haynes may have upset Auld with a series of successful 'nutmegs' that had left the Scotsman trailing. Then, just nine minutes from the end, Haynes and Auld clashed right in the corner of the pitch in front of the main stand. Haynes was keeping possession, shielding the ball, and Auld was niggling him with a certain amount of gusto.

Haynes, who was used to this sort of provocation, rarely retaliated, but on this occasion something must have snapped. He turned on Auld, throwing numerous punches and Auld exploded, replying with a head butt, which knocked Haynes out cold, with blood coming from his nose and mouth.

A nearby Fulham player, Maurice Cook, went to remonstrate with Auld and fell victim to another head butt, which broke his nose, flooring him too. Auld had actually been forced to leap up to get to Cook's height to deliver the 'Glasgow kiss'. Both Fulham players lay toe to toe on the deck, and Auld himself pointed to the dressing room, knowing full well what was coming from referee Egan. He wasn't wrong.

Alan Mullery takes up the story as if it were yesterday: "John was playing great, and Auld was frustrated. John had the ball in the corner, right up against the corner flag. He put his foot on the ball resting against the flag with Bertie Auld trying to kick it. Anyway John thrusts his ample backside at him and Auld steps back and kicks him from behind straight in the how's your father's!

"John lost his temper, turned and punched Auld who gave him the head butt. George and I were in reasonable distance, but Maurice Cook tore past us, and grabbed Bertie Auld and he knocks him out as well."

After the mayhem died down and Haynes had received treatment from the trainer, he too was sent off for the only time in his career. Auld had a history of several previous dismissals. Haynes was helped off, more than sent off, with the Fulham physiotherapist desperately throwing water in his face to bring him fully round. Cook departed on a stretcher. The nineteen remaining players saw out the last few minutes.

Haynes requested a personal hearing, and was supported by Bobby Robson, Maurice Cook and Bobby Keetch, amongst others. The disciplinary panel sat in January 1964, and the verdict was as follows: "From the evidence adduced, the commission was satisfied that Haynes struck Auld after provocation and that Auld retaliated by butting Haynes and later struck Cook and that the referee was justified in the action which he took."

The commission took into account the players' respective records. Haynes, with his clean record, received only a seven-day suspension; Auld, with his more colourful history, was banned for four weeks.

The clash must have cleared away some cobwebs, as just five days later against rock-bottom Ipswich Town, Fulham scored an exhilarating ten goals. Amazingly, Haynes was not amongst the scorers. Because it was Boxing Day, very little was reported about this slightly surreal game, apart from the fact that Graham Leggat scored three goals in the space of four minutes, which established a First Division record. Bobby Howfield also completed a hat trick. Ipswich's only goal came from a back pass that got stuck in the mud. It was a day of amazing scorelines throughout the First Division, but 10–1 outstripped them all. In true Fulham style, they lost the return match at Portman Road 2–4 forty-eight hours later.

By the end of the year, Fulham had improved their league position to fifteenth, and the cry "Haynes for England" was going up all around the country. The next generation of youngsters was coming through the Fulham ranks alongside Alan Mullery: Bobby Keetch, John Dempsey, Fred Callaghan, Steve Earle and Rodney Marsh. The future for Fulham looked very bright indeed.

However, it was not easy for the younger players to get to know the Fulham and England skipper, as Steve Earle remembers: "There was already an established 'family' of senior players, for example Macedo, Langley, Lowe and Leggat, and they played snooker, golf and socialised together. John was quite quiet off the pitch and it was difficult to get to know him.

"The only real chance the younger players had to integrate with the seniors was if they were playing for the reserves due to injury or team changes. John was of

Maurice Cook and Haynes arrive at FA headquarters in London for the Fulham captain's disciplinary hearing. (This picture, which appeared in the newspapers at the time, is actually two photographs pasted together!)

course Fulham captain and at the height of his England powers, and because he was also quite fit, he very, very rarely played for the reserves. Hence it was quite hard to establish a rapport with him initially."

January

Fulham secured a place in the next round of the FA Cup with a 4–1 home success over Third Division Luton Town; it wasn't as easy a ride as the scoreline suggests, and for a considerable time there was only one goal in it. The two late goals that cemented Fulham's place in the next round were scored by Bobby Howfield and Maurice Cook, both from accurate corners taken by Johnny Haynes. Fulham picked up a home league point the following week in a 1–1 draw with West Bromwich Albion, Haynes orchestrating many spirited thrusts.

At Highbury, Haynes notched his fifth goal of the season in a 2–2 draw with Arsenal. On a frosty pitch, Fulham were quickly two goals down and seemingly wearing the wrong type of boot. Two Arsenal efforts had also pinged back from the crossbar. However, boots were changed at half-time and Fulham fought back to snatch their first-ever point at Highbury after fifty years of trying.

The equaliser came when George Cohen took a free kick, Maurice Cook headed the ball down and the Arsenal defence hesitated, allowing Haynes to pick his spot and shoot home in a crowded penalty area. The press said of the error-strewn encounter that Haynes was the only player to show poise on a difficult surface. In the freezing conditions, Scottish international Graham Leggat picked up yet another injury.

A week later Fulham were dumped out of the FA Cup in the fourth round by Blackburn Rovers at Ewood Park, and another chance of a Wembley appearance disappeared for Haynes. Fulham played poorly and Haynes was completely subdued. The score was 0–2, but could well have been more. Fulham had lost at Blackburn by the same score in the league three months earlier.

February

Haynes had no chance to improve on this poor performance, as he missed the following week's 2–1 home victory over Leicester City because of the suspension meted out to him by the FA following his confrontation and sending off with Bertie Auld. It was one of only two league matches he would miss all season.

Alan Mullery is the star

One of the reasons for Haynes' bright displays was the return to form of Bobby Robson, but the main reason was the superb support he was receiving from the consistent and hard-working Alan Mullery. Haynes certainly recognised it—but so did other clubs.

Spurs manager Bill Nicholson contacted Fulham with a 'name your price' offer for the twenty-two-year-old. General manager Frank Osborne quickly referred the matter to Tommy Trinder, who was appearing in pantomime in Sunderland. Trinder immediately dashed Spurs' hopes and quashed the idea that Mullery might leave Fulham.

He said: "Mullery is twenty-one [sic] and quite irreplaceable. There was no point in putting a ridiculous price on him because he is absolutely vital to us. Mullery is a great player and will become even greater before the World Cup in 1966. We are certain that he'll be a must for England. I am sure he will be as vital to us as Johnny Haynes. Remember, we refused £100,000 when Johnny was wanted in Italy; we have never regretted this."

Haynes returned to the side at Bolton after suspension and played well, with plenty of astute passes. After going a goal down early on, Fulham crafted an equaliser, and a gem of a through pass by Haynes allowed Bobby Howfield to net a deserved goal after half an hour. However, a momentary lapse in concentration gave Bolton a 1–2 victory in the dying seconds. The decider was scored by current PFA boss Gordon Taylor.

The press were very sympathetic, saying that if Fulham had made use of the opportunities prised open by Haynes, they would have won comfortably. How he emerged from this match with no reward was a mystery.

After a blank weekend due to the FA Cup fifth round, Fulham played Blackburn Rovers at the Cottage in midweek. Rovers were on good form and lying second in the league. Fulham hoped to avenge the cup knockout three weeks earlier. Alf Ramsey was present to watch Haynes' form yet again. Haynes almost had a goal, hitting the post with a cracking low drive. In the end, there were two goals in the last nine minutes, with Johnny Key salvaging a point for Fulham in a 1–1 draw.

Fulham then gave Stephen Earle a debut the following Saturday and Rodney Marsh was brought back for a rare game. It made little difference against Nottingham Forest, as Fulham frittered away numerous chances and lost 0–2. It was the same story week after week. One report commented: "It was certainly not the fault of Haynes who stood head and shoulders above everyone else for all-round ability and sizing up the situations around him. His long, slanting crossfield passes were object lessons in accuracy."

His hands-on-hips gestures were much in evidence in Nottingham. Neither the young, inexperienced forwards, who lacked the class of Graham Leggat, nor the old, past-it forwards, were on Haynes' wavelength. The headlines suggested that his art was wasted. It was a very worrying result, as these were the first goals Forest had scored at home that year, and this was their first home victory since November.

For the Blackpool match the Cottage pitch was in a very poor and muddy state due to bad weather. Haynes failed to dominate this one, but the pitch condition never allowed him to really stand out. Some said that he had yet to fully recapture his England form, although his passes were accurate.

However, there were several touches from the master craftsman, and he did create the goal with a shrewd pass to Graham Leggat, who moved the ball on to Steve Earle, who coolly shot his first Fulham goal into the corner.

The 1–1 draw had been a poor spectacle in terms of taking chances and the press didn't waste time highlighting the paucity of scoring ideas, but overall, considering the conditions, neither side looked like a relegation candidate. However, Fulham had only won once since Boxing Day and had started to drop down towards the danger zone again.

March

Fulham and Johnny Haynes broke a major record the following week when they won at Stamford Bridge for the first time in fifty-three years, covering thirteen attempts. Haynes revelled in the open spaces and Fulham played with a very positive approach. In a fine 2–1 win, the eighteen-year-old Steve Earle was once again on the scoresheet with Brian O'Connell also scoring, both goals being crafted by Graham Leggat, now fully fit again.

Alan Mullery is transferred

In the next home game, Fulham played a rejuvenated Liverpool who were sitting in second place and chasing the title. It was a cold, wet day and the pitch was virtually waterlogged. Haynes was playing well and was bang on form, using all the space available. "He has never played better," said the media. In the first half it had been a joy to watch Cohen, Haynes and Mullery plot Liverpool's downfall. However, there was a dramatic twist.

The first cracks in the love affair between Fulham and Haynes occurred in the dressing room at half-time. Mullery told Haynes that although he did not really want to move clubs, he was leaving and signing for Spurs after the game. Fulham weren't financially stretched at the time, and the transfer wasn't necessary, although matchday attendances, as part of a nationwide pattern, were currently in decline. Haynes finally realised on that day that the ambitions of his Fulham Football Club were severely limited.

He returned to the dressing room before coming out for the second half to try and find out whether there was any truth in what Mullery had told him. Fulham proceeded to put on their finest show of the season, and the hopeful champions were given a severe drubbing, being completely outplayed in all departments.

The Cottagers won 1–0, thanks to a Reg Stratton goal after a Jim Langley free kick had been blocked. The two best shots of the match came from chief architect Haynes, whose delightful shielding of the ball limited Liverpool's chances of a comeback. Only Lawrence in the Liverpool goal kept the score down.

Of Haynes, the press remarked, "Johnny Haynes touched the pinnacle of his matchless ability—how on this form can England leave him out against Scotland?" This was the message that Haynes was sending to Alf Ramsey and the Fulham board: look what we can achieve if we keep the youngsters and this squad together.

After the victory, Haynes as captain stormed back and confronted manager Beddy Jezzard about the rumours. Jezzard knew nothing about the proposed transfer, but he made further enquiries and the awful truth dawned that, despite what Trinder had said publicly just a few weeks earlier, the chairman and the Fulham board had privately sold Mullery behind the back of the team manager and the captain, virtually forcing him to go, as "the money was needed." At the time the £72,500 fee was a British record for a half back. Fulham did indeed have a debt of around £30,000, but this was significantly less than the Mullery fee.

Trinder apparently told Mullery that the cash was needed to put a covered stand on the Hammersmith end terrace of the ground. Whilst this was true, the stand cost only £25,000 when it was erected a year later, a third of Alan Mullery's transfer fee. Alan recalls: "We had just beaten Liverpool and we should have been on a high, but there was a very subdued atmosphere in the dressing room. I got one of the lads to clean my boots; I had to take them with me, as I was signing for Spurs that evening.

"There were just looks in the communal bath and I think John was probably browned off more than anyone. John was still England's captain at the time, George's England career was just taking off and I had Under-23 caps. John assessed the situation and said 'We've never been a great big buying club but here we are selling one of our best up and coming young players. Hold on, what are we doing?'"

Jezzard was privately furious with the board's stance, and was now considering his future with the club. Haynes was close to Jezzard, and had the utmost respect for him as a man, a footballer and a manager. The relationship between Haynes and the Fulham board of directors was never quite the same after that day.

Fulham snatched a 2–2 draw at Villa Park the following Saturday, with two opportunist goals by Leggat, which marked his personal century of league goals. There was no mention of Haynes, who was allegedly still furious about the events of the week before. The match saw a debut for Fulham favourite Fred Callaghan, who was given the unenviable job of replacing the departed Mullery.

A must for England

On Good Friday, fifth-placed Manchester United visited the Cottage, and Haynes shook himself out of his personal malaise to produce one of his best performances of the season. The game was a delight, played at an unyielding pace in front of an eager 41,000 crowd.

Haynes gave Fulham the lead with his sixth goal of the season. He scooped a free kick into the middle and it was only half-cleared by Nobby Stiles. The ball fell straight back to him, he shot brilliantly on the turn from twenty-five yards, and the ball rocketed into the roof of the net, curling over the hopelessly stranded United goalkeeper Gaskell.

The strong United side fought back to lead, but Steve Earle again proved his promise from the wing with a headed equaliser just inside the far post from a superbly accurate Haynes free kick delivered from near the corner flag. Bobby Robson, back at right half, revived memories of his England partnership with Haynes, the two trying all they knew to gain the ascendancy in midfield. After this 2–2 thriller, the press said that Johnny Haynes was on international form, and had hit one of the finest goals seen at Craven Cottage that season.

The following day, Easter Saturday, saw a swift return to the Cottage for Alan Mullery, just two weeks after leaving Fulham, to vie with his old pal Haynes.

In the absence of Dave Mackay, Mullery was made Spurs captain for the day. He recalls: "We were shaking hands, he was my hero and here we were just two weeks later. If it had been six months it would have been different. The thing was Bill Nick had said to me 'Get close to Haynesey, let him know you're there and don't let him play.' As a matter of fact he scored that day. I think there was mutual respect, we shook hands and tossed the coin—but then it was down to business."

Back so soon? Mullery, now Spurs, greets Haynes, still Fulham. The game took place just two weeks after Mullery's shock departure that had upset Fulham's loyal captain.

In what was described as a piquant fixture, the press decided that Haynes won the duel by the narrowest of margins. For the second consecutive day, Haynes, overflowing with ideas, rarely wasted a pass, and added to his goal tally following a rare error by Mullery.

Mullery stopped a Maurice Cook effort near to the goal line; he tried to clear as Haynes came in from his blind side, but mis-kicked and only succeeded in dropping the ball on to Haynes' left foot, and the next second the ball was nestling in the back of the net. It

Haynes is delighted with his equalising goal against Tottenham that earned Fulham a 1–1 draw.

In flying action against West Ham. In a 2–0 win, Haynes scored for the third successive home game.

was a sad day for Mullery, who was booed throughout the match, the crowd being unaware that his transfer had been enforced and that he had never wanted to leave.

Haynes' goal was his seventh of the season, and the press sent out a message to the England manager, "If Haynes keeps up this goalscoring threat, Ramsey will *have* to take notice." Fulham should have secured both points instead of one in the 1–1 draw. This was still a Fulham side that could go places.

Certainly the wily Haynes had stolen the show. The press said: "Haynes, once again, has recovered the subtle touch which made him, until his accident, the master creator and provider. Time after time he attracted the ball like a magnet before putting his fellow forwards free with an unerring eye for a gap. He has a genius for the unexpected, and he twisted and turned this match to his own liking."

The two matches took a lot out of Fulham and there were some injuries, including Jimmy Langley again. On Easter Monday, Fulham played five reserves at Old Trafford and lost 0–3 to Manchester United; Haynes, who picked up a nasty knock, was described as dispirited and disinterested. The injury caused him to miss his second league game of the season, the single-goal defeat to Sheffield United at Bramall Lane.

The subsequent Fulham match programme was quick to cock a snook at the merchants of doom who predicted that Johnny would never return to his old form following his serious accident. In the end, despite the seemingly endless calls for his reinstatement, Alf Ramsey left Haynes out of his side to play Scotland at Hampden Park, which England lost disappointingly 0–1.

April

Instead, in the penultimate home game of the season, Haynes scored his eighth goal of the campaign in a 2–0 victory over West Ham. The Hammers had reached the FA Cup final and weren't taking any undue risks with injury; they were also without Johnny Byrne and Bobby Moore, both away on England duty.

Haynes, buoyed by the talk of a return to the England fold, played very well again. On a bumpy pitch which did no favours to either side, the fast-thinking captain opened up West Ham time and again, and only keeper Jim Standen stood between Fulham and a bigger score.

He continued to be frustrated by some of the journeyman talent around him. The press said: "Haynes underlined the fact that he is still the best inside left in the country. He split the West Ham defence open time and time again, unfortunately no Fulham player got into the right position to complete his artistry."

Fulham took the lead on the half-hour when Haynes' accurate corner was nodded on by Dave Metchick, and although John Bond blocked the ball on the line, defender Bobby Keetch followed up to head home. Haynes was then forced to take on the mantle of goalscoring himself, and clinched the win when he took deliberate aim and scored with a fine, punchy drive with his right foot from over twenty yards which beat Standen all the way. He had now scored in three successive home games.

The final two league games, with nothing to play for, saw Haynes winding down. In a 0–4 defeat at Wolves, he got in a few shots, and in an entertaining game with Stoke City that finished 3–3 and saw two more goals from the impressive Steve Earle, Haynes was a model of accuracy, but generally quiet.

A very satisfactory season, considering

Fulham finished an unremarkable fifteenth, but were a massive eleven points clear of the two relegated clubs. They had lost only twice at home all season, had beaten champions Liverpool, taken points from Manchester United, Everton and Tottenham at the Cottage, and also won at fifth-placed Chelsea.

They had improved defensively at the Cottage, conceding just twenty-three goals all season. However, they had won only twice away from home, a record that was only better than that of relegated Ipswich Town.

It had been an unsettled side and twenty-seven players had been used. There was a mixture of inexperienced youth, players who were perhaps not quite good enough for the First Division, and others whose best days were behind them. Haynes wanted this problem to be finally addressed.

He had to be quietly satisfied with the forty league games he had played following his season out of football. He was also the second highest goalscorer. He looked forward eagerly to the telephone call from Alf Ramsey.

May to June

The clamour for recall gained further momentum during the summer of 1964, when the England team failed in the four-country Nations Cup in Brazil, primarily because of inaccurate passing. After losing to Scotland in the British Championship, the England team put a meaningless ten past the hapless USA. But against true opposition in the form of Portugal, they only managed to scrape a 1–1 draw; they then lost 0–1 to Argentina, after being hammered 1–5 by Brazil. The *Sunday Mirror* was so confident about Johnny Haynes' recall that its headline read, "It's skipper Haynes again!"

The fickle journalists began to turn the heat up on Alf Ramsey, asking, "Who better to provide the class than Haynes?" Even if he did not return as England's captain, a position in the team in a midfield capacity had to be found for him, they said, adding, "If the need is there for a link man (deep lying) to assemble and deliver from defence, and to polish, prime and supply the attack—who has more suitable qualifications?" Other articles summed up the situation perfectly: "Haynes—does England need him?"

Written off by Alf Ramsey

Alf Ramsey had become the manager of England in April 1963. Although there was much clamour for Haynes' return to the England team, the recall never arrived. One possible reason was that the dour Ramsey was less enamoured of the cocksure, free-spirited Haynes, perhaps thinking that he was too much his own man, and not the archetypal team-member. This reason was dismissed. Those who knew Ramsey understood that it had nothing to do with individuals; he required a team that was a complementary set of parts.

Some said that perhaps the reason was his age, but Haynes was still under thirty. Some thought that maybe he would be past his best at thirty-one when the World Cup was held in 1966, but centre half Jackie Charlton and full back Ramon Wilson were only a few months younger, and they both made the final eleven. This reason was also dismissed.

The third possible factor was his individual style of play. It was difficult to see how Haynes, even at his best, could have fitted into the England team that eventually won the 1966 World Cup. Alf Ramsey eschewed the sort of wing play for which Haynes' studious passing was designed. Width was achieved by movement that turned opposing flanks, not long balls played inside the full backs.

Interestingly, however, the supposed reason came from Ramsey himself—fitness to play football at international level. George Cohen remembers Ramsey asking him about Haynes: "Alf was still experimenting with his midfield, and he asked me about John, how well he was doing week in and week out. Considering the severity of his injury, I thought John was playing exceptionally well, delivering eye-catching performances, and almost back to his best. Alf had been to one of our games, but shook his head and said, 'He's not fit, George, and I don't think he'll ever be properly fit again.'"

Cohen was pretty shocked by that response: "After all the work John had put in, and although he had lost a little pace, he had lost none of his repertoire. I thought he would be upset to hear what Alf said, but when I told him he shrugged his shoulders and whilst walking away said, 'Alf's a good judge.' Contrary to what some people have written, Alf never held anything against John Haynes."

Haynes later in life spoke about this conversation with candour. "Sir Alf never picked me and he was quite right. I wasn't the same player after the accident." Although listeners were never really sure whether he was joking or not, he often said, "I played for seven years on one leg."

The right leg had been a problem, and he admitted, "I've never really had full extension on that leg since. I was never the same, the leg kept collapsing underneath me. There was no way I could have played international football, although it took me a very long time to accept it."

Roy Bentley knew he was right: "After his injury he couldn't 'go both ways' any more like he had done. He could feint to the left, but couldn't go round to the right like before and it was little wonder that it began to affect his legs and hips later in his career. To go round to the right, John had to go in virtually a full circle!"

George Cohen, whose England career was just beginning when the curtain was being brought down on the Haynes era, said: "It speaks volumes of the man that he knew his limitations and played to them. Whatever had happened and whatever compensations he would have had to have made, he was still able to play the ball—to feet, inside the full back, lay a beautiful knock-off to you, anything like that. That's why one of the greatest managers we've had, Bill Nicholson, not known for his sentiment, would have bid a huge amount of money for him."

Haynes is off to Spurs?

July

If Alf Ramsey didn't want Haynes in his England side, other First Division clubs did, and one of those was Tottenham Hotspur. In the summer of 1964, John White, their outstanding, scheming, Scottish inside forward, was tragically killed by lightning at the age of twenty-six whilst sheltering on a golf course. Three weeks before the new season, Tottenham boss Bill Nicholson offered Fulham between £90,000 and £100,000 for Haynes, then almost thirty, to fill the gap.

Mullery remembers: "Manager Bill Nicholson asked me, 'Do you think he would come to Tottenham,' and I said, 'Well, *I* did!' You have to remember Spurs were huge in those days, getting 60,000 crowds every week. He would have fitted in beautifully, and I would have been delighted. I am sure if Tottenham had got him, they would have gone on to win more things before 1967. John White was a similar sort of player to Johnny

Haynes, great passer of the ball and great control."

Haynes was frustrated by Fulham's lack of ambition, and could not see himself being able to challenge for any domestic honours while in this ramshackle side. The team was at a transitional stage, and the sale of Alan Mullery had left him feeling angry and let down.

The opportunity to join Spurs had many advantages. He would team up once again with Alan Mullery, a player he respected, and he would have a strong chance of gaining domestic honours; Tottenham had finished fourth in the previous season. There was also the possibility of European football, another chance for him to show his skills on a bigger stage. Spurs had competed in Europe the previous season, and were looking to strengthen their team for a further assault.

He would also be linking up again with the Spurs goal-scoring machine, Jimmy Greaves, with whom he had an almost telepathic understanding when playing for England. Most of all, the move would increase his chances of regaining the spot he really cherished—a place in the England side. Even his playing colleagues at Fulham urged him to go to Spurs for one last hurrah.

Ironically, the move would have taken Edmonton-born Haynes to the club he was meant to join as a boy. Manager Bill Nicholson said afterwards: "I went for Haynes because he was still one of the best midfield organisers in the game. There wasn't anyone in British football with more awareness. He always seemed to be two moves ahead and have a clear picture of everything that was going on around him."

The transfer would have been a record deal between British clubs at the time, but Fulham turned the substantial offer down. "That was bad business," remarked Haynes later, thinking Fulham should have cashed in. He added: "I think a change might have been good for me then, it would have been an interesting move at that stage of my career, but I couldn't get away and that was that, sometimes you're not given all the details."

George Cohen recalls: "Tottenham had just offered £100,000 for him. It would have been a very, very good move for John. The club couldn't bear to think that he was going anywhere else other than Fulham Football Club; it wasn't a good thing for the club to do anyway.

"Yet it would have been a terrific move for John. It would have given him another good couple of seasons at top level with possible European football and it would have been £100,000 to a club that needed money. But we all understood the sentiments of the club. During training he asked me what I thought, and I told him: 'It will be a good move for you, the club will get £100,000, but it's the sentiment, John; I can understand the sentiment.'"

Very much later in life, a modest Haynes was more reflective: "I'm glad they didn't [let me go], looking back, because if I'd gone to a club like Tottenham, the fans would have expected something special and I'd have struggled to deliver."

Haynes asks for a transfer

By rejecting the bid, Trinder deprived Haynes of the chance of crowning his career with a trophy of some kind. There was a huge swathe of public sympathy for him, and he was shocked that Fulham had turned down the large fee. There were very strong rumours circulating that Fulham's firm stance had upset the loyal Haynes so much that he had actually requested a transfer. Trinder was emphatic, "No, no, a thousand times NO."

Haynes had, however, signed a new two-year contract with Fulham only weeks before, and he found little support from either the press or the Football League. Both were firm in their belief that the players had almost gone on strike for firm contracts, and they maintained that having secured them, they should stand by those commitments; players couldn't have it both ways.

The Football League secretary, Alan Hardaker, was blunt in his assessment of the situation: "If Haynes wants a transfer within weeks of signing a new contract with Fulham it emphasises once again what the league have always maintained; and that is that the Professional Footballers' Association simply negotiates for the favoured few. This is creating a false image of the real stalwart players of the league of which there are plenty."

When rumours of a transfer request leaked out, Fulham fans flared up and phoned the club to protest, and shareholders sent telegrams to the chairman demanding a meeting. Mullery had gone, and Trinder was worried that if Haynes also departed, the fans would stop coming, and the remaining star players like Tony Macedo, George Cohen and Graham Leggat would want to move on as well, as Fulham would have proved itself to be a selling club with little or no ambition. The shareholders were demanding to be put in the picture, many believing the club was way behind the times.

Haynes was actively involved in a number of discussions with Tommy Trinder to resolve his problems. It was a time of significant unrest at Craven Cottage, as Spurs were also turning their attentions towards George Cohen, and had tabled an offer of around £80,000. Fulham rejected this offer as well, which caused Cohen to consider requesting a transfer. Cohen had not signed a new contract at the time and so there was speculation that he, too, might depart. The press said, "The wide boys are speculating that Haynes will be a Spurs player for the big kick-off—will Trinder stand fast?"

Away from football, Johnny's long relationship with Eileen Farmer drifted to an end. Eileen's parents moved to Australia and she had to make a choice. She wanted to marry, and would have remained in England for that, but at the time Johnny did not wish to make the commitment, and so she travelled with her parents to the other side of the world.

23: Hanging on
1964–65

23: Hanging on 1964–65

Following the transfer speculation of the previous season, Haynes appeared to have resisted the urge to move to Spurs. However, he didn't turn out for the pre-season trial match, which saw the first team score a 3–1 victory over the reserves, with the club citing an 'ankle injury'. It seemed that there were still matters behind the scene that had to be resolved. No-one really knew what the next chapter in Haynes' colourful career was going to bring.

August

The season started unspectacularly, as the polished cup winners West Ham came to Craven Cottage and won 1–2. Haynes' play was described as accurate, but the press agreed that he failed to stamp his authority on the game and had been clearly outshone by his West Ham and England counterpart Johnny Byrne. He had been shackled once again by the robust Eddie Bovington.

Play was poor and at one stage slow hand-clapping broke out in this, the very first game of the season. Haynes looked isolated and appeared to be still searching for the intelligent co-operation that had eluded him for several seasons at the Cottage. He picked up an injury in the 2–2 draw at Birmingham and missed Fulham's second trip to the Midlands on the Saturday, which also ended in a 2–2 draw, against West Bromwich Albion. The only bright spot was that Dave Metchick had scored in all three games.

September

The first win of the season was achieved when Birmingham returned to the Cottage during the following week. Young Metchick scored a fine hat trick in the 3–1 win, his second goal being a header from a perfect left-wing centre from Haynes.

Haynes opened his account for the season with a goal in a scrappy 2–1 victory at home to Manchester United which was recorded for television. In a tetchy encounter, Fulham came from behind at half-time, and Haynes shot the winner twelve minutes from the end with a ground shot from twenty-five yards that took a deflection off Nobby Stiles to beat goalkeeper Dave Gaskell. Despite these victories, Fulham were still an unhappy club off the field, and Tommy Trinder was constantly involved in a stream of discussions with dispirited and disaffected players.

Fulham fought out a tough draw in midweek with Sheffield United 1–1, but at the weekend the team still seemed to be in a black mood at Chelsea, who played for an hour with ten men. Haynes had another poor game, some reports saying that he tried to dominate but couldn't shake off the attentions of a young John Hollins.

Haynes was the victim of several crude tackles from behind by Ron Harris and was generally outshone by the young Terry Venables. Other reports were less complimentary, saying that Haynes had just disappeared from the game. To add insult to injury, Chelsea won 0–1. Haynes still had the appearance of a man who wished he was somewhere else.

In midweek things became even bleaker as Fulham went down 1–2 to bogey side Sheffield United at the Cottage. Haynes supplied the pass for Rodney Marsh who eventually, if rather ungainly, beat three United defenders before slotting home; but as usual the defence went to sleep and allowed United two quick goals to win the game.

Johnny Haynes is staying

There were further discussions between Tommy Trinder, Haynes and other senior players, and after a final 'peace meeting', it was declared that differences had been resolved. It seemed to work in the short term, as Fulham went straight out to record their first away win of the season, 3–2 at Nottingham Forest.

Haynes appeared to be back to top form, stamping his authority on the game from the start. He was switching the attack and delivering the usual flow of deadly, made-to-measure passes. Twice in the first half he put Dave Metchick clean through, but the young forward couldn't control the ball.

However, the pass by Haynes to Rodney Marsh for the equaliser twenty minutes from the end was described as a gem. Marsh also netted a solo winner just two minutes later. Although Haynes didn't score, the press considered that he stood out as the architect of this fine victory. One report said, "The ice cool Haynes with a wonderful sense of positional play looks a cert for an England recall."

The revival didn't last, and in typical Fulham style they crashed 1–4 at the Cottage the following week to a mediocre Stoke City team. Reserve goalkeeper Dave Underwood and Bobby Keetch had nightmare matches, donating gift goals to the Potteries side.

Haynes' shoulders dropped again. The press commented that they'd never seen him so ineffective nor had they seen him fail so completely to rouse the forwards, who were described as a thing of shreds and tatters. After the game, manager Bedford Jezzard dodged questions about his future, and Tommy Trinder (rarely for him) would not be interviewed.

October

On the Monday evening, Haynes played against Tottenham for the first time since they had tried to sign him in the summer. He was very sharp early in the game, made chances and floated in free kicks and crosses galore, but the receiving forwards put them all into the crowd.

It was easy to see why he was so frustrated by being made to stay. He faded towards the end, with Fulham 0–3 down, but did supply one final goal-bound missile that was handled on the line by Spurs full back Cyril Knowles. Jim Langley missed the resulting penalty; it was that kind of night.

Haynes acclaims Bobby Howfield's goal against Blackpool in the 3–3 draw.

Fulham decided to whitewash the goal nets before the next home game to make them stand out for the forwards. They then came from behind to beat Leicester City 5–2, their best win and performance of the season. Although Haynes didn't score, he looked much more like the general, and the third goal arose when Gordon Banks failed to hold a scorching shot from Haynes on a wet surface, following a downpour, and Brian O'Connell netted the rebound.

Haynes made his mark on the match with his highly specialised brand of smooth, flowing football—and watching the game was the VIP of British soccer, England team manager Alf Ramsey.

Early in the month, the push for Haynes' return to the England fold gathered momentum once again. A poor England performance at Windsor Park Belfast, where they were lucky to scrape a 4–3 win against Northern Ireland, was followed by an equally uninspiring 2–2 home draw against Belgium. Again the cry rang out for Ramsey to end Haynes' two-year international exile; the question was repeated, "Haynes—does England still need him?"

The press went further: "Whether he returns as captain is irrelevant, do England need Haynes, the player?" Some declared that Haynes was essential to boost Ramsey's flops. Alf Ramsey, however, robustly ignored the baiting and stuck to his guns. England went on to lose just one of their next twenty-five matches, a run which culminated in the World Cup final in July 1966.

Fulham's form was still very erratic, and they drew with lowly Reading in the League Cup with Haynes rested. He returned in an ignominious performance at Roker Park, where Fulham drew 0–0 with struggling Sunderland. The press attested that it was only Haynes' well-conceived direction that kept Fulham in the hunt at all. The draw certainly wasn't an ideal thirtieth birthday present for him.

This match was followed forty-eight hours later by an embarrassing exit from the League Cup at the hands of Roy Bentley's Reading in the replay at Craven Cottage. Fulham were three down before Bobby Robson's consolation goal. The match was described as just awful.

Frank Osborne retires

For general manager Frank Osborne, the recent events proved to be enough. As he was facing criticism of Fulham's performances and the club's financial situation he decided to retire after sixteen years.

At the time he was the third longest-serving general manager in the entire Football League. Bedford Jezzard stepped upstairs to become manager, and team coach Arthur Stevens took on the role of caretaker team manager. Haynes saw another link with his long past disappear.

Stevens had a relatively easy start with a 2–0 home victory over no-hopers Wolves, and Haynes had a good first half. The following week, however, against Midlands opposition again, Fulham crashed 0–2 at Aston Villa, even though they played against ten men for part of the match. Haynes had another quiet game. The worst news was an injury to Graham Leggat which would keep him out of the Fulham side for three months. Although Fulham were lighting no fires, they were sitting in a fairly comfortable fourteenth position at the end of the month.

November

In the next game, league champions Liverpool came calling and at last, almost three months into the season, the real Johnny Haynes began to emerge. He provided glimpses of genius and played superb football, providing the kind of passes that begged for conversion.

The forwards were initially slow to react, so Haynes responded with a gem of a goal himself. He brought the ball through the midfield, twice exchanged passes with Rodney Marsh and then slammed the ball into the net at breakneck speed. The effort was described as a left-footer of splendid accuracy.

Sadly, Fulham sat back after this and allowed Liverpool a lucky equaliser, courtesy of a Macedo error in the last ten minutes of the 1–1 drawn game. At least he had made a headline again: "Masterly Haynes puts brakes on Strong and Co."

At Hillsborough the following week, it was sadly back to normal; Haynes had one flashing, low drive saved at full stretch by Ron Springett, but the forward line lacked cohesion, and the papers said, maybe for the first time ever, that Haynes looked an ordinary player.

Against fellow-strugglers Blackpool the following week, Fulham tore into the Seasiders to lead three-one after an hour, but had to play with ten men in the second half as Steve Earle couldn't overcome a foot injury.

Haynes' glorious through ball gave Stan Brown the opportunity to increase the lead, but he sliced wide with just the goalkeeper to beat. Haynes then did the same for his mate Trevor Chamberlain, but he, too, fired into the crowd.

Sensing this could be their day, Blackpool took full advantage and fought back to draw 3–3. All Blackpool's three goals came from a very young, flame-haired 'little red beacon' called Alan Ball. Haynes fired in a final shot on the wet surface that flashed just wide of the post.

Haynes is disciplined by the club

Johnny Haynes was at an all-time low, and following Frank Osborne's departure, the Spurs transfer raised its head again. Within the club, words were exchanged, the atmosphere became heated and for once Haynes probably overstepped the mark in some of the ensuing debates. In an effort to prove that not even the great Haynes was bigger than Fulham Football Club, he was disciplined and suspended from playing for two weeks.

The Fulham programme, which had so often praised the great man to the heavens, was hardly mentioning him at all. Haynes accepted this indignity and used the time to have a cooling-off break. Predictably, in the absence of the general and captain, Fulham lost both matches, the first 0–2 at Blackburn Rovers.

December

In the second match of his suspension, Fulham went down 3–4 at home to Arsenal. The Arsenal defeat was a typical Fulham performance, two goals ahead and then two goals behind. Fulham played wholeheartedly in Haynes' absence, but when the going got tough in the final stages they sadly missed his influence and experience.

He returned to the Fulham side at Upton Park following his fortnight's penance, but for the second time that season he was completely outplayed by his younger playmaker opponent Johnny Byrne, who again scored both West Ham goals. Haynes was also overworked by his own side.

Back on the Craven Cottage pitch after his club suspension, Haynes warms up for the match against West Bromwich. He played his heart out, creating two first-half goals and scoring the third himself.

Almost every Fulham attack radiated out from Haynes, and he played himself to a standstill. To be fair however, West Ham played well, and their 0–2 victory took them up to fourth place in the table.

It was now seven games without a win, and the warning signs were once again on the wall for Fulham. There was just no real striking power in attack. The attack was missing Maurice Cook, Graham Leggat, Brian O'Connell, Steve Earle and Johnny Key, who were replaced in the forward line by Bobby Howfield, Fred Callaghan and Trevor Chamberlain. It was worrying, and long before the end Haynes was described as a picture of despair; his dejection communicated itself to his weary colleagues.

The danger was lessened to a degree the following week, when Fulham beat a poor West Bromwich Albion side 3–1 at Craven Cottage. In the first half Haynes was inspired, and he created both goals. The first was a beautiful pass to Rodney Marsh, which enabled him to

The clincher. Haynes scrambles home Fulham's third goal in the 3–1 victory over West Bromwich Albion.

score a fine individual goal in Corinthian style. Haynes then arrowed a shrewd free kick over the Albion defence to Bobby Howfield for the second goal.

Albion staged a revival, but Haynes was not done, rattling in a scrambled clincher from Trevor Chamberlain's accurate centre. Haynes took the lion's share of the credit for the victory and was without doubt the man of the match.

It proved a temporary reprieve. Fulham were beaten twice over Christmas by polished Burnley, failing to score and conceding five in the process. Many games throughout the country had been postponed because of the snow and ice, and Fulham probably wished that these two had been as well.

The away performance was truly awful, with the attack non-existent. Burnley's Willie Irvine helped himself to a comfortable hat trick in the 0–4 victory at Turf Moor. In the 0–1 defeat at the Cottage, Bobby Keetch was sent off after a violent clash with Irvine, after his mis-communication with Tony Macedo had presented the Irish striker with Burnley's winner. There were barely 10,000 in attendance.

Tommy Trinder was heckled and jostled, as the supporters were now as pent-up as Haynes. The press were not slow to realise the problems, and commiserated: "It's been a frustrating season so far for Haynes, he needs more quality and support and an experienced marksman." Without the injured international Leggat, he had no-one.

Jezzard calls it a day

The events leading up to Christmas proved too much for the genial Bedford Jezzard, and having been in the manager's seat for just two months he announced that he was not only quitting Fulham but also leaving football altogether to go into the licensing trade full time.

Apart from the occasional testimonial match, Jezzard never returned to Fulham. Johnny Haynes' mood, already depressed, was further disheartened by the departure of his close friend. Acting manager Arthur Stevens, Trevor Chamberlain and the now veteran Bobby Robson were the few remaining links with his earliest days at the Cottage. By the New Year, Fulham had slipped to a precarious eighteenth in the division.

January

Poor weather delayed the post-Christmas start, but further embarrassment was heaped on Fulham when the First Division side, including Johnny Haynes, were knocked out of the FA Cup in the third round 0–2 at Fourth Division Millwall, after a mistake-ridden 3–3 draw at Craven Cottage.

Haynes was lost in the cup-tie atmosphere, unable to play Millwall's type of game. In the first match, Fulham had waltzed into a three-one lead, but then conceded a penalty which Millwall and Harry Cripps contrived to miss. It seemed to galvanise the south London opposition, and two horrendous handling errors by Tony Macedo gifted Millwall another bite at the cherry.

In the replay just forty-eight hours later, Haynes tried hard to swing the match in Fulham's favour. He had one twenty-five-yard shot palmed away by Millwall goalkeeper Alex Stepney, and another effort punched away by the keeper at the very last minute. The home side were supported by a fervent 31,000 crowd, and two goals in the last quarter of the match sealed Fulham's fate. By this time Haynes had very little confidence that Fulham would ever invest in the team and thought that his Wembley cup final dream was finally over.

The following Saturday, when Fulham faced Tommy Docherty's vibrant young Chelsea colts at Craven Cottage, the midweek exertions seemed to have taken their toll on Haynes. He tried to use all his experience, but was uninspired and rarely in the game. The eager young visitors, with their fresh legs, won the game by the odd goal, 1–2. The victory took Chelsea to within a point of league leaders Leeds United. Some

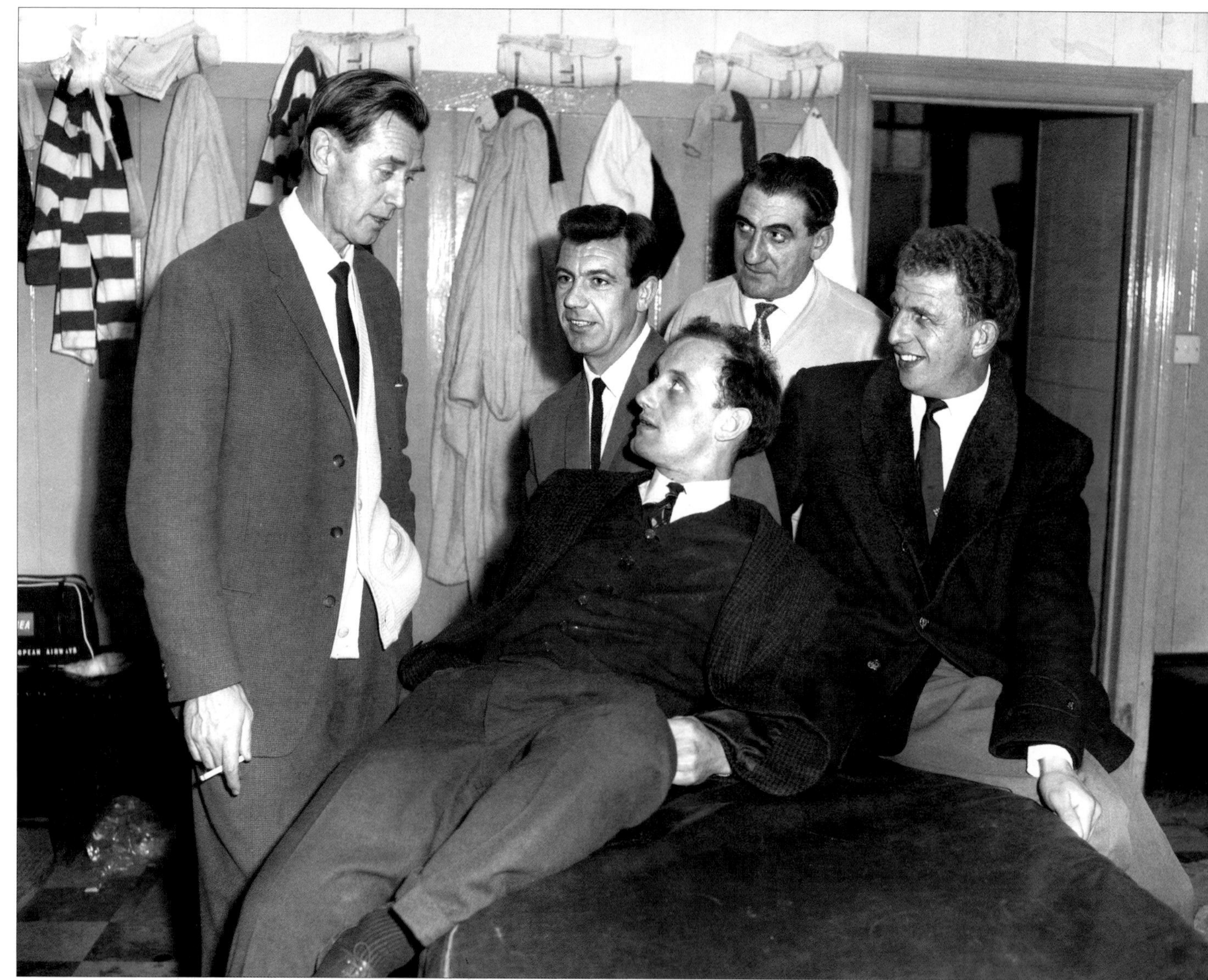

The dapper, cigarette-smoking new manager, Vic Buckingham, talks in the dressing room with players Haynes, Chamberlain and Cook, and (at back) assistant manager Joe Bacuzzi. The relaxed atmosphere was deceptive. Within six months, under the new management, only Haynes remained at the club.

supporters had seen enough, and before the end of the match many were chanting "Trinder must go," and the happy, family club were, without a shadow of a doubt, in crisis again.

The Vic Buckingham era

Haynes' career began to take a darker turn with the appointment as manager of the former Tottenham player Vic Buckingham, who had been a guest player for Fulham during the war. Fulham had allegedly made an approach to Northampton Town for the club's (and Wales') manager, Dave Bowen, but the Northampton club had refused to release him and Bowen stated he was content to remain where he was, probably sensing what a poisoned chalice Fulham were at the time.

Buckingham was appointed soon after. He was an educated man, described as a dandy or beau, always very well dressed, with pocket handkerchief. He ate foreign food and dined at the best restaurants. He used long words which few players understood, and was definitely his own man.

He liked the sound of his own voice, and later in his tenure some of the players would run a book on how long his half-time team talks would last. He was going to do things his way. His personality clashed with that of Haynes almost as soon as he arrived.

Buckingham was of the opinion that Haynes ruled the roost at Fulham, and he decided that there was going to be only one leader—him. He considered that Haynes exerted an unhealthy influence on all Fulham's affairs and this would have to change.

The down-to-earth Haynes had little time for Buckingham's training routines or his 'fancy dan' ways. Buckingham, however, was as stubborn and hard-nosed as Haynes, and fireworks were never far away. George Cohen, however, recalls: "Vic's arrival was terrific for me. We had a manager who was deadly serious—will, want and desire. He brought in discipline and coaching. Although he and Haynes didn't really get on, I think there was mutual respect."

Buckingham had been managing Ajax in Holland, and arrived bang on kick-off time for his first match as manager, following a delayed flight from Amsterdam. Fulham recorded a victory for his first game in charge. In fact it was a relatively easy victory, Fulham overcoming Nottingham Forest 4–1. Haynes had one of his better games, and a fine pass by the maestro down the left wing enabled Marsh to execute another of his special solo goals for the third. It gave Fulham a rare double for the season. Ironically, Haynes was the only forward on the day *not* to score, but that was considered rough justice!

February

A fortnight later, all eyes were on legend Stanley Matthews playing his final game, five days after his fiftieth birthday. In the match at Stoke's Victoria Ground he was marked fairly by Jimmy Langley. It all looked promising for Fulham early on, when, in a repeat of the move from the previous week, Haynes gave a peach of a pass for Rodney Marsh to saunter through and sweep Fulham ahead.

In the end, however, Fulham let the game slip. Stoke equalised, and then a superb Matthews pass enabled John Ritchie to put Stoke ahead. Finally, a dreadful mis-kick by Fulham's young John Dempsey, in just his third game, allowed a Stoke player to run half the length of the field for the third. In the 1–3 defeat, Haynes was described as the prime passer but was no doubt playing second fiddle to Stan that afternoon.

With just two wins in thirteen games, there was little hope of a win against Tottenham, but Fulham produced their performance of the season to see off their visitors by 4–1 in a wind-affected game. Bolstered by the return of Graham Leggat, Haynes had another good match against the club he still desired to join, and helped Fulham score three times in an incredible eight-minute spell after a goalless first half.

Johnny Key was the hero, with two thundering twenty-yard drives. The first Key goal came in the first minute of the second half from Haynes' reverse pass, and then Haynes combined with Key for the winger to cross and give Maurice Cook his goal.

Haynes got through a great deal of work, and the press said that he implored Fulham and drove them to giddy heights. It was an unhappy return for Alan Mullery, and Haynes got what he wanted, one last opportunity to post a message to Spurs—come and get me!

The following week Fulham went down at Highbury, as was usual, this time 0–2. The press reported that Haynes looked the best of a poor bunch. Haynes posted his fourth goal of the season whilst taking part in a 1–5 midweek defeat at Leicester, who gained ample revenge for the trouncing they had received at Craven Cottage earlier in the season.

It was an incredibly poor show by Fulham; Leicester had not won in their last thirteen matches, and had lost eight out of their last nine. However, they turned on the style and scored four goals in the first half-hour, with centre forward Goodfellow hitting a hat trick. When Leicester took a breather and the defence watched and retreated, Haynes ventured forward to shoot Fulham's goal. However, Fulham conceded again after half-time; it was their sixth successive away defeat.

Fulham subsequently beat off some of the fears of relegation with a scrappy 1–0 win over Sunderland at Craven Cottage. In a match to forget, Haynes created many chances down the middle but none was taken. At least it was two points in the bag, but Fulham were still in an uncomfortable seventeenth position.

March

Two weeks later, Johnny Haynes played well in a 2–2 draw at the Cottage against Leeds United, one of the league's better teams fighting for the championship. He didn't score but had an early shot kicked off the line. He also created the second goal when Maurice Cook mis-kicked following his clever free kick, and impressed a media pack by clicking his forward line into action. They said, "He is still the best in the game and dictated much of the play." Forty-eight hours later, despite hitting the bar at Old Trafford with a stinging shot, Haynes and Fulham offered little in a 1–4 defeat.

Against Liverpool at Anfield, Haynes upped his game again. Fulham shocked the home crowd by going two goals ahead. First Haynes took Cook's pass and put Rodney Marsh through for a simple goal. The Haynes and Marsh combination had been working well for several weeks, and had generated a number of goals.

Haynes kept a high tempo going for as long as possible, and with shrewd first-time distribution enabled Fulham to grab a second. However, the inevitable happened: Haynes faded without the support, and despite missing a penalty Liverpool stormed back and took the match 2–3.

Thankfully, some fears of the drop were eased when Fulham beat a lacklustre Sheffield Wednesday 2–0 at the Cottage, and things looked even better when Fulham garnered a further point in a 0–0 draw with virtually doomed Wolves at Molineux during the week.

April

With a little more heart, Fulham travelled to fellow-strugglers Blackpool, but were soundly beaten 0–3. Johnny Haynes started the match with some devastating distribution, but fell away after receiving no response.

Fulham in danger yet again

Fulham were slipping badly. Their home form was keeping them up, but their horrendous away displays were rooting them firmly in the relegation area—again. Since beating Wolves in November, they had won just five out of twenty-three league games, and gained only fifteen points out of a possible forty-six.

The next match was vital. It was on a Friday evening, against Blackburn Rovers at the Cottage again. Blackburn always seemed (as in 1958 and 1961) to visit the Cottage at this stage of the season for

Haynes congratulates Johnny Key (left) on his goal at home to Everton as a snow flurry subsides. Rodney Marsh celebrates in his own fashion. The goal in a 1–1 draw gave Fulham the point they needed to once again avoid relegation.

critical games. Bobby Robson scored his first league goal of the season with a twenty-yard shot, but soon Blackburn fought back and led two-one. Haynes had been frustrated up to this point and had seen all his craft blunted, but he somehow found an extra gear, and in a frantic finale Fulham scored twice in seven minutes.

First Haynes equalised with a fine angled drive from the left under goalkeeper Fred Else's body which flew into the net via Blackburn defender Keith Newton's boot. Then, just as quickly, Haynes fed Rodney Marsh, who netted a trademark solo goal. It was a great turnaround and gave rise to a critical 3–2 victory.

Survival again

It was still touch and go, however, and Fulham picked up just one point over Easter, following two games against Everton. In the 0–2 defeat at Goodison, Haynes was praised for his persistent promptings, but little else. The 1–1 draw with Everton at the Cottage took place on a cold, grey day and some snow fell. Snowflakes were landing on Haynes, and a wag in the crowd said that his hair was turning white. Sadly this was true, as Haynes appeared to have aged during the season. Most agreed it was hardly surprising, in view of what had gone on around him.

The point garnered from the Everton game guaranteed Fulham's safety, but in truth they had survived solely on the inadequacies of others rather than by their own positive efforts, with Birmingham City finding no form at all in the final weeks.

In the last home game, Fulham drew against Aston Villa 1–1 at the Cottage, and the season ended as it had started, with the slow handclap. Fulham survived in the end by four points, but they finished just two places off the bottom again. Haynes' goalscoring total was a reasonable eight.

Summary

It was clear that Johnny Haynes had served up a very sporadic and indifferent season, and had only impressed when the England manager and his assistants had been present or when one of the top five clubs were in opposition, as if to prove that he could still compete with the best and outwit some of the tightest and most professional defences. A number of times he had hardly turned up or dominated fixtures as he had done the previous season.

Many considered that he still harboured a deep resentment at not being allowed to leave at the beginning of the season and this had exhibited itself in his play.

With Fulham's dismal league showing and lack of investment, Haynes, who would be thirty-one in October and was approaching the veteran stage, had little to look forward to. His last chance to join a major club or play for England again had probably gone, and it seemed as if he would end his career as a Fulham player. The *Fulham Chronicle* astutely observed that his dejection would inevitably develop into depression.

The end of the season was made even more difficult for him when his old pal Trevor Chamberlain decided to call it a day after Buckingham's arrival, having only played around forty games in the last five seasons.

After the season ended, Haynes demonstrated he was not yesterday's man by appearing in the fifty-year-old Stanley Matthews' final retirement match against an international all-star side.

24: Dropped, but no drop 1965–66

Haynes (left) brushes up his heading skills with full back Barry Mealand (third left) and new boys (from left) Mark Pearson, John Ryan and Terry Dyson.

24: Dropped, but no drop — 1965–66

Johnny Haynes had reconciled himself to the fact that he would now probably end his career at Fulham and that his England days were over. Ramsey's team targeting the 1966 World Cup was beginning to take shape and they were now unbeaten in nine games, having conceded very few goals in the process.

Perhaps Haynes' indifferent form the previous season had been down to an injury. During the close season he had undergone a foot operation. He redoubled his efforts to prove that he was still a quality player. It was going to be even harder this season as experienced players Maurice Cook and Jim Langley had been discarded with indecent haste by Vic Buckingham, with seemingly no adequate replacements.

Buckingham removes the captaincy from Johnny Haynes

At the start of the season Vic Buckingham decided to remove the captaincy from Haynes—who had held it for nearly a decade—and hand the honour instead to England team member George Cohen. George recalls: "It wasn't a problem for John; there was no resentment and he said, 'Don't feel badly about it, George.' You never needed to tell him anything on the field anyway. Mind you, I was probably captain in name only—you couldn't be a captain to Johnny Haynes!"

Previous page: Pre-season high jinks with great mate Bobby Keetch.

August

Fulham opened the season with a visit to Blackpool. After a goalless first half, Johnny Key gave Fulham the lead early in the second half with a shot from Johnny Haynes' defence-splitting through pass. Then, at one goal behind, Key this time turned provider, sending in a cross for Haynes to flick the ball into the corner of the net between Blackpool keeper Waiters and the post in the very last minute to earn Fulham their first point of the season in a 2–2 draw.

Against Blackburn in midweek, Stan Brown netted the first in the tenth minute with a fine header after running forty yards to get on to the end of a swirling cross from Haynes. Two further goals put Fulham firmly in command, and before half-time it was four. Haynes pushed through a superb forty-yard pass, Key latched on to it, and again beat the Blackburn keeper Else. Fulham eventually won 5–2.

Manager and former captain discuss tactics before the Blackpool match at Bloomfield Road.

Haynes' flicked goal in the last minute earns Fulham a 2–2 draw at Blackpool.

Haynes is Fulham's first player to be substituted

Against the young Chelsea at Craven Cottage, Fulham were outplayed and were three goals down by the interval. In the second half, heat and tempers rose, and Ron 'Chopper' Harris scythed Haynes down from behind. This gave rise to an injury that left him limping. As a consequence, Haynes made history in the match by becoming the first Fulham player ever to be substituted when Graham Leggat took the field in the first minute of the second half. Fulham could make no inroads and lost 0–3. The injury was a bad one and caused Haynes to miss the next four league games.

September

As usual Fulham struggled without their star, and picked up just one point in those four games. At Bramall Lane, Fulham began to put too much of the physical side into their second-half performance, and both Johnny Haynes, in his comeback game, and Rodney Marsh were booked for unseemly skirmishes on the touchline, and Fulham went down again, 0–2.

An amazing game followed the next week, when Fulham lost 3–6 at home to Aston Villa after leading three-two with a Graham Leggat hat trick. Haynes was frustrated by the whole episode, and his body language clearly showed it.

Against Sunderland at Roker Park at the end of the month, Fulham were a goal behind until the dying seconds. Then Haynes intercepted Johnny Key's cross, pulled the ball down, sidestepped two Sunderland defenders and put over another perfect crossfield pass for Bobby Robson to slam home the equaliser with virtually the last kick of the game. This earned Fulham a 2–2 draw. Haynes' performance again brought rave reviews, many commentators calling yet again for his return to the England fold.

October

Early in the month, Fulham carved a welcome win against West Ham. After a goalless first half, an own goal gave Fulham the lead, and Johnny Haynes added a second. Graham Leggat fired in a shot, and Hammers defender Dennis Burnett only cleared the ball back to Haynes, who promptly despatched it back into the net with great precision. A late third from Leggat gave Fulham a 3–0 victory. Unfortunately they lost their second London derby the following week to Arsenal 1–2.

In the League Cup against Northampton Town in midweek, Terry Dyson put Fulham on their way in the seventeenth minute, when he hit home Haynes' pass from twenty yards. The press reported that Haynes fashioned most of the goals in the 5–0 victory with a

Despair from the West Ham defence, but joy from Haynes, as an own goal sets Fulham on the road to a 3–0 victory.

Despite this goal scored by Haynes with a fierce shot, Fulham crashed to a 1–4 defeat at home to fellow strugglers Northampton Town.

superb display of inside forward play. Centre half John Dempsey responded to being asked to play up front with an opportunist hat trick in the comprehensive win.

Against Everton on the Saturday in a tetchy match, Fulham came from behind, and finally, from an astute Haynes corner, the mobile Dempsey took Rodney Marsh's juggling near-post flick-on and bundled in Fulham's winner in a penalty box scramble. Everton's Colin Harvey was sent off and Fulham won 3–2. Although Haynes worked hard in the following week's display at Old Trafford, it was an off-key performance and Manchester United won 1–4 without too much difficulty.

Against Newcastle United at the Cottage in the final game of the month, just as the game appeared to be petering out into a goalless draw, the persistence of Haynes prised open the Newcastle defence.

Newcastle's Ollie Burton needlessly brought Haynes down just inside Fulham's own half by pulling his shirt. Haynes rose quickly, and planted a sixty-yard free kick on to the head of Bobby Robson standing on the edge of the Newcastle area. Robson headed the ball goalwards, the ball bounced awkwardly in the box, and some slack Newcastle defending allowed Johnny Key to accept the knockdown and screw a shot across goalkeeper Dave Hollins into the corner of the net.

A second goal by Leggat quickly followed after Haynes had been involved with Key and Dyson, and Fulham ran out 2–0 winners. Alf Ramsey was amongst the 20,000 crowd, probably checking on George Cohen, but he witnessed another superb Haynes display, worthy of an England recall. It was the third home victory in a row in the league, and it saw Fulham rise slightly to eighteenth at the end of the month.

First-ever League Cup goal

November

Against Aston Villa in the League Cup at Craven Cottage, Fulham took the lead right on half-time, when Johnny Haynes scored with a sweetly hit volley with the outside of his foot from Johnny Key's crossfield pass, the ball finding its way through a gap between Villa keeper Colin Withers and the post. It was his first-ever League Cup goal after six seasons of trying. Fulham couldn't press home their advantage and a late defensive slip gave Villa a 1–1 draw.

At the weekend, Fulham were truly hammered 2–6 at the Hawthorns, and then they returned to the Midlands forty-eight hours later for the League Cup replay. Haynes worked tirelessly pushing Fulham along, and just before half-time a Haynes flick was turned away from the goal line by Villa full back Charlie Aitken. Villa raised their game in the second half and won 0–2 on a wet and greasy pitch.

Against Nottingham Forest on the Saturday, Haynes switched to the unfamiliar number eight shirt. Rodney Marsh obliged on the half-hour with his first goal of the season, soaring above the Forest defenders to bullet home a fine header from Haynes' precision corner. Haynes hit the post twice in the match, and appeared to have scored the winning goal late in the game, when he netted following a lobbed pass from Terry Dyson.

However, despite few complaints from the Forest players, the referee decided to disallow the goal for an apparent infringement by Graham Leggat on the Forest keeper, Peter Grummitt. Haynes was denied in the last minute when Grummitt fingertipped a back-header over the bar, and Fulham only managed a 1–1 draw. Haynes received no press mentions the following week in a drab 0–1 defeat by Sheffield Wednesday at Hillsborough.

Fulham had no luck in the last match of the month during the league visit of Northampton Town. In a disastrous performance, Rodney Marsh was forced to play in goal after Tony Macedo broke his jaw. Fulham were already a goal down at this point but somehow managed to contrive an equaliser. Substitute Dyson,

Johnny Key and John Dempsey combined, ending with Haynes shooting home through a ruck of players; this was as good as it got. Fulham could not overcome their troubles and more defensive howlers handed the match to the Cobblers 1–4. Fulham had not won at all in the month, and Haynes was now struggling and frustrated at the displays going on around him.

December

Early in the month, after a 2–3 defeat at Stoke where Haynes played with a number nine shirt for the first time in his Fulham career, Fulham took on championship-chasing Burnley at the Cottage. Fulham were outplayed, and Burnley took an early lead. Fulham's equaliser in the twenty-sixth minute was fortunate, Burnley's Gordon Harris putting through his own goal whilst trying to prevent Terry Parmenter's left-wing centre reaching Johnny Haynes. Although some statistics credit this goal to Haynes, he clearly made no contact, and most reports have this down as an own goal.

Burnley had stretched their lead to four-one before Mark Pearson managed to pull a goal back for Fulham fifteen minutes from time, after Burnley keeper Adam Blacklaw had failed to hold a sharp shot from Haynes. Pearson was then dismissed for arguing about a penalty award. It was another poor performance, ending 2–5.

The rumblings of a first major fallout between manager Buckingham and Haynes began to appear the following week. Against Everton at Goodison, rumours abounded that Haynes would be dropped for the match, but in the end he took his place in the side, though operating in an unfamiliar inside right/right wing position. It wasn't very effective either, especially as he was up against England full back Ramon Wilson. Fulham played poorly and lost 0–2. They were even worse after Christmas and were soundly beaten 0–5 at Leicester, though Haynes was praised, alongside Bobby Robson, for "a few ideas."

By the end of the year, Fulham were rock bottom, were showing no form at all, and hadn't won for two months. Although Haynes still looked like Fulham's most creative player, he knew that it would be very hard to pull himself and the Fulham team out of this tight spot.

January

A brief respite followed on New Year's day with a 1–0 victory over Arsenal at the Cottage. Haynes had a shot cleared off the line early on. After Graham Leggat had been fouled midway through the first half, Haynes tapped the free kick to him, and his first-time effort thundered through a wall of defenders high into the net just inside the post, beating the partially unsighted Arsenal goalkeeper's despairing dive.

This impetus failed to continue. Fulham lost 0–1 at Burnley, where Haynes was frustrated by the forwards' lack of awareness, and the following week against Manchester United at the Cottage they lost by the same score. Haynes was brought down in the box when his shirt was clearly grabbed and the incident appeared to be a glaring penalty, but the referee waved play on.

Anguish for Haynes at a missed opportunity against Arsenal turned to delight at the final score of 1–0 to Fulham.

Fulham then made a swift and undignified exit from the FA Cup, losing in the third round 1–3 to Sheffield United at Bramall Lane. Haynes put in one piledriver that was well saved, and therewith Fulham's resolve seemed to melt away.

Dropped for the first time

Manager Buckingham was still experimenting with the side. None of the forwards was doing well and the team had scored only twice in the last six matches. Following another abrasive 'exchange of opinions', Buckingham omitted Haynes for the match against Blackpool at the Cottage, which ended 0–0. At least this saw the return of Steve Earle after a long absence and the arrival of Les Barrett. George Cohen recalls: "I personally don't think Vic Buckingham was trying to humiliate Haynes; the only reason why he would have left him out of the side would have been that he sincerely thought he wasn't playing well enough."

February

Buckingham also left Haynes out of the game against Chelsea, which ended 1–2 at Stamford Bridge. The move, with Mark Pearson as Johnny Haynes' replacement, hadn't worked and Buckingham reluctantly recalled Haynes to the side for the next match, at Spurs a fortnight later.

Although returned to the line-up, Haynes was wearing the unfamiliar number nine shirt and playing as a deep-lying midfield player. Fulham were soon three goals down but replied with three goals in an amazing eight minutes.

For the third, Les Barrett took a Haynes pass from an opening created by Pearson and thundered the ball in for the equaliser. Fulham very unluckily lost 3–4. At this point it looked like curtains for Fulham, as they were six points adrift at the bottom of the table with just thirteen games to go. However, a revival was once again about to start.

Haynes plots the great escape

At home against league leaders Liverpool, who were closing in on the title, Haynes created the first goal in ten minutes. He won the ball in midfield and exchanged passes with Graham Leggat, before moving forward to almost the corner flag, where he glanced up and sent over a head-high teasing cross. Steve Earle moved in between two Liverpool defenders to score with a glancing downward header, squeezing his effort between Lawrence and his near post.

Although it was heart-stopping stuff, Earle scored a controversial second goal and Fulham produced a coupon-busting 2–0 victory. George Cohen remembers the match well: "Part of this was due to Vic Buckingham's decision to play Johnny out wide on the right. The reason was unknown, but it did make a difference to the team." Liverpool were so rattled that centre forward St John was sent off in the last few minutes for punching Pearson. Fulham then had to wait another fortnight for the next game.

March

At Villa Park, the Fulham team started where they had left off against Liverpool. Within two minutes Graham Leggat had given Fulham the lead with a trademark downward header from a Haynes free kick. After a Villa equaliser, Haynes floated in another accurate corner, the Villa goalkeeper dropped the ball, and Steve Earle scored with a shot on the turn. This enabled Fulham to go in at the interval two-one up.

Just after half-time Haynes beat two Villa midfield players with a beautiful body swerve, Brian Nichols picked up the pass and as the ball came across, Leggat helped the ball on, and Earle, again with ample time, converted easily. Two further late goals gave Fulham a resounding 5–2 victory, their equal highest away win in the First Division.

In the next home game against Sunderland, Haynes destroyed the visitors with his distribution. Although he didn't score, he had an involvement in all the goals in the 3–0 win, and from two more of his slide-rule efforts Mark Pearson and Bobby Robson both rattled the Sunderland bar. Haynes, unsurprisingly, was voted man of the match; "What precision passing!" commented the *Evening Standard.*

A confident Fulham then beat West Ham 3–1 at Upton Park. After a goal close to half-time, Fulham doubled their lead just thirty seconds after the interval. It was a goal to really set the crowd talking. Les Barrett took a superb pass from Haynes, controlled the ball immaculately and beat three West Ham defenders for speed, including Bobby Moore, before moving into the box and crashing a shot high into the roof of the West Ham net wide of Jim Standen in the West Ham goal. Fulham, although still in the relegation zone, had moved up one place.

Two critical Haynes goals beat West Bromwich

April

Against West Bromwich at Craven Cottage, Fulham snatched an early lead. Johnny Haynes took a pass from Les Barrett following a brilliant overlapping run by Brian Nichols. Haynes ran the ball into the box, and smashed a beautiful side-foot cross-shot into the net, ending up smiling flat on his face amongst the photographers beside the goal.

After an Albion equaliser, their defence once again unwisely allowed Haynes time on the ball, and again he put in an unchallenged shot. The ball clipped Albion's centre half Campbell on the heel, spun and rocketed past the wrong-footed and stranded Albion keeper.

Haynes, who had not scored for three and a half months, had come up with two goals in the 2–1 win when they were really required. It was fitting that the goals came on that day, as he had just been named the *Evening Standard* footballer of the month for March. A Fulham side that had been in desperate trouble only

Haynes scores the winning goal against West Bromwich Albion with a shot from the edge of the penalty area that was deflected past the Albion goalkeeper. The 2–1 result was a fifth successive win.

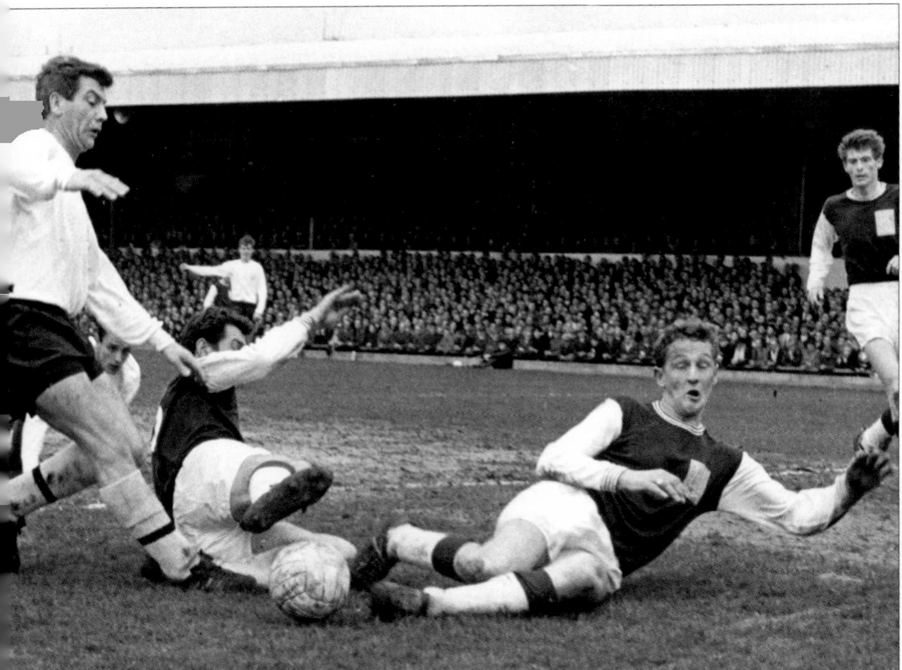

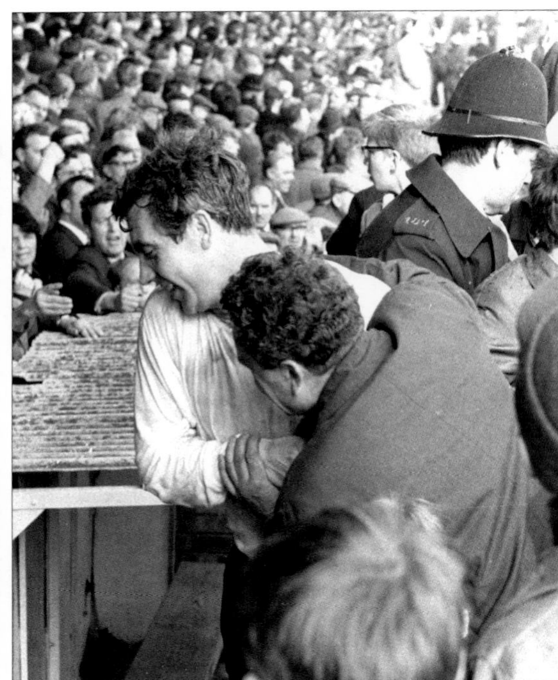

In the make-or-break clash at Northampton Town, Haynes' experience and determination finally cracked a resolute Cobblers side, and at the final whistle, after a 4–2 victory, he ran off the pitch much contented at a job well done.

a month earlier had now won five league games in a row.

Against a strong Leeds United at Fulham on Good Friday, Haynes badly bruised a leg muscle in the first half, disrupting the team's rhythm. He did not reappear for the second half, and Allan Clarke made his first Fulham appearance as a substitute. The team badly missed Haynes' craft, and his absence was keenly felt in the eventual 1–3 defeat. Fulham's winning run was finally broken. Haynes would miss the next three vital games in the relegation dogfight.

Fulham did very well in two of these fixtures, especially in the backs-to-the-wall 1–0 victory over Leeds United at Elland Road and the 4–2 home win over Sheffield Wednesday. However Fulham sank back into the mire with a shattering 0–4 defeat in a re-scheduled match with Leicester at Craven Cottage just forty-eight hours later.

It was now either Fulham or Northampton for relegation. In the virtual decider at Northampton's County Ground, Fulham were two-one down at one stage and could have been further behind. Haynes' experience finally wrested control away from the Northampton midfield and he began to pull the strings, sweeping passes to both wings. Fulham finally took a one-goal lead with only a minute to go.

Northampton sent everyone up for a final corner, but the move broke down. Haynes picked up the ball and his clever pass found Steve Earle unmarked in the centre circle; Earle ran half the length of the field to secure his personal hat trick and the fourth in a critical 4–2 win.

His 500th Fulham appearance

At Nottingham Forest, Haynes recorded his 500th appearance for Fulham. This figure included only league and FA Cup games and didn't take into account the nine League Cup games he had also played in.

Haynes' pass helped to create the first Fulham goal and he had another shot held on the line. Sadly he was injured again after thirty-three minutes, and had to leave the field. Fulham thankfully won 2–1, a victory that virtually guaranteed their First Division survival. Haynes felt compelled to say, "I can't ever remember Fulham playing as well as they are now."

The club programme commented that the last eleven games had proved that his value to football had not diminished an inch, and that in fact many people had still been campaigning for his return to the England team for the World Cup. The Fulham editorial stated emphatically, "No need to quote our opinions on the subject!"

Of his 500 games, Haynes said: "Basically the game hasn't altered much. These systems have made the game tighter undoubtedly, but beating defences has always been a problem. In fact I would say that five or six years ago I was more tightly marked than I am now."

The programme also discussed Haynes relinquishing the captaincy rather than having it removed by Buck-ingham, but Haynes didn't bite, and with candour suggested: "Yes, I seem to enjoy my football more. There's not so much responsibility. I was skipper for ten years, and it makes a change to be just one of the team. Being captain during a relegation battle is tough going, I can assure you."

Fulham are safe yet again

One last push was all that was needed. Haynes, nursing a calf injury, only played in the match at home to Stoke City after receiving a pain-killing injection. In a very tense and frustrating game, in which George Cohen was carried off on a stretcher early on, Fulham finally secured a point in a 1–1 draw thanks to Allan Clarke's first goal for Fulham just eight minutes from the end. Fulham were saved yet again.

Haynes has a shot blocked at Nottingham Forest, where Fulham continued to play as well as they had ever done. It was Haynes' 500th appearance, and the 2–1 victory virtually guaranteed Fulham's survival in the First Division.

Another milestone

May

In the last match of the season at Newcastle, Johnny Haynes reached another significant milestone: by playing in the 1–1 draw, he surpassed Eddie Lowe's record for the total number of games played for Fulham FC in all competitions. He now had 512 to his credit.

Summary

There was no doubt that Haynes had played a major role in this escape. Somehow Fulham had clawed themselves upwards to finish twentieth yet again, and beaten the drop at the very last. Haynes said after the nerve-wracking season had ended: "I don't think we've ever been as close [to relegation] as we have been this time. It has been a great run and although I think the ball has run for us, I can't remember Fulham playing any better than this."

Vic Buckingham was still trying to clamp down on the happy-go-lucky style at the Cottage and Haynes was uneasy with the approach. Within a year of his arrival, Buckingham with his abrasive personality had also disposed of Fulham characters like the dashing Bobby Keetch and clown prince Rodney Marsh, two of Johnny's close friends.

Fulham closed the season with a sponsored tour of Asia. Haynes scored once on the trip in a 5–3 win over Sheffield Wednesday.

More frustration for the maestro in the final home match against Stoke City, but the 1–1 result ensured Fulham's annual safety.

25: A bit of a struggle
1966–67

25: A bit of a struggle 1966–67

A happy Haynes had taken part in Fulham's annual cricket fixture with Putney and his side had doggedly held on for a draw against determined opposition. In the main pre-season friendly against promoted Millwall, Fulham fought back after being two down to win 4–2. Haynes scored the third to put Fulham ahead for the first time with a full-blooded shot from well over thirty yards that the goalkeeper never saw.

Fulham also completed a short pre-season tour of Belgium, winning one match and losing one. The initial game against Olympic Charleroi resulted in a 4–2 victory, with Haynes' name once again on the scoresheet. He looked in good trim and ready for a better season.

Dropped again by Vic Buckingham

August

For the opening match of the season against Everton at the Cottage, Buckingham dropped a bombshell and removed Haynes from the team on the eve of the game, and went as far as to say privately that Fulham were a better team without him! Buckingham was convinced, wrongly, that he was not giving his all or pulling his weight. Haynes' team-mates protested vigorously that it wasn't the case, but Vic Buckingham wouldn't listen.

Without Haynes' spark, Fulham found it even harder to break down the Everton defensive wall, and created few scoring opportunities. England World Cup star Alan Ball, making his debut for Everton following a British record transfer of £110,000 only days before, scored the goal which gave Everton their win.

The Fulham crowd were chronically aware of the absence of craft and guile, and began chanting "*We want Haynes*" as the game began to ebb away from the home side. Haynes could be seen reading a newspaper at the players' entrance on the corner of the pitch, looking far removed from the whole episode. Fulham lost the game 0–1.

Haynes demanded to see chairman Tommy Trinder to discuss his position. He had been invited to the boardroom, where a silverware award was to be presented to George Cohen for his World Cup exploits. Haynes was going to be given an award as well, marking his fiftieth England cap, even though, bizarrely, he had won it more than four years earlier! Haynes did not show up, but the presentation to Cohen went ahead.

It was probably Buckingham's decision to drop Haynes that began to isolate the manager from some of

A dropped Haynes nonchalantly reads his newspaper whilst his colleagues toil unsuccessfully against Everton in the summer sunshine. The crowd vociferously called for Haynes, but on this day he could do nothing to prevent a 0–1 defeat.

Fulham's late winner at Stoke is seconds away. Haynes shoots from long range, the goalkeeper can only palm the ball out and Allan Clarke is on hand to slam the rebound home. The 2–1 away win was Fulham's first of the season.

the senior players. Haynes did meet Trinder during the week and was predictably re-instated for the next game, which Fulham lost 0–3 at Burnley. There could only be one winner in a contest between Buckingham and Trinder's favourite son. It was no surprise that Haynes remained long after Buckingham had departed.

Steve Earle recalls: "After one match that we had lost, Buckingham lined up all the players in order of seniority. He asked me as one of the youngest players in the team how I thought Johnny Haynes had performed on the Saturday. I mumbled something about 'probably not up to his usual highest of standards,' which was true.

"Johnny objected to this kind of humiliation and it naturally provoked a response from him. It all began to get a bit heated and when we looked for the manager to intervene and calm things down, Vic had sneaked out of the room and left us to it. That's the way he was, particularly with Johnny.

"I think John felt bad about how it had all escalated and afterwards took me out to a pub lunch at Barnes to have scampi and chips. I hardly said a word; I was awestruck that he'd taken me."

At Stoke on the Saturday, with just fifteen minutes remaining and Fulham a goal down, Graham Leggat took a superb Haynes through pass and scored with a lovely shot from the edge of the area just inside a post. Then, as the final seconds were approaching, Haynes fired in a magnificent low shot from well outside the area through a clutch of Stoke defenders. Stoke's keeper Farmer could only beat out the shot and the ball fell nicely to Allan Clarke following up and he slammed it in from close range for a 2–1 win. Haynes also played well in the return match at Craven Cottage against Burnley, creating chances in an exciting 0–0 draw.

September

Haynes received a kick against Sheffield United at the Cottage in a real stinker of a game, which Fulham lost 0–1. The injury rendered him ineffective and as it was now taking him longer to recover from knocks, he missed the next two league games against Nottingham Forest and West Bromwich Albion. Both these were away from home. Fulham lost both, conceding seven goals in the process.

Haynes, the unfit substitute

A strange story emerged regarding that trip to the Hawthorns. A Fulham player called in sick at the very last moment. Fortunately, the injured Haynes had travelled with the party, and had to be named as the emergency substitute. Kitted up, he hobbled over to the bench. Fortunately he was not called upon to play, but it would have been interesting if he had been.

His eventual return saw a slight upturn in Fulham's fortunes, and they obtained a 2–2 draw at home to a fluent Leeds side and a 1–1 draw at Newcastle.

October

Against Spurs on the opening day of the month, after going a goal down in the second minute, Fulham came back strongly and in the tenth minute were awarded a free kick. Johnny Haynes put in a beautifully weighted cross, and Steve Earle headed in a magnificent goal from six yards. Late in the game Earle headed just over from a Haynes cross. Despite impressive play from all the forwards, the defence had a torrid time, and Spurs won rather fortunately 3–4.

In the League Cup at Craven Cottage four days later, Second Division Wolves were never in the game. Fulham produced a glorious exhibition of attacking football from beginning to end, with devastating finishing. Earle scored the first with a rasping volley from ten yards from a sweet Haynes pass, and Fulham triumphantly breezed through to the next round with a resounding 5–0 win. The match saw the debut of Jimmy Conway.

Things got better still at the weekend in the trip to Liverpool. At one-all, Haynes started the move for the

The moment Haynes knew that Fulham would leave Anfield with a point. Liverpool forward Roger Hunt has just missed an easy chance—and Haynes jumps for joy.

second goal with a perfect pass out to the wing to Allan Clarke, who cut inside and skilfully beat four Liverpool defenders, before drawing Tommy Lawrence from his goal and rolling the ball arrogantly past him. Fulham put on one of their best displays of the season, fighting hard to secure a 2–2 draw.

Fulham were a team in full flow, and were soon into their stride against the Hammers the following Saturday. They took the lead in the tenth minute. Allan Clarke's crossfield ball found Haynes, who chased and pulled the ball back, and from his tempting low centre Earle casually side-footed the ball wide of the goalkeeper.

After a Hammers equaliser, Haynes also had a part in the goal which gave Fulham the lead. His fiercely-struck shot looked to be going just wide, until the Hammers full back Dennis Burnett stuck out a leg and turned the ball tidily into his own net. Bobby Robson and Haynes dominated the midfield, and Fulham ran out 4–2 winners.

At Hillsborough, Fulham took the lead early on. Les Barrett picked up Clarke's flick-on, and drew out the Sheffield Wednesday keeper. Barrett then squared the ball unselfishly to Haynes, who hammered it left-footed through a crowded penalty area into the net from eighteen yards. It was his first goal of the season in twelve appearances. Fulham pinched another away point in a tenacious 1–1 draw.

The only downside to the accomplished performance was an injury to man-of-the-match Haynes ten minutes from time, which caused him to leave the field and be substituted by Mark Pearson. The injury meant he missed the midweek League Cup defeat at Blackpool and the following week's derby against Chelsea, which Fulham unluckily lost 1–3.

Fulham were scoring a number of goals, but their overall form was still erratic, and by the end of the month the team, with only two wins, lay just outside the two relegation places.

November

On Guy Fawkes Day there were fireworks at Upton Park on Johnny Haynes' return. The maestro cleverly tapped a free kick sideways, Jimmy Conway sold the

Haynes' first goal of the season came at Sheffield Wednesday on October 22nd; it secured a 1–1 draw. Again it's a trademark strike from the edge of the penalty area. This one was a left-foot strike.

Another clincher from Haynes, another last-minute goal, another strike from outside the penalty area—the fourth goal in the 4–2 Christmas victory over Leicester City at a misty Craven Cottage. This one is a right-foot strike.

dummy by jumping over the ball, and this set up Fred Callaghan, who blasted in through a gap in the West Ham wall from twenty-five yards. Fulham led at this stage, but in the end were soundly beaten 1–6, England World Cup star Geoff Hurst scoring four goals.

The team recovered the next week at home to Aston Villa. After a goalless first half, Haynes bamboozled the Villa defence and pulled them out of position, then stabbed a cross over to Les Barrett, whose quick return cross was netted by Mark Pearson. A minute later Fulham scored again. Haynes provided a waist-high pass to Allan Clarke, who hooked the ball over his shoulder and turned. He finally crashed the ball powerfully home on the volley past the bewildered Colin Withers in the Villa goal, a truly superb individual effort. It had been a total reverse of the previous week and Fulham recorded a 5–1 victory. Unfortunately Haynes picked up another niggling injury, which caused him to miss another London derby, the 0–1 defeat by Arsenal at Highbury.

A fortnight later, in the next home game against Manchester City, Haynes, back from injury, was involved in the move with Jimmy Conway that gave George Cohen a rare goal for Fulham's first score. He was involved in the third goal as well. He took Macedo's throw and found Barrett with a sublime pass on the left wing, and the unmarked Clarke hammered Barrett's accurately placed cross superbly past City goalkeeper Dowd.

Haynes completed the scoring himself with his second goal of the season, another long-range shot from over thirty yards that whistled in past the despairing Dowd's hands with virtually the last kick of the match. Fulham had scored three goals in an eighteen-minute spell in a convincing 4–1 win. The maestro had proved that he was definitely still a force to be reckoned with.

December

The following Saturday at Bloomfield Road, Johnny Haynes split the Blackpool defence with a telling through pass; Steve Earle took the ball in his stride before swerving to the left and the right and finally planting a perfectly placed shot past Tony Waiters in the Seasiders' goal. It proved to be the only goal of the game.

In the next home match against Southampton, Haynes didn't score, but was always given too much space in the centre of the pitch. He responded by striking a long shot from a free kick into a crowded goalmouth and it was deflected into the goal by Allan Clarke. Another positive performance gave rise to another home win in a 3–1 victory.

At Goodison against Everton the following week, Fulham were three down at half-time and truly second best. In the second half they turned the tables. Haynes and Conway were involved in the move that culminated with the unmarked Clarke heading Les Barrett's precise centre into goal twelve minutes from the end.

Clarke turned provider five minutes later, linking up with Haynes, who put Barrett through with a glorious pass to squeeze a super shot inside the post, giving Everton keeper Gordon West no chance. Fulham just lost out 2–3 in a thriller.

On a frosty Boxing Day at Filbert Street, Haynes' dangerous corner was headed out and the ball fell nicely to Fred Callaghan who returned it venomously into the top corner for Fulham's first goal against Leicester; Fulham recorded yet another impressive away win 2–0.

In the return match the following day, Fulham went a goal down early on, but then Haynes won a tackle with Leicester's Rodrigues, and before he could be tackled again, he put in an exquisite centre, allowing

Concentration against Stoke. A bandaged Haynes comes out on top on New Year's Eve in an impressive 4–1 victory.

Graham Leggat to equalise with a trademark jack-knife header.

Fulham wasted no time in going ahead, and the second goal was a carbon copy of the first: a headed goal from Leggat, following another perfectly flighted corner from Haynes. After Leicester had equalised, Leggat completed his hat trick.

Leicester were coming back strongly for a third goal, but Haynes had the last word and sealed the win with a tremendous shot in the last minute. He was surrounded by Leicester defenders, but threw them all off balance by feigning a pass. He moved the other way instead, found himself a yard of space and hit a swerving shot from twenty-five yards, which gave Gordon Banks no chance at all. The late strike saw Fulham home 4–2.

It was a sad occasion for Haynes, as Fulham recorded the death of their former player and trainer Frank Penn, who had joined the club as a winger in 1915 and remained at the club in various capacities, mainly as trainer, for fifty years.

On New Year's Eve, Stoke were the visitors to the in-form Cottagers. Fulham were once again a goal down, but recovered. Haynes floated in a centre to the near post, Leggat powered a typical head on it, and the ball shot goalwards, only to rebound off Maurice Setters. However, before any Stoke defender could react, the alert Leggat whipped the rebound into the net. Haynes, heavily bandaged, provided an object lesson in passing and helped Fulham to a splendid 4–1 victory.

Buckingham and Haynes appeared to be steering Fulham in the right direction. They had now won six of their last seven league matches and were playing strongly. Haynes' admirers were still insisting that in this form he was good enough to slot into the current England set-up.

Although Fulham were an average fourteenth at this stage, they sat just six points behind third-placed Stoke, the team they had just seen off comprehensively. For Haynes and Fulham, things were the brightest they had been for years.

Graham Leggat departs

January

The new year brought the shock news of goalscorer Graham Leggat's sudden departure. Despite five goals in his last two games, Leggat had been sold to Second Division Birmingham City for a paltry £15,000, and the move ended an eight-year association with the club. Haynes and Leggat were good friends and golfing partners; Haynes did not agree with Buckingham's decision.

Although it is hard to assess whether Leggat's departure affected Haynes' form, he had a very quiet month, and Fulham picked up just one league point from three games. Against Bradford Park Avenue in the FA Cup third round, Fulham were leading two-one but were under pressure from the Fourth Division side. Thankfully, two minutes from time, Park Avenue finally succumbed when Haynes fired in another of his characteristic rocket shots from the edge of the box. Fulham were relieved to survive 3–1.

February

Fulham started the month at home to Newcastle United, and both they and Allan Clarke were rejuvenated. After Clarke had given the Cottagers an early lead, Johnny Haynes sent in a floating free kick, and Steve Earle lost his marker to score with a corking header.

In the second half, Clarke quickly added a third, and Haynes added the fourth himself in the fiftieth minute, when he arrowed a low twenty-yard drive into the corner of the net from a narrow angle. Clarke completed his hat trick eight minutes later, after a very sweet move involving Haynes, Earle and Fred Callaghan. Although Newcastle had been poor opposition, this was still a stunning 5–1 victory for the refreshed home side.

At Tottenham, the game of the season unfolded. Fulham were a goal down early on to Alan Gilzean. They immediately went on the offensive and were rewarded for their pressure in the seventeenth minute. Haynes swept out a fine pass to George Cohen, and his low cross was controlled well by Clarke, who turned the ball neatly back to Haynes supporting the move. Haynes hit a beauty, a first-time shot from outside the

Yet another long-range shot from Haynes as he scores a late third goal for Fulham in the gloom in the 3–1 cup victory at Bradford Park Avenue.

The Haynes power drive is in evidence again at Tottenham where he scored with this magnificent strike that Pat Jennings in the Spurs goal never saw. It brought the first equaliser. Fulham were very unlucky to be on the wrong end of a 2–4 score.

box, which gave Pat Jennings in the Spurs goal no chance at all.

The match was marred somewhat by the sending off of Fred Callaghan and Terry Venables. Fulham were level for long periods and lost to two late goals, one in the last minute. Haynes had been outstanding throughout the match, a game that Fulham were very unfortunate to lose 2–4. Haynes had now scored four in his last eight matches.

Fulham also played well the next week in the cup-tie against Sheffield United at Craven Cottage. Haynes hit the bar and the post in the most one-sided 1–1 draw

Haynes (at left) watches his shot cannon back from the Sheffield United crossbar in an FA cup-tie that Fulham should have won easily. In the end, the home side were saved by an Allan Clarke goal just two minutes from time in a 1–1 draw.

Haynes hits the bar against Sunderland with a rare header, but Fulham go on to win 3–1.

you could ever see. Fulham were unlucky not to score ten.

Fulham were playing very well at home and next took on the mighty Liverpool. From a cross, Haynes' headed flick found Les Barrett in the penalty area. Barrett picked the ball up, flicked it into the air, swivelled and put in a shot on the volley that the Reds goalkeeper Tommy Lawrence got close to, but couldn't stop. Fulham drew a pulsating match 2–2, thanks to a last-minute own goal by the Liverpool captain Ron Yeats, but had clearly deserved at least a point. Despite this, they had slipped down to sixteenth place at the end of the month.

March

Following two postponements for heavy rain, Fulham finally lost their fourth-round replayed FA Cup tie against Sheffield United 1–3 at Bramall Lane. On the evening before the match, manager Buckingham ordered the players to bed, but turned a blind eye when Johnny Haynes strolled out into the night arm in arm with a well-known actress who was appearing at the local theatre.

Fulham lost two early goals to poor defending. Haynes hit one tremendous shot that beat Alan Hodgkinson in the Sheffield goal all the way, but the ball fizzed inches wide of a post. Despite a goal pulled back by Fred Callaghan, Fulham eventually lost to a late goal. A despondent Haynes considered that this had been his final chance for FA Cup glory, and alongside Bobby Robson he began to resign himself to the fact that his dream of a Wembley appearance with Fulham was now truly over.

Three days later, in humid and hot weather at Chelsea, Eddie McCreadie kicked an Allan Clarke header off the line, following a Haynes free kick. Bobby Robson and Haynes were dominating the midfield, but over-elaboration in front of goal meant that Fulham had to settle for a draw in a 0–0 result.

In a 1–2 defeat at the Cottage by Sheffield Wednesday, Haynes had a frustrating game where nothing went right, but he was slowed down because of a knock he had taken. This caused him to miss the next away fixture against Southampton, where Fulham played very poorly without his guidance and lost 2–4.

In the Easter home fixture, and in front of an almost record crowd of 47,290 against Manchester United, Haynes raised his game to international standard once more. Fulham took the lead as early as the eighteenth minute, when following a foul, Haynes floated a free kick perfectly into the goalmouth and Clarke slipped in front of the United veteran Bill Foulkes and out-jumped him to plant in a perfectly headed goal.

After George Best had levelled the score, Fulham took the lead again in the second half. George Cohen started an attack with a pass to Haynes on the right. Haynes ran through and slid a perfect pass out to Mark Pearson, who in turn flicked a perfect fourth pass to Barrett in the penalty area. Barrett hesitated briefly and then drove the ball into the roof of the net; United did not know what had hit them. Fulham were denied by a late Nobby Stiles goal, but they more than deserved their share of the spoils in a 2–2 draw.

April

Sunderland proved that they were the April Fools on

Haynes scores in the 1–1 draw at Villa Park to mark the occasion of his 500th league match. (Without wishing to labour the point, it's yet another shot from outside the box!)

the first day of the month. Johnny Haynes hit the bar with a strong header, and fortunately Fulham secured a win for the first time in ten matches (including the cup), with a 3–1 score.

Haynes' 500th league match—and a goal

At Villa Park, it was Haynes' 500th league match, and he characteristically turned in a man-of-the-match performance. He put Fulham ahead as early as the ninth minute. The goal followed a sparkling move between Fred Callaghan and Allan Clarke, and from Callaghan's centre Haynes hit home a twenty-yard strike through a ruck of players. The goal was his eighth of the season. Fulham took a point in a 1–1 draw.

It was now really end-of-season stuff, and a goalless draw with Arsenal was followed by a 0–3 defeat at Manchester City. Little was seen of Haynes in either match.

Fulham wound down against relegated Blackpool. Clarke who had already scored, was just wide from an excellent Haynes free kick. After Blackpool had equalised, Clarke scored his second goal of the game to give Fulham the lead again, and it was a gem. A crossfield pass was missed by Blackpool's centre half Glyn James, Haynes nodded the ball forward into the path of Clarke, and the striker fired a strong cross-shot into the corner of the net. The torpid match ended in a disappointing 2–2 draw, but the point Fulham gained secured their place in the top flight for yet another season.

Bobby Robson retires

May

The season ended with a 1–3 defeat by Sunderland in a tired game at Roker Park and a kickabout fixture and 2–3 loss against eventual runners-up Nottingham Forest. It was the final game in a long and distinguished career for Bobby Robson, who had joined Fulham at the same time as Haynes in 1950. Robson was calling it a day in England after almost seventeen years. This was another blow for Johnny Haynes, but it was clear that he himself was not contemplating retirement.

Summary

Fulham finished the season in a disappointing eighteenth position; they had slipped badly since Christmas having won only two league games. Haynes had another very good season, playing in forty-one of the forty-eight games. He was now playing as a deep-lying creator, but with a number seven on his back instead of his usual number ten. He had contributed another seven league goals, mostly trademark long-range blasters from outside the penalty area.

By his own admission he had found the long season hard, and the pace was just starting to tell. By moving deeper, he could still control games but he was unable to cover as much ground as he once did.

26: Down but not out 1967–68

26: Down but not out 1967–68

Johnny Haynes was on great form in Fulham's pre-season tour of Germany. The tour was completed with a 4–1 rout of Tennis Borussia. Allan Clarke scored a hat trick, with Fred Callaghan scoring the other goal. Haynes was the man of the match, cutting the defence to ribbons with telling passes.

Clarke scored as early as the fifth minute, when Haynes lobbed the ball forward for him, and he sent a header flashing into the net. Then a Haynes/Clarke move put the home defence in a panic and enabled Fred Callaghan to score with a low twenty-yard drive.

After the interval a fine crossfield pass by Callaghan found Haynes, who slipped the ball through to Clarke for him to push it home. Clarke's hat trick came from a low fifteen-yard drive, which rocketed into the net off a defender's boot. Haynes was also in tip-top condition in the other pre-season friendly at Walsall where Fulham drew 1–1.

August

The season did not start well and Fulham looked very lethargic, taking just one point from their opening three matches: a home defeat at the hands of promoted Wolves 1–2, a 0–3 defeat at Sunderland, where Terry Parmenter was ordered off with Jim Baxter, and a 1–1 draw at Chelsea that was only achieved thanks to a deflected shot from Stan Brown in the last ten minutes.

Previous page: It's January and new manager Bobby Robson (centre) chats with Tony Macedo and Johnny Haynes, who only a few months previously were his playing colleagues.

Johnny Haynes contributed a couple of free kicks and shots in the Chelsea match, but little else. Matters looked ominous; forty-eight hours later, however, the real Haynes emerged. After leading at home to Sunderland, Fulham were one-two down. Haynes persisted, however, and his reward came in the sixty-fifth minute, when he hit a long pass downfield over everyone's head. The ball was somewhat clumsily brought down by Mark Pearson and pushed into the path of the eager Les Barrett who shot home his second goal of the night from six yards, with the Sunderland defence appealing unsuccessfully for offside.

On this occasion neither team would settle for a draw, and it turned out to be Fulham's night when thirteen minutes from time the tireless Brown hit a long pass high into the goalmouth, and Allan Clarke climbed above two Sunderland defenders to head the ball down. It fell to Haynes, so often the cool head amongst all the hustle and bustle, and he placed his volley with arrogant accuracy into the only gap there was, just inside the far post, from twelve yards. Fulham won 3–2, and the first exciting win was on the board.

September

Unfortunately, the ageing Johnny Haynes had picked up an injury in the Sunderland thriller, and this caused him to miss the next three games. At Leeds, Billy Bremner was sent off, but Fulham lost against ten men. Like a blast from the past, Fulham's injury list lengthened, but they were unlucky to lose 2–4 to top-of-the-table Sheffield Wednesday during the following week. Fulham were in trouble, but bounced back with

Johnny Haynes (in background) can only watch as another Fulham effort goes narrowly wide at Stamford Bridge. A late goal from Stan Brown secured Fulham a 1–1 draw.

A dramatic goal from Haynes against Sunderland gave Fulham a late winner in the 3–2 victory. Terry Parmenter watches Haynes' celebration.

the game of the season, a 2–1 victory over star-studded Everton, Bobby Moss scoring the dramatic winner in injury time.

At Leicester, Haynes returned after injury with immediate effect. Fred Callaghan's free kick soared down the centre of the pitch into the Leicester box; their hesitant defence allowed the ball to bounce once, and Haynes stole in front of a defender to head it past Peter Shilton from six yards with a deft flick. Allan Clarke added a second, and Leicester's late goal never really threatened Fulham. Haynes had given another man-of-the-match performance in a 2–1 win. However, this wasn't consolidated and the team lost their next two games, at home to West Ham 0–3, in a match where nothing went right for Haynes, and 0–2 at Burnley where Clarke missed a second-half penalty.

October

September was followed by three more league defeats. In the first, after going a goal down to West Bromwich Albion at the Cottage, Fulham equalised when Johnny Haynes received the ball and, from his right-wing centre, Steve Earle breasted it down to set up Allan Clarke, who scored with a fine shot from twenty yards. Tony 'Bomber' Brown pinched a winner for Albion, but Haynes was unlucky to see his last-gasp jabbed shot hit the post, and the rebound scrambled away. The game ended 1–2.

Haynes' final goal in the League Cup

Fulham then made the long trip to Fourth Division Workington in the third round of the League Cup. Fulham took the lead in the seventeenth minute with a direct Johnny Haynes free kick from twenty yards. The doughty northern side fought back to equalise and take the lead. Fulham were rescued by a Steve Earle goal which produced a 2–2 draw, but could have lost had the referee not ruled out a third for Workington in the last minute. Haynes' goal would prove to be his last in the League Cup.

Fulham had little luck in the next league game, going down 1–2 to Newcastle at St James's Park. Haynes was on particularly good form in the first half, spraying passes everywhere. The stress was relieved a little when Fulham disposed of Workington 6–2 in the League Cup replay, after at one stage being two-all.

Haynes makes it look easy, stealing into the Leicester defence and heading past Peter Shilton for Fulham's first goal in the 2–1 victory over the Foxes.

At the weekend, George Cohen was away on international duty with England, and so Haynes took over the captaincy for the home match against Manchester City. After a goalless first half, the classy northern side scored four in the rain in the second half to win 2–4. The press was quick to acknowledge Haynes' fine contribution to the match, but stressed, "He can't do it all," and urged manager Buckingham to quickly find an infusion of new blood.

The forward line was playing well, but as during the Fifties the problems appeared to be at the back. This was demonstrated perfectly when Fulham went to Highbury the following week. On a rain-sodden pitch, Fulham took the lead only to ship two loose goals. Then Jimmy Conway took Haynes' astute through pass and cleverly beat Arsenal centre half Ian Ure, before scoring with a well placed cross-shot from twelve yards.

Unfortunately, two further defensive blunders saw Fulham two goals behind again. However, ten minutes after half-time, they came right back into it with the goal of the match. Haynes scooped the ball out cleverly to Clarke, and he hit a rasping first-time volley from an almost impossibly narrow angle that beat goalkeeper Furnell. After going close to four-all, Fulham eventually lost 3–5. It was now six league defeats in a row, with Fulham occupying their customary bottom-of-the-table position at the end of the month.

Off the field

If events on the pitch were taking a downturn, at least Johnny Haynes' personal life was on an upsurge. The Queen's Elm pub in Chelsea was a wonderful, vibrant place, run by Irish novelist Sean Tracey. It was a haunt for many of the leading media, showbiz and sporting personalities of the day. Johnny Speight was always there on Saturdays and other regulars were the cartoonist JAK, actor Stanley Baker and actress Julie Christie.

Twenty-two-year-old Libby Tucker, a lady from Connecticut, had been working for the BBC in New York and had moved to London to study acting. She was introduced to Haynes by Paul Shields (chairman of Indigo Film and TV). At first she knew nothing of his footballing career, and regarded him as a typical bachelor.

Johnny was in a relationship at the time with a lady named Patsy who was from New Zealand and worked for a chauffeur business in London. Soon, though, he was calling Libby "the love of his life." A few months into their relationship, Libby acquired a flat above a bank close to the Queen's Elm, where she lived from Monday to Friday. Johnny stayed with her at the flat during the week.

Libby soon became a devoted Fulham supporter and was often accompanied to matches by Johnny Speight. She attended all the home games and some away fixtures as well. Rose, Haynes' Mum, would take her reserved seat in the Stevenage Road stand, and Libby would often watch matches from the Cottage.

When Libby was first dating Johnny, he had a regular invitation to a gentlemen's luncheon club. The hub of the gathering were Tom Wilson and Jimmy Hill. They met once a month, and among the six or eight regulars were playwrights Willis Hall and Keith Waterhouse, Michael Parkinson and the sports journalist Ian Wooldridge. Guests such as Ron Greenwood and Jackie Charlton were often invited. In those days, the lunches were held at the White Elephant restaurant, in the centre of London.

Ramsey wishes he could have turned the clock back!

November

Fulham sprang a major surprise by going through the whole month unbeaten. The team started in tremendous fashion, disposing of league leaders Manchester City 3–2 to reach the quarter-final of the League Cup.

In the league at Coventry, home winger Morrissey committed a foul, and Johnny Haynes' quick free kick found George Cohen upfield. Cohen moved the ball quickly forward to Steve Earle, and from Earle's cross, Allan Clarke positioned himself cleverly and rose superbly to head home. New signing Joe Gilroy then headed a second. Haynes was revelling in the room given, and was providing made-to-measure passes all over the pitch.

Fulham and Haynes were in dominating form, and were well worth their third goal five minutes from the end. In a glorious five-man move involving Haynes and Mark Pearson, Clarke volleyed in a magnificent goal just inside a post, giving goalkeeper Glazier no chance. The 3–0 victory was just what the doctor ordered.

The following week, Clarke scored in just fourteen seconds against Nottingham Forest. The win was consolidated in the second half when Haynes' shrewd pass found Les Barrett, and from his hard, accurate centre Clarke, again escaping his marker, veteran Bobby McKinlay, nonchalantly nodded in. The 2–0 win had been another impressive performance.

At Stoke Fulham made it three league wins in a row. It was a tough and close encounter, but in the end hard-working Fulham ground Stoke down and won the match ten minutes from time. Barrett's cross was mis-headed out; Haynes evaded Eric Skeels' tackle and prodded a shot past Banks as he advanced. It proved to be the only goal.

The media were full of praise for Haynes' quality display; many suggested—yet again!—that he was worthy of an England recall. One reflected: "How Alf Ramsey must have wished he could have turned the clock back ten years and taken Haynes back." Another excellent 1–0 victory had pulled Fulham out of the bottom two.

Haynes was pleased for the team, but cast aside claims that Fulham's new £10-a-point incentive scheme had contributed to the upturn in form. He added: "The bonuses made no difference; I put it

The Fulham programme that reported on the victory at Stoke commented that Haynes took the headlines for his inspirational display. The maestro scored the only goal of the game just ten minutes from time. He got to the ball as he was being tackled by Stoke's Skeels and prodded the ball past goalkeeper Banks.

down to tightness in the defence. We haven't conceded one in three games now. We had been going to away matches, thinking how many we would lose by. We went to Stoke wondering how many we would win by, there's the difference."

Fulham closed the month with a 1–1 draw at home in the League Cup quarter-final against Second Division Huddersfield.

December

Fulham were very unlucky not to dispose of mighty Liverpool at the Cottage early in the month. In this match, George Cohen received the injury that would ultimately end his career, and a fan ran on to the pitch to attack Les Barrett. Allan Clarke gave Fulham a lead, but prolific scorer Tony Hateley equalised for Liverpool in the last few minutes in a 1–1 draw. The form carried over into the League Cup quarter-final replay, but Fulham were unluckily edged out 1–2 after extra time.

At Wolves it was the old story, Fulham going ahead and then gifting two goals to the opposition. In the second half, a touch of England class by Johnny Haynes brought Fulham's equaliser on the hour. Haynes scooped Pearson's pass into Moss' run. Moss let the ball drop before volleying a superb equaliser into the roof of the net from eight yards. Haynes was once again singled out for praise along with the tenacious Fred Callaghan. It was a very undeserved 2–3 loss, and an exasperated Haynes said, "What do we have to do to win?"

Against Chelsea at the Cottage just before Christmas, Fulham were again two goals down in the first half, but played well to fight back for the draw. For the first, Jimmy Conway began the move, beating John Boyle and Peter Osgood before finding Haynes on the right wing. Haynes chipped the ball accurately into the centre. Young Bobby Moss came storming through, rode a tackle from Ron Harris, and buried a ferocious dipping volley over goalkeeper Bonetti that he hardly saw.

Haynes limped out of the derby four minutes from the end, after receiving another crack on his already injured shin. He had been doubtful for this match but had agreed to play considering the club's position. The 2–2 draw had been a brave performance. Haynes was equally determined to play in the next match.

At Tottenham on Boxing Day, Fulham as usual went two behind, but showed excellent resilience to come

In a break from real football, Haynes was a member of the team that took part in the TV programme Quiz Ball. The team was Chappie D'Amato (Fulham director), Haynes, Joe Gilroy and commentator Harry Carpenter. The four are pictured here with quizmaster David Vine.

Haynes concentrates, framed by Leeds keeper Gary Sprake and Joe Gilroy. The maestro could not weave his magic on the day, and Fulham lost 0–5.

back yet again. After Joe Gilroy had pulled a goal back before half-time, Fulham grabbed an equaliser in the first minute of the second half when Spurs defender Dave Mackay was penalised for a foul; from Haynes' deftly floated free kick, Mark Pearson stooped low to score with an awkward glancing header that seemed to totally baffle Spurs keeper Pat Jennings. It had been another terrific display in the cold, winter mud to earn a 2–2 draw. Haynes went down with a heavy cold shortly after the game.

In the final game of the year against Spurs at home, Haynes was clearly not himself although he still played well, helping Fulham to the impetus of a third-minute goal. In the second half he did not emerge, and Bobby Moss substituted for him. Haynes said afterwards, "My legs felt like lead." A great deal of Fulham's rhythm and class disappeared with him. One reporter said, "Without Haynes, the team looked like a collection of characters in futile search of an author!"

Fulham slumped to a 1–2 defeat following a late goal from Jimmy Robertson. It was beginning to look bleak. Despite playing fairly good football, Fulham had not won at all in the month and were not making inroads into the teams lying just above them. They were, once more, back in the relegation places.

January

Fulham's season appeared to disintegrate completely after that, and the new year opened with a 0–5 defeat at the Cottage by a sublime Leeds United side. It was the first time that Haynes' shoulders had really slumped, and he was visibly exasperated at the team's terrible display, one that Vic Buckingham described as the worst Fulham performance he had seen. At least the team had a fortnight to lick their wounds.

The home game against Leicester at the Cottage was a four-pointer, a vital relegation game. However, there were two hammer blows, inasmuch as both Haynes and leading scorer Allan Clarke were missing. George Cohen attempted a comeback, but lasted only forty-five minutes. Fulham were again very poor and Leicester weren't much better. Without their chief schemer and chief scorer, an impotent Fulham recorded a disastrous 0–1 defeat to a second-half breakaway goal.

Vic Buckingham is sacked

Following the Leicester defeat, Vic Buckingham was relieved of his duties. Haynes shed few tears over his departure; although Haynes recognised that he had tried to rebuild a new Fulham side, he had dispensed with too many players too quickly and alienated himself from senior players.

John Dempsey recalls Buckingham's treatment of Haynes near to his departure as a manager: "One game Johnny Haynes was injured for the Saturday game, and on the Friday we were having a team meeting. Haynes came into the room, and Buckingham told him he was 'dead wood' and asked him to leave, which astounded me, with Johnny being the former club captain and an England player! But that was Vic Buckingham, and that's how he worked."

The return of Bobby Robson—as manager

There were a number of names flying around for Buckingham's replacement, but the name on most people's lips was that of former player and favourite Bobby Robson, who had left Fulham just the previous May. Even the press speculated: "Is Robson the Mr X of Fulham?"

The speculation was not allowed to mount for long, and the next day the club formally announced that Robson had indeed been appointed on a three-year contract. Robson saw his task as "to save a club that has been too long on the bread line." His appointment came just eight months after he had played his final game for Fulham.

What a baptism of fire Robson had for his first game, a home third-round FA Cup tie against non-league Macclesfield Town! Fulham were like jelly for the majority of the game and were twice behind. The equaliser came courtesy of the referee from a very soft penalty.

Thankfully the pace and fitness told on Macclesfield in the end, and thirteen minutes from time Haynes snapped in a shot after a quick wall pass with Joe Gilroy on the edge of the penalty area, shooting into the bottom left-hand corner. It was the vital third in an ultimate 4–2 win. It would prove to be Haynes' last FA Cup goal at the Cottage.

Bobby Robson returns to Fulham as manager and takes a training session at the Harrods sports ground. Haynes (second left) seems determined to make a success of the new set-up.

Fulham on the rack again

February

At West Ham in the first game of the month, Fulham's limitations were cruelly exposed by a rampant Hammers side. However, Fulham took a surprise lead in the eighteenth minute against the run of play in virtually their first attack. A deflected shot by Les Barrett gave Fulham a corner. The ball was punched out by the West Ham keeper Bobby Ferguson only as far as Johnny Haynes, who turned it back first time into the penalty area, where Steve Earle pivoted neatly to guide it home. On the half hour Fulham were still one goal ahead, but in the next thirty minutes they conceded six.

Five minutes later, in a crazy match, it was Fulham's turn to score. Good scheming work by Haynes and a deft pass from Joe Gilroy provided a goal for Allan Clarke, and he scored with an excellent left-foot volley from eighteen yards that was in the net before goalkeeper Ferguson had moved. West Ham scored near the end, leaving Fulham on the receiving end of a 2–7 trouncing. Even Haynes' efforts could not ignite a side like this and many journalists commented that they had never seen Johnny Haynes so subdued; it was hardly surprising. The press said plainly of Fulham in general and Haynes specifically, "The days of miracles are almost over."

Before the next match, at home to Burnley, Fulham signed centre half Reg Matthewson from Sheffield United. Early on Fulham were again a bag of nerves, but these nerves were settled when they took the lead in the eighteenth minute. They were awarded a free kick, and Haynes floated the ball into the penalty area from outside the box, where Earle headed it neatly in just inside the left-hand post.

Fulham then performed their time-honoured trick of giving away two goals, but this time they turned the match around with three of their own. Haynes looked back to his best. Clarke equalised and then Fulham took the lead. A long shot by Jimmy Conway was deflected to Haynes via a Burnley defender. He seemed to be in an offside position, but didn't wait and scored with a brilliant effort, taking the ball around the goalkeeper and netting from the narrowest of angles.

The referee initially disallowed the goal, but the Fulham players persuaded him to talk to a linesman and after a long consultation, he awarded it. Despite a goal from Burnley in the last minute, the match resulted in a very welcome 4–3 victory.

The fourth-round FA Cup tie at Fulham against Portsmouth ended goalless and was a complete non-event, but the replay at Fratton Park was a far more fiery affair in which goal-bound shots from Clarke and Haynes were blocked. Finally, a quarter of an hour from time, goalkeeper John Milkins rose from a crowded goalmouth to tip a Haynes header on to the bar. Fulham, despite playing very well, bowed out 0–1 in front of 43,000. The twin towers of Wembley must have seemed like a distant dream.

The unlucky defeat against Second Division opposition had drained a great deal of confidence out of the Fulham side, and at the weekend they were again disappointing in a 1–2 defeat at the Hawthorns.

Haynes scores from the narrowest of angles, after rounding the Burnley goalkeeper. Fulham won a thriller 4–3 to ease their relegation fears.

Haynes stood out as the only player likely to turn the game around.

It was now looking very dark indeed for Fulham, but as usual they sprang a surprise with a midweek win against struggling Sheffield Wednesday to stop the rot. In one raid in the first half, from a chance fashioned by Brian Nichols and Clarke, Haynes' twenty-yard low drive rattled the post with goalkeeper Peter Springett well beaten. Fulham finally beat Wednesday with two goals very near the end of the game.

In a flowing move, Haynes combined with Earle, who fed Clarke with a fine pass. Clarke beat one defender and then another, finally deceiving Springett with a low left-foot shot from the edge of the eighteen-yard area into the corner of the net.

Fulham could see a chink of survival light glimmering after the 2–0 win, but they still remained bottom of the table.

March

At Southampton on a Friday evening, Fulham were again without striker Allan Clarke, and were, needless to say, the usual two goals behind, but within sixty seconds they were back in the game. Saints defender Dennis Hollywood brought down Les Barrett in the penalty area and Johnny Haynes, in Clarke's absence, deputised as penalty-taker and converted from the spot, just inside a post. As Fulham's desperation increased, Southampton began to show a few signs of nerves, but Fulham couldn't find the equaliser. The 1–2 defeat pushed them further into the mire.

A rare picture of Haynes taking a penalty. He scored with this one at Southampton, but Fulham still lost 1–2. It was the last penalty he took for the club.

Fulham and Haynes battled hard at Manchester City, but found themselves on the end of a 1–5 defeat.

During the week, in a critical encounter, Fulham lost 0–1 to relegation companions Sheffield United at the Cottage. It was a very large nail in their coffin.

On the Saturday at champions-elect Manchester City, Fulham began brightly with Haynes in particular spraying around a fine collection of passes. Then he beat City defender Kennedy and slotted the ball through the home defence. Clarke collected it, and turned centre half George Heslop, before taking the ball around keeper Ken Mulhearn, and sliding it into an empty net from a narrow angle. It was a picture goal, worthy of winning any match, and even the City supporters joined in the applause. Haynes and Jimmy Conway battled superbly all afternoon in midfield, but the team had no luck; they even had a ludicrous penalty decision awarded against them. The team were fading fast now and ended up on the receiving end of a 1–5 score.

Despite signing his old friend Johnny Byrne from Crystal Palace on the eve of the transfer deadline, manager Robson could not inspire Fulham and they lost the next home match as well, to a mediocre Arsenal on a windy day at the Cottage by 1–3.

April

Fulham started the month with an uninspiring 1–1 draw with struggling Coventry at the Cottage; they should have secured both points, but their finishing let them down. It was a game that they really needed maximum points from. On Good Friday, title-chasing Manchester United came to Fulham and showed no mercy, winning easily 0–4.

At Nottingham Forest the next day, Fulham played well and were very unlucky not to win the game, having to settle instead for a 2–2 draw. Then came the bad news that Johnny Haynes was struggling with a knee injury. The veteran Haynes couldn't recover quickly enough and missed the 0–3 defeat at Old Trafford. Fulham now looked a doomed side.

However, the tail still wagged, and at the weekend Fulham turned the form book upside down, beating an impressive Newcastle team at the Cottage. It was one-way Fulham traffic in the first half and Allan Clarke gave the home side the lead. During a spell of sustained pressure, Fulham forced numerous corners, and from one on the half-hour Haynes produced a perfect in-swinger and Clarke glanced home his and Fulham's second with his head. The 2–0 win gave them a toe-hold.

They then confounded the critics and journalists by winning again without Haynes, 3–2 at Bramall Lane, after being two goals behind with only twenty minutes left, dragging United firmly into the fire. Could Fulham pull it out of the hat yet again?

They had to travel to one of the toughest venues in the league to attempt a third consecutive victory—Liverpool. Fulham were now riddled with injuries and unable to field anything like their best side. Despite his injury, Clarke gave them the lead in the thirteenth minute with another superb goal. He took a lofted Haynes pass, beat the Liverpool offside trap, and skilfully rounded Liverpool keeper Tommy Lawrence, before guiding the ball high into the empty net. Haynes tried his best, but was rendered ineffective after taking another kick on the recurring injury. Fulham lost 1–4, and it was now virtually all over.

Fulham are finally down

May

On May Day evening against Stoke City at Craven Cottage, a patched-up Johnny Haynes played, but was pretty ineffective in a side full of the usual makeweight reserves and injured players. They were finally relegated to the Second Division following a 0–2 defeat.

In the last post-relegation home game against Southampton at the Cottage, Bobby Robson took Haynes out of the side and made him manager for the day whilst he embarked on rebuilding the team. He said: "Johnny knows the game, and what we are looking for, and it seems an ideal arrangement." Haynes also missed Fulham's last game in the First Division, a 1–5 defeat at Everton, again assuming a mentor's role, trying to piece together ideas for the following season.

Still the cry: "Haynes for England"

Even in a badly struggling side, Johnny Haynes was able to show that despite the advancing years, he was still one of the best passers, thinkers and ball players in the top division. Many journalists believed that England's midfield at the time, even with the likes of Alan Mullery, Martin Peters, Colin Bell and Alan Ball around, could still have benefited from having Haynes alongside them—a compliment indeed. This book bears witness to the number of goals that Haynes, now almost thirty-four, had continually schemed and crafted for his colleagues. The cry "Haynes for England" was still being heard, albeit faintly, in some quarters.

Haynes had spent five years propping up the Fulham side, trying to coerce top-flight performances from his dwindling band of warriors. For many years he had watched helplessly as starlets like Mullery and Rodney Marsh had been sold, whilst First Division and international class players like Jim Langley, Graham Leggat and Bobby Robson had followed; the club had also lost players of the calibre of Tony Macedo and (through injury) George Cohen. None of these stars had been adequately replaced.

Fulham had refused to bolster their paper-thin squad with the purchase of quality replacements, relying on free transfers, reserve and youth players, who were often not even of Football League quality, let alone First Division.

Although still a bright star, Haynes no longer had the guile and pace to supplement such heavy losses in personnel. It was hardly surprising that Fulham's decline mirrored that of its finally fading star. Haynes had become a prisoner of the romance he had done so much to create. Spurs allegedly tried once more in 1968 to link Haynes with the ageing Greaves, but Fulham again stepped in and blocked any possible move.

Haynes for England, or Haynes for America. The end of the season was a time of turmoil for our hero.

Off to America?

During the close season, former Manchester United and Leeds player Freddie Goodwin, now in charge of American side New York Generals, was in England to offer Haynes a contract. This time the club sportingly allowed Haynes to make his own decision whilst on holiday in Tangier.

For many reasons he ultimately turned the offer down. In true Fulham style, he said: "Sentiment shouldn't really be allowed to enter into it, but I shall probably end my career still a Fulham player. My feelings for the club will not make that a hardship."

27: Manager and a testimonial 1968–69

At the pre-season photo call, Haynes shows just how easy it is to be a photographer—but what would the club's photographer have thought about that? (But then, who took the picture?)

27: Manager and a testimonial 1968–69

Johnny Haynes felt that relegation might have done the club some good, and that it wouldn't be the first time a relegated side had emerged stronger for the experience. He maintained, "Although some of last season's results seem to contradict this, I still feel we have a strong and well-balanced side. All we need is the confidence that comes from a good start." He would start the season as skipper in the continuing absence of George Cohen.

He was about to begin his nineteenth season as a Fulham player, and was still as excited as anyone else—as enthusiastic as the young seventeen-year-olds in the juniors team. The club had also granted him a very well-earned testimonial match.

He had found it difficult later in his playing career to adjust to the new young players, who had newfound freedoms. He always thought they should earn their colours, and keep quiet until they had completely learned their trade.

He had a number of arguments with the strong-willed and petulant Allan Clarke, so much so that Clarke wrote a damning press article after he had left the club to go to Leicester. Clarke praised both George Cohen and Bobby Robson as mentors, but said of Haynes, "There was a permanent clash of temperament." He explained, "It affected younger players; he could make a mistake, but he felt no-one else should."

Clarke, an England international in his own right, wasn't going to be browbeaten: "He wasn't going to frighten me as he had some other youngsters. He would hand out embarrassing scoldings by yelling the width of the pitch. Our rows often carried on at half-time, and Vic Buckingham often had to intervene. It used to carry on all the time, and my favourite phrase was, 'It never Haynes but it pours.' Haynes not only refused to suffer fools gladly, but also declined to suffer the human mistakes of any player very gladly. We were soon bristling at each other when the pressures on the field—and believe me there were always plenty—brought us to the test."

However, Clarke also paid tribute to Haynes' commitment: "Haynes used to get tensed up before a match and so did I. Perhaps if there had been eleven like us in the Fulham team, we wouldn't have struggled so much every season." Even the genial Irishman Jimmy Conway was forced to admit, "Johnny was a very nice man, but he was very, very difficult to play with."

One very sad event at the start of the season didn't put Haynes in the best of spirits. Manager Robson hadn't confined his changes to the playing squad, and one major departure was that of coach Arthur Stevens. Stevens had been at Fulham even longer than Haynes, as a player since 1947 and coach and friend since retiring in 1959. For Haynes, this severed another link—virtually the last—with his past.

August

Bristol City were the first visitors of the season. Fulham scored their opening goal of the season early on, a goal carved out of sheer persistence rather than much else. New signing Frank Large found Jimmy Conway on the wing. Conway passed the ball inside allowing Johnny Haynes, faced with a phalanx of defenders, to squeeze in a pass-cum-shot that rebounded in the goalmouth; from the ensuing scramble Joe Gilroy deflected the ball home from close range. Haynes was standing out like a colossus with his quality distribution and unlimited energy, and was soon the target for some rough tackling.

Robson finally withdrew the bruised Haynes from the fray with fifteen minutes to go. Despite his age, Haynes had looked the only class player on view, an opinion not lost on the media when they commented on the 1–0 win.

At Aston Villa, Haynes was again on superb form, working at a frantic pace, prising open the Villa defence at will and putting in a colossal amount of effort. After one three-man move, he put in a cross that left three Fulham forwards with an open goal; none of them could convert, and Haynes hung his head as he saw his good work being frittered away. He then received a crack on the ankle that lessened his grip on the game. The 1–1 draw was the least the Cottagers had deserved. After a boring 0–0 at home to Hull City in which Haynes had again sparkled, Fulham entertained Bolton.

The evergreen Haynes worked prodigiously putting the skids under Bolton every time he received the ball. However, things didn't go to plan and despite having most of the play, Fulham slumped to their first defeat, 0–2. The press said, "The result was so tough on Haynes, again looking the best player on the pitch by a country mile."

Off to Brighton or Queens Park Rangers?

There had been further rumours within footballing circles that Haynes would leave Fulham imminently. Following the summer transfer talk with Freddie Goodwin, Fulham announced that Brighton and Hove Albion had made a bid for him that the club had allowed him to consider. Thankfully, Haynes turned down the opportunity once more.

That should have been the end of the turmoil, but there was a further cheeky bid for Haynes' services, this time from Bill Dodgin at the helm of recently promoted Queens Park Rangers. Rangers had made a woeful, struggling start in the First Division and certainly could have used Haynes' craft and experience.

This time, however, Fulham turned down the approach from their west London rivals immediately, without referring the offer to Haynes. Robson said, "He's essential to my plans, we certainly wouldn't want to lose him." Following the Bolton match, the media agreed, stating, "Fulham would be the biggest fools in football if they parted with Johnny Haynes."

Haynes' 600th game for Fulham

Late in the month at Bramall Lane another milestone was passed when Haynes took the field against Sheffield United for his 600th game for the club. The team didn't play badly, but Haynes looked very subdued on the night. Fulham drooped to a 0–1 defeat, and most agreed that it had been a fairly inauspicious way for Johnny to mark the occasion.

Matters came to a head at Millwall at the weekend when Fulham conceded two comical goals to lose this London derby. They never recovered from those mistakes, and even Haynes mockingly applauded the second Millwall goal.

The match was proving heartbreaking for Haynes, the oldest player on the pitch but still looking the best. He went through his entire range of gestures and looks at the malaise going on around him. He was forced to play defender, midfield player and forward almost on his own. He was trying to "plug more holes than you would find in a leaky roof." The 0–2 defeat meant that it was already five games without a win.

September

At newly promoted Oxford United, Johnny Haynes again dominated the midfield, and ran himself into the ground. He was peppering the Oxford goal with shots, but was finding ex-Chelsea goalkeeper Jim Barron in magnificent form, saving everything the maestro could throw at him.

After losing a goal in the second minute, Fulham did everything but score, the forwards having no luck. Including the League Cup defeat at Orient, it was now six games without a goal. Only Haynes, yet again, came out of the match with top honours, and the press were frank: "This master of soccer science is too good for the rest of the team."

Haynes had talked, at the beginning of the season, about the importance of a good start. Fulham had hit rock bottom with this 0–1 defeat, and this was exactly what he *didn't* want. At this stage, a dreary Fulham did not look capable of staying in the Second Division, let alone making a quick return to the First.

Some pressure was alleviated on the following Friday evening with Malcolm Macdonald's first Fulham goal in the 1–0 win over Crystal Palace, but the team returned once more to their shot-shy ways at high-flying Derby in midweek and were again edged out 0–1. At the weekend, Haynes showed improved form at Blackpool where the weather and pitch conditions proved ideal for his repertoire of crisp and precise passing. Two Jimmy Conway goals gave Fulham a well-earned point in a 2–2 draw.

Against Blackburn Rovers at the Cottage, Haynes had a hand in the goal six minutes after half-time

Haynes watches Malcolm Macdonald score against Crystal Palace—Fulham's first goal in 660 minutes. The 1–0 win relieved some pressure from captain Haynes.

when Macdonald scored. Frank Large picked up a poor throw from Blackburn keeper Blacklaw and fed Haynes. Haynes drove the ball into the penalty area immediately, where it found Macdonald. The young forward cleverly controlled the ball, swivelled round and crashed it into the net in virtually one movement. It was a point gained in a 1–1 draw, and Fulham had squeezed themselves out of the bottom two.

October

However, fortunes did not improve for Johnny Haynes or the club in the month with Fulham picking up just one point in three games from Birmingham 4–5, Sheffield

Determined action from Haynes in the 1–1 draw at home to Blackburn Rovers.

United in midweek 2–2 and Norwich City 1–3. Haynes missed the first of these through a niggling injury, but press mentions of him were few and far between in the other two matches, and with only one win in thirteen league games manager Bobby Robson decided that changes were needed.

Robson rests Haynes

At Middlesbrough, Robson gambled and made the decision to drop Johnny Haynes and make Reg Matthewson team captain. Haynes played for the reserves instead, and scored in a 4–1 win over Chelsea. The change had little effect on the fortunes of the first team, who put in another poor performance in a 0–2 defeat.

The press seized upon Haynes' absence, and it was inferred that there had been a difference of opinion between manager Robson and the former England skipper. Haynes did return the following Saturday in a desperately poor goalless draw with Bury, when the club programme appeared to be backing Robson's resolve to experiment with the available resources in any way he saw fit. It said: "He cannot afford to let sentiment, or his personal regard for a player's ability to stand in his way." By the end of the month Fulham had slipped to bottom of the table.

November

Robson stuck to his guns the following week against Portsmouth at Craven Cottage and once again decided to omit Johnny Haynes, this time in order to accommodate new boy and striker Vic Halom. It seemed to work and Fulham put in an improved performance in a 2–2 draw.

This move finally caused a clash between Robson and Fulham's most recently appointed director Eric Miller. Bobby Robson had been thinking that this Fulham team needed a more direct approach in the Second Division, and had to get the ball into the penalty area more quickly.

He also thought that everything was still flowing through Haynes in the centre of the field and the short passing was not bringing results. He honestly believed that Haynes was now past his best and, at thirty-four, should be 'rested' for a while, a nicer word than 'dropped'.

"Fresh faces and a new approach" was Robson's policy. Miller was angry and appalled, calling the idea madness. It put the two on an inevitable collision course. After Robson rejected further suggestions from Miller over the signing of new players, the end was in sight.

Bowing to the pressure, Robson recalled Haynes in the disappointing 0–2 defeat at Carlisle where Fulham lost to two set-pieces. Miller had flown to Carlisle in his private jet. After the match, Haynes did not return with the defeated team but accompanied Miller by air.

Bobby Robson was crudely sacked during the following week. Although he was managing his long-term friend, Robson said later, "He [Haynes] wasn't difficult to manage, and there was definitely no falling out. If I left him out of the side, he would have accepted it. He definitely didn't want me to be sacked."

Haynes the caretaker Fulham manager

The major surprise was that the board, after dismissing Robson, turned to Haynes and asked him to take over. Haynes was stunned by the request, but after considering it overnight, he agreed to take over the role of *caretaker* player/manager on his own terms—a strict understanding that Fulham continue to search for a full-time manager whilst he was in post. The Fulham directors agreed to this.

A sombre Haynes spoke to a number of journalists, and said: "I have accepted the job on the understanding that they [Fulham] will carry on looking for a permanent manager. I felt I owed it to the club to help out. I would not do this for anyone else but Fulham. ... I don't see why we are bottom of the division, but we are, and we have to get out of it. ... I shall pick the team tomorrow—all I can tell you about it is that I will be

The new manager gets down to work.

Player/manager Haynes leaves the field after an inspiring display at home to Huddersfield that saw Fulham achieve a 4–3 victory—the club's first win in over two months.

playing. Maybe if things work out well I'll be tempted to stay on as a manager—but that's not definite. If things go badly, I certainly won't be tempted. The only reason I'm in the position is that Bob has gone, and there's no one else.

"It is well known that management has never really appealed to me, but Fulham are in trouble, and after nearly twenty years here, I should try to do something to help. Bobby's dismissal shows what a perilous business this side of the game can be. You live on results and the players are on their own once they are out on the field. This is why I have never even considered becoming a manager before."

When Haynes accepted the post of manager, an interesting statistic arose, inasmuch as the golden inside forward Fulham trio of the Fifties—Bobby Robson, Bedford Jezzard and Johnny Haynes—had now *all* managed the club. Haynes' first match in charge was the home fixture against Huddersfield Town, and one of his first moves was to appoint Fred Callaghan as temporary captain. He was also quick to bring in Bill Dodgin, junior, as coach, after he had resigned from the turmoil at Loftus Road.

Fulham gave away a simple goal early on, but this time they came back well. Eight minutes later they were level, when from Haynes' crossfield pass, Johnny Byrne gained possession and neatly sidestepped Terriers centre half Roy Ellam before putting in a tight cross-shot from a narrow angle, and the ball found the net just inside a post. Haynes was spraying passes in all directions, and his work rate was described as magnificent.

From yet another superb slide-rule Haynes pass, Fulham took the lead just three minutes before half-time. Jimmy Conway shot Fulham ahead with a fifteen-yard low cross-shot from the corner of the penalty area that gave Huddersfield goalkeeper Terry Poole no chance. Huddersfield levelled again, but Halom edged Fulham in front once more. Then Fulham made it four.

This time Haynes' beautifully flighted free kick was knocked down, and Cliff Jones, unmarked but looking offside, beat the advancing keeper from six yards. Despite a late Huddersfield goal, Fulham held on for the win. Haynes had crafted three of the goals in a 4–3 victory. It was Fulham's first win in over two months.

Understandably, Haynes' role was seized on by the press, who enthused: "Rarely has he played so well. Certainly he cannot have covered so much ground, expended so much sweat in inspiring his side as he did yesterday." Another report said, "He tackled their troubles with a real thirst for a fight. Haynes was magnificent, shouting and urging, directing and cajoling, chasing and tackling—yes, he really tackled!"

Haynes said afterwards: "This is very tiring work, and harder than one thinks. I haven't even had time for a drink yet because I've had to get out four teams this week." He finished on a cautionary note: "I wasn't conscious of my role as player/manager, but I hope the board find a new manager—soon."

Forty-eight hours later, Fulham picked up another point in a goalless draw with Preston at Deepdale, where Haynes had a fierce shot blocked on the goal line. In poor playing conditions it was a good point to win.

Haynes said afterwards: "I was well pleased with our showing tonight, an away point is always welcome … and in fact we did enough to win. … I thought we played better than on Saturday against Huddersfield, we were tighter at the back, and didn't give much away. Our general pattern of play showed that we have the spirit and style still."

Fred Callaghan recalls the match with a smile: "We had got a draw, a good result at Preston, and as skipper he said to me, 'Take all the lads out for a drink.' Anyway we were all leaving without him, when he came running up and said, 'Hang on, you've left me out.' I said, 'But you're the manager now!' but he said, 'I'm with you.' Even though he'd been England captain, he was always just one of the lads."

The match set things up well for the London derby against high-flying Charlton at the Valley at the weekend. It proved a disaster. Fulham unluckily went three goals behind, one a disputed penalty and one a wicked deflection. Fulham pulled one back when Haynes took a free kick and the ball found its way to Terry Parmenter; his shot was deflected and found Vic Halom, who squeezed the ball in just inside a post.

Fulham could never quite get back within striking distance and eventually went down 3–5. Poor refereeing by the colourful Roger Kirkpatrick had contributed to the defeat. Haynes displayed the first signs of stress as he picked arguments with the official throughout the game, and was lectured twice for refusing to accept his haphazard decisions.

The following week Haynes played his reported 600th game (this was based on a count of just league and FA Cup matches, which excluded League Cup ties). Haynes said, "I don't keep count."

He again confirmed that he didn't see himself as manager and before the Cardiff game he said: "There is one certain thing—as long as I have the job, I will spare no effort to get the club out of trouble. I care too much about Fulham to make a half-hearted approach to the problem. … Looking at the problems from a manager's chair gives you an entirely different view, but I haven't changed my opinion that we have the players and the morale to do the job."

December

Despite the rhetoric, Fulham went down 1–5 to a vibrant Cardiff City side at Craven Cottage, and this time Haynes' form was dragged down. Chairman Trinder had been booed and catcalled throughout the match, and afterwards the directors held a lengthy crisis meeting. Johnny Haynes and Bill Dodgin were both in attendance to discuss the playing situation. The post mortem went on late into the night.

Club secretary Graham Hortop insisted that the gathering had been nothing more than a routine board meeting but Trinder admitted that a great deal of time had been spent discussing the day's performance. Haynes left before some of the others and snapped at waiting reporters: "I am saying nothing." Dodgin left over an hour later.

Johnny Haynes resigns!

The Cardiff capitulation proved to be enough for Haynes, who this time had failed to inspire as player/manager, and his own form had been seriously affected. He mulled over his position on the Sunday and immediately sought out the board on the Monday and stated his wish to stand down from the post, recommending them to appoint Bill Dodgin as manager on a full-time basis. Haynes' tenure as caretaker player/manager had lasted a mere four matches and seventeen days. His father, Eddie, had been seriously ill following a heart attack earlier in the year, which had added to the overall burden.

"John was never manager material," said Bobby Robson. "He didn't like the office work, the paperwork and really even the coaching!" His girlfriend Libby agreed: "He wasn't comfortable with the position. He just wanted to be a player and a team-mate. He didn't have future aspirations of managing." Haynes later in life concurred, "I didn't like it. I valued my health too much. I saw what it did to other people."

Bill Dodgin appointed manager

The club agreed with Haynes' recommendation, and Dodgin became Fulham's fourth manager in only eleven months. Dodgin initially agreed to take the position on a match-by-match basis. Ironically, Bill Dodgin had wanted Haynes as a player at Queens Park Rangers just two months earlier; now he was managing Haynes at Fulham.

At Norwich on a frozen pitch, Haynes was scheming well on the difficult surface, but again nothing went right for the Cottagers. Mike Pentecost broke a leg and Norwich's second goal came from a needless penalty. Haynes was frustrated at the goings-on that day, and finally earned himself a booking for continually arguing with the refereeing decisions. It was, however, another defeat, 0–2.

The next week was just as depressing—a 0–3 defeat by Middlesbrough. At least George Cohen provided some uplift as he returned to the fray, though he didn't look fully right.

Nevertheless, over Christmas Fulham received one present with a 2–0 win over Birmingham City. After Fred Callaghan had given Fulham the lead, Haynes assisted in the second. A defender in the penalty area blocked his initial shot near goal, but Halom swooped upon the rebound to thump the ball emphatically in from ten yards.

The end-of-year match away at struggling Bury was already billed as a four-pointer. Fulham's cause wasn't helped when Vic Halom headed an own goal in the first half. Then Haynes was injured in a tackle. He did not appear for the second half, being replaced by a half-fit Johnny Byrne. Without him the side fell to pieces and conceded four second-half goals in a 1–5 pasting. At the end of the year, Fulham for the second successive season looked like a team without hope.

Over to you! Haynes is relieved to hand over the managerial reins to Bill Dodgin, junior. If nothing else the change enabled him to get his maracas out and spend a rattling good time (below) with colleagues at a supporters' club function. Pictured are Les Barrett, John Dempsey, Haynes, Johnny Byrne, Jimmy Conway and Fred Callaghan.

A final FA Cup cameo and goal

January

Johnny Haynes, half fit at best, managed to put his injury to one side to play in the prestigious third-round FA Cup tie at First Division Sunderland. Fulham were stricken by injuries and illness. It looked as if it would be the usual story when Bobby Kerr put Sunderland ahead after just seven minutes. Amazingly, Fulham completely turned the tables, and two minutes later young Irishman Brendan Mullen equalised. Then Haynes stepped in.

He picked up a misdirected pass from Sunderland's Ian Porterfield and whipped the ball straight down the middle of the field for Mullen to score with a firm shot on the run. Then Sunderland goalkeeper Montgomery made a hash of an awkward right-wing cross that was flighted just underneath the crossbar. He palmed the ball out, and Haynes calmly slotted the rebound in.

Before half-time it was four. Fred Callaghan took a free kick; Haynes worked the ball cleverly on to hero Mullen, who in turn astutely squared the ball for Stan Brown to ram joyfully home. Fulham only had to play out the second half to record the shock third-round result of the afternoon in a 4–1 rout.

Haynes looked rejuvenated and appeared to be in England form. The headlines exclaimed, "Fulham you're fabulous—and Haynes, you're great." After the game he said, "Nobody marked me! They must have thought I couldn't play any more. I had the freedom of the park—it was just like my heyday!" It would be the last goal Haynes would ever score in the FA Cup.

There was no doubt that he had played a blinder and merited all the headlines the following day. On the Monday he said: "We didn't expect to win; it just wasn't on the cards. We came hoping for a replay, but the boys showed that we have the ability to do much

This early goal from Haynes at Portsmouth was the highlight of the match for the visitors, which they eventually lost 1–3. It proved to be his only league goal of the season.

better in the league now. … Sunderland were far too stereotyped, we took them easily in the end."

Fulham had a fortnight to build on this success, but 'normal' service in the league was quickly resumed. It looked encouraging at Portsmouth when Fulham took the lead with an early goal hammered in by Haynes, after a clever three-man move involving Mullen and Les Barrett, but that was as good as it got. Fulham were again poor defensively in a 1–3 defeat—and the effort would prove to be Haynes' only league goal of the season.

With that Sunderland victory, he must have thought that despite Fulham's league form there might be some progress in the cup. At a packed Cottage against the Cup holders, First Division West Bromwich Albion, he once again proved his class.

After Albion had taken the lead through Asa Hartford, Haynes plotted the equaliser. A short corner reached Haynes, and from his clever in-swinging cross, the ball soared out of goalkeeper John Osborne's reach and led to a superb headed effort from the diminutive Stan Brown that flew into the top right-hand corner of the net.

The nearest Fulham came to taking the lead was a snap shot from Haynes from close in that Osborne threw up his hands instinctively to save; in the ensuing scramble, the ball was hacked away. Haynes then had another chance, but unluckily hit a post. Finally Fulham were right out of luck when Tony Brown headed Haynes' in-swinging corner off the line.

Just when it looked as if Fulham could pull off yet another big surprise, Albion substitute Rees secured his side's passage into the next round with a late winner. Fulham had been desperately unlucky in the 1–2 defeat, but Haynes now knew that with Fulham in this lowly position he would never play at Wembley in an FA Cup final.

Haynes walks off

February

Against Carlisle at the Cottage, Fulham gave one of their worst displays for years and were inevitably trailing, when Bill Dodgin, exasperated by events on the pitch, called on a substitute midway through the half. Dodgin had wanted Malcolm Macdonald to be replaced by Jimmy Conway, but Johnny Haynes suddenly walked off the pitch with a shrug of the shoulders and disappeared into the tunnel, leaving the bemused Dodgin to continue without his midfield general and having to continue with the ineffective Macdonald.

The official club statement was that "Haynes had taken a bad knock and would have had to have come off anyway. Therefore it had been inappropriate to substitute anyone else, as his knee might have 'gone' completely."

The truth was that Haynes was totally fed up with the whole episode, and since every member of the team was playing so badly, and *anyone* could have gone off, he decided to take the decision himself and go! Fulham eventually lost 0–2.

It was also Macdonald's last game for the club, and for a long time he was a bitter man. He knew he had been raw and incredibly naïve about the game, but he felt that Haynes had never seen beyond his boyish arrogance and enthusiasm. In the last two games that

Haynes scores for the reserves against Southampton, during his period of 'rest' from first-team action.

he played for the club Macdonald was stranded on the left wing. He only had about three touches during the Carlisle game; Haynes wouldn't even pass the ball to him.

Later in life Macdonald said: "I still think he said and did some rotten things to me, but I reacted to them and they helped me to become a better player. So I've got to say, thank you, Mr Haynes, for being a bastard to me."

Little was seen of Haynes in the 0–1 home defeat by Charlton, but he came to life in the midweek home victory over Preston North End. He took a clever free kick, the Preston defence failed to clear the crossed ball, and it was edged across to Barry Lloyd who prodded in the winner from seven yards. The brace were Lloyd's first goals for the club, and his first in league football. Haynes had given the team a tiny glimmer of hope in a 2–1 win.

George Cohen retires

March

This awful season came to a head in a 0–6 debacle at Ashton Gate where Fulham lost to Bristol City. The ageing Fulham team were run off their feet by a young athletic City side and they had no answers. George Cohen finally admitted defeat after failing to overcome a knee injury for over a year, and retired from the game.

Haynes 'rested' for the remainder of the season

After this massacre, and with the miasma of relegation beginning to descend once more on the Cottage, Bill Dodgin made the brave decision to omit the former England captain Haynes from the doomed side for the remainder of the season. There may have been an injury involved, but Dodgin and Haynes were close friends; it was more likely that Dodgin had decided to start rebuilding Fulham for the future, and to spare his mate any more agonising matches like the Bristol debacle.

April

To retain fitness levels, Johnny Haynes still continued to turn out sporadically for the reserves and scored a couple of goals. In the last game of the season whilst the Fulham first team were capitulating at Selhurst Park, he played and scored in a 1–1 draw for the Fulham reserve team against Luton reserves at Kenilworth Road in front of over 1,500 spectators, double the normal attendance. Despite a couple of wins against promotion-chasing Millwall and Cardiff City, the sorry Fulham side did indeed suffer a second successive relegation.

Haynes' future was definitely in doubt, and even before the season had closed it was widely rumoured that QPR were ready to snap up the former England star on a free transfer to spearhead their return to the First Division following their disastrous relegation after a single season in the top flight.

Haynes' testimonials

A number of events were held in Johnny Haynes' testimonial year. Initially, way back in September, there had been a boxing dinner organised by Len Mancini. The profits for the night were presented to him by Walter Winterbottom. The evening was attended by numerous football stars from London clubs present and past, and Jimmy Hill and Walter Winterbottom gave speeches. There was also a dance at Hammersmith town hall in March, with tickets priced at 7/6d (37½ pence). This was followed by a civic lunch on the 18th of the month. A personal tribute was given by the Mayor of Fulham.

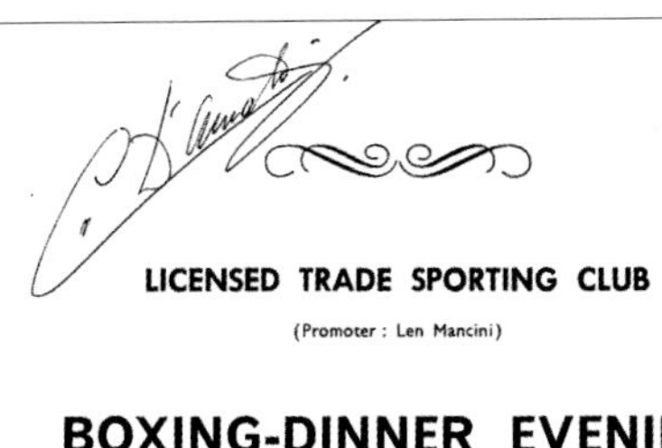

LICENSED TRADE SPORTING CLUB

(Promoter : Len Mancini)

BOXING-DINNER EVENING

IN AID OF

JOHNNY HAYNES
TESTIMONIAL FUND

(BOXING DIVISION)

CONNAUGHT ROOMS

MONDAY, 16th SEPTEMBER, 1968

Menu

Haynes was a great fan of the fight game and boxing evenings featured during his testimonial year.

A boxing night with friends and stars, including Johnny Byrne (standing third left), Dave Underwood (fourth left), Reg Weller (seventh left), George Cohen (ninth left); and Johnny Speight (seated left) and Dave Metchick (seated second right).

OFFICIAL PROGRAMME 1/- APRIL 28th 1969

20 seasons

JOHNNY HAYNES SOUVENIR

Fulham Past v Present (7 p.m.)

Johnny Haynes' XI v
Bobby Moore's XI (8 p.m.)

Fulham F.C.'s Ground
Craven Cottage

The testimonial match at Craven Cottage showed just how much Haynes was revered by Fulham fans, and almost 25,000 attended the memorable evening.

Chairman Tommy Trinder presents Haynes with his gold watch in recognition of his many years of service to Fulham.

Alf Ramsey and Walter Winterbottom were amongst the guests. Libby recalls the time: "It was all great fun and there were loads of darts matches!"

The Big Match

On Monday, April 28th, and for one night only, all the misery and depression of Fulham's second successive relegation was forgotten, as Craven Cottage rocked to the carnival atmosphere of Johnny Haynes' testimonial match. A crowd of nearly 25,000 packed into the Cottage for this momentous evening. Apart from their cup-tie against West Bromwich, it was Fulham's highest attendance of the season. A special club programme was produced in black and white.

Many tributes were made to the maestro—Johnny the Greatest, the Magician, and the Miracle Worker. The club conceded that the decline in their own status had probably coincided with the inevitable decline in Haynes' career.

Describing Haynes as the man who took over England when the country's national sport was at its lowest ebb following defeats by Hungary, the club stated: "It was the Haynes-led team which gave England back its self-respect and more. This was the foundation on which others were fortunate to be able to build. He can be proud of that, and we are proud of him.

"Here is a man respected and envied by his fellow professionals, club mates and opponents both. Their view of him is the ultimate in compliments—we mortals can only stand in awe."

Libby remembers the evening well: "The stands were packed and we looked forward to the game, but it was beyond our expectations. When Johnny ran on to the field, the crowd started chanting 'King, King, King.' I believe he was really chuffed!"

The heavyweight bout of the evening was an All-London Big Match between Johnny Haynes' XI and Bobby Moore's XI. The game produced a 7–4 result with, naturally, a goal for Haynes; the opposition did not try too hard to prevent him scoring.

Libby was glad it was Moore in 'opposition': "It seemed natural to see Bobby Moore, as we had been out with him socially. We went to several events with Bobby and his first wife Tina. They had a great mutual respect for each other. There was a great deal of showmanship in the game and the crowd loved Johnny!"

The Football League's president Len Shipman presents Haynes with a statuette to mark twenty years' service to football and to Fulham.

The testimonial match raised £11,000. Johnny used a significant proportion of it to invest in the Tommy Benfield bookmaking business.

After the game Tommy Trinder said sadly, "Could we have foreseen George Cohen getting injured? Could we help Johnny Haynes getting old?" Caught up in the excitement of the night, an emotional Trinder presented Haynes with a gold watch from Aspreys that the club had asked him to pick out for himself, and said: "Johnny Haynes is Fulham's finest ever player. … I hate to think my crystal ball will let me down, and I predict that Johnny Haynes will be the highest paid player in the Third Division. … I have told Johnny I want him to stay, and now it is up to him."

Haynes, although flattered, had always said that he would retire rather than play for the reserves and replied: "I cannot decide anything without a couple of days to think the matter over." Thankfully, just a few days later, he re-signed for Fulham for a further year. General manager Graham Hortop said, "We are *very* pleased he is stopping with us … Johnny feels he has at least two more seasons of league football left in him."

At FA headquarters, Haynes was given a statuette by the Football League president Len Shipman to celebrate his twenty years at Craven Cottage, and for services to the English game in general and Fulham Football Club in particular.

BY APPOINTMENT

FULHAM FOOTBALL CLUB

sole supplier of Johnny Haynes
to football
for 19 years

—and proud of it!

Summary

Haynes had worked exceptionally hard up until the Christmas period to keep the ailing Fulham side afloat, but time appeared to be catching up with even this great man. From January onwards, he became more of a peripheral figure and he seemed to have admitted defeat by February. It was no great surprise when Bill Dodgin withdrew him from the failing team. For the first time in his career, Haynes failed to register a single goal at Craven Cottage all season.

Off the field

Girlfriend Libby now spent most weekends with John at his Epsom home. After Saturday nights with the team members, there were often charity matches on the Sunday. Johnny still persisted with his golf and Libby was happy to caddy. Showing the skills that would later lead to her own interior design business, Libby redecorated the Epsom home.

Johnny was still a slave to mum's home cooking, with a particular penchant for the lemon meringue pies, and whatever event was occurring on the Sunday, Rose would always have lunch waiting.

Johnny Haynes and Libby spent much of the next two summers in Majorca, where they met up with Tommy Benfield and rented a flat by the water. After a bitterly disappointing season, Haynes could at least relax. He did, and said: "This is the good life." However, even on holiday he satisfied his own demanding urge to stay fit. Libby recalls: "Even there, every morning on waking he would go for a one-hour run. He needed to keep fit. On his return he liked his breakfast ready, two fried eggs and tomatoes on toast. He ate well, but never between meals!"

28: Twenty and off
1969–70

28: Twenty and off
1969–70

The annual cricket match with Putney Cricket Club went ahead as usual, with the proceeds going towards Johnny Haynes' testimonial fund. Haynes was the star of the Fulham show, and demonstrated how he could have just as easily become a professional cricketer. Putney batted first and declared at 169–9. Fulham's response was 122 all out. Haynes was the top-scorer for Fulham with a bristling thirty-seven that included five fours.

Haynes' 20th season at Fulham

As he prepared to start his twentieth season with the club, Haynes said, "It should be easier in Division Three!" The Craven Cottage ground looked a picture, and Haynes remarked, "The pitch is as good now as it has ever been in my time." It would be the first time in his career that he would take part in Third Division football. He had chosen, however, not to continue as captain, and the captaincy was given to midfielder Stan Horne, signed the previous season.

August

Against Bradford City on the opening day, there was a keenly contested 0–0 draw. Vic Halom and Johnny Haynes linked well, with the veteran spraying his usual pinpoint passes. Stan Horne and Haynes worked cleverly in midfield. Halom created an opening for Haynes in the first minute and he was unlucky with a twenty-yard shot. In the 3–1 League Cup replay victory over Orient, he limped off with a thigh injury, and when Barry Lloyd came on as substitute it turned the match. Maybe it was a sign of things to come.

However, Haynes returned against Gillingham, and the team showed plenty of class, taking the lead in the twenty-second minute. Horne picked up a throw-in and fed Jimmy Conway, who made a clever dart down the right wing; from his centre, Haynes controlled the ball with his right foot and shot low into the net with his left, all in one movement, scoring his first goal of the season.

After Gillingham had equalised, Haynes kept his side roaring for the winner with keen tackling and shooting. Fulham won 2–1—their first league win of the season—and the reporters were still impressed. One said: "Johnny Haynes, veteran of twenty seasons, showed his vintage best for Fulham in the first half with a production-belt service of passes." Another noted: "It was a cool attractive display of football, with Haynes master-minding the attack as in the good old days!"

Four days later against Southport at the Cottage, it took Fulham just thirteen minutes to take the lead. Haynes supplied the slide-rule pass and Conway collected the ball and hit a left-foot shot wide of Southport's Scottish goalkeeper John Armstrong. Fulham netted a second, but slack defending allowed the visitors a goal back. This forced the home side to up the tempo, and their pressure was rewarded when, with only three minutes to go, Stan Brown leapt high to head home their third from Haynes' pass and Conway's final cross. Fulham won 3–2 but it had not been easy.

Haynes shows his class in his final League Cup game

September

First Division champions Leeds United, an almost unbeatable team, came to the Cottage for a second-round League Cup encounter. Jack Charlton scored the only goal to win the match, but it was a close-run thing. In the second half, Johnny Haynes was beginning to find his colleagues with accurate passes, and the Leeds team were looking stretched for the first time. They were supposed to have one of the best defences, but some of Haynes' passes cut them to pieces. It was his last League Cup game for Fulham.

World Cup winner Jack Charlton, never one to hand out cheap compliments, said: "Fulham were twice as good a team as when we last played them in the First Division. Their work rate was much higher and I am still trying to think why all their moves were not better rewarded. Johnny Haynes is surely the best player ever seen in the Third Division. It is not only his class, but the fact that he is prepared to make the effort too."

Elated by their good performance, Fulham made an enterprising start against Shrewsbury at the weekend,

Still Haynesey after all these years! Above, he appeals with Stan Brown during the match against Gillingham. Below, frustration in the League Cup match against Leeds United, which was lost 0–1 and proved to be his last-ever League Cup match.

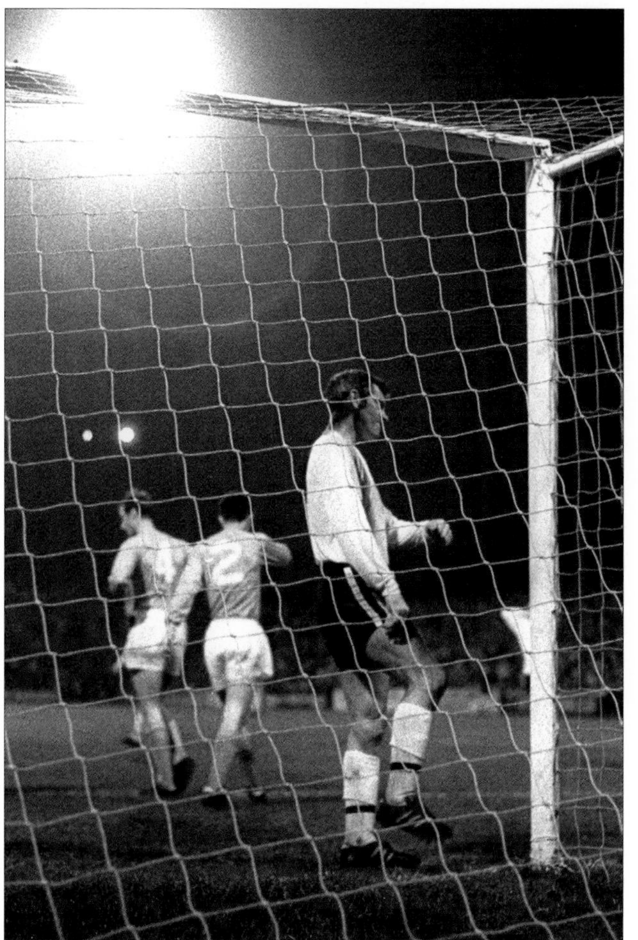

and were twice unlucky not to go ahead in the opening minutes, the first occasion being when Cliff Jones headed fractionally wide from a Haynes free kick. Fulham finally made the breakthrough ten minutes before half-time when Haynes, waltzing through defenders, was brought down unnecessarily in the penalty box by Shrewsbury full back Tony Loska. The resultant penalty kick was converted as usual by Jimmy Conway. Haynes hit a post late in the game. In the boiling sunshine he ran himself into the ground and was clearly exhausted when replaced with a few minutes left. Fulham's 3–1 victory continued their good home form.

It wasn't so good the next week, when Haynes was the victim of a stomach bug, along with many others in the side. He played in the 2–3 defeat against Bristol Rovers at Eastville but was clearly not himself and was withdrawn at half-time.

The team and Haynes, however, made a fantastic recovery and just three days later travelled up to the Shay at Halifax to post a record 8–0 away win. As usual Haynes didn't score in the big win, and judging from the reports he didn't create any goals either. Perhaps this was a night when he didn't need to try too hard. Steve Earle registered five goals on this particular evening, putting himself firmly in the record books. Stan Horne and Haynes revelled in the midfield spaces, and Fulham could afford the luxury of substituting Haynes again with the job comprehensively done.

The final Haynes goal at the Cottage

Buoyed by the success against Halifax Town, Fulham set about Plymouth Argyle. They were behind to a crazy own goal, but fortunately didn't take long to equalise when Haynes' pass found Jimmy Conway, whose accurate centre found Barry Lloyd, and he shot Fulham level from close in. Then, before half-time, they were ahead.

In the second half, it took just eight minutes for Fulham to extend their lead. A move ended with the ball bobbing about in the Plymouth penalty area; it was only half-cleared to Haynes, standing outside the box, and he thundered in a beautiful low half-volley before the despairing goalkeeper, Pat Dunne, could move. In a super game Fulham won 4–3. It was the last competitive goal Haynes would score at the Cottage. Fittingly, this final goal was the 100th that he had scored at his little ground beside the Thames. It was a perfect way to reach his century.

Fulham's storming form continued at Stockport, and they were quickly in front. Earle was fouled on the fringe of the penalty area, and Haynes touched in a beautiful swerving free kick that was met by the striker, whose spectacular glancing header gave goalkeeper Alan Ogley no chance. Quickly it was two. Haynes, Fred Callaghan and Les Barrett caused a catalogue of defensive errors in the Stockport goalmouth, which allowed Conway to run in from the right and score

Opposite: Haynes salutes the Fulham fans following his fine strike for one of the goals in the 4–3 victory over Plymouth Argyle. It was the last-ever competitive goal that he scored at the Cottage. Above: From the edge of the penalty area Haynes hits a powerful shot to score Fulham's goal in the 1–2 defeat at Brighton. It was his last goal for the club.

easily from an acute angle between the goalkeeper and the post. Conway, Earle and Haynes were playing as if Fulham were competing against First Division defences. At this stage of the season, they were totally unstoppable. The eventual 4–1 away win meant that the Haynes-inspired Fulham had rattled in sixteen goals in just three league games.

The month ended on a disappointing note with a 1–3 defeat at promotion rivals Orient. Things looked bright early on, and Fulham took a swift lead. The goal was a carbon copy of the first at Stockport. Haynes swept an accurate free kick from the touchline on to the head of Earle, who darted in front of the Orient defenders and glanced a beautiful header into the roof of the net. Orient to their credit played well and came back with three decent goals of their own. Haynes did however take another knock and his ageing frame was finding it difficult to run off such knocks in matches, and for the fifth time in six games he was substituted.

October

Although he continued to create a few chances, little was seen of Haynes in the month; maybe the injuries were beginning to tell. He did come alive in the last match of the month against Barnsley at Craven Cottage. He forced the visitors' keeper, Brian Arblaster, into a full-length save. He was then just wide again with a volley following a neat headed pass from Barry Lloyd, and just on half-time, his third effort of the half, following yet another pass from Lloyd, was just inches over the bar. He was at his vintage best, showing his shot-shy colleagues how to do it.

His last-ever Fulham goal, away at Brighton

November

Early in the month Fulham visited Brighton and broke away to take the lead in the nineteenth minute. They produced a crisp left-wing move from Les Barrett, and from his centre Barry Lloyd touched a short pass across to Johnny Haynes. Positioned at the edge of the box, Haynes balanced himself beautifully and hammered the ball in. He then took a nasty crack on the ankle, and his influence on the match waned. Fulham eventually lost 1–2, and this would prove to be the last first-team goal ever scored by Haynes for Fulham Football Club.

Haynes had recently celebrated his thirty-fifth birthday, but remarked, "We don't talk about those things!" There were numerous press reports, including the club programme, that the goal scored by Haynes equalled Bedford Jezzard's record of 156 goals for Fulham. In most statistical publications, Jezzard's scoring record is reported as standing at 154 goals for Fulham.

But the Haynes count was inaccurate, and most publications credit the Brighton strike as being his 157th goal. Therefore, Haynes had beaten Jezzard's record with his first goal of the season against Gillingham, and plainly held the current record by at least three clear goals. Whatever the rights and wrongs, Haynes said at the time, "I'm entitled to equal the record, I've been here long enough!"

He received another cameo award when he was nominated as the Third Division's sportsman of the month for his attitude to some rough tackling up at Halifax, when the home side were 0–8 down. Gillette sponsored the award and Haynes received a superb executive briefcase.

The following week at home to Torquay, Haynes gave early intent with a stinger that Torquay goalkeeper Andy Donnelly brilliantly turned round the post. Fulham were not on top form and found themselves a goal down. Despite constant pressure in the second half it looked as if it would all end in tears, but finally, from Fulham's twelfth corner of the half, and just four

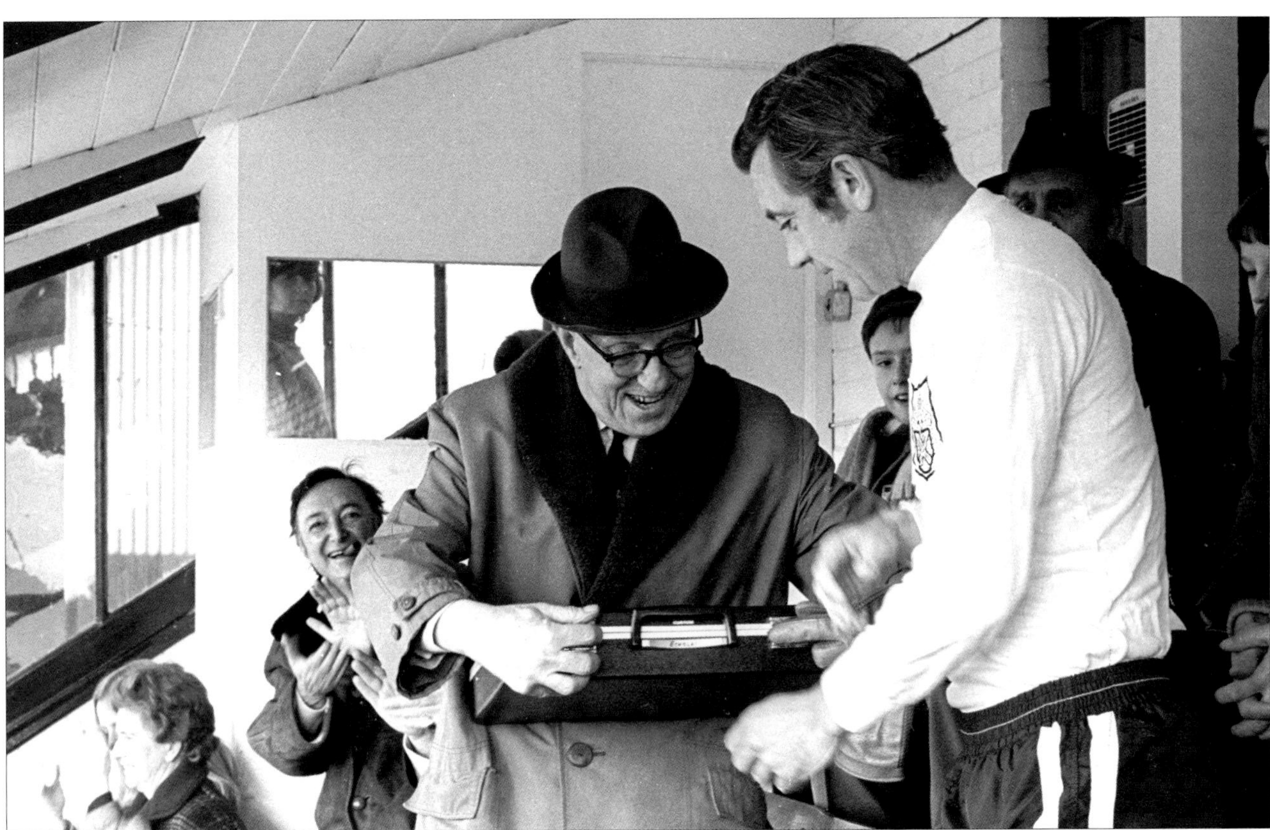

Another award, another presentation. Director Chappie D'Amato does the honours for Haynes' achievement of being the Third Division's sportsman of the month.

minutes from time, Steve Earle rose to rocket an in-swinging Haynes corner into the roof of the net with his head, and a point was saved.

His final FA Cup match

Haynes took part in George Cohen's testimonial, playing for the International XI during the week. Fulham then travelled down to Fourth Division Exeter City to compete in the FA Cup first round. Even at this stage of his career it was a first for Haynes, as he had never before competed in the cup at such an early stage.

He still had the enthusiasm, without any doubt. He worked like a Trojan to keep Fulham in it, but it wasn't their day, and a missed penalty by Jimmy Conway and a fortuitous Exeter goal contributed to their 0–2 defeat. It was Haynes' last FA Cup match, and what a way to go out—ignominiously, on a muddy Fourth Division ground, in front of a sparse crowd of under 10,000!

Three games later, at an icy Rochdale, Haynes 'scored' reputedly one of the best goals of his career six minutes into the second half, a stunning thirty-yard shot into the top corner to restore Fulham's lead. Unfortunately, the Rochdale match was abandoned at 2–2 and the goal was erased, thus never making the statistics or the record books.

December

Haynes played impressively in a Fulham side, now struggling a little after a promising start, that beat Bristol Rovers 3–1. He was described as the master architect feeding the forward line impeccably. It was Fulham's first win in eleven league matches. His form carried over into the match at Gay Meadow the following week against Shrewsbury. Stan Horne touched a ball forward, Haynes floated over a tempting cross and Earle then headed a fine 'goal' but was disappointed to see the effort chalked off for a marginal offside decision. Shrewsbury took an undeserved lead, but the advantage lasted less than a minute; Haynes speared through a pass into the Shrews defence and Earle, on the edge of the area, lunged in for the ball and managed to slot it past the advancing keeper.

Shrewsbury manager Harry Gregg, who had seen plenty of Haynes earlier in his career as a goalkeeper with Doncaster Rovers, Manchester United and internationally with Eire, paid tribute to Fulham, and in particular Haynes, saying, "Fulham are a good footballing side, and Johnny is as skilful as he ever was. Haynes makes the ball do the work; he's a master, as good now as he was in his international days."

The final goal crafted

In the last match of the year against Barrow, Fulham took the lead as early as the seventh minute when John Richardson climbed high to meet a Haynes free kick and put a soaring header into the net. It was the last goal Haynes crafted for his little Fulham team, and he was beginning to look tired.

Fulham ended the year in fourteenth position, ominously near the foot of the table with their meagre points tally, and they were also beset by severe financial difficulties. They were still weighed down by having a number of players tied to First Division contracts, eight of the current senior squad having been with the club in the First Division. The only way the wage bill could be reduced (if a wage drop was not voluntarily accepted), was to offer a player a free transfer instead. Johnny Haynes, as loyal to his beloved club as ever, offered to accept a reduction in his wages if it helped the club's plight.

On a bleak and grey afternoon, a few Fulham diehards witness a 1–1 draw against lowly Stockport County. The match was instantly forgettable, remaining only in the memory as the final game in a Fulham shirt for the maestro, pictured here watching another wasted effort in a dire match.

His last first-team game

January

Against Stockport it was an old pals' reunion. Johnny Haynes' old friend and former England international colleague Peter Broadbent was playing against Fulham, and at the age of thirty-seven also occupying the number ten shirt. Haynes looked rejuvenated and two fine shots from him were superbly blocked by goalkeeper Ogley and finally cleared. Eventually Haynes' influence waned, and he was the victim of a heavy tackle from a Stockport forward. Frustration got the better of him and he reacted with a petulant verbal and physical response to the offending player. He was badly injured by the tackle, but somehow played on and remained on the pitch to the very end. An appalling game of football finished 1–1.

It was terrible to watch Haynes limp from the field with a thigh injury at the end of this farce with a chorus of boos directed at the Fulham team ringing in his ears. The master signed off in front of a small, huddled crowd of 7,000 under a grey, wintry sky, after seeing an untalented bunch of Stockport hoofers bustle their way to a most dismal draw.

It had been about as far away as you could get from the 30,000-plus crowds of the club's heyday. The match had been a mile away from the silken skills and delicate passing that Haynes would have wanted to see. One thing was for certain: the Third Division would never see a player like him again.

The match would remain in the memory for just one reason only, that it proved to be the final game in a Fulham first-team shirt for the maestro, the last of 658 glorious games. Until then Haynes, even at his age, had been miraculously ever-present in the team that season, with thirty-one appearances.

The dwindling band of Craven Cottage faithful who had watched Haynes attempt to shore up a team struggling in the lower reaches of the Third Division might have been hard put to remember those starry peaks of a few years earlier. At this time Fulham were occupying their lowest position for years, just a few points and places off the bottom four in the old Third Division.

February to April

However, a phoenix arose from these ashes, and without Haynes a younger Fulham side, led by Barry Lloyd, was about to embark on an unbeaten fifteen league match run that would take them from this perilous position to the brink of promotion.

It was ironic to think that Fulham's form and unbeaten run had begun when Haynes was out of the side through injury. After sustaining yet another injury to his ankle whilst testing out his injured thigh muscle for the reserves, he was eventually fit enough to return to league action.

He had seen a top specialist about his ankle, and had come away feeling significantly more optimistic about regaining his place. By this time, however, Fulham were on a roll and Bill Dodgin was unable to change a winning side that was playing so well—not even to accommodate the maestro. Haynes understood.

His final competitive Fulham game

The last sad event for Haynes took place in early April, when he stepped on to the Cottage turf for a competitive game for the final time. Playing in a Fulham reserve side that included Ian Seymour, John

Fraser, John Gilchrist, Wilf Tranter, Dave Roberts and Stan Horne, Haynes, at number ten naturally, took part in a 2–1 victory against Norwich City reserves in the Football Combination. Tranter scored both goals. At least the great man stepped off the Cottage pitch for the last time a winner, in this, his final competitive Fulham game.

Even at this late stage, he was his normal proactive and happy self, and right up to the last few weeks was involved in every way with the day-to-day running of the club's activities.

He had been asked during the close season how long he thought he had left at almost thirty-six. He replied: "Three to four years probably, as long as I can keep fit; I am a good trainer, I always have been. I still last the pace well and training is vital. When I can no longer do it, like Billy Wright, I'll pack up. I've always said I enjoy playing, well … perhaps I don't enjoy it as much as I used to, because as I said, it's getting harder and it takes more out of me now, but I still *do* enjoy it—you must do to be in the game at all." The estimate proved to be pretty accurate!

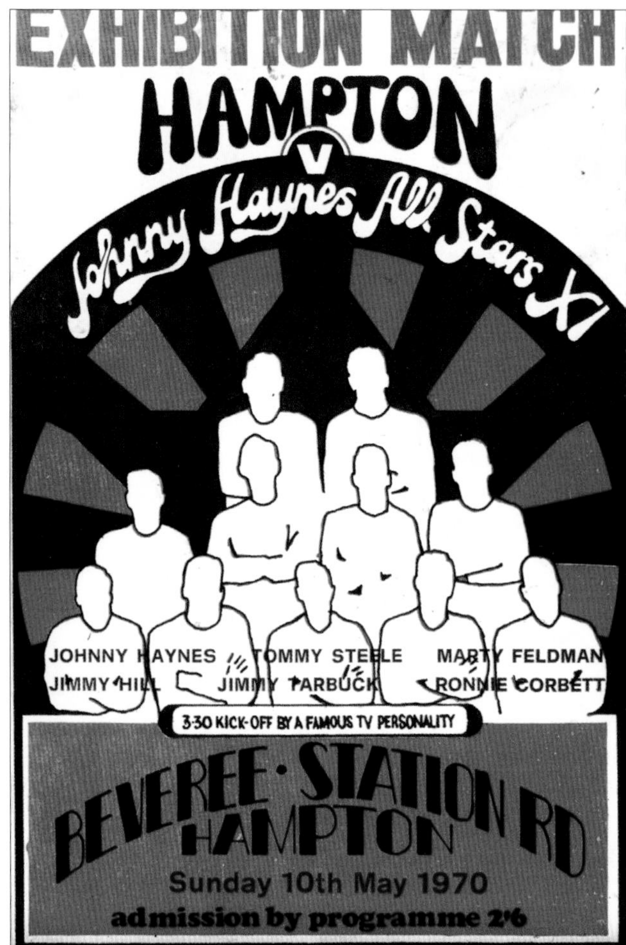

Haynes turned out for charity and exhibition matches many times throughout his career.

Off to South Africa

In the summer of 1970, and in recognition of his loyalty and commitment, Fulham gave Johnny Haynes a free transfer. He had decided to hang up his playing boots and call it a day in British football. His decision ended a magnificent twenty-year relationship and involvement with Fulham Football Club.

He had privately admitted that he had become increasingly disenchanted right at the end with trends at the club and its dramatic drop in status, saying that it had been hard to keep interested. It was widely expected that Fulham's elder statesman would go into business in this country, so it was somewhat of a surprise when he elected to go to South Africa and continue his playing career with Durban City, following in the playing footsteps of his friend Johnny Byrne, and taking note of the views of his friend Bedford Jezzard who admired the country.

Any disappointments he had harboured about his last couple of playing years had vanished by the time the move to Durban had been finalised. He said: "I never had any regrets about staying at Fulham for nearly twenty years. They were a great club and very good to me. But there came a time when I knew that I would have to move when my playing days in the Football League were over. I received a couple of offers, but the best came from Durban City, so I decided to take it.

"I will play for them until the end of their season in October and then I shall be coming home again. If things go well, and I like it out there, it will be up to me whether I go back next March for the new season.

"I've only been to South Africa once before, on holiday. But I have been told that it is a great place to live, and playing for Durban will give me the chance to meet up with my old Fulham friends 'Budgie' Byrne, Tony Macedo and Bobby Keetch. This is really a test period; if I like it, I could go back."

An approach from the then aspiring Southern League club Wimbledon is the only other documented bid for Haynes' services. In early August 1970, Wimbledon manager Les Henley talked terms with him, offering a contract that would make him the highest-paid player in the competition. Henley stated afterwards that he was "confident that the former Fulham star would be joining the club." However, the move never materialised. Many were dumbfounded that an English league club had not come in for him. He was still only thirty-

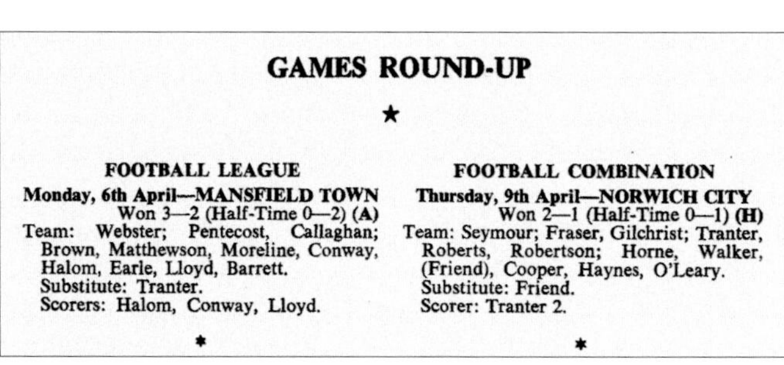

GAMES ROUND-UP

★

FOOTBALL LEAGUE

Monday, 6th April—MANSFIELD TOWN
Won 3—2 (Half-Time 0—2) (A)
Team: Webster; Pentecost, Callaghan; Brown, Matthewson, Moreline, Conway, Halom, Earle, Lloyd, Barrett.
Substitute: Tranter.
Scorers: Halom, Conway, Lloyd.

*

FOOTBALL COMBINATION

Thursday, 9th April—NORWICH CITY
Won 2—1 (Half-Time 0—1) (H)
Team: Seymour; Fraser, Gilchrist; Tranter, Roberts, Robertson; Horne, Walker, (Friend), Cooper, Haynes, O'Leary.
Substitute: Friend.
Scorer: Tranter 2.

*

The final mention of Haynes in the club programme, recording his appearance in a reserve match against Norwich City.

HAYNES
John Norman

5195.

Date of Birth	Where Born	National Registration No.
17/10/34	Town: St. Pancras County: London	

Club	Season	Signed From	Signed To	Remarks	Benefits and Acc. Share Date	£
Fulham	52/3	6.5.52	30.6.53			
do	53/54	1.7.53	30.6.54			
do	54/55	1.7.54	30.6.55			
do	55/56	1.7.55	30.6.56			
do	56/57	1.7.56	30.6.57			
do	[illegible]	[illegible]	[illegible]			
do	58/59	1.7.58	30.6.59	Ben	26.6.59	750
do	59/60	1.7.59	30.6.60			
do	60/61	1.7.60	30.6.61			
do	61/62	1.7.61	30.6.62			
do	62/63	1.7.62	30.6.63			
do	63/64	1.7.63	30.6.64	Ben	5.6.64	1000
do	64/65	1.7.64	30.6.65			
do	65/66/67	1.7.65	30.6.67			
do	67/68	11.11.67	30.6.68			
do	69/70	1.7.69	30.6.70			

Haynes' Football Association record as a professional. A one-club man. Note on the right the two long-service bonuses.

five, and skilful players such as Stanley Matthews had continued to play at a high level for much longer than him.

Many in the game considered that a fit Haynes, who still trained like a teenager, would have been an invaluable asset to another British club, but there were perhaps worries over his influence and personality. It certainly seemed a tragedy that the final chapter of his magnificent career would ultimately be played out in a foreign country.

Haynes left England having never won a major honour, apart from his England caps. He never won a league championship medal, and never qualified to play in Europe. He never played in the FA Cup final, or the League Cup final and he was never voted Footballer of the Year, although he was twice in the top three. The only medals and trophies he ever won with Fulham were those *Evening Standard* five-a-side championships way back in the Fifties.

He had been in preliminary negotiations with Durban as early as March 1970, and by April the South African club were fairly confident that a deal could be struck and that Fulham would release him for the English close season or, more optimistically, would allow him to come to South Africa permanently.

There was initially some criticism that a player of his stature should contemplate going to South Africa. He was accused of wanting a big final payday, and grabbing the cash whilst he could. There was a lot of ill feeling at the time because of apartheid, his move coming as it did hot on the heels of Basil D'Oliveira's exclusion from the England cricket squad to tour South Africa.

Bobby Robson said: "I was amazed and couldn't believe he went to South Africa. It wasn't really a footballing country at the time, there wasn't a big league and it had no big stadiums or clubs, it must have been for the sun and the playboy lifestyle."

So, early in August 1970, twenty years almost to the day after walking into Fulham as a fresh-faced schoolboy, Johnny Haynes left England for South Africa. For Libby it was a difficult time. He left on his own, leaving her in Britain whilst she continued to work.

Even after Johnny had left the country, his mother Rose continued to support Fulham and occupy her customary seat in the Stevenage Road stand.

Haynes had spread his wings at last, and left behind his beloved club and family. One of his first duties as soon as he was settled was to contact the young Fulham team back home, who were going so well in Division Three, and to tell them he was okay and that he would return to England after the season in South Africa was over. After all this time, he was still happy that the new Fulham foundation he had laid was now showing some signs of success, and he was delighted that the club was now fighting its way back up the league towards its rightful position.

Although a new post-Haynes age was about to dawn at Fulham, the club wrote *nothing* about Haynes' departure in the official club programme—perhaps they were trying to make a clean break, and make it all less painful. However, chairman Tommy Trinder, his personal friend, made many references to the maestro in the new season's handbook.

As much of a Fulham landmark as Craven Cottage itself

Tommy Trinder was truly sad at the loss of an old friend. He was pretty lost himself and genuinely found it difficult to come to terms with not having Haynes around the place after twenty years. He confessed that Johnny Haynes was as much of a Fulham landmark as Craven Cottage itself. He paid tribute to his total professionalism.

He said that in the end it was all about loyalty. "It is my belief, as well as my hope, that this is going to be quite a season, but whatever happens it is going to be strange not having Johnny Haynes around.

"In all football there was never a better example of loyalty. He had so many offers to move—and we knew all about them because he would come and tell us about them. But after we had talked them out and we had explained how much we needed him, he always stayed. To give just one example of what this meant, going back about ten years, he could have collected £15,000 for joining AC Milan. How grateful we are, all

Season 69–70, a last team picture for Johnny Haynes (seated second left) at Craven Cottage. In front at left is Barry Lloyd, who captained the team to promotion the following season.

of us. When you think of how many of his fifty odd caps were collected whilst he was in the Second Division, it makes you wonder what those players are moaning about when they insist on a move just because their team has gone down.

"I gather Johnny will be going into business soon [written before Haynes' decision to go to South Africa]. If he is half as good in that field as he was with us, he'll finish up a tycoon! He will always be welcome at Fulham and we are sure his mother will be taking her usual seat in Craven Cottage. She is more than Johnny's mother—she is a Fulham fan."

Ironically, in the first season following his departure, the new young Fulham team back home finally turned the corner after a number of years in decline, and secured promotion back to Division Two under the guidance of Barry Lloyd.

Although there was never a suggestion that Barry Lloyd was as good a player as Johnny Haynes, it was almost as if the Fulham clock had turned the full circle. Here was a young midfielder and former England youth international, slight of build, with a through pass and a cannonball shot when he chose to use it, also wearing the number ten shirt and captaining the team at the tender age of twenty-one.

It was the dawn of a new era, which Lloyd acknowledged. After the promotion-winning campaign he said: "His [Haynes'] presence tended to inhibit younger players. His absence has forced youngsters like Steve Earle, Jimmy Conway and Les Barrett to take on more responsibility, and they have become star players in their own right."

But George Cohen summed it up perfectly: "Do you know, I sincerely believe that the players I played with throughout my career were genuinely proud to think they had a player like Johnny Haynes in their side. It gave them a little status of their own. You could be proud of the fact that you were playing with someone who was bloody unique!"

29: Haynes' South Africa career

JOHNNY HAYNES - Durban City

S.A. SOCCER APRIL/MAY, 1971 Page 4

29: Haynes' South Africa career

Haynes went to Durban City on what was initially a three-month contract. Johnny Byrne, always known as 'Budgie' because of his loquacious nature, felt that Haynes would be a big draw in this part of the world, and made a great sales pitch for him.

Byrne went public in the *Natal Mercury*, stating: "He has everything; his ball distribution is without question the best in the world and that is no exaggeration, he has two good feet and his work rate is high. Obviously he is slower than when he last played for England in 1962, but he is the brainy type of player with almost uncanny positional sense."

Haynes' close friend Bobby Keetch, always up for an adventure and tiring of English football, was also in South Africa and was a significant catalyst in bringing Haynes over. Keetch had been financially enticed and was enjoying life there to the full, and he no doubt had a number of conversations with Haynes about it.

Johnny Byrne had joined Durban City as a player immediately after ending his football career with Fulham in April 1969, and he persuaded the astute club chairman, Norman Elliott, to go for the former Fulham skipper.

Durban City – season 1970

Haynes' arrival in South Africa on 5th August 1970 to play for Durban City had been meticulously planned. His new chairman, a man renowned for exploiting players, made sure that the maestro's introduction to the Durban football scene would never be forgotten.

Haynes recalls: "I flew into Louis Botha airport on a Tuesday morning and Elliott, immediately wanting his 'pound of flesh' from me, decided that I was to be in City's line-up against Arcadia Shepherds that night. Despite the long flight and the Durban heat, I managed to last about an hour. That was my introduction to football in South Africa!" Durban won 3–1.

Elliott, dubbed the 'Silver Fox' because of the grey hair that he had for most of his adult life, had astute business acumen; he had been the founder of Durban City FC and in early 1959 played a major role in the establishment of the semi-professional National Football League (NFL), following a breakaway from the amateur code. Durban City were playing in the NFL, which was a traditional white league, although the year following Haynes' arrival, a league for black players, the NPSL, was formed.

Elliott was one of the province's most colourful sporting personalities and his fame spread throughout the land. Whilst City were being hailed as one of the most exciting NFL clubs, he also involved himself in other sports. He trained boxers at amateur and professional level, thrived in the atmosphere of the 'sport of kings', where his pride and joy was his racehorse named "Up the City", and even relished the thrill of another type of racetrack—hot rods. He was a successful driver and at one stage was the South African Formula Two champion.

The Durban-born businessman had begun importing British football players as early as 1962, but the arrival of 'Budgie' Byrne from Fulham midway through the 1969 season coincided with City's weakest attack since 1962. All the men responsible for the club's sixty-five goals the previous year had left.

As often happened, the departures followed disputes over cash, and three players had walked out, followed by a fourth, Derek Smethurst, who took the opposite direction to Johnny Haynes, arriving in London SW6 to sign for Chelsea. Interestingly, Smethurst played and scored for Chelsea at Craven Cottage in their 2–0 victory in Stan Brown's testimonial match just a couple of months later.

Although Johnny Byrne was officially only a player at the club at first, he took a big interest in its future and helped Elliott secure the services of a number of new players that season. Scottish winger Joe Fascione (ex-Chelsea), midfielder Ron Bolton (ex-Bournemouth) and goalkeeper Tony Macedo (ex-Colchester United) all jetted into the tropical city.

Macedo was, of course, a veteran of 346 league games for Fulham, and was determined to prove himself in his new country despite being hampered by injury during the latter stages of his career. Flamboyant outside-right Greg Farrell (ex-Bury) also signed on, but there were no prizes for Durban City in that 1969 season. Therefore the chairman, who was accustomed to success on the field of play, decided with the help of Johnny Byrne to bring the great Johnny Haynes into his fold.

Haynes recalls: "It was as a direct result of 'Budgie' Byrne that I ended up in South Africa. He contacted me to say that Durban was a great place to be and that I should consider a move. At the age of nearly thirty-six, I literally began a second football career in a foreign country. Initially that took some motivation but when I discovered that Durban City had a great team spirit and that I knew many of the lads from my playing days at Fulham, it felt as though I was back in London."

He played at the New Kingsmead stadium in Durban. Matches were usually played at 3pm on a Sunday afternoon. Durban United and Addington both shared Durban City's ground, which led to some lively local derbies.

Haynes was part of an all-white team, and the referee and linesmen were also white. Although coloured supporters were allowed to watch the matches, they were segregated and each had their own enclosure inside the stadium. Black players could not play with white players.

Haynes was not a political animal, and said at the time: "It's strange really, you hear about it more over here [UK] than you do over there. There are a lot of

Indians in Durban and they account for about a third of our gate." Of the racially segregated teams he said, "Things are changing over there though; it's getting better all the time, even if it is slowly."

The playing standard was about that of the English Third Division, the level Haynes had just left at Fulham. Most matches were fairly easy, except when playing against the top five or six clubs. Cape Town pitches were good, as they had lots of rain, but other pitches toward the north of the country were very hard, and Haynes had to play with rubber studs. All in all, with three sponsored cup competitions he would play in about forty matches a season in South Africa, roughly as many as he would have played in this country.

As he didn't have to work, he augmented the football training by playing golf and squash every day. He still liked training and was only seven pounds over his ideal fighting weight at the height of his powers a decade previously.

A number of his local playing colleagues were not full-time professionals and they trained four evenings a week, most of them having a day job as the wages were lower than those in the English Football League. Haynes lived comfortably in an attractive beach-side apartment. He said later, "I was better off than most and spent my free time playing golf and swimming in the ocean."

Haynes wore the blue and white hooped shirts of Durban. If he had joined QPR in 1969, he could have worn the hoops then. However, unlike QPR, Durban played in blue shorts and blue socks. The club was managed by Martin Deetlifs and he was assisted by Harry Weir, who became a close friend of Haynes and subsequently went to live in retirement in Torquay.

How about that! A league championship medal at last

When Haynes donned the club's famous blue and white hoops for the first time, the team were well on their way to capturing the British Petroleum (BP) sponsored league championship for 1970. With only a handful of games left, there was no real pressure on him, but he integrated into the side immediately, laying on some superb passes for strikers Ronnie Mann and Jim Scott to score. After his debut match, Haynes played his first full game for Durban against Powerlines on August 9th, the game ending in a 1–1 draw.

Deetlifs said of Haynes a couple of weeks after his arrival: "This is our first opportunity to welcome Johnny Haynes officially. In the few games he has played, and on the training pitch, he has shown us what a first-class player he is. There is no doubt that when he settles in and when the other players get to understand him better, he can only be a tremendous asset to us, and a terrific boost to us at this stage of the season, in the position we are in to win the league title."

City clinched the title for the third time in their history, their closest rivals throwing away countless careless points at a critical stage. The South African season ran from February to October, because during the intervening months it was too hot to play. At the awards ceremony, City's new star received his first football medal with great happiness.

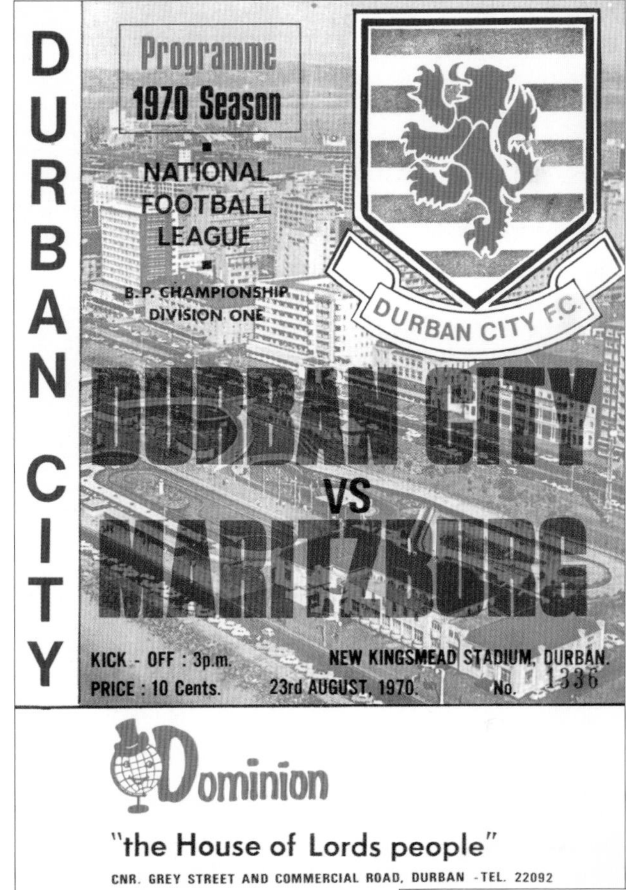

TODAY'S TEAMS

DURBAN CITY (Red, Blue & White)	vs	MARITZBURG (Maroon & White)
MACEDO	1	WILKINSON
MAULLIN	2	PRICE
LOUGH	3	JEFFREY
KEETCH	4	SMIT
FORSYTH	5	JAMES
FASCIONE	6	VARNER
COOKE	7	GREENE
FARRELL	8	DAVIDSON
SCOTT	9	EXALL
BYRNE	10	CHALMERS
HAYNES	11	GEILS

REFEREE: Mr. W. Gultig (Tvl.)
LINESMEN: Messrs. J. McCarney and H. Parker.
KICK–OFF: 3.00 p.m.

In his first season in South Africa, Haynes plays for Durban City against Maritzburg. He lines up alongside former Fulham favourites Macedo, Keetch and Byrne.

Haynes wasted no time in contacting Fulham to inform them that his Durban City side had won the South African League. He quipped, "How about that—a medal at last!" He was delighted at Fulham's progress during the 1970–71 season and hoped to return and see the boys soon.

The National Bowl was a competition sponsored by the United Tobacco Company (UTC) which featured the league's top six clubs. The competition came after City's league campaign, which had finished on September 29th. A portion of the sponsors' money was also set aside each year, either to bring a leading UK football personality to the country or to send South Africans abroad.

For example, in 1972 Alan Hardaker, secretary of the English Football League, would visit the country on a goodwill mission. Prior to this, Alan Wade (the

English FA's director of coaching), Denis Follows (secretary) and referee Jim Finney were also entertained.

A first cup competition victory

On the evening of 24th October 1970, a week after his thirty-sixth birthday, Haynes ran on to Durban's New Kingsmead pitch to face Southern Suburbs in the Life Bowl final; it was the National Bowl trophy, called the Life Bowl that year because Life Cigarettes had put their name on the tournament.

Little did he realise at the time that this was going to be one of the greatest series in the history of South African professional football. As the neatly kitted-out City side surged forward against their comparatively inexperienced opponents, the atmosphere inside the ground matched the electric storms exploding overhead. Prior to kick-off, the referee had received death threats which were ignored. Local Indians were involved and there may have been a recent 'history' between the two clubs.

Triple winners Durban City pose proudly with their trophies. The goalkeeper half hidden by the gap in the picture is Tony Macedo. Other ex-Fulham players are Bobby Keetch (two away on Macedo's left), skipper Haynes (seated third from left) and, on his left, Johnny Byrne.

The Suburbs underdogs fought for every ball, and with Haynes' team just two minutes away from victory an awful mix-up between keeper Tony Macedo and one of his own defenders let in Ernie Phythian. The former Wrexham and Hartlepool striker converted to make the score 2–2, to force extra time and ultimately a replay.

The most celebrated football immigrant to hit the shores of sunny South Africa dragged himself off the field, drenched and disappointed. He had tried his best but the luck had not been on his side. In the Johannesburg replay a week later, the same 2–2 score prevailed after extra time, which meant that the two sides returned to the coast for one final attempt to determine who would take home the 6,000 SA rand prize and the trophy.

At last, after 330 minutes of pulsating soccer and fourteen goals, Haynes had something to celebrate when City finally won the third game 4–2. It had taken all the professional knowledge gained over years on English football fields for Elliott's team, consisting of nine UK men, to triumph over Suburbs, who had in their team six Johannesburg boys, of whom three had never been near a First Division park until that year. A total of sixty thousand fans had witnessed the three games which brought the curtain down on the maestro's first few months of his African soccer adventure.

Haynes returned to England with his trophies in November 1970, and he was at Craven Cottage, bronzed, fit and looking decidedly prosperous, to watch Fulham's first-round FA Cup tie against Bristol Rovers. Unfortunately they failed to put on a show, sliding out of the competition 1–2.

Back in Durban, Elliott was in seventh heaven as he celebrated his club's first league win in nine years. The Bowl victory was City's fifth since 1961 and the outspoken chairman expressed great satisfaction with the magnificent team effort. With Farrell's scintillating runs down the right wing, 'Budgie' and Haynes' brilliant moves in the middle, and former Leyton Orient player Jim Scott's opportunist finishing (he scored an amazing forty-three times), Durban City were back to their best. At the back, Macedo, who conceded just twenty-eight league goals in as many games, was voted Foreign Footballer of the Year. Defender Dave Forsyth (ex-Leyton Orient) had also kept things tight at the back.

Haynes returned to South Africa at the beginning of January 1971 to prepare for the new season, and he actually considered looking for a job during the month to help keep him fully occupied. Byrne, who had scored eighteen times in his first full season, was appointed player/manager shortly afterwards, and one of his first tasks was to hand the captain's armband to his friend Haynes. Byrne reduced his playing commitments and took a closer interest in managing and in the behind-the-scenes activities at the club.

Before the next league campaign, Durban City kicked off their 1971 season with a 'champion of champions' clash against Castle Cup winners Cape Town City on January 29th. This tournament usually pitted the League, Bowl and Cup winners against each other, but this year Bowl finalists Southern Suburbs were included, as Durban had won two out of the three trophies.

Durban City now treble winners

There was great disappointment when Durban City lost their opening match 1–3 in Durban to Cape Town City and there was further disappointment when they were subsequently held to a 1–1 draw by Suburbs up in the 'highveld' city of Johannesburg (highveld meaning the high-altitude Transvaal province, now Gauteng).

However, skipper Haynes rallied his troops for the next two games, and on February 9th he scored his first goal for the club in a 4–0 home drubbing of Southern Suburbs. Three days later, following a great 3–1 win against Frank Lord's Cape Town City, the new Durban City captain was again in a party mood as his side were crowned champion of champions (on goal aggregate) for only the second time in their history. Durban City had now won a 'treble'!

Libby moves to South Africa

Although John was in South Africa, Libby was still spending most weekends at Epsom with his parents, Rose and Eddie, and they were still a family. Libby and Johnny continued a long-distance relationship, frequently exchanging letters, and Johnny would phone home every Sunday night, speaking first to his parents and then to Libby.

Johnny asked Libby to come out to South Africa. Libby recalls: "When he asked me to join him, I called my boss in New York and asked for a three months' leave of absence. He countered with an offer of a huge promotion. He said he needed me there, in London, and I would have to decide between my job and my romance. I went to Durban."

It was a difficult decision for Libby because she had been working in London for almost five years, and apart from the career side, she was very happy living there. In South Africa she continued to work, and started a job with Elizabeth Arden at the large department store Stuttafords. She quickly became friends with the Byrne and Keetch families, and Johnny and she rented a flat from Norman Elliott.

Durban City – season 1971

Just seventeen days after Durban City's treble success Haynes and his team-mates were back in Cape Town, this time to face ex-Newcastle, Arsenal and Stoke player George Eastham's high-octane Hellenic side in their opening league encounter; and what a shock it was for the champions that Friday night at the Green Point Stadium!

Cape Town was the only place in South Africa where matches were played on a Friday evening. It had been a tradition since the team had joined the league in the early Sixties. That evening Hellenic stunned the whole of the South African soccer fraternity by dishing out Durban City's biggest-ever defeat as they scored six goals without reply.

There was a deadly hush over Durban on the morning of February 27th, as if a huge bomb had landed in the middle of the town and stunned everyone into silence. When the news hit the city, the immediate reaction was that Tony Macedo, the rock of Gibraltar, had not kept goal.

Many thought the score was a misprint and that it was impossible for the best goalkeeper in the country to have failed so badly. However, the 'Silver Fox' was fully aware of the battering his team had suffered. It was with great courage and magnanimity that he had stood up to applaud Eastham and his magnificent side as they left the pitch.

Haynes' team enjoyed fanatical support from Durban's Asian community, and when the club found themselves in the doldrums, their charismatic owner would take some of the squad to visit a local witch doctor. Joe Fascione said: "Norman Elliott took me, Bobby Keetch, 'Budgie' Byrne and Johnny Haynes over to some Indian witch doctor in some village somewhere because we were not winning. He was going to change our luck and as it happened it did—we started winning games after that!"

Other muti rituals involved smearing foul-smelling substances on the players' boots or sprinkling ash on the field before important games. "I do recall having our boots taken away on a Friday night and only returned to us an hour before kick-off the next day," said player Richard Gomes.

During March 1971, City recovered well to record three good wins in a row, including a thirteen-goal home thriller against perennial strugglers East London United. Here, the greying Haynes demonstrated that he'd lost none of his ability to beat goalkeepers with his deadly corners and free kicks.

In fact, Johnny foxed the East London defence on two occasions with his unique skills. City were awarded a free kick about two yards outside the penalty area, right in front of the goal. Up stepped the City captain and local player Ronnie Mann. Then, with noted goalscorer Scott darting around as a decoy, the pair cleverly pretended to be arguing over where they should pass the ball, and Mann suddenly tapped the ball to Haynes, who in a flash beat former Scottish international goalkeeper Eddie Connachan with a great shot while his team-mates were still trying to form a defensive wall.

The remarkable final score was 9–4 with no fewer than seven City men on the scoresheet, including raiding-defender Alex Munro (ex-Bristol Rovers) who had only just arrived in the country, and must have been puzzled by all the goals he had witnessed. Perhaps he thought he had joined a rugby club instead! The encounter certainly reminded Haynes of the occasion when he led England to a thrilling 9–3 victory over Scotland almost exactly a decade earlier.

Haynes netted his next goal on April 16th, as City easily beat Arcadia Shepherds 5–2 in Pretoria. Three months later, he made sure his team-mates were well prepared for the return league encounter with title-chasing Hellenic. Revenge was sweet for City. Durban won the game 3–0 but failed by just two points to retain the league title. Durban City finished in third place, surrendering the title to Hellenic and finishing one point behind runners-up Cape Town City.

Haynes plays in a cup final at last

Haynes had proved beyond doubt that he was a very

important cog in City's machine. That season he scored eight league and cup goals and played a vital role as Durban City reached their sixth Castle Cup final, equivalent to the FA Cup final in England. In the early rounds, Elliott's side had thrashed Windhoek City 6–0, and by the time September 25th dawned, there were eleven confident Durban men on the park, despite the fact that their opponents, Cape Town City, were making their third successive appearance in the final.

Castle Cup finals were always played at Johannesburg's Rand Stadium, often regarded as the Wembley of South African soccer. This ground, which was officially opened in 1951, had a 32,000 capacity, and its compactness, which allowed a close, unobstructed view of play from any angle, was one of its outstanding virtues. At the time of writing, the stadium is being upgraded ahead of the World Cup in 2010.

The 1971 Castle Cup final had all the tension and excitement of an English FA Cup final as the two sides played out a breathtaking 3–3 draw. The tide turned against Durban when Dave Forsyth conceded an own goal and then Cape Town netted from the penalty spot to take a three-one lead. But Ronnie Mann grabbed two quick goals to even things out, and, after extra time had failed to produce a winner, the result forced the first-ever replay of a Castle Cup final.

Although the replayed game took place in Durban a week later, Haynes did not get the opportunity to lift the coveted trophy in front of his loyal fans. The home crowd were left shocked and speechless and manager Johnny Byrne deflated when Cape Town took the match 1–2.

Elliott had arranged for some of his squad, including Haynes, to visit a witch doctor before the match. Former player Bobby Cooke, who played in the midfield alongside Haynes, recalls: "The guy threw some bones and said Durban City 4, Cape Town City 2. Haynesey took it as Haynesey would take it, sort of in his stride. 'Budgie' also gave us some muti to burn in our hotel room. But it obviously didn't work!"

Durban City – season 1972

In 1972, Johnny Byrne gave up playing to concentrate on the manager's role. He put matters on a more professional footing, and the club obtained its own training ground and clubhouse. Tony Macedo left for Highlands in 1972. City lost other players too, but recruited two experienced replacements, both wingers: Terry Wharton (ex-Palace, Wolves and Bolton), and fiery Tony Coleman (ex-Doncaster and Manchester City, with whom he had won a First Division title in 1968). For six months in the season they also had the services of ex-England and Ipswich striker Ray Crawford. However, Crawford was at this stage a little past his best.

After the disappointment of not winning the Castle Cup or the BP League championship, the veteran Haynes began the 1972 season with a flourish of goals. Appropriately wearing City's number ten shirt, he scored in three consecutive games, and slowing the games down to his own pace, his side clinched maximum points against Germiston Callies, Durban Celtic and Johannesburg Rangers.

However, on 6th April 1972, then a public holiday (Van Riebeeck Day), a thirteen-year hoodoo was broken when Durban City were beaten by Arcadia Shepherds in a league match for the first time since 1959. On that stifling hot day in Pretoria, Haynes was marked right out of proceedings, but three months later in the return game he bounced back to net one of his side's three winning goals.

City were lying in fourth place in the table, but the arrival of two West Germans, Peter Enders and Wolfgang Gayer, and a Romanian, Laszlo Gergely, all from Hertha Berlin, proved significant, as the Durban club shot up the table on their way to a second league title in three years.

The inclusion of the trio was, however, highly controversial. All three men had been found guilty in the notorious bribery scandal that had rocked the West German game. Although a number of NFL clubs had made it abundantly clear that they did not want the Hertha Berlin stars in South Africa, Elliott, with his cavalier disregard for principles, was quite happy to employ them.

Durban City are league champions again

Haynes was delighted when Gayer notched a hat trick against Port Elizabeth City on August 11th. The midfield trio of Haynes, Cooke and Milne were superb, and indeed five weeks later Durban City were crowned league champions following a very tough 3–2 home win against the Germiston Callies side; both Haynes and Gayer found the net in this game. They regained the championship from their old rivals Hellenic by two points, with the emerging Berea Park one further point adrift.

Another knock-out tournament victory for Haynes

Earlier, on 26th August 1972, the first of the season's competitions, the Coca-Cola Shield, was decided. This competition was played on a home and away basis from the first match right through to the final. The competition was similar in stature to the original League Cup (now Carling Cup) in England. It had only been introduced in 1965 and was originally a province-based competition. The opponents in the final were Berea Park.

In the first leg, despite the fact that Durban City had started as outright favourites, they looked anything but certain to clinch things after a goalless draw. The main difference between the two sides in Pretoria was that City had Haynes in their side, and his enthusiasm for the game remained undimmed; as the master of the quick penetrative pass, he stretched the home defence on a

Right in front in 1972—champions Durban City in their blue and white hoops, with a delighted Haynes right in front. At least Haynes wasn't the victim of a 1972 hairstyle, unlike most of his colleagues.

number of occasions. Unfortunately, Terry Wharton missed two relatively easy scoring chances.

However, the second leg in the Durban sunshine at New Kingsmead went very much according to plan as City, shocked by an early first-half Berea goal, stormed back in the second half. Their pressure was eventually rewarded, and following a well-placed Haynes free kick, Andy Milne nodded home. A minute earlier, Wharton made up for his previous misses by blasting home a great goal from thirty-five yards; two goals in two minutes were just what was required.

The last few minutes did produce a few panicky moments, but the home side held their own and at the final whistle the partisan crowd spilled over the barricades, evaded the dogs and policemen and carried Haynes, the Durban City captain, shoulder-high from the field. Moments later, the maestro collected the first knock-out competition winners medal of his long career—and how well he deserved it!

Surrounded by press cameramen, he held the heavy shield up for the packed crowd to see. This was a great moment for Haynes and all the City fans. He was also presented with a cheque for 100 SA rand, having been chosen as the tournament's 'Coca-Cola Kid' that season. It must have tickled him to be labelled the kid at almost thirty-eight!

The winner of this award for the most outstanding player was selected by an NFL panel, following recommendations from all the league's sub-committees in the country. Importantly, the selectors took the players' behaviour into account as well as their playing ability.

The judges must have taken into consideration the general punch-up that occurred in the tense and exciting final that started with Tony Coleman lying injured on the ground following a vicious kick from Berea's Jimmy Turner. Haynes ran fifteen yards to throw a punch at Turner and then the players from both sides paired off in a general slugging match.

Turner, renowned for his fairly vicious temper, later said: "I had a dust-up with one of the Germans and Haynes came straight towards me. In his career, he had never hit anybody but he hit me. After a few minutes of fighting, it was sorted out. The strange thing was we were friends; we always kept in touch with one another!"

Victory in 1972 meant that Durban City had secured a kind of grand slam, the feat, never before accomplished by a team in South Africa, of winning four titles: the Coca-Cola Shield, which had eluded them since 1965, the league (which they had first won in 1959), the Castle Cup (won the first time in 1960) and the National Bowl (won the first time in 1961).

Haynes reaches a second cup final

City reached yet another Castle Cup final after disposing of arch-rivals Hellenic in the two-legged semi-final. It was not an easy passage by any stretch of the imagination.

The initial leg at Durban finished uneventfully 1–1. The second leg at the Green Point Stadium, however, was not without incident—there were sixty-six fouls, four bookings, a disputed penalty and extra time! Due to the fact that Haynes had not played, there always seemed to be a little touch of midfield control missing. This gave rise to a 2–2 draw.

The man with the golden boot bounced back in the August 30th decider when he placed a precious forty-yard upfield pass at the feet of Alan Skirton (ex-

Arsenal and Blackpool) who made no mistake from close range, and Durban were victorious 1–0.

Manager Budgie Byrne was determined this time around to bring glory to his fans in a cup final against fierce local rivals Durban United. It didn't go to plan.

Durban United had the match all sewn up, but allowed City to sneak an equaliser through Alan Skirton seconds from the final whistle to level the scores at 2–2. The first real scoring opportunity had come after fifteen minutes when a neat through ball from Haynes found Wharton just inside the penalty area, but his fierce shot was pushed around the post. Unfortunately, City's captain was tightly marked during the game, one of the reasons for United's superiority in the midfield.

The generally authoritative Haynes appeared tremendously jaded. Fans cheered when he made a sporting gesture by kicking the ball out of play to enable an injured opponent to get attention, but this was not the final the former England captain had wished for. The crowd were kept on their feet throughout this thrilling encounter, and for the second successive year the final went not only to extra time, but also to a replay.

On October 7th the score was again 2–2 after ninety minutes. However, City faded remarkably in extra time, allowing United to score three further goals, thus ending Haynes' opportunity of earning a medal in South Africa's equivalent of the English FA Cup. Johnny Byrne was devastated by this second successive cup final defeat.

It had still been great fun for Haynes, as he recalled later: "At Fulham I played in a few FA Cup semi-finals but never won anything. It was therefore wonderful to win the knock-out shield in Durban. It was a different class. I also really enjoyed playing in those Castle Cup finals, especially at the Rand Stadium where the atmosphere was superb. But I was disappointed that we were unable to beat our opponents on those two occasions."

Haynes is South Africa's Foreign Footballer of the Year

After another terrific season, Haynes was voted South Africa's 1972 Foreign Footballer of the Year. Harry Weir praised Haynes' dedication to remaining fit and competitive, and was impressed with his personal training regime.

Both the UK star imports, Haynes and Byrne, were very likeable fellows who were wonderfully gifted players, but they were vastly different in character. Budgie didn't enjoy hard training but he did enjoy a drink, lived life to the full and was everyone's friend. Haynes was more reserved and highly disciplined and never allowed his fitness to wane.

Haynes' ill-concealed annoyance with any performance that did not match his own high standard might have bred discontent in many other South African clubs, but to City he remained 'the skipper', and he still pulled off those accurate forty-yard passes which changed a midfield movement into an almost certain goal. Chairman Norman Elliott became his long-standing friend, and said: "He was very special; a great player, who could pass the ball with unbelievable accuracy. We remained pals right through the years."

Former Fulham team-mates Terry Dyson and Haynes snapped when they met up again to play for Wealdstone.

Byrne's theories on man management were sometimes as whimsical as his manner of playing. He once asked John if he could criticise him at a team meeting so that the rest of the players, who were in awe of Haynes, would think themselves in good company when the manager took them to task.

Haynes reluctantly agreed. "Remember," said Budgie, knowing his friend's short fuse, "Whatever you do, don't reply. It's only pretend." Came the day, and Byrne was in the middle of dressing him down when he started answering back. What was meant to be a dummy run became a full-scale slanging match as both men argued and nearly came to blows!

A stopover in Wealdstone

After completing the 1972 season with Durban City, Haynes returned to Britain and surprisingly signed for then Southern League Wealdstone in November of that year. He was expected to play for the club until the end of January 1973, before returning to Durban to play for a further season.

In the event he only appeared in three matches for the club, one in each month. He made his debut against Dorchester Town on November 18th, in a Southern League game that Wealdstone lost 2–3; he was not one of their scorers. He appeared again just before Christmas against Wimbledon, the club that had tried to sign him before his departure to South Africa, in a Mid-Surrey Floodlight League match that Wealdstone lost 0–1.

His final appearance was in early January against Hillingdon Borough also in a Mid-Surrey Floodlight League game, which Wealdstone drew 0–0. The media admitted that it had been a small reminder of his illustrious past. Haynes himself called it an enjoyable form of training.

During this brief sojourn in Wealdstone, Haynes played alongside former Fulham players Terry Dyson and Bobby Moss. Although he played only three times that season, he was expected to return to Wealdstone at the end of the next South African season, but this failed to materialise.

Haynes was a happy man, and exclaimed, "It's about the perfect set-up; eight months in the sunshine out there, four months back home." He returned home each year to see his parents, friends and relatives and to holiday in Majorca.

"Get out your top hat!"

Johnny Haynes had left South Africa quite quickly in order to fulfil his playing commitment with Wealdstone, leaving Libby in South Africa. In one of his phone calls, he finally asked her to marry him. They had already been together for five years and Libby says she would have married him after a year. She responded with a stylish "I'll think about it."

Naturally, that was a 'yes', and Libby sent a telegram back to Haynes: "*Get out your top hat!*" She had to give notice at work in order to hurry to Britain. It gave her little time to issue invitations and make plans.

On December 28th, Johnny Haynes and Libby Tucker were married at Epsom Registry Office. Tommy Benfield was Johnny's best man, Francis Whitney was Libby's maid of honour and Bobby Moore was a guest. Libby's father and mother, two brothers, nieces and nephews all flew in from America. Close friends Sheila and Tom Norton, who owned the Epsom pub, and Paddy Holter, Libby's friend from the BBC, also attended.

From Johnny's side there was Rose and Eddie and Uncle Jack. Ex-Fulham goalkeeper Dave Underwood was present, as well as a number of Johnny's former team-mates. Unfortunately the party-loving Byrne and Keetch families remained in South Africa.

The reception was in a hall upstairs in the pub in Epsom, and Fred Callaghan recalls "copious quantities of scampi and champagne". Following this, family and close friends returned for an additional mini-party at the Haynes home in Epsom. The newly-weds then left to spend their wedding night at a country inn.

Next morning, fitness fanatic Haynes still went swimming in the inn's pool (it was December!) before breakfast. Libby's family stayed with Eddie and Rose at Epsom. They all met up the next day, as everyone knew that Johnny and Libby would soon return to South Africa, and Libby always considered family time important.

Durban City – season 1973

In 1973, Durban City slumped to their worst finish ever as numerous players left the club. As champions, they may have been trying to secure more money from Elliott, who was having none of it. During this internecine feud between players and management, the three German players were transferred to Hellenic, and prolific scorer Ronnie Mann returned to Durban United. Johnny Byrne himself departed controversially and suddenly early in the season to take up the manager's hot seat at Hellenic.

Although the team started the season on a real high, putting six goals past both Berea Park and Durban Celtic, with Haynes on the scoresheet on both occasions, they were subsequently bundled out of the Coca-Cola Shield in the first round, faded in the Castle Cup and ended up a fairly dismal ninth out of fifteen in the league table, registering just thirty-nine goals. They had won only one more game than the bottom club, finishing a disastrous seventeen points below the champions Cape Town City. The championship-winning side of the previous season had come apart at the seams.

Toward the end of the year, Libby became anxious to return to London and start her acting career. Although South Africa had been an exciting adventure, she had never wanted to live there for long. She remembers that Johnny was always saying, "Just one more year."

A visit from the All Stars

Midway through that year, Malcolm Allison's boycott-busting and flamboyant British All Stars soccer circus arrived in the country to play four matches. The All Stars included the likes of Frank McLintock (Queens Park Rangers), George Armstrong (Arsenal), Rodney Marsh (Manchester City) and Don Rogers (Crystal Palace). Johnny Haynes, together with a number of locally based Britons, was called up to join the squad. Games were played against a South African-born XI, a Natal XI, an NFL XI and an African XI.

Former Bury and Blackburn player Jimmy Kerr, who featured as a player, coach and manager, and was mentor of the South African Stars, said: "Haynesey was one of the finest players I ever saw. His ability to distribute the ball with pinpoint accuracy was phenomenal."

In early September 1973, Haynes made one of his last appearances for Durban City, and once more he was the star of the game as Elliott's side defeated local rivals Durban Celtic 2–1. He continued to show how dexterous he was at shielding the ball, despite being

Wedding day delight with bride Libby Tucker—and Bobby Moore.

repeatedly kicked by an opponent and getting little protection from the referee. He was still the prime architect, and created the second goal which was a beautifully taken overhead kick by Jurgen Sperlich.

Durban United – season 1974

Next season, Haynes joined Durban United on a free transfer. The reasons why he left City are not fully known, but there may have been a series of issues, including the departure of his friend Byrne. At United, he was generally used only as a substitute when the game was dead and buried. Sometimes it was puzzling to see him spending most of his time on the bench.

But, according to Greg Farrell, he assisted manager Bill Williams with coaching. Farrell remembers: "He was very good; he helped the coaching staff a lot and many of the young players like me were very grateful.

The British All Stars who toured South Africa in 1973. Standing: Malcolm Allison, Frank McLintock, Gary Sprake, Geoff Hurst, George Eastham, Don Rogers, Tony Burns, Derek Dougan, Ron McKinnon, Johnny Byrne; front: Rodney Marsh, Johnny Haynes, Alan Whittle, Willie Hunter, George Armstrong, Tony Coleman.

Haynesey was in and out of the side but don't forget he was getting on a bit. I think he was not all that well, I'll be quite honest with you."

However, in late May 1974, the player who could still change the direction of any game was selected for a full game against his former club. And just to prove that he still had plenty of fuel left in his tank, the veteran star rose to the occasion by giving an excellent display in green and white and helping United defeat the Blue and White hoops 2–1.

Durban Celtic – season 1974

A few weeks later Haynes, due to lack of action on the pitch, decided to quit United and exchange the green and white for the gold and black of Durban Celtic. In mid-July, he significantly scored his first goal with a fine header. He also placed a perfect corner for Ian Bender to score, although Celtic lost the game against a rampant Arcadia side.

Durban Celtic, a young athletic side comprised almost entirely of South Africans, had won promotion into the top flight in 1972, and Haynes, who was by this time almost forty, was about eighteen years older than the majority of his team-mates. However, he was still keen to demonstrate that he had the power to dominate games.

A former Celtic player recalls the time well: "Haynes was old and used to just stand around and ping the ball all over the place. Although he did not do much running, he was a different class. On many occasions, he was a substitute but we used him and he worked for us in the right midfield. I'll never forget his beautiful crosses."

The same man, however, also described Haynes as a fairly miserable guy, who wouldn't talk to anybody and just read the paper on his own.

Norman Elliott and his cronies put severe financial pressure on Durban Celtic when they ruthlessly denied them use of the New Kingsmead stadium on the crowd-pulling Sundays. This move forced the club to play its home games in front of meagre midweek fans, but they battled on to complete the season in tenth position—still one place and one point above rudderless Durban City. However, they were still sixteen points away from league winners Arcadia Shepherds.

The writing was now firmly on the wall, and at the end of the 1974 season, following heavy financial losses, the Celtic club amalgamated with Maritzburg. The name of Durban Celtic disappeared.

The Maritzburg team had finished strongly in 1974, third in the league. This union meant training in Durban, but playing home matches at the Jan Smuts Stadium in Pietermaritzburg some fifty-five miles away where, significantly, in 1879 the country's very first civilian football club, Pietermaritzburg County, had been established. Most Maritzburg players still lived in Durban. Johnny played under a chairman named Mitch Mendonides, and the manager and coach was

Berry Mills, who went on to become one of Johnny's close friends.

His marriage is over

It was a time of change for Johnny Haynes off the field as well. He had been married late in life—at the age of 38—but his marriage to Libby was damaged and broke down just eighteen months after the wedding. They were divorced on 22nd November 1974.

A year later Johnny asked Libby to re-marry him, but she had already started a new life. She stayed in South Africa for a while, but remarried and now lives in Naples, Florida, with her English husband Tony and family. She still holds with great affection memories of those 'magical times' with John.

Maritzburg – season 1975

As Haynes entered the final phase of his very long career, he continued to train as hard as he possibly could, was a model professional right to the end, and still always wanted the ball.

Player Grant McDade recollects: "When you get to forty, most guys battle to run around the block but Haynes was phenomenal at training. He kept up with us youngsters and never ran out of steam. When running between beacons we would always cheat by a yard or so, but Haynesey would dash from point A to point B and make sure he actually touched them. We would say 'Haynesey, man, just cheat a little', but he would never. He was an amazing guy, a legend, but a very, very difficult team member. He used to crap on you if you didn't give him the ball!"

Haynes' young team-mates used to play a joke by hiding his immaculate clothes after he'd meticulously hung them up in the changing room before a game, something which infuriated him.

During 1975, Maritzburg's manager Peter Balfour faced one of the toughest decisions of his soccer life. His dilemma was whether to rest the forty-year-old link man, who was now understandably slowing, and replace him with his own young son, Brian, who played in the same position.

In the end sanity prevailed, and Haynes spent more and more time on the substitutes bench together with manager Balfour. On one of those occasions the former Fulham star demonstrated just why he was regarded as a gentleman both on and off the field.

A Martizburg team group. Haynes is second right in front.

Brian Balfour recalls with affection: "Before the game Johnny suggested that we go and put the kit out for the team. At Maritzburg we didn't have a kit man but it wasn't our job to hang the shorts and shirts in the dressing room. That wonderful gesture by the former English international made me realize just what a great man he was, and that day will always be special to me."

England's first £100-a-week player never actually discussed retiring, preferring just to drop hints about playing more golf. However, as he approached his forty-first birthday the pressure to quit the beautiful game intensified. Grant McDade explains, "Towards the end of the season he played a couple of matches and then just said, *'Now that's it.'*"

Although they were rarely in contention for the league title, Maritzburg with Haynes finished a very creditable third in the league once more. However, they failed in the cup competitions. Therefore Johnny unfortunately did not win any honours whilst at Maritzburg. The white South African NFL league eventually folded two years later, in 1977.

George Cohen summed it up: "He would have still had a great presence of mind, he loved football and whatever stage he was in his career he would have wanted it to be 'right', and if he couldn't, then he'd give up. This is the sign of a good player, knowing when 'I've had enough of this.'"

Johnny Haynes marries again

During his final playing year at Maritzburg, Johnny Haynes met a divorcee at a social gathering who was helping a friend sell tickets for a boxing match. Her name was Marjorie Green. Haynes bought a ticket, but she didn't know who he was. They had lunch together but only saw each other now and again. However, a relationship developed and after a courtship of two years, they married in February 1976. The wedding took place at Marjorie's sister's house, with only family and close friends present. Marjorie had a nine-year-old daughter, Karen, from her previous marriage, and Johnny became a stepfather for the first time. Marjorie said: "Karen adored him."

Johnny Haynes retires

Very soon after the wedding, Johnny Haynes finally stopped playing at the age of forty-one. Having joined Fulham at fifteen, he had played professional football for over a quarter of a century. Perhaps the early death of his father at sixty-three had made him contemplate his own retirement. He decided that he wanted to finish completely with soccer. His Uncle Jack, who had first taken him to Highbury and White Hart Lane, managed to get out to South Africa to see him play in his final years, but his parents never made it.

In June, during his final playing days at Maritzburg, John received a phone call telling him that his father Eddie had died at home. He was dreadfully upset, but

A forty-third birthday picture with wife Marjorie; left: happy holiday memories.

insisted in playing on, not wanting to let any of his team-mates down. Johnny's reliable pal Uncle Jack arranged the funeral.

Johnny said later in life, after returning to Scotland: "The idea of becoming a manager didn't really occur. I just played for as long as I could and that was it. Then I became a spectator; playing the game was my big interest, once I'd finished playing that was the end of it—I wasn't interested in doing anything else at all. The first couple of years I was there, City went great guns and I thoroughly enjoyed playing in the cup finals in the Rand Stadium. I had a great time over there, playing into my forties."

Johnny Haynes had nothing much to do with serious football after that, and all he really did was to tune in to the World Service to pick up the English football results, in particular those of his beloved Fulham FC. He also went over to Harry Weir's house every Wednesday to read the sports pages. Harry had three daughters and they regarded him as one of the family.

Coaching the youngsters

After Haynes had hung up his well-used boots for good there was one final cameo. He did not want to do any professional coaching, but Wimpy, and maybe also Coca-Cola, paid him to coach young schoolboys after lessons (ages around twelve and thirteen). At first he was reluctant, but Marjorie thought that it would be good for "Johnny Haynes to put something back into the South African game."

Johnny did this on and off for a few years. Some say that the coaching continued right up until 1980, and that he kicked his last ball in anger at the age of forty-six. Amongst those coached were Marjorie's two nephews. Johnny also coached a team of teenagers, and invariably they were league and cup winners.

More time for golf

John was engaged in the Tom Benfield bookmaking business, not actively but as a sleeping partner. In 1976 they sold their shops to the Tote, which helped to set Haynes up financially. He had no business interests in South Africa and decided to spend his new-found leisure time working on his golf handicap at the Royal Durban golf club. He spent many hours on the golf course, where his obsession with the perfect fairway

Consolation from Haynes for Les Strong in the Wembley dressing room before Fulham's FA Cup final appearance in May 1975. Strong had played in every match up to the final, but injury kept him out of the Wembley showpiece.

drive (like the perfect pass) sometimes led him to storm off for an early drink!

In the spring of 1977, John's mother Rose passed away at the Epsom home, less than two years after her husband. She had been greatly affected by Eddie's passing and had suffered a stroke soon afterwards. She was just sixty years old. As Johnny was no longer actively playing, he and Marge returned home to conduct the funeral arrangements personally, and organise the sale of the Epsom home.

Trips back to England – and a Fulham cup final

Haynes was a great sun-worshipper. Every year John and Marjorie would spend four weeks in Marbella. There were two trips to Mauritius and a four-week sojourn to the south of France in 1980. Marjorie introduced Johnny to the delights of skiing. They went to Saalbach, usually with Marjorie's sister and her husband. It became an annual event.

Often John and Marjorie would travel via London to drop in on John's friends and acquaintances. One of their most important trips back was in celebration of Fulham finally reaching an FA Cup final, the occasion that had eluded him twice in his twenty years at the

Johnny and his dog Robbie, pictured in 1985.

club, but which had been achieved in less than five years after his departure.

Marjorie found Johnny a very deep and complicated man. They were both strong-willed and independent people, and they were beginning to find it difficult to live together. By 1984, after ten years, Johnny Haynes' second marriage was on the wane.

During this period, Johnny Haynes took his usual skiing holidays in Austria, and on one occasion, when Marjorie could not go because of an injury, her sister travelled with Johnny and another couple. Whilst on the Austrian slopes, Johnny Haynes was reunited with Avril, whom he had met whilst recovering from his car crash twenty years previously, and his second marriage was over.

After their divorce, Marjorie and Johnny remained friends, but she did not see him for twenty years. Johnny, however, kept in regular contact with his stepdaughter Karen, and met the eldest of her three daughters. After returning to Scotland, he visited South Africa again on several occasions between 1985 and 1990 to see friends and to see 'Robbie', the dog he had given to Marjorie as a present during their marriage. Marjorie feels that Johnny might well have stayed in South Africa but for that meeting in Austria. She steadfastly maintains that she is not bitter about the way it all ended, but she has not married again.

Postscript

Most people in South Africa considered that they had been privileged to see Johnny Haynes, even in the twilight of his playing days. They could only speculate as to how brilliant he must have been in his prime. Nevertheless, he provided admiring fans with numerous glimpses of his golden touches while with Durban City and other clubs.

In 2006 Norman Elliott died of Alzheimer's disease, aged seventy-nine. Over 500 people attended his lavish wake at the Durban Country Club, including many former City players, some of whom were still probably awaiting their signing-on fees or bonuses.

Conversations abounded in every nook and cranny about the controversial 'Silver Fox', his twenty-two trips to Britain to recruit stars like Johnny Haynes, and the demise of Durban City in 1988.

30: Back in Britain

30: Back in Britain

Paradoxically, like much else in his life, Johnny Haynes settled in Scotland, not England, for the remainder of his days on his return to Britain in 1985. At this stage of his life he did not appear to be nostalgic for life in London. He said, "I'd always had friends in Edinburgh while I was playing for Fulham."

He lived this part of his life out of the limelight, enjoying the quiet life, perhaps reasoning that he'd already had his fair share of the glare of publicity. He was very happy living in Edinburgh, and said that he felt totally at home there. Seeing that he masterminded the greatest humiliation of the Scots at football to the tune of 9–3 he had amazingly been given absolution. Haynes smiled and said: "I was a bit worried about the reception I'd get, because I did nasty things to them on the football field!"

John's third partner, Avril, had dry-cleaning and office-cleaning businesses, and he always assisted in these, sometimes delivering door to door. Although he had been remunerated as well as anyone in his day, the riches he secured still didn't safeguard his future. It is also thought that he didn't keep up all of his National Insurance contributions during his fifteen years in South Africa.

This, coupled with an urge to keep busy, gave rise to his 4am excursions in a delivery van well past his pensionable years. Some say that he delivered laundry to Rangers and Celtic players who probably didn't know or remember who he was. A very nice press quote put it perfectly: "Those who saw him in the twilight hours when he began his shift might not have known it then, but know it now: there passed a great British footballer of his day, one of the finest of all time."

Johnny Haynes didn't seek out a position as a football pundit. Even in later life he frequently vetoed opportunities to appear on television which was surprising given his intelligence and eloquent speaking. He also never sought to air his footballing opinions in public and appeared to be only really interested in reviewing the nostalgia of matches played in the Sixties and Seventies, appearing with his old England pal Bobby Charlton in *Bobby Charlton's Scrapbook* with Dickie Davies.

Despite this reluctance to remain in the limelight, he would nearly always appear at, and be actively involved in, worthwhile charity functions. Steve Earle said: "He was also offered considerable sums to make

Haynes receives a bronze statuette from George Best during the Evening Standard tribute dinner at the National Sporting Club at the Café Royal in March 1993.

public appearances, and to attend golfing weekends and the like. It would have made him more money, but he wasn't really interested. He wasn't bothered by the sideshows."

Haynes liked to watch Hearts play football at Tynecastle, but later on this was limited to only a couple of games a season. Over half a century since joining Fulham, he said, "I've become Scottish enough to be a firm Hearts supporter, but when the Saturday scores come up the absolute priority is still to see how Fulham got on. It's the first result I look for up here." Later on in life, he was more interested in Scottish rugby.

The Fulham supporter

For ten or so years before Mohamed Al Fayed acquired Fulham Football Club in 1997, the club had been in perilous straits. There had been real possibilities of mergers with other clubs and even of the club disappearing altogether. For many of these years, Haynes was a true friend of Fulham supporters, and was one of the figureheads in the Fulham 2000 campaign that fought for the club's very existence and helped keep it going.

He pledged his name, support and goodwill to the campaign, taking part in as many functions as time and practicalities would allow, in order to keep Fulham's plight in the forefront of publicity. He joined supporters on a famous boat trip up the Thames to a match at Orient in a 'Don't Kill Fulham' initiative. His efforts, together with those of hundreds of others, eventually led to Al Fayed's purchase of the club in 1997, and the subsequent years of stability—and a return to the top flight.

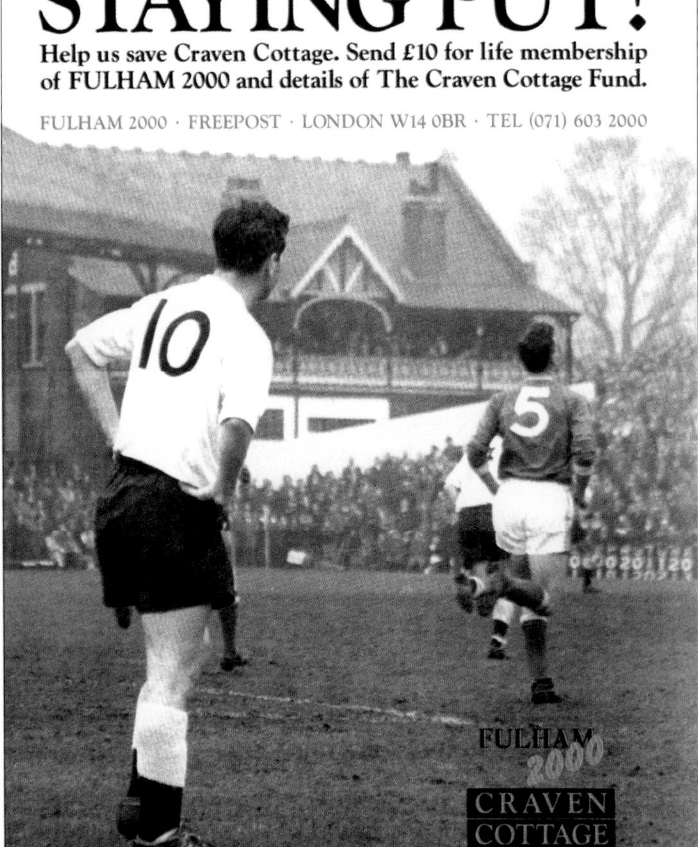

Haynes put his full backing behind the Fulham 2000 campaign.

'Don't Kill Fulham' was the message surrounding the boat trip to Orient in 1995—a message heard in Parliament! Joining Haynes on the trip were George Cohen and Jimmy Hill. The picture at left shows Haynes about to be interviewed by the originator of Fulham Clubcall, Ken Myers.

Right: one of Fulham 2000's campaigners, Alan Williams, chats with the maestro outside Craven Cottage. Above: Hundreds of celebratory first-day covers, produced on behalf of Fulham 2000, were individually signed by Haynes.

Haynes sees Fulham back in the top flight

Johnny Haynes was as delighted as anyone when Fulham's exciting young side under the stewardship of Jean Tigana returned to their rightful position in the top flight after a long absence of thirty-three years. In their first year after promotion, Haynes ventured south in 2001 to watch Fulham play well and beat Newcastle United 3–1.

He sat as an honoured guest next to Fulham's saviour Mohamed Al Fayed, and was reportedly impressed with the pace of Louis Saha, Luis Boa Morte and Barry Hayles. One can't help but wonder whether his mind drifted back to that epic FA Cup encounter with Newcastle forty-five years previously and the pace and movement of Chamberlain, Robson and Hill.

Above: Haynes is feted by chairman Mohamed Al Fayed at the Newcastle match in November 2001. The picture below, taken at the same occasion, features a happy maestro chatting with Gary Piper, Fulham's chaplain, who, just a few years later, would be conducting a memorial service for the great man. Also in the picture is Fulham photographer Ken Simpson.

A number of Fulham football legends were introduced to the crowd in April 2002. A waving Johnny Haynes (above) once more treads the famous Craven Cottage turf. In front of him are Fred Callaghan and Les Barrett. Also in the picture are Maurice Cook and Stan Brown. At right is ever-cheery Tosh Chamberlain, delighted to meet his great mate again. Below: In the foreground is Stan Brown, whilst behind him Haynes meets up again with his great playing companion Roy Bentley, whom he once described as Fulham's best ever signing.

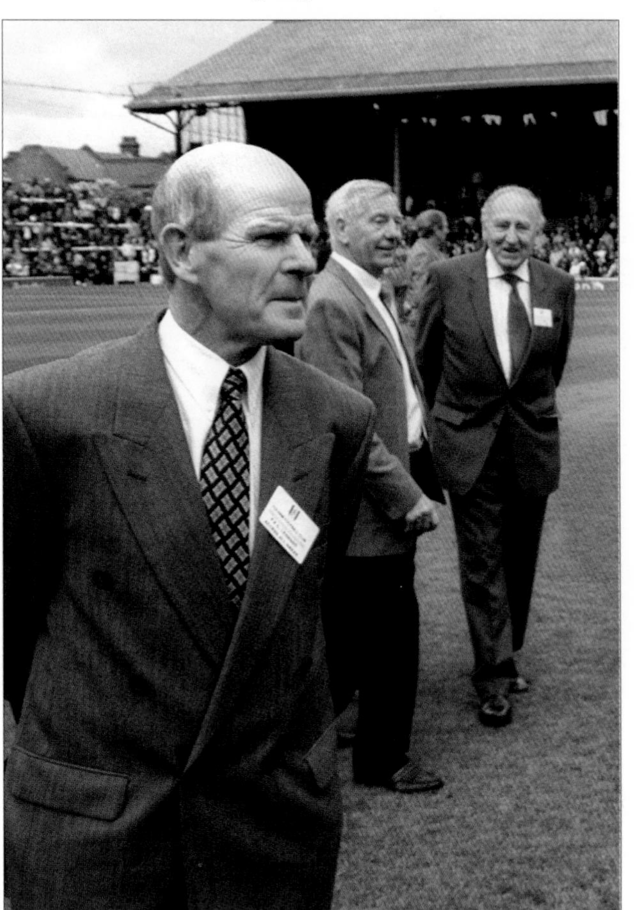

Soccer's Hall of Fame

In 2002 Haynes became an inaugural inductee to the English Football Hall of Fame in recognition of his football talents and impact on the national game. The Hall of Fame is housed at the National Football Museum in Preston. Its aims are to celebrate and highlight the achievements of top British footballers and those who have played for their country. New members are added each year, with a ceremony described as the Oscars of English football being held in October.

The members of the Hall of Fame are selected by a panel made up of some of the biggest names in the game including Sir Alex Ferguson and Sir Bobby Charlton. To be considered for induction, players and managers must be thirty years of age or older and have played or managed for at least five years in England. Johnny Haynes' name sits comfortably beside other great players of his time, as well as those from other eras. The names include: Gordon Banks OBE, George Best, 'Dixie' Dean, John Charles CBE, Sir Bobby Charlton CBE, Peter Doherty, Duncan Edwards, Sir Tom Finney OBE, Jimmy Greaves, Denis Law, Nat Lofthouse OBE, Billy Wright CBE, Sir Stanley Matthews CBE, Bobby Moore OBE and Dave Mackay.

A 'legendary' visit to the Cottage

One of Haynes' last trips south from Edinburgh was to Craven Cottage in April 2002 for the Premiership match against Leicester City. He was one of a number of Fulham legends introduced to the crowd that day. It must have been poignant for Haynes to see the way little Fulham's ground down by the river had been transformed into an exciting stadium, whilst still retaining those homely, friendly qualities that had drawn him to start his illustrious career there all those years ago.

Happy days, full of smiles.
Above: the publication of a Dennis Turner Fulham history book was celebrated at the Cottage, and Haynes, looking fit and in great form, delights his audience which included, pictured here, his partner Avril and politician (and Sheffield Wednesday supporter) Roy Hattersley.
Right: happy reminiscences with lifelong Fulham fan David Roodyn and Haynes' former team-mate Bobby Keetch.
Below: John and Avril enjoy a night out with Tommy Benfield.

Johnny Haynes' reflections

"Regrets? I have a few, but then again too few to mention." (From the song *My Way.*)

From the man who (like his hero Sinatra) always did it *his* way, a few reflections:

On football in general:

"I thought I was the luckiest man alive. I got paid to do what I love best—playing football."

On missing out:

"Of course I would have liked to have played in an FA Cup final at Wembley, and of course I would like to have played in the World Cup in England ... that would have been interesting."

On the modern balls and pitches:

Haynes' only real envy was the perfect pitches on which today's players are able to play.

"There was so much more we could have done with the ball then, instead of playing in deep mud or on almost bare earth in the spring, there are players today who could not have coped back then."

"I'd love to play in today's game. I think I'd find a lot of space to put my foot on the ball and pass it around. I think I might enjoy working with the modern ball. It's difficult to explain to players just how heavy and brutal the old ball was. Once we played on a mud heap at Port Vale and even Tosh, who could kick a wall down, couldn't move the ball more than ten or twelve yards. Roy Bentley, who played centre forward and centre half for us, had a forehead covered in scar tissue."

Speaking further on the cumbrous footballs, Haynes said: "Mind you, I'd be much more accurate now with these balls they play with. Ours were like great lumps of lead, wet cannonballs in the mud."

On his club Fulham:

Haynes had no regrets: "I suppose things could have worked out differently, but I was happy at Fulham and playing for them didn't affect my international career so there didn't seem to be much point in moving elsewhere, although if the maximum wage hadn't been lifted I'd have gone to Italy.

"Not that I've ever bothered much about money. The game was the thing. I just loved playing. I don't envy the wages in football today."

"As far as transfers went—at that time you didn't have much choice. I was always in the position where the club didn't want to sell or cash in on me. So if the club weren't willing to sell, that was the end of the story. You couldn't stand up and say you wanted to go."

"I was at Fulham for my whole career and thoroughly enjoyed it. I didn't think I'd be happier or that I'd enjoy myself any more at another club, and that's one of the reasons that I stayed. We didn't actually win anything, but we had some success. We got to the FA Cup semi-final twice, we got promotion and we stayed in the top flight for almost ten years—and I enjoyed it.

Playing for another club wasn't that important to me. I was happy at Fulham and happy in London. If the club showed a little lack of ambition, then, in a way, so did I; I was just as guilty as them."

On today's superstars:

Haynes looked upon the life of modern footballers with no envy and there was not a shred of rancour from him at the mention of the money today's players can command: "Good luck to them. They are of their time, as I was of mine."

"Then was then, now's now; money didn't bug me in those days. I simply enjoyed playing football, playing alongside such a great bunch of talented blokes. Today I'm comfortable; I've no complaints at all."

Haynes grinned at the present wage packets: "No regrets at all, good luck to them, it's only numbers. In my day you could buy a Jag for £600, and a lovely suburban house for six grand."

"The whole scene of football has taken off completely in the last five years or so; with television rights there is so much money in the game. I'm delighted for the players. As long as TV stays interested in football, then the money will be there. The players are worth it, because if they weren't, you wouldn't get any football. If there is somebody there to put up the money, then the players must get their fair share."

On the treatment table:

"It was the cruciate ligament in the right knee that did for me. They used to stitch them together, but it didn't work like the operations today. For me it was a big struggle and I was, more or less, playing on one leg."

On honours:

"I must be one of the few England captains who have finished up with nothing, I must be honest. A distinguished playing career, yeah, but you've probably got to do a bit more than that. Tom Finney and Stan Matthews were two of the few who just got a knighthood for football. How does it leave me? It does worry me a bit that some people have MBEs and OBEs. It gets to me. Yeah. I can look at some of the lists in football and find it very hard to work out. But that's the way it goes, I suppose."

On agents and loyalty:

"Loyalty is a thing of the past in football. Players make a fortune from moving to a different club, it's hard to see anyone staying in one place for a great length of time—unless they are very well paid. I stayed at Fulham for the entire duration of my career; I don't think it's very fair to compare the two ages. It's a pity there is not more loyalty shown by players but you can hardly blame them for wanting to get the best deal they can."

"Football is a completely different game to what it was when I was playing. For instance today's agents hold a huge amount of power. When I was at Fulham I had an agent, but he only looked after my off-field activities."

"The difference in what the spectators and players earn means that there is now more difficulty in identifying with the players. We used to socialise amongst supporters at Fulham."

On why it was all such great fun back then:

Haynes would definitely have adorned the modern game, but in the true Fulham style of the Fifties and Sixties he said: "But would it have been such fun?"

"I remember one season we scored 100 goals and didn't come top! We couldn't work it out until someone pointed out we had conceded 100 goals as well. It was great fun, wasn't it?"

"We were never a good side. We were in the Second Division for the best part of the 1950s and although we got plenty of goals and played a lot of good football, we let in plenty too."

"These days and those days are obviously very different, in that in those days Fulham were a selling club. We did buy one or two players but on the whole we were a selling club. If you sell your best players you don't do as well as you could do."

On the modern game:

"It's a different game now, no long balls, keeping possession is what matters. I don't think football is more skilful, but they're all very fit and a lot more organised; but that often means twenty players bunched in a strip thirty yards either side of the halfway line. It makes it much harder to play."

Haynes was asked whether there were players that still excited him. He replied: "Not in England, a few in Italy; the Mancini of seven or eight years ago, Del Piero before his injury, Zidane; people who think about the game, look for space—and then do something."

There would be no prizes for guessing who he sees in them...

31: *Playing statistics*

Fulham

Johnny Haynes made a record 594 league appearances for Fulham.
He played 658 games in all, and scored 158 goals.

Appearances:

Season	Football League	FA Cup	Football League Cup	Total
1952–53	18	1		19
1953–54	41	3		44
1954–55	37	1		38
1955–56	40	2		42
1956–57	33	2		35
1957–58	38	7		45
1958–59	34	4		38
1959–60	31	2		33
1960–61	39	1	1	41
1961–62	38	6	1	45
1962–63	8	1		9
1963–64	40	2	1	43
1964–65	39	2	2	43
1965–66	33	1	4	38
1966–67	36	3	2	41
1967–68	34	3	5	42
1968–69	28	2	1	31
1969–70	27	1	3	31
TOTAL	**594**	**44**	**20**	**658**

Goals:

Season	Football League	FA Cup	Football League Cup	Total
1952–53	1			1
1953–54	16	2		18
1954–55	8	1		9
1955–56	18	1		19
1956–57	5*			5
1957–58	15	1		16
1958–59	26			26
1959–60	10			10
1960–61	9			9
1961–62	5	1		6
1962–63				0
1963–64	8			8
1964–65	5			5
1965–66	6		1	7
1966–67	6	1		7
1967–68	5	1	1	7
1968–69	1	1		2
1969–70	3			3
TOTAL	**147**	**9**	**2**	**158**

*Some statistics mark a Johnny Haynes goal at Rotherham United in February 1957 as being an own goal.

Appearances and goals by division:

Division	Appearances	Goals
First Division	335	59
Second Division	292	96
Third Division	31	3
TOTALS	**658**	**158**

Goals by number:

		Goals
Four-goal hauls	1	4
Hat tricks	5	15
Braces	15	30
Single goals	109	109
TOTAL		**158**

Goals by home and away:

Season	Craven Cottage	Away Grounds	Total
1952–53	1		1
1953–54	11	7	18
1954–55	5	4	9
1955–56	7	12	19
1956–57	3	2	5
1957–58	12	4	16
1958–59	20	6	26
1959–60	6	4	10
1960–61	8	1	9
1961–62	2	4	6
1962–63			0
1963–64	7	1	8
1964–65	4	1	5
1965–66	6	1	7
1966–67	3	4	7
1967–68	3	4	7
1968–69		2	2
1969–70	2	1	3
TOTAL	**100**	**58**	**158**

England

Under 23:	P 8	W 7	D 1	L 0	goals 8
England 'B':	P 5	W 2	D 2	L 1	goals 0
Football League:	P 13	W 8	D 1	L 4	goals 7

Full England caps:

WCQ = World Cup qualifier; WCF = World Cup finals; BC = British Championship; F = friendly; **G** *= Haynes goals*

	Opponents	Date	Location	Match	F–A	G	Details	Shirt
	Belgium	*17 Jun 1954*	*St Jakob Park, Basle, Switzerland*	*WCF*	*4–4*		*Unused reserve*	*21*
	Switzerland	*20 Jun 1954*	*Wankdorf Stadion, Berne*	*WCF*	*2–0*		*Unused reserve*	*21*
	Uruguay	*26 Jun 1954*	*St Jakob Park, Basle, Switzerland*	*WCF*	*2–4*		*Unused reserve*	*21*
1	Northern Ireland	2 Oct 1954	Windsor Park, Belfast	BC	2–0	1	Start	10
2	Northern Ireland	2 Nov 1955	Empire Stadium, Wembley	BC	3–0		Start	8
3	Spain	30 Nov 1955	Empire Stadium, Wembley	F	4–1		Start	10
4	Scotland	14 Apr 1956	Hampden Park, Glasgow	BC	1–1	1	Start	10
5	Brazil	9 May 1956	Empire Stadium, Wembley	F	4–2		Start	10
6	Sweden	16 May 1956	Råsunda Stadion, Solna	F	0–0		Start	10
7	Finland	20 May 1956	Olympiastadion, Helsinki	F	5–1	1	Start	8
8	West Germany	26 May 1956	Olympiastadion, Berlin	F	3–1	1	Start	8
9	Wales	14 Nov 1956	Empire Stadium, Wembley	BC	3–1	1	Start	10
10	Yugoslavia	28 Nov 1956	Empire Stadium, Wembley	F	3–0		Start *(off 30 mins)*	10
11	Republic of Ireland	8 May 1957	Empire Stadium, Wembley	WCQ	5–1		Start	10
12	Denmark	15 May 1957	Idrætsparken, Copenhagen	WCQ	4–1	1	Start	10
13	Republic of Ireland	19 May 1957	Dalymount Park, Dublin	WCQ	1–1		Start	10
14	Wales	19 Oct 1957	Ninian Park, Cardiff	BC	4–0	2	Start	10
15	Northern Ireland	6 Nov 1957	Empire Stadium, Wembley	BC	2–3		Start	10
16	France	27 Nov 1957	Empire Stadium, Wembley	F	4–0		Start	10
17	Scotland	19 Apr 1958	Hampden Park, Glasgow	BC	4–0		Start	10
18	Portugal	7 May 1958	Empire Stadium, Wembley	F	2–1		Start	10
19	Yugoslavia	11 May 1958	Stadion J.N.A., Belgrade	F	0–5		Start	10
20	U.S.S.R.	18 May 1958	Lenin Stadium, Moscow	F	1–1		Start	10
21	U.S.S.R.	8 Jun 1958	Nya Ullevi Stadion, Gothenburg, Sweden	WCF	2–2		Start	10
22	Brazil	11 Jun 1958	Nya Ullevi Stadion, Gothenburg, Sweden	WCF	0–0		Start	10
23	Austria	15 Jun 1958	Ryavallen Stadion, Boras, Sweden	WCF	2–2	1	Start	10
24	U.S.S.R.	17 Jun 1958	Nya Ullevi Stadion, Gothenburg, Sweden	WCF	0–1		Start	10
25	Northern Ireland	4 Oct 1958	Windsor Park, Belfast	BC	3–3		Start	10
26	U.S.S.R.	22 Oct 1958	Empire Stadium, Wembley	F	5–0	3	Start	10
27	Scotland	11 Apr 1959	Empire Stadium, Wembley	BC	1–0		Start	10
28	Italy	6 May 1959	Empire Stadium, Wembley	F	2–2		Start	10
29	Brazil	13 May 1959	Estádio Jornalista Mário Filho, Maracanã, Rio de Janeiro	F	0–2		Start	10
30	Peru	17 May 1959	Estadio Nacional Coloso de José Díaz, Lima	F	1–4		Start	10
31	Mexico	24 May 1959	Estadio Olímpico Universitario, Mexico City	F	1–2		Start	10
32	USA	28 May 1959	Wrigley Field, Los Angeles	F	8–1	1	Start	10
33	Northern Ireland	18 Nov 1959	Empire Stadium, Wembley	BC	2–1		Start	8
34	Yugoslavia	11 May 1960	Empire Stadium, Wembley	F	3–3	1	Start	8

	Opponents	Date	Location	Match	F–A	G	Details	Shirt
35	Spain	15 May 1960	El Estadio Santiago Bernabéu, Madrid	F	0–3		Captain	8
36	Hungary	22 May 1960	Népstadion, Budapest	F	0–2		Captain	8
37	Northern Ireland	8 Oct 1960	Windsor Park, Belfast	BC	5–2		Captain	10
38	Luxembourg	19 Oct 1960	Stade Municipal, Luxembourg City	WCQ	9–0	1	Captain	10
39	Spain	26 Oct 1960	Empire Stadium, Wembley	F	4–2		Captain	10
40	Wales	23 Nov 1960	Empire Stadium, Wembley	BC	5–1	1	Captain	10
41	Scotland	15 Apr 1961	Empire Stadium, Wembley	BC	9–3	2	Captain	10
42	Mexico	10 May 1961	Empire Stadium, Wembley	F	8–0		Captain	10
43	Portugal	21 May 1961	Estádio Nacional, Jamor, Lisbon	WCQ	1–1		Captain	10
44	Italy	24 May 1961	Stadio Olimpico, Rome	F	3–2		Captain	10
45	Austria	27 May 1961	Praterstadion, Vienna	F	1–3		Captain	10
46	Wales	14 Oct 1961	Ninian Park, Cardiff	BC	1–1		Captain	10
47	Portugal	25 Oct 1961	Empire Stadium, Wembley	WCQ	2–0		Captain	10
48	Northern Ireland	22 Nov 1961	Empire Stadium, Wembley	BC	1–1		Captain	10
49	Austria	4 Apr 1962	Empire Stadium, Wembley	F	3–1		Captain	10
50	Scotland	14 Apr 1962	Hampden Park, Glasgow	BC	0–2		Captain	10
51	Switzerland	9 May 1962	Empire Stadium, Wembley	F	3–1		Captain	10
52	Peru	20 May 1962	Estadio Nacional Coloso de José Díaz, Lima	F	4–0		Captain	10
53	Hungary	31 May 1962	Estadio Braden Cooper Co., Rancagua, Chile	WCF	1–2		Captain	10
54	Argentina	2 Jun 1962	Estadio Braden Cooper Co., Rancagua, Chile	WCF	3–1		Captain	10
55	Bulgaria	7 Jun 1962	Estadio Braden Cooper Co., Rancagua, Chile	WCF	0–0		Captain	10
56	Brazil	10 Jun 1962	Estadio Sausalito, Viña del Mar, Chile	WCF	1–3		Captain	10

Pre Captaincy	Played 34	Won 18	Drawn 10	Lost 6	F 85	A 43
During Captaincy	Played 22	Won 12	Drawn 4	Lost 6	F 64	A 31
Total	Played 56	Won 30	Drawn 14	Lost 12	F 149	A 74

Johnny Haynes 18 goals — 1 hat trick, 2 braces, 11 single goals

Grand total for England (including Under-23, 'B' and Football League) and Fulham: 740 games and 191 goals.

Memories are made of this.

32: Epilogue

32: Epilogue

Johnny Haynes had always looked after himself. Just prior to his seventieth birthday he admitted that he enjoyed the odd liquid refreshment, but he didn't smoke cigarettes and usually had just one cigar a week. He had a massive love for oranges and would go to the market every few weeks to get crates of them. He would mix fresh orange with vodka and make his own screwdrivers every night; otherwise, he stuck to coffee. He loved swimming as a way of keeping fit.

His knees, like those of a number of players of his era, were troublesome. He said, "You know within yourself once you're past your sell-by date. One knee never fully recovered from a road accident I had forty years ago and I needed surgery for the other last Christmas. Otherwise I feel great."

He added sharply with a smile, "I suppose I'm getting old now. I was knackered the other night after *watching* two games on television." He continued to love watching all sport on television, especially football, but had to endure the soaps for a few hours, as Avril, his long-standing partner, was a keen fan. He managed to shoehorn in some UK Gold programmes and admitted an admiration for *Fawlty Towers.*

Haynes used to like classic films like *Casablanca* and *Gone with the Wind*, and was a great lover of musicals, *Guys and Dolls* and *High Society* for example. He rarely visited the cinema, reckoning the last film he'd seen was *Out Of Africa,* and that had been almost twenty years earlier. He still listened to the crooners, admitting that Sinatra remained his favourite, but he had a liking for Pavarotti and even Michael Bolton, and also admitted to listening to Classic FM in the car.

Letters and fan mail still continued to drop through Johnny's letterbox. In 2003 he said: "The only letters you usually get as a footballer are for autographs. In fact, I still get them. At least two a day come through that letterbox. It's a surprising amount of mail for someone of sixty-nine who hasn't kicked a ball for 30-odd years. It makes me very proud."

Celebrations

In October 2004, Johnny Haynes celebrated his seventieth birthday in style, in the company of his long-time friend Sir Bobby Robson. Nine days previously, in a private ceremony at Dalkeith, he and Avril had been married.

In September 2005, to celebrate her sixtieth birthday, Johnny's first wife Libby flew to Scotland with husband Tony to have dinner with Johnny and Avril in Edinburgh.

A star fades away

The following month, on the afternoon of his seventy-first birthday, at around 3pm, Johnny Haynes appeared to lose consciousness whilst at the wheel of his car in Dalry Road, Edinburgh, where he had chosen to make his home. The resultant loss of vehicle control and subsequent collision with a light goods vehicle was to cost him his life. His wife Avril, travelling as a passenger, was severely injured.

The accident was witnessed by a doctor who managed, using CPR, to restart Johnny's heart. He was rushed to Edinburgh Royal Infirmary and placed on a ventilator. During the next thirty hours, many tests were conducted by medical staff, but at 9pm the following day, when these exhaustive tests all produced negative results, his life-support machine was switched off. Trevor Chamberlain said, "I was only talking to him a few hours before the accident and we were laughing and joking as normal. I can't quite believe he's gone and I'll miss him always."

Homage at Craven Cottage

Within hours, the gates at the front of the Cottage were adorned with a mass of tributes of all kinds, mostly from grateful supporters who had had the privilege of watching him. A few days later at Craven Cottage, the picturesque Thamesside ground which he graced for so long, homage was paid to Fulham's greatest player. A minute's silence was held and perfectly observed, a giant number ten shirt was laid out on the pitch and Trevor Chamberlain placed a wreath at the edge of the centre circle before the kick-off. The match was against mighty Liverpool and Fulham duly played as Haynes would have wished, and sent the fans home a little less downcast with a 2–0 victory.

Johnny Haynes is laid to rest

The funeral took place on October 27th at Basil Spence's Mortonhall crematorium in Edinburgh. Then after, appropriately, *How Great Thou Art*, *Jerusalem* and *Abide with Me*, Johnny Haynes was laid to rest. The final piece was *Amazing Grace,* which could so easily have described him as a passer of a football, as well as his manner off the field.

The funeral was attended by many of football's greats, including the England manager Sven Goran Eriksson, Sir Bobby Charlton CBE, George Cohen MBE, Sir Bobby Robson CBE, Alan Mullery MBE, Dave Mackay and of course Trevor Chamberlain. Johnny's former wife Marjorie travelled from South Africa, and her daughter Karen from California also attended. Karen and Marjorie met on a dull and overcast day at a hotel, but the sun shone brightly on the day of the funeral, and, as Marjorie said, "It was most appropriate for a man who loved the sun."

This was followed by a memorial service in January 2006, held at St Paul's Church in Hammersmith. The church was packed, and amongst those attending were former colleagues Stan Brown, Fred Callaghan, Trevor Chamberlain, George Cohen, Maurice Cook, Ken Craggs, Jimmy Hill, Barry Lloyd, Dave Metchick, Barry Mealand, Alan Mullery, Brian Nichols, Tom Wilson and Harry Weir. The service was conducted

Homage to Fulham's greatest son. 22nd October 2005, Fulham v Liverpool at Craven Cottage.

JOHNNY HAYNES

1934 - 2005

Memorial Service
St Paul's Church
Hammersmith
Sunday 22 January 2006

by Fulham's own lifelong supporter, the Reverend Gary Piper, who perfectly captured the mood of the occasion, which was of great sadness at Haynes' passing mingled with great pride and gratitude that such a genius had been part of 'our club'. Inspiring tributes were spoken by Jimmy Hill, Dennis Turner, George Cohen and Trevor Chamberlain. A memorial service for the maestro was also held in Durban, where he was still remembered with much fondness.

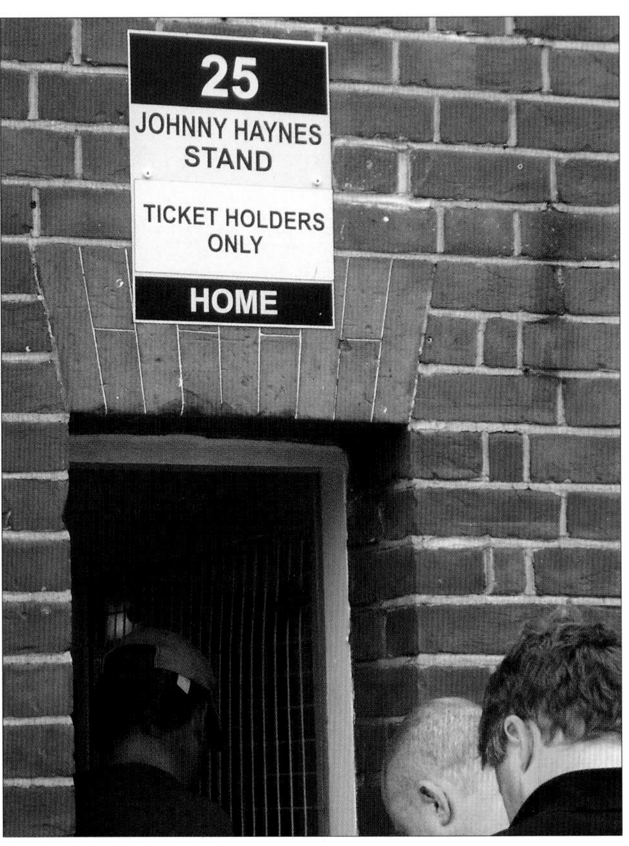

The Stevenage Road stand is dedicated

On 27th November 2005, a few weeks after its centenary year, Fulham Football Club announced that the Archibald Leitch-designed Stevenage Road stand at Craven Cottage would be renamed The Johnny Haynes Stand. The dedication took place on the day of Fulham's home match with Sheffield United on 26th August 2006.

This move would have found favour even with the modest Haynes, who once said: "I have to say that I see other grounds such as Bristol City (Ashton Gate) that has a John Atyeo stand or the Billy Wright one at Molineux and I think I would love something like that before I leave this earth."

Remembering Brave Johnny Haynes

isn't it strange how emotions can change
like a blink in the wink of an eye
when just for a moment your world it stands still
no matter how hard you may try

I was back in a place in a whole other space
and the haunts of my footballing past
in the back streets of Fulham we'd play on those streets
and we thought that it always would last -
but there at the ground there was barely a sound
by the gates where the tributes all lay
just reporters and fans with their heads in their hands
and I'm lost and can't think what to say

he was awesome prolific imposing terrific
all the times that I saw Johnny play
when the rafters would ring they would bellow and sing
at the Cottage some long ago day -
there's a picture in flight you're in black and in white
in the colours of country and team
is it really all gone will your memory go on
when I wake will they say it's a dream?

you were there at the top you were so hard to stop
in mud and in snow or in rain
and whatever is said there are goals in my head
that will linger and always remain -
there was Tony Macedo and your old mate Tosh
there'd be Langley and Robson and Hill
there are memories of Cup games and flags on the bank
I can capture it all and I will

and the bloke in his coat in that old rowing boat
collecting the ball from the Thames
the closeness the banter the wags in the crowd
they are days that we won't see again -
for you were the heart of it so much a part of it
Johnny I'm shattered and sad
you were one of the first games that I ever saw
and the thought of it now makes me glad

glad to remember some hopeless defender
left strewn by your pace and that shot
you were lethal in flight like a thief in the night
you were marked liked some penalty spot

but isn't it great how your memory is saved
in footage your legend remains
your name echoes loud - and I'm down but I'm proud
Remembering brave Johnny Haynes

Crispin Thomas, Football Poet

The Tributes

Johnny Haynes played in the good days when football wore a smile. Anyone who went to Craven Cottage when Haynes was king will tell you the same. He always remained loyal to the unfashionable club that had given him his chance in the game, and thus failed to win the trophies his talents deserved. Fulham had been his trial and his joy, and he readily accepted the bad days alongside the good days, realising that lives were not dependent on football success.

The Fulham team at the time were often characterised as 'Haynes and ten others', but in fact he played alongside such very good players as Tony Macedo, George Cohen, Jim Langley, Bobby Robson, Alan Mullery, Roy Bentley, Eddie Lowe, Archie Macaulay, Bedford Jezzard, Rodney Marsh, Allan Clarke, Graham Leggat, and the sporadically brilliant Trevor Chamberlain. Haynes modestly pointed out that when the Fulham team included the above players, he could claim to be in the best of company.

Roy Bentley agrees with that: "John couldn't look or be a great player without having other really good players around him to enable him to do his job properly; he needed targets to find, intelligent players able to find the right positions on the field. We had happy, intelligent players, all one big family. Johnny just lived for Fulham."

Johnny Haynes was never given an honour for his services to football, something that still irks many inside and outside the game, including public figures, managers, former players and supporters. It seems a scandal that the footballing authorities that now hand out honours like sweets gave so little recognition to Haynes, who set the highest standards of behaviour both on and off the pitch. Despite never receiving a knighthood or *any* other official recognition, he left a legacy of memories.

Here are just a few.

Sir Bobby Robson CBE:

I am very distressed by this news [his passing]. Johnny and I joined Fulham together in 1950. He was one of the greatest passers in the history of football and would have been great in today's game.

He was without doubt one of the greatest players this country has ever produced. He ranks alongside Wright, Matthews, Charlton, Finney, Lofthouse and Moore, great club men and international players. He loved the game and was a sensational player.

Alan Mullery MBE:

He was the only reason I went to Fulham as a young boy of fifteen leaving school. He was my hero, the captain of England and Fulham. The word great rolls off the tongue quite easily these days, but he really was. He was the best passer of a ball I have ever seen—I don't know anyone who could pass a ball as accurately. Anyone who saw him will know what a great player he was. He will never go from my memory.

England have been lacking a player of his calibre ever since.

I think he had extra-sensory powers as a player and he was the greatest passer of a ball I have ever known. He could lay it to within six inches of a colleague. A yard wasn't good enough for Johnny. He could send a forty-yard pass inside the full back to the winger streaking in towards goal. He was a world-class player.

He was the all-time greatest player for Fulham, and was the first-ever superstar footballer. He really was a true legend. He was the first to have a sponsored car and used to date film stars too. We all looked at him with envy.

Roy Bentley:

If they talk about players being ten years ahead of their time, Johnny Haynes was probably fifty years ahead of his. Whatever system or formation a team could play today, he would have fitted into it. He would probably have been even better in today's football. The only role that he wouldn't have liked would have been up front on his own in a 4–5–1 system. He would have probably devised a playing system of his own—'the Haynes method'.

When I moved back to centre half, an easier position on the field, it was an ideal place to watch him. It was like watching a snooker player building a break, he was three shots [moves] ahead of the play, judging the angles and getting himself in the best position.

Bobby Moore OBE:

Once you got used to watching that perfection, you realised the rest of the secret. John was always available, always hungry for the ball, always wanting to play. He was the master. I loved watching the player and later I learned to love the man. The two go together. I could never feel that close to anyone I did not respect.

George Cohen MBE:

John was a magnificent footballer. I cannot explain to people just how good he was. He had terrific vision and knew exactly what he was going to do before the ball reached him. He was the greatest foot-to-ball player I've ever seen and his ability to read the game was second to none. To be honest there wasn't much he wasn't good at!

His vision was just outstanding. If you think of him in the same way as Pelé then you would come close.

I have a hundred individual memories of the beauty of John's play. One stands out for the sheer perfection of his skill. It was a charity match which, but for that one second, has faded completely from my memory. The ball came to him at speed on a wet, slippery surface but with the slightest of adjustments, one that was almost imperceptible, he played it inside a full back and into the path of an on-running winger. I looked at our coach Dave Sexton on the bench and he caught my glance and shook his head as if to say 'fantastic'. Haynes could give you goose bumps on a wet night in a match that didn't matter.

He'll be known as one of the all-time world class players. Anybody who picks a world eleven without him in it doesn't know what they are talking about.

Fred Callaghan:

We have had some top class players at the Cottage over the years, George Best, Rodney Marsh and Alan Mullery, but even they will tell you that Johnny Haynes was the greatest. If I was ever to be asked what Johnny Haynes will be remembered for, the answer would be a simple one. He will forever be remembered as the greatest player to grace the field at Craven Cottage, past, present and future.

Jimmy Hill OBE:

He was really just wonderful. He had a special skill and he was a lovely young man. He was not arrogant or conceited in any way. He adored the game of football and, to be honest, he mastered it, the difficult parts especially. Haynes just dictated most games he played in with his magnificent tactical brain, control and passing ability.

I would have Johnny Haynes in my team every time. I've never seen a better passer of the ball; his passes were so often productive ones that led to goals.

Rodney Marsh:

I've never known a more dedicated footballer than Johnny; as a provider Johnny was supreme. He only let you have the ball when you could make use of it. His quickness and ability to make the most of a situation was phenomenal. His mind was often three passes ahead of the ball and I mean that quite literally.

Let me put it simply. Johnny was David Beckham, Patrick Vieira and Paul Scholes rolled into one, and that's no exaggeration.

He had sublime skills. He could pass a ball any distance with pinpoint accuracy, score regularly, tackle, beat people and organise everything. In fact there wasn't anything he couldn't do. Johnny stood head and shoulders above any other player in those days.

The only person in recent years to get anywhere close to Johnny was Glenn Hoddle. The main difference between them was that Haynes scored more goals and he played in two World Cup finals. Johnny had amazing vision and he was one of football's gentlemen in days when sportsmanship and fair play meant a whole lot more than they do today.

Bobby Keetch:

His great hero is Tom Finney, and I think John stands comparison. Like Finney, he has been given a retrospective accolade. It's only in recent years that people have come to realise they were both truly great players. Can you imagine a time when we were able to take footballers of that calibre for granted!

I think John was the best passer of the ball I ever saw. His accuracy was remarkable over distance and the weight and speed of the ball was always perfect. He was the master of the long, defence-splitting pass. It's been lost to the game in recent years, but I saw Ruud Gullit playing at Chelsea and he hit a couple of forty-yarders to feet that had men of my age remembering John.

When people ask me about him, I tell them that he was a perfectionist and sometimes he achieved perfection. Not many of us can say that.

Trevor Chamberlain:

More than anything I am proud to say Johnny Haynes was like a brother to me and, if I am honest, I was totally in awe of him.

Birthdays and Christmases were never forgotten and we were always looking out for each other. If you went out of your way to be a friend to Johnny Haynes, rest assured he would do the same for you. People talk of Johnny as a real gentleman, but people close to him never recognised it, because more than anything he was such a dear friend.

Fulham chairman Mohamed Al Fayed:

In these days of the modern game and the hyperbole that the Premiership commands, words are often used cheaply. But when I say that Johnny Haynes was truly 'The Maestro', one of the greatest players ever to grace a football pitch and one who brought joy to many, many thousands of spectators, it is not an exaggeration. Johnny Haynes will forever be remembered as Fulham's greatest son.

Chris Coleman (Fulham manager at the time of Haynes' passing):

We have lost one of football's finest players. He was Fulham's greatest-ever player and one of the best to pull on an England shirt. He'll be greatly missed. There will never be another but his contribution to this club and to the game of football will never be forgotten.

Tom Greatrex (spokesman for the Fulham Supporters Trust):

With the hyperbole of the modern Premiership, big words are often bandied about very cheaply, but it is no exaggeration to say that Johnny Haynes was one of the greatest ever footballers, who brought pleasure to thousands. His dedication, skill, professionalism, grace and charm—both in his playing days and in retirement—serve as a poignant reminder to many of today's footballers about what true greatness really means.

The Fulham supporter:

The fact that I can remember individual goals and inch-perfect passes despite the mists of forty years testifies to how brightly that talent shone.

Ian St John (Liverpool and Scotland):

Johnny could have scored more goals in his career if he had pushed up further and he certainly had the ammunition for it. However, you always got the feeling he was happy in the middle of the field directing the traffic. He was a special player and he knew how to conceal his passes. They talk about Ronaldinho today as the master of disguise, but Johnny was doing it forty years ago. He could turn on a sixpence, look right and suddenly the ball would be flying to the left wing. Everyone knew he was a special player.

Jimmy Greaves (Spurs and England):

Forget David Beckham or Glenn Hoddle. Johnny Haynes was the best passer of the ball the game has ever seen.

Johnny and I had a great understanding; we could read each other like a book. If Bill Nicholson had succeeded in signing him in 1964, I have no doubts he would have been the cornerstone of another great Spurs team. Johnny also rejected a move to AC Milan and spent his entire career at Fulham, which was odd because in the early Sixties he was just about the most famous man in the country.

Johnny Haynes was the proverbial jewel in the crown of English football, a player touched by genius. His left foot was so sharp he could have opened tin cans. It was said of Whistler that he mixed his paints with brains. That was what Johnny did with his football. His style was graceful, colourful, and he orchestrated every telling move.

Denis Law (Manchester United and Scotland):

He was one of the best inside forwards of his or any other generation. He was also one of the best passers of a ball you could possibly imagine.

On top of which he was an absolute gentleman on and off the pitch. A lovely, lovely guy, although I didn't think he was such a lovely guy at Wembley in 1961 when England edged us in that twelve-goal thriller [for 'edged' read a Haynes-inspired 9–3 rout]. Johnny was magnificent that day. When I had my cancer, Johnny was one of the first people to ring me; that's the kind of man he was.

Strangely, he didn't get the plaudits other lesser players received, but if he'd played his club football at Spurs or Arsenal he would have been the icon he deserved to be.

Gordon Taylor (chief executive of the Professional Footballers' Association):

As a person, Johnny was always a gentleman, and as a footballer, a class act. He could be well satisfied that he made a massive contribution to English football. I was fortunate enough to play against him. Not only was he a great England player and captain, but he was a loyal, one-club man. He was not driven by money, it just happened that Tommy Trinder valued him and made him the first £100-a-week player.

Ken Jones:

Haynes was a star performer, appearing in the mind's eye as an outstandingly gifted inside forward, an immaculate passer, who possessed a sixth sense on the football field and a way of going about life that made people warm to him. The essential thing about Haynes was something you hardly ever read on the obituary page, the simple fact that he made it a pleasure to know him.

Hugh McIlvanney:

There was for me always an aura of the genuine original about him. In companies of his choosing he was uninhibitedly gregarious, with an insatiable enthusiasm for winding up his companions and a generous tolerance for being wound up in turn, but the sincere reaching out was done from the contained strength of a firmly, at times stubbornly independent nature.

What would he be worth today?

Johnny Haynes was the David Beckham of his generation, perhaps even more famous, and had he been born two generations later he would now be earning £200,000 a week, with huge personal endorsements adding to his fortune each time he changed clubs.

He was a football scholar, an academic, and he studied the art and practised it. In the Premiership he would have loved the training regime and fitness aspects, the modern all-weather training facilities, the advances in medical treatment, the perfect pitches and balls. He would have been a true giant in the Premiership. One journalist recently remarked that any club wishing to buy the Premiership Johnny Haynes in 2008 would have to start the ball rolling at around £60 million. He wouldn't have been far wrong.

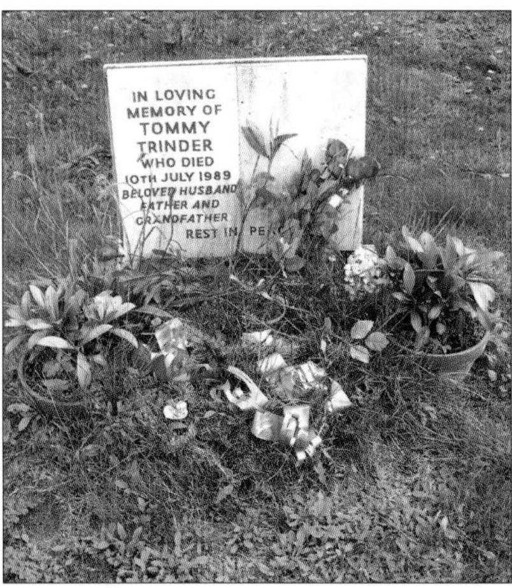

Tommy Trinder

Haynes admired Tommy Trinder as almost a father figure. He knew he cared deeply about the club and Tommy would literally have broken the bank to keep 'his favourite son'.

Haynes and Trinder made headlines that day in 1961 when Haynes became a £100-a-week player, and they remained close always. In a way, during that era the name of Trinder the chairman was almost as important in show business as the name of Haynes on the playing field. Tommy Trinder CBE, a great comic, passed away in July 1989. His final resting place is remarkably modest, tucked away unnoticed in the corner of a cemetery between Weybridge and Hersham in Surrey. The small headstone makes no mention of his life's work, of his lifelong attachment to Fulham Football Club, or of his place in football's history. The flowers are plastic and the grave appears untended.

Flowers at the Cottage gates, October 2005.

A tribute

In January 2008, plans were said to be well advanced for a fans' tribute in the form of a statue to the maestro, which would take its proper place at Craven Cottage, as a fitting and permanent memorial to Fulham's greatest son.

10

Fulham's Craven Cottage ground, November 1960. The programme covers are from Johnny Haynes' first and last matches for the club